BRIDGES:
DOCUMENTS OF THE
CHRISTIAN-JEWISH DIALOGUE

Studies in
Judaism and Christianity

Exploration of Issues
in the Contemporary Dialogue
between Christians and Jews

Editors
Mark-David Janus, CSP, PhD
Yehezkel Landau, D.Min
Michael McGarry, CSP
Peter Pettit, PhD
Rena Potok
Elena Procario-Foley, PhD
Rabbi Stephen Wylen

A STIMULUS BOOK

Bridges:
Documents of the
Christian-Jewish Dialogue

Volume Two
Building a New Relationship (1986–2013)

Edited by Franklin Sherman

A STIMULUS BOOK

PAULIST PRESS ◆ NEW YORK ◆ MAHWAH, NJ

Cover image by Orhan Cam / Shutterstock.com

Cover design by Lynn Else

Book design by Celine M. Allen

Library of Congress Cataloging-in-Publication Data

Bridges : documents of the Christian-Jewish dialogue / edited by Franklin Sherman.
    v. cm.
  "A Stimulus book."
  Includes bibliographical references and index.
  Contents: v. <1> The road to reconciliation (1945–1985) —
  ISBN 978-0-8091-4732-8 (alk. paper)
  1. Judaism—Relations—Christianity. 2. Christianity and other religions—Judaism.
I. Sherman, Franklin.
  BM535.B725 2011
  261.2'6—dc22

                                                                    2011011015

ISBN Volume 2: 978-0-8091-4818-9 (paperback)

Published by Paulist Press
997 Macarthur Boulevard
Mahwah, New Jersey 07430

www.paulistpress.com

Printed and bound in the
United States of America

Contents

PART ONE

Protestant Statements

NORTH AMERICA

PART TWO

Roman Catholic Statements

VATICAN DOCUMENTS

Selected Papal Addresses or Writings

Pope John Paul II

Pope Benedict XVI

PART THREE

Orthodox Christian Statements

PART FOUR
Ecumenical Christian Statements
(Protestant–Catholic–Orthodox)

PART FIVE
Joint Christian-Jewish Statements

PART SIX

Jewish Statements

Preface

by Franklin Sherman

The advances in Christian-Jewish relations in the years from 1986 to the present have paralleled and extended those of 1945–1985, as presented in the first volume of this two-volume collection.[1] New church bodies have been heard from, others have updated their views, and there is now also an array of Jewish statements (Part Six below).

A striking example of the distance that has been traveled since 1945 can be seen in the Roman Catholic sphere. When the Second World War ended, it was unimaginable that twenty years later, in 1965, a global council of the Roman Catholic Church would authoritatively reject the "teaching of contempt" toward the Jewish people and begin an unprecedented rapprochement with them. As a sign of the remarkable progress since then, that same church in 2013 was able to elect as pope a person with lifelong experience in Christian-Jewish dialogue, who on his very first day in office wrote a letter of fraternal greetings to the chief rabbi of Rome. "I strongly hope," the new Pope Francis wrote, "to be able to contribute to the progress of the relations that have existed between Jews and Catholics since Vatican Council II in a spirit of renewed collaboration and in service of a world that may always be more in harmony with the Creator's will."[2]

Similar examples of dramatic change can be given from the Protestant and Eastern Orthodox spheres, such as the Evangelical Lutheran Church in America's 1994 statement repudiating Martin Luther's anti-Jewish views[3] or the remarkable message of Patriarch Alexy II of the Russian Orthodox Church entitled "We Must Be in Unity with the Jews."[4]

To be sure, there have been conflicts and controversies between Christians and Jews during this period, some of which are chronicled in the surveys offered by the three introductions that follow. But always the will to build a new relationship has triumphed in the end over such difficulties. What has been learned is that, in the words of one of the statements, "Jewish-Christian relations are not a 'problem' that is going to be 'solved,' but rather a *continuing process* of learning and refinement."[5]

This volume, like its predecessor, does not present itself as exhaustive. Some statements have been omitted because they largely duplicate others, and some, regrettably, because of their length. For statements issued after the publication of this volume, the reader is urged to consult online resources such as www.jcrelations.net or www.ccjr.us/dialogika. Please see the latter also for an important document from the immediate post–World War II period recently translated into English, the Schwalbach Theses.[6]

As in the first volume of this collection, statements dealing primarily with the Middle Eastern situation are not included, even though Christians have recognized how central the State of Israel is to contemporary Jewish identity. Statements of this nature are very numerous and would require a volume or volumes of their own, including careful historical contextualization.

As in Volime 1, the spellings "anti-semitism" and "anti-Semitism" found in various documents have been updated to "antisemitism."

It should be noted that what is commonly called "the Holocaust" is referred to in most of the documents (Christian as well as Jewish) as "the Shoah," a Hebrew term meaning "catastrophe." An explanation of this usage may be found in note 1 on page 137 below.

Comments on Selected Statements

The three introductions that follow, each written by an eminent scholar in the field of Christian-Jewish relations, present overviews of the specifically Protestant, Roman Catholic, and Jewish documents in the present volume. Offered here are brief comments on the other sets of documents in the collection: Orthodox Christian, Ecumenical Christian, and joint Christian-Jewish.

Orthodox Christian. Since the terms "orthodox" and "orthodoxy" are used in both Christian and Jewish contexts, the term "Orthodox Christian" is used here rather than simply "Orthodox" to avoid any confusion with Orthodox Judaism. It refers to the third great family of Christian tradition in addition to Roman Catholicism and Protestantism. Included in this designation are the churches of Eastern Europe such as the Greek, Bulgarian, Serbian, Ukrainian, and Russian Orthodox Churches, as well as others in the Eastern

Mediterranean area such the Syrian Orthodox and the Copts (Egypt).

Like Orthodox Judaism, Orthodox Christianity is not typically inclined to make formal statements on the issues of the day; rather, guidance is sought in the wisdom of scholars and religious leaders. Thus in the present collection we have the already-mentioned address of the Patriarch of Moscow and All Russia, Alexy II, in New York in 1991, "We Must Be in Unity with the Jews" (Document 61, presented here in English translation for the first time). Also remarkable is the address of Ecumenical Patriarch Bartholomew of the Greek Orthodox Church at the United States Holocaust Memorial Museum in Washington in 1997 (Document 62); two other of his addresses are presented as well.

A notable development in Orthodox Christian-Jewish relationships has been the holding of a series of international meetings of academicians from each community. Six such consultations have been held since 1977, most recently in Thessaloniki, Greece, in 2003, and Jerusalem in 2007. The written product of these meetings has been a series of communiqués summarizing the discussion rather than formal statements; thus they do not fall under the normal rubrics of the present collection. However, one of the communiqués, that of the 2007 meeting, is included as an example (Document 83).

Ecumenical Christian. This term is used for statements whose issuing bodies include at least two of the three main expressions of Christianity: Catholic, Protestant, and Orthodox. These may be Protestant and Orthodox, as in the World Council and National Council of Churches statements (Documents 67, 68, 70, and 71 below); Catholic and Protestant, as in the joint statements from Hungary (Document 69) and Argentina (Document 75); or other combinations. Particularly broad in sponsorship is the "Charta Oecumenica" issued in 2001 by representatives of substantially all the Christian bodies in Europe. An excerpt from this lengthy statement, namely, the section on relations to Judaism and Islam, is provided in Document 72.

Of special interest in the Ecumenical Christian category is the statement issued in 2002 by the Christians Scholars Group on Christian-Jewish Relations, a free-standing ecumenical group of some forty-five years standing (Document 73). This statement was explicitly crafted in response to the pioneering Jewish statement *Dabru Emet* (Document 94). Entitled "A Sacred Obligation: Rethinking Christian

Faith in Relation to Judaism and the Jewish People," it provides an overview of nodal points in contemporary Christian-Jewish relations.

Interfaith Statements. The term "interfaith," as distinguished from "ecumenical," is used to refer to organizations that include Jews as well as Christians. Noteworthy among these is the International Council of Christians and Jews (ICCJ), whose origins go back to the issuance of the famous "Ten Points of Seelisberg" in 1947 (Document 56 in Vol. 1 of this collection). More than sixty years later, the ICCJ undertook to update the Ten Points for a new situation, especially the now multi-religious character of Europe. The resulting statement, known as "The Twelve Points of Berlin," is presented in Document 84 below.[7]

Other interfaith documents found in this section include three of the many statements on current topics issued by the International Catholic-Jewish Liaison Committee, namely those on the Family, the Environment, and Religious Freedom (Documents 76, 77, and 79). Also of special interest is another document presented here in English translation for the first time, the 2010 statement by the Federation of Swiss Protestant Churches and the Swiss Federation of Jewish Communities, "Journeying Together in Mutual Respect" (Document 85).

As with Volume 1 of this collection, I would like to express special thanks to my friends and collaborators, the writers of the Protestant, Catholic, and Jewish Introductions that follow—Alice L. Eckardt, Philip A. Cunningham, and Michael S. Kogan—as well as Peter A. Pettit for Hebrew transliterations. It is our common hope that the project of making available this documentation of the Christian-Jewish dialogue of the past almost seventy years will contribute to the further realization of a mutually beneficial relationship between the two communities.

Notes

1. *Bridges: Documents of the Christian-Jewish Dialogue*, Vol. 1, *The Road to Reconciliation (1945–1985)*. New York and Mahwah, NJ: Paulist Press, 2011.
2. March 15, 2013. See http://www.news.va/en/news/pope-christians-cannot-be-anti-semitic.

3. Document 5.

4. Document 61.

5. Document 83, p. 452 below (italics added).

6. See www.ccjr.us/dialogika-resources/documents-and-statements/ecu-menical-christian/1229-schwalbach. The Schwalbach Theses were issued in 1950 as a German revision and expansion of the Ten Points of Seelisberg. For further materials in German, see Hans Hermann Henrix and Wolfgang Kraus (eds.), *Die Kirche und das Judentum*, Bd. II. *Documente von 1986 bis 2000* (Paderborn: Bonifatius-Druckerei and Gütersloh: Gütersloher Verlags-Haus, 2001) and the online continuation at www.nostra-aetate.uni-bonn.de/kirchliche-dokumente.

7. The Twelve Points form part of a longer document entitled "A Time for Recommitment: Building the New Relationship between Jews and Christians." The full text is available at http://www.ccjr.us/images/stories/ICCJ_Time-for-Recommitment.pdf.

Franklin Sherman *is Founding Director of the Institute for Jewish-Christian Understanding at Muhlenberg College. He served previously as Tutor and Lecturer at Mansfield College, Oxford, and as Dean of the Lutheran School of Theology at Chicago. He is the author of* The Promise of Heschel *and other studies of Judaism and Jewish-Christian relations, and edited the volume of* Luther's Works, American Edition *that contains Luther's writings on the Jews and Judaism.*

Building a New Relationship:
A Protestant Perspective

by Alice L. Eckardt

"Time to Turn," the title of the 1998 statement by Austria's Protestant Church of the Augsburg and Helvetic Confessions (Document 18 below), is a perfect phrase to emphasize as we read, think about, and utilize the Protestant documents in this collection. Time to turn *away* from the evils of anti-Judaism and antisemitism; time to turn *away* from supersessionist (replacement) and triumphalist theology; time to turn *toward* a new future in which Christians and Jews will "walk a common way" by *returning* to God, who offers a new beginning.

In the years since 1985 numerous Protestant churches have made or are continuing to make that turning, moving further along the trails broken in the earlier period and making significant theological advances. Many fundamental beliefs have been reformulated quite profoundly by North American Protestants and those of Europe and Australia. Their statements recognize serious needs: the need to address both clergy and congregations about the issues that have been at the core of enmity and separation between Christians and Jews; the need to express genuine repentance for defamation and evils done; the need to make significant changes so as to build a new and positive relationship between the two faiths.

It is clear that those who produced these statements have wrestled at length with thorny issues and long-established theology, including the "teaching of contempt" and supersessionism, missionary efforts to convert Jews, and lack of knowledge about contemporary Judaism in its various forms and teachings. The authors have not hesitated to issue new and often radically altered faith affirmations that include expressions of readiness to learn from Jews about the central texts of Judaism and their teachings; to affirm God's unrevoked covenant with the Jewish people; to recognize Jesus and his teachings as an embodiment of Judaism in his time; to advocate respectful dialogue with Jews; and to search for mutual understanding.

Throughout we find strong professions not only of the common roots of the two faiths but also of their continuity. The concept of covenant between God and the two peoples, Jews and Christians— whether viewed in terms either of one covenant encompassing both communities or two equally authentic covenants—emphasizes the con- tinuing validity and role of the people Israel in today's world and acknowledges their primary place in covenantal history.

Because of the multiple topics covered and the scope of all that is dealt with, no summary will do justice to this collection. Each docu- ment needs to be read for its own contributions, as well as in light of its particular time and place of origin. Even so, we find that there is much commonality in the topics covered, the wrongs acknowledged, and the affirmations made.

Overview of the North American Statements

As I have read and reread these statements I have sensed something of a fundamental difference in tone between those from North America and those from Europe. Those from the United States and Canada seem generally more forward-looking and positive in their approach. That is, the prime emphasis is on new expressions of faith and on what should be done now, while not ignoring the central prob- lematic issues inherited from the past. In Europe, on the other hand, a prime emphasis is on confessing the evils perpetrated against the Jewish people, which in turn spiritually defiled the Christian faith. Also emphasized, however, are present efforts to overcome those failings, including a new appreciation of the Jewish faith and its adherents' con- cern for applying it to human society and world events.[1]

The Episcopal Church was the pioneer among American denomi- nations in issuing a statement on Christian-Jewish relations in 1964 (prior even to the Second Vatican Council's *Nostra Aetate*) that denounced antisemitism as a "direct contradiction of Christian doc- trine" and renounced the charge of "deicide" against the Jews (see *Bridges*, Vol. 1, Document 8). Fifteen years later, its General Convention spoke about the church's many spiritual and historical ties to "the seed of Abraham" (Vol. 1, Document 22). In the present volume we find in the same church's 1988 *Guidelines* (Document 3 below) much more extensive advice for the dialogue with Jews. Because the Episcopal Church has "a tradition of respect for truth wherever found," a "careful listening" to the other's expression of faith is called for, so as not to bear false witness against them. There is an imbalance in the relationship, the *Guidelines* note: whereas Christianity requires an understanding of the Judaism underlying its own origins, Judaism does not require an understanding of Christianity in the same way. As Christianity gradually emerged from Judaism, it replaced Judaism's biblical interpretations with its own. This led to a supersessionist conviction of having displaced its forerunner. The church needs to recognize Jesus as a Jew who accepted the Hebrew scriptures as authoritative, though he interpreted them in "fresh and powerful ways." The church needs also to learn how Rabbinic Judaism developed out of Pharisaic Judaism in the Common Era. It needs to discard the long-held arguments that Judaism was or is only a dry legalism which has been "abrogated" by God; it needs also to renounce its teaching of contempt, along with the long history of hatred and persecution of Jews. This is a powerful statement indeed.

The Presbyterian Church (U.S.A.), in its 1987 statement (Document 1), focuses on the assertion that through Jesus Christ the church was "engrafted into the people of God" created by the covenant God made with Abraham, Isaac, and Jacob; hence it insists that "Christians have not replaced Jews." Despite the separation of the Jewish and Christian communities in the first centuries of the Common Era, the church continued to utilize much of the language, liturgy, and thought forms it received from its Jewish forebears. However, by the third century supersessionism had become the "predominant and orthodox understanding of God's relationship with the Jews" and led to the church's "long and deep complicity" in the proliferation of anti-Jewish attitudes and actions through its "teaching of contempt" for Jews. It is that teaching, the Presbyterian statement asserts, that "we now repudiate." In its place the Presbyterians put forward five positive affirmations pointing to the commonalities of the two faiths: the same God, a shared covenant, irrevocable election, the reality of the reign of God, and yet the waiting for fulfillment of the messianic redemption of the world. Both peoples are "elected by God for witness to the world," and are to serve as "a light to the nations."

The United Church of Christ (also 1987, Document 2) agrees that Christianity is not a "successor religion" to Judaism, because God's covenant with the Jewish people is not rescinded but "remains in full force." The Christian Church (Disciples of Christ) statement of 1993 (Document 4) acknowledges the "enormity" of the problem that originated in the early church's renunciation of Judaism and denunciation of Jews as "blind" and "obstinate." It calls attention to how these attitudes were greatly augmented and given legal force over the Christian centuries through restrictive laws, imposed ghettos, and expulsions, and notes that the Third Reich reenacted all of these discriminations prior to establishing the death camps.

As the churches have undertaken the task of revising their theologies in light of the Christian-Jewish dialogue, we find many new positive themes. The Methodists (Document 6) put emphasis on Christianity's rootedness in biblical Judaism, on Jesus as a devout Jew, and on the validity of both covenants (though the Christian covenant is "radically new"), as well as on the further development of both living faiths over the centuries. This statement, "Building New Bridges in Hope" (1996) follows up on the strong Methodist statement of 1972 (*Bridges*, Vol. 1, Document 13), and expresses the hope that relationships may be raised to "the highest possible level of human fellowship and understanding."

"Bearing Faithful Witness," the statement by the United Church of Canada (2003, Document 9 below), also rejects all theology that expresses contempt for Jews and Judaism. It argues that although God's "reconciling mission in Jesus Christ...opened the door in a new way" for those outside the original covenant with Israel, God did not abandon or revoke that earlier covenant, for God is faithful. The Canadian statement forthrightly acknowledges the presence within its own church body of anti-Judaism and antisemitism as well as a deeply rooted anti-Jewish interpretation of New Testament texts.

The Alliance of Baptists' statement (2003, Document 8) has similarities to the European statements in its focus on the admission of guilt regarding Baptists' own participation in transmitting the anti-Jewish polemic found in the New Testament, in usurping the biblical promises given to Jews, and in ignoring the nineteen hundred years of Judaism's post-New Testament development. The Baptists confess to sins of indifference and inaction in face of the horrors of the Holocaust. They pledge themselves to work against all of these sins, to seek genuine dialogue with the Jewish community, and to consider "appropriate forms of Christian witness" for our time.

A particularly powerful declaration acknowledging "in pain" Martin Luther's "anti-Judaic diatribes and violent recommendations" against the Jews was made by the Evangelical Lutheran Church in America (ELCA) in 1994 (Document 5). The church rejects Luther's "violent invective" and expresses its "deep and abiding sorrow over its tragic effects on subsequent generations," including its appropriation by modern antisemites. The ELCA commits itself, in this declaration, to a relationship of "love and respect" toward the Jewish people. Its subsequent "Guidelines" (1998, Document 7) offers concrete suggestions on how to maintain and enhance that relationship.[2]

The European Statements

The European churches are, of necessity, much more committed to facing up to their failure to make any interventions on behalf of their Jewish neighbors during the years of National Socialism and the Shoah, as well as admitting the long negative relationship of church and synagogue in prior centuries. Seven of the statements of this kind were issued on the fiftieth or sixtieth anniversaries of key historical events—the 1938 pogrom (*Kristallnacht*); the liberation of Auschwitz; and the end of World War II. These statements emanate from the Protestant churches in Poland, Italy, and Austria as well as the regional German churches (*Landeskirchen*).

The Protestant Church of the Palatinate (1990, Document 12) admits having done nothing to oppose the deportation of Jews from its area to a concentration camp in southern France. Moreover, after the end of the war most of its citizens "avoided coming to terms" with all that the German nation had inflicted on other nations, on dissenters, on the weak and ill, and especially on the Jewish people. Hence, the Holocaust "deeply shakes" Christian self-understanding; indeed it shows where "Israel-oblivion" led.

Austria's Protestant Church of the Augsburg and Helvetic Confessions (1998, Document 18) finds it incomprehensible that its churches, which had themselves suffered during the Counter-Reformation, did not protest against the all-too-visible crimes of *Kristallnacht* when the victims were "abandoned" by all. The Hungarian Reformed Church (1990, Document 13) also recalls its sixteenth-century trials, noting that forebears compared their own sufferings with that of

Jews. It sadly recalls, and repents for, its failure to intervene when some six hundred thousand Hungarian Jews were being decimated in the closing years of the Holocaust. Hence it stresses the necessity of resisting the "temptation of Christian antisemitism, the most dangerous form." The outcome of Christ's crucifixion must be reaffirmed as tearing down the wall separating the two peoples.

Poland's Reformed Church (1995, Document 15) insists on the need to give "truthful witness" to the terrible events of the years of the Second World War. It remembers with "deepest sorrow" the Jews slaughtered in "our homeland," admitting that most of the population was indifferent due to the centuries-long anti-Judaism which held every Jew guilty for Christ's death. In contrast, the Polish church quotes John Calvin's observation that "the Jews knew justification by faith from their own experiences." It also speaks in sorrow about the Polish people's suffering under two totalitarianisms, and the "martyrdom of fellow Poles" following the war.

Along with such confessions of guilt and repentance, all of the European statements also make very positive assertions regarding Christian relations with Jews and Judaism and call attention to the important shared beliefs.

In 1950 the Protestant Church in Germany was the first Protestant body to reject the long-established teaching that God had cut off Israel and replaced it with the church, which became "the true Israel."[3] In the year 2000 this body, representing some twenty Lutheran, Reformed, and United church bodies throughout Germany, commemorated the fiftieth anniversary of that proclamation (see Document 19). In so doing, it reiterated that God's promise to Israel "remained in force" following Christ's crucifixion, for God remains ever faithful to his choosing Israel as "his people." The statement also rejects all attempts to "close the book" on German history before 1945, since it is the "disastrous tradition of estrangement from Jews and enmity toward them" that burdens current efforts to establish a new relationship. The statement expresses gratitude for Jewish interpretations of and commentaries on the Hebrew Bible/Old Testament, which help Christians gain a "deeper understanding" of it. A special feature of this statement is its reference to its "sisters and brothers of Jewish descent" whom it identifies as "witnesses" to the indissoluble bond of the church and "God's permanently chosen people Israel."

The Church of Sweden, in a 2001 study document titled "The Ways of God,"[4] reviews the Jewish background of Jesus and the common rootedness of Christianity and Judaism. It then surveys three basic models according to which the relation of God's covenant or covenants with Jews and Christians has been or can be understood: "replacement theology," "parallel covenants," and "roads converging at the end of time." Such models, it notes, are to be tested not only by fidelity to the New Testament but also by their effects on the actual historical relationship of Jews and Christians. In relation to the latter, replacement theology is especially found wanting. Ultimately, the Swedish statement reminds us, the core of all faith is something mysterious, a "secret of God" before which both Jews and Christians should feel humble.

The statement by the Federation of Swiss Protestant Churches (Document 16) inaugurated a Day of Encounter and Discovery to emphasize the "unique and enduring relation" between the church and the Jewish people, and to foster a better understanding of the "goal of the Christian journey with Judaism," for both peoples see the world as God's creation, and look forward to its fulfillment. The Swiss Federation admits that we cannot wipe out the past with its evils, but we can discard all "anti-Judaic enmity" and do *teshuvah*—overcome earlier evil—by a lengthy process of "shared suffering and growing reconciliation."[5]

Some Comments on Selected Themes

Conversion and Covenant

On the vexed question of conversion, always a sensitive one for Jewish partners in the dialogue, we find a mixed record in these documents. There are no absolutist assertions insisting on converting Jews to the Christian faith. But there are multiple commitments to continue publicly proclaiming Jesus as "the savior of all people," as in the Lutheran Church in Australia statement of 1996 (Document 23). Also the Hungarian Reformed Church (Document 13) argues that "Christians should not be expected to abandon proclaiming the New Testament's confession that 'Jesus Christ is Lord.'" This church expresses the hope that the two communities will not be separated from each other forever, for "we and our Jewish brothers are bound together by God's choice and by his covenant." The Episcopal Church

(Document 3) insists that it must bear witness to God-in-Christ among all peoples, but rejects "coercive proselytism" and endorses "mutual witness" through dialogue. The United Methodists also assert that Christians are called to witness to all people, yet they add that they may "never presume to know the full extent of God's work in the world" and must recognize that God also works outside the church.

The United Church of Canada (Document 9) affirms that "the Holy Spirit calls us to give faithful witness concerning God's reconciling mission in Jesus Christ" through whom the door is opened in a new way "to those previously outside the covenant." But God's covenant with the Jewish people is "irrevocable." The European Lutheran Commission in 1990 (Document 14) states that "God empowers us to mutually witness to our faith, trusting in the free working of the Holy Spirit." Consequently, though dialogue may lead to one persuading the other, any Christian witness must be done "with due respect for the convictions and faith of their Jewish partners."

We also find in a few of the statements some evidence of vacillation, ambiguity, or even internal contradiction. This may be due in part to the drafting and amending process by which such statements are produced. Thus while the Presbyterian Church (U.S.A.) asserts in Document 1 that Christians are "engrafted into the people of God established by the covenant with Abraham, Isaac, and Jacob," it subsequently affirms that Christ established a "new covenant." Also, while both peoples are elected by God to "witness to the world," the new covenant requires Christians to call all people to faith in Jesus Christ. (The statement itself acknowledges that there is a tension here.)

The same issue is wrestled with again, and at some length, in the recent statement by the Presbyterian Church in Canada (2011, Document 10). The Westminster Confession of Faith's affirmation of the "one covenant of grace embracing Jews and Gentiles" is reaffirmed and is used to undergird the assertion of the "unique role" of Jews in God's salvation and healing for the world. Jews thus "have not been supplanted and replaced by Christians in the one covenant." Both peoples "worship and serve the One Living God." But the Canadian Presbyterians also insist that Jesus Christ is the unique, final, and "sole mediator of the one covenant embracing both Jews and Gentiles." The church's commission is "to bear witness to our Lord to all peoples" without arrogance and with humility.

In contrast to the caution and/or ambiguity of the foregoing statements, open opposition to any mission efforts to convert Jews is voiced by the Protestant Church of the Palatinate (Document 12) and the Austrian Protestant Church (Document 18). The first of these churches asserts that the mission command in Matthew 28:19 to "make disciples of all nations" is misunderstood if Israel is counted among the "nations," which for Jews is synonymous with "Gentiles." Christian witness to Jesus "must not separate him from his people or put him in opposition to his people," for when we separate the two "we set ourselves against our Lord." Indeed, Jesus is a "fulfillment and living interpretation of the Torah," not a witness against it. The Austrian Church also affirms the "permanent election of Israel as God's people"; hence, it states, "mission to Jews is theologically not justifiable and must be rejected as a church program."

The Land and the State of Israel

The documents included in the present collection do not include the respective churches' numerous pronouncements on specific issues in the Middle East, but they do include discussions of the biblical promise of the land and its realization in the State of Israel. The European Lutheran Commission on the Church and the Jewish People, meeting in Romania in 2004, issued a "Statement on Antisemitism and Anti-Zionism" (Document 20) that expresses "deep concern" about the increase in antisemitism in Europe, and sees anti-Zionism as a current manifestation of it. The commission speaks of its "close and lasting ties" with the Jewish people and the State of Israel, along with its "inherent relationship" with Palestinian Christians. But it notes a frequent unbalance favoring the Palestinian point of view in its churches. It especially laments the "intolerable equation of the Israeli government's present policies with the National Socialist policy of annihilation," along with challenges to the Israeli state's very existence. The Commission asserts the "right and obligation" of Israel to "protect itself and its citizens from terror."

Similarly, the Lutheran World Federation statement on "Antisemitism and Anti-Judaism Today" (Document 26) expresses great concern about the "ongoing conflict" and the sufferings it imposes on both Israelis and Palestinians, and it urges both parties to "seek a just agreement." But it acknowledges the "importance of the land of Israel to the Jewish people and its central place in the promises of God." And it recognizes that this is a "central element of Jewish faith," not a "racist ideology."

Sometimes only one sentence is allotted to the subject, as in the 2009 Uniting Church in Australia's affirmation of the right of the State of Israel and a Palestinian state to exist "side by side in peace and security" (Document 24). The Protestant Church of the Palatinate and the Hungarian Reformed Church in their statements (both 1990; Documents 12 and 13) defer questions about the State of Israel for future consideration, though in their text the Hungarians do express joy that their nation has established diplomatic relations with Israel.

A Trialogical Approach

A unique statement is the Anglican Communion's "The Way of Dialogue" (1988, Document 25), as it gives equal attention to Christian relations with Islam as it does to Christian relations with Judaism. In its presentation and explanation of Islamic teachings, of particular interest to Christians is its description of Muslim devotion to Jesus and his mother Mary, and Muslim acceptance of Jesus as the "promised Messiah of Hebrew scripture" though not as Son of God. Islam rejects Jesus' crucifixion both as a historical fact and as theologically significant. While it affirms God's "special relationship" with the Jewish people, it views the Bible as textually corrupted and therefore "no longer valid." But it does not reject the concept of the "suffering of God's righteous prophets," and affirms the positive value of suffering for others or in the cause of God.

Christians need to understand, the Anglican statement points out, that Islam is a missionary religion that is spreading rapidly and widely, and that many Muslims believe Islam supersedes Christianity, just as Christians have believed their faith replaced Judaism. The statement acknowledges that over the centuries Christians have held both a distorted image of Islam and "outright animosity" to it. For any dialogue to be possible, Christians must first learn more about Islam from its primary sources.

Islam's early ideals of religious tolerance, the statement notes, can and should carry over to just treatment and the assurance of basic human rights for minorities in present-day Muslim societies.

With regard to Judaism, the Anglicans affirm that for Christians Judaism can never be just "one religion among many others." It needs to be respected as a still living and developing religion with great spiritual and intellectual vitality. Moreover, Judaism is a people and a civilization as well as a faith community and must be understood and appreciated in all these dimensions. Particular praise is given to the biblical scholarship by both Jews and Christians in recent times which provides a new and different assessment of the first-century Judaism out of which Christianity emerged.

Work Yet to Be Done

All too often these statements, which are intended to educate in the present and shape the future, receive little attention from those to whom they are addressed—both clergy and laity. Indeed, some groups' statements openly acknowledge that not all of their members or congregations are prepared to agree with the thinking and recommendations presented.[6]

Awareness of the continuing need for changes in preaching and teaching and in the entire practices of church organizations and their parishes is clearly recognized by the European Lutheran Commission on the Church and the Jewish People in its statement of 1990 (Document 14). It notes that a "reappraisal of history, especially that of theology, is imperative if we want to attain credibility for the church and to reform our common life in Europe." Poland's Evangelical Reformed Church admitted in 1995 (Document 15) that the accusation of "Jew = God-murderer" was still being heard in its churches. The Protestant Church in Germany, in its statement in the year 2000 (Document 19), notes that the tradition of "estrangement and enmity" continues to burden all efforts for a new approach to the Jewish people. The Lutheran Church of Australia (1996, Document 23) admits that Lutheran church papers "naively and uncritically" published German anti-Jewish propaganda before and during World War II, and that Australian Lutherans stressed the "doctrinal gulf" between themselves and Jews. It urges its members to confess and repent for the church's silence regarding both the Holocaust and its ongoing sins of prejudice against the Jewish people, acknowledging that bigoted information about Jews is still accepted by some Australian Lutherans. The

Lutheran World Federation, in the statement issued by its 2001 international conference (Document 26), warns that "antisemitism and anti-Judaism [are] present in every church and society" represented at the conference.

Both the Waldensian Protestant Church in Italy (1998, Document 17) and the Swiss Protestant Churches (1997, Document 16) recognize that we are only at the beginnings of the changes needed; others will come in successive phases. The will to undertake these changes needs constant renewal and requires a "long process of reconciliation."[7]

Congregations and church members should give close attention to the statements presented here, both those of their own denomination and others. For like Paul's letters to the young churches, these are letters from fellow Christians speaking about the further light and truth breaking forth about God's word for our world today.

Notes

1. While the Australian churches follow the perspectives of their European origins to some extent, they appear not to have been quite as strongly affected by the historical factors.

2. Clearly the Lutherans—in their various national bodies, in the European Lutheran Commission on the Church and the Jewish People, and in the Lutheran World Federation—have been the most persistent of all Protestant denominations in their efforts to reject former anti-Judaic stances and to embrace new theological positions. This is evident even in the number of documents issued: seven in the current volume of *Bridges* in addition to the eight in Volume 1.

3. See *Bridges*, Vol. 1, Document 5.

4. The Swedish document is not included in the present volume on account of its status as a study document rather than an official statement. The text may be found online at http://www.bc.edu/dam/files/research_sites/cjl/texts/documents/protestant/church_of_sweden_2001.htm.

5. Another important European Protestant document not included in this volume because of its length needs to be mentioned. Entitled "Church and Israel: A Contribution from the Reformation Churches in Europe to the Relationship Between Christians and Jews," it was issued in 2001 by the Community of Protestant Churches in Europe (CPCE), also known as the Leuenberg Church Fellowship. It offers in-depth coverage of the entire subject of Christian-Jewish relations: the history and theology of the relationship

over the centuries, consideration of theological attempts to clarify the relationship, and recommendations for how the foregoing should affect the worship, preaching, teaching, and educational programs of the churches. The full text in both German and English may be found at http://www.leuenberg.eu/sites/default/files/doc-162-1.pdf.

6. In the U.S. the statements of the Presbyterian Church (U.S.A.) and the United Church of Christ initially met with "firestorms" of protest, which made it necessary for these churches to conduct regional open meetings to discuss the issues.

7. In the 1970s when Dr. James Parkes was asked how long he thought it would take for the necessary changes in Christian theology to be made and take effect, he unhesitatingly replied "several hundred years" (Parkes, *Voyage of Discoveries* [London: Victor Gollancz, 1969], pp. 128–29). Such hard-headed realism may be disheartening, but acceptance of it is perhaps the only force that will keep Christians working to eradicate the problem.

Alice L. Eckardt *is Professor Emerita of Religion Studies at Lehigh University. She is the author, and coauthor with A. Roy Eckardt, of studies of Christian-Jewish relations and of the Holocaust, including* Burning Memory: Times of Testing and Reckoning *and* Long Night's Journey Into Day: A Revised Retrospective of the Holocaust.

Building a New Relationship: A Catholic Perspective

Philip A. Cunningham

My introductory essay in *Bridges*, Volume 1, discussed pre-1986 Roman Catholic documents in terms of four overarching themes: (1) an eternal covenant; (2) the condemnation of antisemitism; (3) the interpretation of the Christian Bible; and (4) education. Since the documents presented in this second volume further develop these themes, they continue to provide a useful way of surveying the later texts.

First Theme: An Eternal Covenant

During the twenty-six years of his pontificate, Pope John Paul II constantly reiterated that the Jewish people's covenantal life[1] with God has never been revoked or abrogated. This began with his address to the Jewish community in Mainz, Germany on November 17, 1980 (*Bridges*, Vol. 1, Document 34) and recurred frequently in his subsequent writings.[2]

The most iconic of John Paul II's affirmations of the ongoing vigor of Jewish covenantal life came on March 26, 2000, when, according to Jewish custom, he inserted a prayer in the Western Wall in Jerusalem (Document 37 below). Its concluding words are a formal pledge of the Roman Catholic Church to the Jewish people delivered at the holiest site of Judaism: "...we wish to commit ourselves to genuine brotherhood with *the people of the Covenant*" [italics added].[3]

His successor Pope Benedict XVI not only made his own the words of John Paul II's Western Wall prayer,[4] he, too, acknowledged Judaism's continuous covenantal life in his own writings. Thus, during his address at the Great Synagogue of Rome on January 17, 2010 (Document 43), he spoke of the Nazi incarceration of Roman Jews in these words: "The extermination of the people of the Covenant of Moses,[5] at first announced, then systematically programmed and put into practice in Europe under the Nazi regime, on that day tragically reached as far as Rome."

Closely related to the covenant theme is a stress in Catholic statements on the close spiritual affinity between Judaism and Christianity. This was powerfully stated by John Paul II during his visit to the Great Synagogue of Rome (Document 27): "[T]he Church of Christ discovers her 'bond' with Judaism by 'searching into her own mystery.' The Jewish religion is not 'extrinsic' to us, but in a certain way is 'intrinsic' to our own religion. With Judaism therefore we have a relationship which we do not have with any other religion. You are our dearly beloved brothers and, in a certain way, it could be said that you are our elder brothers."

This same sentiment was expressed later by Pope Benedict XVI during his address at the Roonstrasse Synagogue in Cologne, Germany (Document 38):

> We must come to know one another much more and much better. Consequently I would encourage sincere and trustful dialogue between Jews and Christians, for only in this way will it be possible to arrive at a shared interpretation of disputed historical questions, and, above all, to make progress toward a theological evaluation of the relationship between Judaism and Christianity. This dialogue, if it is to be sincere, must not gloss over or underestimate the existing differences: in those areas in which, due to our profound convictions in faith, we diverge, and indeed precisely in those areas, we need to show respect for one another.

Second Theme: The Condemnation of Antisemitism

If *Nostra Aetate* (*Bridges*, Vol. 1, Document 30) in 1965 could be criticized for denouncing antisemitism without explicitly admitting any Christian culpability for it, Catholic documents increasingly engaged in self-examination as the years passed. The fiftieth anniversaries of events preceding and during the Second World War provided many occasions for both the Vatican and national bishops' conferences to ponder Catholic actions and inactions a half century earlier. The post-conciliar attitude of remorse is strikingly evident in materials dating from the fiftieth anniversary of *Kristallnacht* in 1988 through to the Great Jubilee of 2000.

Penitential self-reflection was also strongly encouraged by Pope John Paul II. On November 10, 1994, he issued an apostolic letter, *Tertio Millennio Adveniente* (On the Coming of the Third Millennium), which set forth an ambitious multiyear plan to prepare for a Great Jubilee in the year 2000: "[I]t is appropriate that, as the Second Millennium of Christianity draws to a close, the Church should become more fully conscious of the sinfulness of her children, recalling all those times in history when they departed from the spirit of Christ and his Gospel and, instead of offering to the world the witness of a life inspired by the values of faith, indulged in ways of thinking and acting which were truly forms of counter-witness and scandal."[6]

The remembrance of the Shoah[7] and the legacy of Christian contempt for Jews and Judaism were clearly among the collective sins that the pope had in mind. For instance, a few years earlier he had told the new ambassador from the Federal Republic of Germany that "For Christians the heavy burden of guilt for the murder of the Jewish people must be an enduring call to repentance; thereby we can overcome every form of antisemitism and establish a new relationship with our kindred nation of the Old Covenant" (Document 30). These sentiments were now woven into preparations for the Great Jubilee of 2000 and explicitly or implicitly informed the continuing series of bishops' statements marking Shoah-related anniversaries.

Kristallnacht or the "Night of Broken Glass" occurred in Nazi Germany on the night of November 9–10, 1938. Many historians consider this planned series of attacks on Jewish synagogues and businesses to be the beginning of the Shoah. The bishops of West Germany, Austria, and Berlin marked the fiftieth anniversary of this rampage with "Accepting the Burden of History" (Document 58). After recalling that Catholic teaching rejected Nazi racism and that the bishops of the time struggled to defend Christianity against Nazi attacks, the bishops posed the searing question: "But was this enough…in the face of burning synagogues and thousands of abused Jewish fellow-citizens? …Would not public protest, a clearly recognizable gesture of humaneness and sympathy, have been the duty demanded from the Church's office as guardian?" They went on to declare that "We have to accept the burden of history. We owe this to the victims, whose sufferings and death may not be forgotten."

Two years later, to commemorate the twenty-fifth anniversary of *Nostra Aetate*, the Catholic bishops of Poland issued a pastoral letter on Catholic-Jewish relations (Document 59). After recognizing that Poland had become "for many Jews a second fatherland," they lamented that "in our century this particular land became the grave for several million Jews. Not by our wish, and not by our hands." The bishops expressed their admiration for the "hundreds, if not thousands" of Polish Catholics who sought to aid Jews but "paid for this with their own lives and the lives of their loved ones." Yet, despite these "heroic examples" the bishops acknowledged that there were also those who "remained indifferent to this incomprehensible tragedy":

> We are especially disheartened by those among Catholics who in some way were the cause of the death of Jews. They will forever gnaw at our conscience on the social plane. If only one Christian could have helped and did not stretch out a helping hand to a Jew during the time of danger or caused his death, we must ask for forgiveness of our Jewish brothers and sisters…We express our sincere regret for all the incidents of antisemitism, which were committed at any time or by anyone on Polish soil. We do this with the deep conviction that all incidents of antisemitism are contrary to the spirit of the Gospel.

The bishops rejected the notion of a particularly virulent Polish type of antisemitism, recalling that Poles themselves "were one of the first victims of the same criminal racist ideology of Hitler's Nazism." They urged that Polish Christians and the surviving Polish Jews should be united by "blood spilled together, the sea of horrific suffering and of injuries shared," and should actively pursue dialogue in order to eliminate "distrust, prejudices and stereotypes," thereby "opening the way to cooperation in many fields."

In 1997, a group of French Catholic bishops issued a "Declaration of Repentance" (Document 60) to mark both the fiftieth anniversary of "The Ten Points of Seelisberg" (*Bridges*, Vol. 1, Document 56) and also the imminent sixtieth anniversary of the passage of anti-Jewish legislation by the collaborationist French government in Vichy in 1940. They opened with this ringing declaration: "The time has come for the church to submit her own history, especially that of this period, to critical examination and to recognize without hesitation the sins committed by members of the church, and to beg forgiveness of God and humankind." While acknowledging that by February 1941 France was defeated and partially occupied by the Nazis and that "the hierarchy saw the protection of its own faithful as its first priority," the bishops characterized this move as a "retreat into a narrow vision of the church's mission." Therefore, Catholic clergy, "caught up in a loyalism and docility which went far beyond the obedience traditionally accorded to civil authorities, remained stuck in conformity, prudence and abstention." The French bishops felt "obliged to acknowledge objectively today that ecclesiastical interests, understood in an overly restrictive sense, took priority over the demands of conscience—and we must ask ourselves why."

Although they denied "a direct cause-and-effect link" between the historic Christian teaching of contempt and the Shoah," the bishops candidly stated that "it is a well-proven fact that for centuries, up until Vatican Council II, an anti-Jewish tradition stamped its mark in differing ways on Christian doctrine and teaching, in theology, apologetics, preaching and in the liturgy. It was on such ground that the venomous plant of hatred for the Jews was able to flourish." They declared, "Today we confess that such a silence was a sin…We confess this sin. We beg God's pardon, and we call upon the Jewish people to hear our words of repentance."

Although sometimes commentators erroneously speak of such statements in terms of an "apology" or "asking for forgiveness," the realization of the burden that requesting forgiveness would place on survivors or their descendants, who could not possibly speak for the murdered victims, militated against making any appeals to Jews directly. Instead, these documents asked that Jews hear Catholic expressions of contrition and sinfulness and new resolve, but prayers of forgiveness were directed, almost without exception, only to God. This is vividly the case with John Paul II's prayer at the Western Wall in 2000 (Document 37).

In 1998, the Commission for Religious Relations with the Jews issued a long-awaited Vatican statement on the Shoah. Compared to the forthright self-criticisms from several national bishops' conferences, this statement, "We Remember: A Reflection on the Shoah" (Document 49), seemed to many observers to be overly measured. Critics pointed to such sentences as "At the end of this Millennium the Catholic Church desires to express her deep sorrow for the failures of her sons and daughters in every age" as seeking to absolve the church "as such"[8] from the sins committed by its members. There was also criticism of the document's effort to rigidly distinguish between anti-Judaism and antisemitism, of its lengthy defense of Pope Pius XII in footnote sixteen, and especially of its weak response to the question of whether Christians had done all they could to help Jews: "Many did, but others did not."[9]

Cardinal Edward Idris Cassidy, president of the Pontifical Commission for Religious Relations with the Jews, discussed such concerns in an address to the American Jewish Committee on May 28, 1998. Replying to criticisms that "We Remember" did not sufficiently address the role of the Christian "teaching of contempt" for Jews over the centuries, Cardinal Cassidy gave a frank historical summary that would have benefited the actual document:

> There can be no denial of the fact that from the time of Emperor Constantine on, Jews were isolated and discriminated against in the Christian world. There were expulsions and forced conversions. Literature propagated stereotypes; preaching accused the Jews of every age of deicide; the ghetto which came into being in 1555 with a papal bull became in Nazi Germany the antechamber of the extermination.
>
> It is also true that the Nazis made use of this sad history in their attacks on the Jewish people, adopting symbols and recalling events of the past to justify their deadly campaign. It is also true, I believe, that a part of the indifference shown toward the mass deportations and brutality which accompanied these forced movements of helpless and innocent people was a result of the age-old attitudes of Christian society and preaching toward those considered responsible for the death of Jesus.[10]

The cardinal's use of the phrase "the Christian world," rather than simply "the church," echoed the document's phrases "members of the Church" or "sons and daughters of the Church." He explained this usage as follows: "[W]hen we make this distinction, the term 'members of the Church' does not refer to a particular category of church members, but can include according to the circumstances popes, cardinals, bishops, priests, and laity...We do not speak of the Church as sinful, but of the members of the Church as sinful—a distinction you may find hard to understand, but one which is essential to our understanding of the Church."[11]

In the Catholic ecclesiological tradition to suggest that as a mystical communion the church is sinful is tantamount to denying that the Holy Spirit dwells within it. However, when confronted with the enormity of the Shoah and the magnitude of Christian participation in it, the reaffirmation of transcendent realities can seem out of place, if not offensive. Indeed, the challenge of this question gave rise to a major study by the Vatican's International Theological Commission in conjunction with the Great Jubilee of 2000. Entitled "Memory and Reconciliation: The Church and the Faults of the Past," it reasoned:

> The Church is holy because, sanctified by Christ who has acquired her by giving himself up to death for her, she is maintained in holiness by the Holy Spirit who pervades her unceasingly...One can distinguish, however, the holiness of the Church from holiness in the Church...
>
> Without obscuring this [transcendent] holiness, we must acknowledge that due to the presence of sin there is a need for continual renewal and for constant conversion in the People of God. The Church on earth is "marked with a true holiness," which is, however, "imperfect."...Thomas Aquinas makes clear that the fullness of holiness belongs to eschatological time; in the meantime, the Church still on pilgrimage should not deceive herself by saying that she is without sin.[12]

The figure of Pope Pius XII has been another debated topic. The controversy over whether the wartime pope should be canonized has periodically roiled Catholic-Jewish relations. One such episode occurred in December 2009 when Pope Benedict XVI formally recognized the "heroic virtue" of Pius XII, an initial step in the Catholic process of canonization. In an interview shortly afterward, Benedict explained:

[O]ne can still always ask, "Why didn't he protest more clearly?" I believe it was because he saw what consequences would follow from an open protest. We know that personally he suffered greatly because of it. He knew he actually ought to speak out, and yet the situation made that impossible for him.

At the present time, we have new, clever people who say that, while [Pius XII] did save many lives, he had old-fashioned ideas about Jews that fall short of Vatican II. But that is not the question. The decisive thing is what he did and what he tried to do, and on that score we really must acknowledge, I believe, that he was one of the great righteous men and that he saved more Jews than anyone else.[13]

In contrast, an op-ed by two Jewish writers that same year stated, "A saintly life? Hardly. Pope Pius failed to act in a saintly fashion in one very crucial respect: He did not give Jews the help he could and should have during the Holocaust."[14]

In its exhibit on the subject, the Holocaust Memorial Museum in Jerusalem, Yad Vashem, placed new signage in 2012 to describe both sides of the dispute:

The Pope's critics claim that his decision to abstain from condemning the murder of the Jews by Nazi Germany constitutes a moral failure: the lack of clear guidance left room for many to collaborate with Nazi Germany, reassured by the thought that this did not contradict the Church's moral teachings. It also left the initiative to rescue Jews to individual clerics and laymen. His defenders maintain that [his] neutrality prevented harsher measures against the Vatican and the Church's institutions throughout Europe, thus enabling a considerable number of secret rescue activities to take place at different levels of the Church. Moreover, they point to cases in which the Pontiff offered encouragement to activities in which Jews were rescued. Until all relevant material is available to scholars, this topic will remain open to further inquiry.[15]

Pope Pius XII is also linked to the story of a Jewish woman named Edith Stein, who was canonized by Pope John Paul II in the same year of 1998 that "We Remember" was issued. An atheist by the time she reached adolescence, she went on to earn a doctoral degree in philosophy. Her writings as a university professor would appeal to the future John Paul II. She embraced Catholicism in 1922 and eventually was accepted as a novice in the Discalced Carmelite Order where she took the religious name of Teresa Benedicta of the Cross.

On April 12, 1933, she wrote a letter to Pope Pius XII "as a child of the Jewish people who, by the grace of God, for the past eleven years has also been a child of the Catholic Church." She urged the public condemnation of Nazi antisemitic propaganda and actions. "Is not this idolization of race and governmental power which is being pounded into the public consciousness by the radio open heresy? Isn't the effort to destroy Jewish blood an abuse of the holiest humanity of our Savior, of the most blessed Virgin and the apostles?"[16]

By 1942, Sister Teresa had fled to the Netherlands for safety. But after the Dutch Catholic Bishops read a statement in all churches in July of that year denouncing National Socialist antisemitism, the Nazis rounded up Catholics of Jewish ancestry in retaliation. Sister Teresa died in Auschwitz on August 9, 1942.

Her canonization by John Paul II on October 11, 1998, was contentious. To some it seemed that she represented the Catholic ideal of the perfect Jew: one who had been baptized. Others saw her sainthood as part of a Catholic initiative to Christianize the Holocaust itself—a process that was thought to include the canonization of a Catholic priest, Maximilian Kolbe, and the presence near Auschwitz of a Carmelite convent.

The traditional Catholic process of canonization is applicable only to Catholics. This does not mean that there are no non-Catholic saints, only that the Catholic Church never developed a mechanism for recognizing them. If John Paul sought to give the church's highest honor to victims of the Shoah, this custom would allow him to identify as saints only those who had been baptized as Catholics.

In his homily for her canonization (Document 34), John Paul stressed the reason for her death: "Because she was Jewish, Edith Stein was taken with her sister Rosa and many other Catholic Jews from the Netherlands to the concentration camp in Auschwitz, where she died with them in the gas chambers." In the pope's thinking, her feast day on August 9, the day of her death, should be the occasion to honor all the Jewish victims of the Nazis: "From now on, as we celebrate the memory of this new saint from year to year, we must also remember the Shoah, that cruel plan to exterminate a people—a plan to which millions of our Jewish brothers and sisters fell victim. May the Lord let his face shine upon them and grant them peace."

John Paul's commitment to fostering Catholic-Jewish rapprochement is most vividly seen in the events that occurred early in Lent during the Great Jubilee of 2000. On March 12, 2000, the First Sunday of Lent, an unprecedented "Mass of Pardon" was celebrated by all the leaders of the Vatican in St. Peter's Basilica to confess and seek God's forgiveness for the sins Christians had committed in the previous thousand years.

Included in this communal "examination of conscience," which is the Catholic cognate of the Jewish concept of "a reckoning of the soul" (*cheshbon hanefesh*), were "Sins against the People of Israel." Cardinal Cassidy prayed that "in recalling the sufferings endured by the people of Israel throughout history, Christians will acknowledge the sins committed by not a few of their number against the people of the Covenant and the blessings, and in this way will purify their hearts." The pope replied with a prayer of remorse and commitment that two weeks later he repeated at the Western Wall in Jerusalem (Document 37). There, John Paul prayed in the Jewish manner by inserting his written petition into a crevice of the Western Wall. The petition was sealed with the papal seal and personally signed. After asking God's forgiveness for the suffering caused by Christians to God's Jewish children, he wrote, "we wish to commit ourselves to genuine brotherhood with the people of the Covenant." Clearly, the pope understood these iconic actions at the two central sites of both faiths to be a solemn pledge for the future. His pilgrimage to Israel was repeated in 2009 by his successor Pope Benedict XVI, who also prayed at the Western Wall and visited Yad Vashem (Documents 41 and 42).

The sheer number of Catholic ecclesiastical statements from 1985 to the present condemning antisemitism, especially in the context of the Shoah, is striking. They have taken the few words in *Nostra Aetate* that the church "decries hatred, persecutions, displays of antisemitism, directed against Jews at any time and by anyone," and have begun to apply them critically to the Catholic community itself.

Third Theme: The Interpretation of the Christian Bible

Since 1985 there has also been continuing development in terms of Catholic teaching on biblical interpretation concerning Jews and Judaism. Prior to that point, largely driven by the statements of the Pontifical Commission for Religious Relations with the Jews (*Bridges*, Vol. 1, Documents 38 and 39), Catholic documents were especially concerned with New Testament texts describing the crucifixion of Jesus, the Pharisees, and the Judaism of Jesus' time. This remains an issue, as seen in John Paul II's statement to the Pontifical Biblical Commission in 1997 (Document 32 below) that "erroneous and unjust interpretations of the New Testament relative to the Jewish people and their presumed guilt circulated for too long, engendering sentiments of hostility toward this people."

More recently, Catholic ecclesial texts have devoted attention to the complex relationship between the two parts of the Christian Bible and their interpretation. This often includes a stress on the incompleteness of God's plans for the world, which at the end of days, at the "eschaton," will achieve their ultimate fulfillment. (This perspective is known technically as "futurist eschatology.") Two major studies of the Pontifical Biblical Commission (PBC) are especially important.

In 1993, the PBC released "The Interpretation of the Bible in the Church" (see Document 47). This study stressed that since "Holy Scripture, inasmuch as it is the 'word of God in human language,' has been composed by human authors in all its various parts and in all the sources that lie behind them...Catholic scriptural scholarship freely makes use of the scientific methods and approaches which allow a better grasp of the meaning of texts in their linguistic, literary, socio-cultural, religious and historical contexts" (I, A; III). It understood the process of scriptural interpretation as "overcoming the distance between the time of the authors and first addressees of the biblical texts, and our own contemporary age, and of doing so in a way that permits a correct actualization of the Scriptural message so that the Christian life of faith may find nourishment" (II, A, 2). When a sense of the meaning of a text on its own terms has been gleaned, its significance or implications for today's church still must be "actualized," or brought into dialogue with today's world.

In discussing this process of actualization, the PBC set forth an important axiom: "Particular attention is necessary, according to the spirit of the Second Vatican Council (*Nostra Aetate*, 4), to avoid absolutely any actualization of certain texts of the New Testament which could provoke or reinforce unfavorable attitudes to the Jewish people." To put it another way, if someone comes away from reading the New Testament with antagonism toward Jews, then that person's reading is incorrect.

In 2001 the PBC published a document of such length that it constituted a small book. Therefore only a small but key section is excerpted in this volume (see Document 50). As its title suggests, "The Jewish People and Their Sacred Scripture in the Christian Bible" represents the most extensive ecclesial consideration to date of the interrelation between Christian-Jewish relations and the study of the Bible. Its treatment of the topics of fulfillment and prophecy is remarkable.

"It would be wrong," the PBC states," to consider the prophecies of the Old Testament as some kind of photographic anticipations of future events. All the texts, including those which later were read as messianic prophecies, already had an immediate import and meaning for their contemporaries before attaining a fuller meaning for future hearers." Rejecting the notion that one can prove things about Jesus by citing prophetic passages, the study declared that this longstanding practice "has contributed to harsh judgments by Christians of Jews and their reading of the Old Testament: the more reference to Christ is found in Old Testament texts, the more the incredulity of the Jews is considered inexcusable and obstinate."

The PBC could argue this way because it understood the New Testament as continuing the biblical process of "rereading" earlier scriptures in the light of contemporary circumstances:

> Although the Christian reader is aware that the internal dynamism of the Old Testament finds its goal in Jesus, this is a *retrospective* perception whose point of departure is not in the text as such, but in the events of the New Testament proclaimed by the apostolic preaching. *It cannot be said*, therefore, that Jews do not see what has been proclaimed in the text, but that the Christian, in the light of Christ and in the Spirit, discovers in the text an additional meaning that was hidden there [italics added].

If Christians read their "Old Testament" retrospectively through a Christological lens, it is also the case that Jews read their Tanakh retrospectively through the lens of the rabbinic tradition. Therefore, "Christians can and ought to admit that the Jewish reading of the Bible is a possible one, in continuity with the Jewish Sacred Scriptures from the Second Temple period, a reading analogous to the Christian reading which developed in parallel fashion. Both readings are bound up with the vision of their respective faiths, of which the readings are the result and expression."

Thinking in terms of cognate traditions of Jewish and Christian interpretations of scripture also has consequences for each community's respective messianic expectations:

> The definitive fulfillment will be at the end with the resurrection of the dead, a new heaven and a new earth. Jewish messianic expectation is not in vain. It can become for us Christians a powerful stimulant to keep alive the eschatological dimension of our faith. Like them, we too live in expectation. The difference is that for us the One who is to come will have the traits of the Jesus who has already come and is already present and active among us.

The PBC here stresses that the ultimate fulfillment of all God's intentions lies still in the future. Most notably, Christians and Jews are seen to have converging expectations about the end of days, but on the basis of different "traits" mediated by their respective traditions.

Finally, the PBC encouraged Christians and Jews to learn from each other's traditions of biblical interpretation. Without adopting each other's respective lenses, "Christians can, nonetheless, learn much from Jewish exegesis [interpretation] practiced for more than two thousand years, and, in fact, they have learned much in the course of history. For their part, it is to be hoped that Jews themselves can derive profit from Christian exegetical research."

The possibility of Christians and Jews "profiting discerningly"[17] from each other's interpretive traditions was a regular theme in Pope Benedict's writings. Not only as Cardinal Joseph Ratzinger did he give a glowing foreword to the 2001 PBC study, but as pope he stressed the common biblical heritage of Jews and Christians in a number of papal addresses (e.g., Documents 38 and 43). In a 2011 book he was quite direct: "After centuries of antagonism, we now see it as our task to bring these two ways of rereading the biblical texts—the Christian way and the Jewish way—into dialogue with one another, if we are to understand God's will and his word aright."[18]

These important developments in Catholic biblical teaching lead naturally to our fourth theme.

Fourth Theme: Education

In both Volume 1 of *Bridges* and in this second volume, almost all Catholic documents assert the importance of correct and thorough education. Here I will simply draw attention to three very significant educational guidelines put forth by bishops' committees of the United States Conference of Catholic Bishops.

In 1988, the Bishops' Committee on the Liturgy released *God's Mercy Endures Forever: Guidelines on the Presentation of Jews and Judaism in Catholic Preaching* (Document 55). After discussing the Jewish roots of Catholic liturgy and giving a general overview of difficult scriptural texts in terms of Christian attitudes toward Judaism, it suggests how homilists can approach the lectionary readings during Advent, Lent, Holy Week, and Easter with sensitivity to the concerns of the post–*Nostra Aetate* church. This document, which is not as widely known as it deserves, is notable for expressing more than ten years earlier many of the same principles found in the 2001 PBC study.

Also in 1988, the Bishops' Committee for Ecumenical and Interreligious Affairs published "Criteria for the Evaluation of Dramatizations of the Passion" (Document 56). This text applies principles articulated in Vatican and papal documents to the scripts and productions of passion plays. It sets forth Catholic biblical standards on the utilization of the four distinct Gospel passion narratives, noting in particular that a "clear and precise hermeneutic and a guiding artistic vision sensitive to historical fact and to the best biblical scholarship are obviously necessary. Just as obviously, it is not sufficient for the producers of passion dramatizations to respond to responsible criticism simply by appealing to the notion that 'it's in the Bible.' One must account for one's selections."

Regrettably, this axiom was not much honored during the 2004 controversy over the movie *The Passion of the Christ*, which drew heavily on non-biblical materials and combined elements from the four Gospels in ways that heightened their anti-Jewish potential.[19] The episode revealed that many young Christians were unaware of how the epithet "Christ killers" had victimized Jews for centuries, probably because *Nostra Aetate* and corresponding Protestant documents had thoroughly excised it from teaching materials. Perhaps what this indicates is a need to teach about past Christian anti-Judaism and its modern repudiation so that students can recognize any signs of its resurgence.

In 2001, the Bishops' Committee on Ecumenical and Interreligious Affairs released "Catholic Teaching on the Shoah: Implementing the Holy See's 'We Remember'" (Document 57). As the title suggests, this document provided guidelines for Catholic education about the Shoah. It included detailed curricular recommendations and concise treatments of such topics as "Framing Issues Properly and Sensitively," "The Church, Its Members, and Responsibility for the Shoah," "Guilt and Responsibility," and "The Construction of Memory."

Different Catholic dioceses around the world have developed many educational programs that simply cannot be presented in a single volume. In addition, there have been numerous scholarly curricular initiatives at Catholic universities around the world that are not part of this collection of ecclesial materials.

Reservations and Renewal:
The Growing Pains of Transformed Perspectives

In Volume 1 of *Bridges*, I suggested that beginning with *Nostra Aetate*, Catholic magisterial teaching regarding Jews and Judaism has unfolded in four overlapping movements: (1) *repudiation* of the teaching of contempt; (2) *ramifications* of this repudiation for education, scripture, ecclesiology, and so forth; (3) *remorse* for the harm caused by previous teachings and practices; and (4) *renewal* or the development of theologies based on the conviction that Jewish covenantal life is salvific for Jews while being mysteriously related to the saving work of Jesus Christ. The Catholic documents up to 1985 published in Volume 1 of *Bridges* were mostly from the first two of these "movements," while this second volume presents ensuing materials that include the third and fourth movements. In considering these later texts, however, it seems necessary to revise the fourth of these categories to *reservations and renewal.* This is because in the first decade of the twenty-first century some leading Catholic figures and a few minor ecclesiastical documents questioned the trajectory launched by *Nostra Aetate.*

In the United States, many underlying reservations surfaced after the publication of a report in August 2002 called "Reflections on Covenant and Mission."[20] This report is not included in this collection because it was not an official statement of the United States Catholic bishops, although it emerged from an official consultation of the Bishops' Committee on Ecumenical Affairs and the National Council of Synagogues and was made public after going through the normal procedures for such texts. The study had been composed shortly after some Christian groups had announced campaigns to encourage Jews to convert to Christianity. The Catholic portion of the joint statement explained why such endeavors were not undertaken by the Catholic Church: "A deepening Catholic appreciation of the eternal covenant between God and the Jewish people, together with a recognition of a divinely-given mission to Jews to witness to God's faithful love, lead to the conclusion that campaigns that target Jews for conversion to Christianity are no longer theologically acceptable in the Catholic Church."

The paper cited numerous papal and Vatican statements and also the important 2001 address by Cardinal Walter Kasper to the official Vatican liaison committee with the worldwide Jewish community (Document 51): "The only thing I wish to say is that [Vatican teaching] does not state that everybody needs to become a Catholic in order to be saved by God. On the contrary, it declares that God's grace, which is the grace of Jesus Christ according to our faith, is available to all. Therefore, the Church believes that Judaism, i.e., the faithful response of the Jewish people to God's irrevocable covenant, is salvific for them, because God is faithful to his promises."[21]

This approach struck some Catholics as denying the universal saving significance of Jesus Christ for all humanity. Over the next several years a series of articles and even some ecclesiastical actions sought to interpret *Nostra Aetate* in a restrictive manner so as to assert the necessity of Christ for salvation. I have elsewhere charted these developments in detail,[22] but here it will suffice to list the various strategies employed to constrict the application of *Nostra Aetate*:

    a. subordinating it to other conciliar documents and/or inflating its continuity with received traditions

    b. disregarding post–*Nostra Aetate* official ecclesial documents

   c. being unconcerned with the history of post–New Testament Judaism and/or of contemporary Jewish self-understanding

   d. invoking the Letter to the Hebrews in a supersessionist fashion to circumscribe the Letter to the Romans upon which *Nostra Aetate* largely depended

   e. preferring a realized eschatology over a futurist eschatology, especially when speaking of what has already been "fulfilled" by Christ

   f. seeing an intention to convert the other as part of interreligious dialogue

   g. understanding "covenant" in terms of promises rather than as a continuing relationship; thus calling into question the ongoing validity of the Sinai covenant after Christ[23]

Several actions consonant with these ideas occurred roughly in the years 2005–2010. For example, in August 2009, the Vatican approved a change in the *United States Catholic Catechism for Adults*. It had originally stated that "the covenant that God made with the Jewish people through Moses remains eternally valid for them." This was replaced by a quotation from Romans 9:4–5: "To the Jewish people, whom God first chose to hear his Word, 'belong the sonship, the glory, the covenants, the giving of the law, the worship...'" A "Backgrounder" prepared by staff at the U.S. Conference of Catholic Bishops explained the change in this way: "The prior version of the text might be understood to imply that one of the former covenants imparts salvation without the mediation of Christ, whom Christians believe to be the universal savior of all people."[24] Although this explanation invoked a soteriological rationale, the effect of the revision was to question whether the covenant at Sinai remained "eternally valid." The implication was that Torah observance was no longer valid for Jews.

   Similarly, staff of the Bishops' Committees on Doctrine and for Ecumenical and Interreligious Affairs issued "A Note on Ambiguities Contained in 'Reflections on Covenant and Mission.'" A desire to assert that Catholics should always hope for Jewish conversions to Christ seems to have been a primary concern of its authors. Thus, as originally released the document stated:

> *Reflections on Covenant and Mission* proposes interreligious dialogue as a form of evangelization that is "a mutually enriching sharing of gifts devoid of any intention whatsoever to invite

the dialogue partner to baptism." Though Christian participation in interreligious dialogue would not normally include an explicit invitation to baptism and entrance into the Church, the Christian dialogue partner is always giving witness to the following of Christ, to which all are implicitly invited.

Almost immediately, an unprecedented unanimous letter from all the American rabbinic movements and Jewish advocacy organizations was sent to the bishops warning that "once Jewish-Christian dialogue has been formally characterized as an invitation, whether explicit or implicit, to apostatize, then Jewish participation [in dialogue] becomes untenable." The Jewish leaders were also dismayed that the "Note on Ambiguities" appeared "to posit that the Mosaic covenant is obsolete and Judaism no longer has a reason to exist." The leadership of the bishops' conference replied quickly with a statement affirming that "Jewish covenantal life endures till the present day as a vital witness to God's saving will for His people Israel and for all of humanity." They also declared that "Jewish-Catholic dialogue, one of the blessed fruits of the Second Vatican Council, has never been and will never be used by the Catholic Church as a means of proselytism—nor is it intended as a disguised invitation to baptism." In an unheard of action, the episcopal leaders also ordered the removal of the sentences about explicit and implicit invitations to baptism from "A Note on Ambiguities."

Most regrettably, after a special bishops' synod on the Middle East held in the Vatican in October 2010, Melkite Archbishop Cyril Bustros, a synod participant, wrote, "As for the idea of the chosen people, it is clear, according to Christian theology and especially to St. Paul, that after Christ there is no longer one particular chosen people!"[25] This claim effectively denied that Jews have an ongoing covenantal life with God.

Pope Benedict XVI did not endorse such minimizations of *Nostra Aetate*. Some observers had raised questions in this regard when in 2008 he promulgated a revised Tridentine Rite Good Friday intercessory prayer for Jews (Document 40). ("Tridentine" refers to the practices and prayers deriving from the Council of Trent, 1545–1563.) Unlike the post–Vatican II Good Friday intercession used by 99 percent of the world's Catholics, which prays that Jews, "the first to hear the Word of God,…may continue to grow in the love of his name and

in faithfulness to his covenant," the new formulation for the preconcil-
iar rite asks that Jews "may recognize Jesus Christ as savior of all men."
Although unclear at the time of its release, it was subsequently
explained that this prayer was not meant to spark Catholic efforts to
convert Jews today. As Cardinal Walter Kasper explained in the
Vatican newspaper (Document 53), in an article published at the
request of the pope,

> Such petitions for the coming of the Kingdom of God and for
> the realization of the mystery of salvation are not by nature a
> call to the Church to undertake missionary action to the
> Jews....So in this prayer the Church does not take it upon her-
> self to orchestrate the realization of the unfathomable mystery.
> She cannot do so. Instead, she lays the *when* and the *how*
> entirely in God's hands. God alone can bring about the
> Kingdom of God in which the whole of Israel is saved and
> eschatological peace is bestowed on the world [italics in the
> original].[26]

Pope Benedict later wrote explicitly on the topic of whether
Christians should seek to convert Jews today. He affirmatively cited the
opinion of a Cistercian Abbess of Mariastern-Gwiggen in Austria
(Document 44):

> Hildegard Brem comments...as follows: "In the light of
> Romans 11:25, the Church must not concern herself with the
> conversion of the Jews, since she must wait for the time fixed
> for this by God, 'until the full number of the Gentiles come in'
> (Rom 11:25)."

This papal opinion has been reiterated by Cardinal Kurt Koch, current president of the Pontifical Commission for Religious Relations
with the Jews, who has stated, "there cannot be any organized mission
to [convert] the Jews[27]....The rejection in principle of an institutional
Jewish mission does not...exclude Christians from bearing witness to
their faith in Jesus Christ also to Jews, but they should do so in a humble and unassuming manner, particularly in view of the great tragedy of
the Shoah" (Document 54). This distinction between a conversionary

"mission" to Jews and giving "witness" to one's Christian faith is crucial in the context of interreligious dialogue. Obviously, both Jews and Christians must "witness" to their respective faith experiences and traditions; otherwise, what would be the purpose of conversing about religious matters? The point is that in dialogue the intention of the participants is to learn more about the other, not to harbor desires to convert the other away from his or her religious identity. This has been put very powerfully by Cardinal Walter Kasper (Document 52): "[W]e Catholics became aware with greater clarity that the faith of Israel is that of our elder brothers, and, most importantly, that Judaism is as a sacrament of every otherness that as such the Church must learn to discern, recognize and celebrate."

In 2012, in his apostolic exhortation, *Ecclesia in Medio Oriente* (Document 45), Pope Benedict contradicted the claim of Archbishop Bustros that "there is no longer one particular chosen people!" The pope wrote that our "close bonds [with Judaism] are a unique treasure of which Christians are proud and for which they are indebted to *the Chosen People*. The Jewishness of the Nazarene allows Christians to taste joyfully the world of the Promise and resolutely introduces them into the faith of *the Chosen People*, making them a part of that People" [italics added].

The Election of Pope Francis

The world was stunned when Pope Benedict XVI announced on February 11, 2013, that he no longer had the "strength of mind and body" to continue in the Petrine ministry and would retire from the papacy. It had been almost six hundred years since the last pontiff had stepped down from the Chair of St. Peter, rather than serving until death.

Another astonishing event occurred on March 13, 2013, when the College of Cardinals elected Jorge Mario Bergoglio, SJ, the cardinal archbishop of Buenos Aires, to succeed him. Not only was he the first pope to be elected from the Americas, he was also the first member of the religious order of the Society of Jesus (the Jesuits) so chosen. As a further amazing development, the new pope chose Francis of Assisi as his papal namesake, the first time in history that any pope had selected the saint of simplicity, poverty, and church reform as his guiding model.

It soon was learned that Cardinal Bergoglio had been very active in ongoing dialogue with the Jewish community in Argentina. A book of his dialogues with Rabbi Abraham Skorka had been published in 2010 and was quickly translated from the original Spanish into many other languages.[28] It could be said that Francis was the first pope in history to have as an adult engaged in serious, theological conversations with Jewish religious leaders.

During the first year of his pontificate, Francis has spoken and written with great sincerity of the church's familial relationship with the Jewish people (see Document 46). His comments reflect the personal friendships he has enjoyed with Jews in Argentina. He reiterated that Catholics "hold the Jewish people in special regard because their covenant with God has never been revoked" and insisted that "dialogue and friendship with the children of Israel are part of the life of Jesus' disciples." Contrary to some theologians who preferred to disregard post–*Nostra Aetate* ecclesial statements, Francis thanked God for "the publication of a series of documents to deepen the thinking about theological bases of the relations between Jews and Christians." Such theological discourse is important for Christians, he said, because "God continues to work among the people of the Old Covenant and to bring forth treasures of wisdom which flow from their encounter with his word."

In response to a question from an Italian publisher, Pope Francis movingly explained "that God has never neglected his faithfulness to the covenant with [the People] Israel, and that, through the awful trials of these last centuries, the Jews have preserved their faith in God. And for this, we, the Church and the whole human family, can never be sufficiently grateful to them." In other words, Christians should thank God that Jews remained faithful to God despite awful trials—trials that were inflicted upon them for centuries by Christians who believed God had cursed Jews for faithlessly rejecting the gospel! These sentences suggest that Catholic thinking about Judaism may be entering into an increasingly candid and humble phase, one that stresses the need for ongoing personal friendships.

Clearly, despite occasional setbacks, the creative ferment begun by *Nostra Aetate* in 1965 is still unfolding. There can be no better way to celebrate its fiftieth anniversary in 2015 than for Catholics to vigorously renew the quest to implement its principles and to follow through on its implications.[29]

Notes

1. I use the term "covenantal life" both to indicate the intimacy and durability of a covenant that includes God as a participant and to bypass the unhelpful debate about whether to think in terms of a model of a single covenant in which Jews and Christians abide together or a double covenant in which Judaism and Christianity are seen as distinct and perhaps unconnected covenanted communities. I say "unhelpful" because the debate tends to objectify "covenant" as a legal contract rather than understanding it theologically as a relationship in which life is shared.

2. For a wide-ranging collection of John Paul II's writings on Jews and Judaism, see Eugene J. Fisher and Leon Klenicki, eds., *The Saint for Shalom: How Pope John Paul II Transformed Catholic-Jewish Relations: His Complete Texts on Jews, Judaism, and the State of Israel, 1979–2005* (New York: Crossroad, 2011).

3. For a photograph of this prayer, now preserved at Yad Vashem, the Holocaust memorial museum in Jerusalem, see: http://yad-vashem.org.il/yv/en/exhibitions/bearing_witness/featured_artifacts_john_paul_II.asp.

4. "Address to Delegates of the Conference of Presidents of Major American Jewish Organizations," February 12, 2009 (available at http://www.ccjr.us/dialogika-resources/documents-and-statements/roman-catholic/pope-benedict-xvi/471-b1609feb12) and "Address at the Great Synagogue of Rome," January 17, 2010 (Document 43 below).

5. It should be noted that several of the affirmations of Jewish covenantal life by both John Paul II and Benedict XVI specifically invoke Moses or the gift of the Torah at Sinai. As will be discussed below, some Catholics in the past decade have discriminated among the various biblical "covenantal moments," attempting to argue that only the promise to Abraham (that many nations would bless him) was permanent, whereas the Torah covenant at Sinai was conditional and impermanent. However, such picking and choosing among the various biblical expressions of covenanting with God are not supported by the words of John Paul and Benedict, who plainly include the Torah as intrinsic to Judaism's ongoing covenantal life.

6. John Paul II, *Tertio Millennio Adveniente* (1994), §33.

7. Catholic documents tend to prefer the Hebrew term Shoah, or devastating whirlwind, when discussing the "Holocaust," as it is typically called. Biblically, "holocaust" refers to burnt sacrifices offered to God, a theologically offensive connotation in the context of the Nazi genocide of Jews.

8. A phrase used by John Paul II in an address to a special Vatican conference on "The Roots of Anti-Judaism in the Christian Milieu" (Document 33): "[I]n the Christian world—I am not saying on the part of the church as such—erroneous and unjust interpretations of the New Testament relative to the Jewish people and their presumed guilt circulated for too long..."

9. See, for example, the response of the International Jewish Committee on Interreligious Consultations (IJCIC) [Document 91 below]. On the last point, drafts of "We Remember" originally (and more accurately) read, "Many did, many more did not." It was revised during the protracted vetting process of the drafts among the various curial offices.

10. http://www.ccjr.us/dialogika-resources/educational-and-liturgical-materials/classic-articles/1138-cassidy1998may28.

11. Ibid.

12. Excerpted from sections 3.2 and 3.3 of the report. For the full text see www.ccjr.us/dialogika-resources/documents-and-statements/roman-catholic/vatican-curia/281-memory.

13. Benedict XVI and Peter Seewald, *Light of the World: The Pope, the Church, and the Sign of the Times: A Conversation with Peter Seewald* (San Francisco: Ignatius Press, 2010), 110.

14. Debórah Dwork and Eric Greenberg , "Church's Misguided Honor," *The Philadelphia Inquirer*, January 5, 2010.

15. "Yad Vashem Statement Regarding Updated Text on the Panel about the Vatican" (July 1, 2012). Available at: http://www1.yadvashem.org/yv/en/pressroom/pressreleases/pr_details.asp?cid=752.

16. Available at: http://www.baltimorecarmel.org/saints/Stein/letter%20to%20pope.htm.

17. Pontifical Commission for Religious Relations with the Jews, *Notes on the Correct Way to Present the Jews and Judaism in Preaching and Catechesis in the Roman Catholic Church* (1985) [*Bridges*, Vol. 1, Document 39], II, 6: "Christian identity and Jewish identity should be carefully distinguished in their respective reading of the Bible. But this detracts nothing from the value of the Old Testament in the Church and does nothing to hinder Christians from profiting discerningly from the traditions of Jewish reading."

18. Benedict XVI, *Jesus of Nazareth: Holy Week: From the Entrance into Jerusalem to the Resurrection* (San Francisco: Ignatius Press, 2011), 35.

19. See my "A Challenge to Catholic Teaching" in Philip A. Cunningham, ed., *Pondering the Passion: What's at Stake for Christians and Jews?* (Franklin, WI, and Chicago: Sheed & Ward, 2004), 143–56.

20. Available at: http://www.ccjr.us/dialogika-resources/themes-in-todays-dialogue/conversion/1093-ncs-bceia02aug12.

21. See also his words in November 2002: "So from the Christian perspective the covenant with the Jewish people is unbroken (Rom 11:29), for we as Christians believe that these promises find in Jesus their definitive and irrevocable Amen (2 Cor 1:20) and at the same time that in him, who is the end of the law (Rom 10:4), the law is not nullified but upheld (Rom 3:31). This does not mean that Jews in order to be saved have to become Christians; if they follow their own conscience and believe in God's promises as they understand

them in their religious tradition they are in line with God's plan, which for us comes to its historical completion in Jesus Christ." "Christians, Jews and the Thorny Question of Mission," *Origins* 32/28 (December 19, 2002): 464.

22. "Official Ecclesial Documents to Implement Vatican II on Relations with Jews: 'Study Them, Become Immersed in Them, and Put Them into Practice,'" *Studies in Christian-Jewish Relations*, 4/1 (2009); http://ejournals .bc.edu/ojs/index.php/scjr/article/view/1521/1374.

23. Adapted from "Official Ecclesial Documents," 13–14.

24. All of the relevant texts may be found on *Dialogika*, the online resource library of the Council of Centers on Jewish-Christian Relations. See: http://www.ccjr.us/dialogika-resources/documents-and-statements/roman-catholic/us-conference-of-catholic-bishops and http://www.ccjr.us/dialogika-resources/themes-in-todays-dialogue/conversion.

25. "Peace for the Holy Land: The Promised Land and the Chosen People—The Two-State Solution," November 11, 2010. Available at: http://www.ccjr.us/dialogika-resources/themes-in-todays-dialogue/isrpal/898-bustros 2010nov11.

26. This, incidentally, echoed the thinking of several council fathers during the Second Vatican Council's deliberations on September 28–29, 1964. See: http://www.ccjr.us/dialogika-resources/documents-and-statements/roman-catholic/second-vatican-council/na-debate.

27. Echoing the 2002 dialogue document, "Reflections on Covenant and Mission"—"campaigns that target Jews for conversion to Christianity are no longer theologically acceptable in the Catholic Church."

28. Jorge Mario Bergoglio and Abraham Skorka, *On Heaven and Earth: Pope Francis on Faith, Family, and the Church in the Twenty-First Century* (New York: Image Books, 2013).

29. In addition to these comments, see also my Editor's Notes to particular documents in Part Two below.

Philip A. Cunningham *is Professor of Theology and Director of the Institute for Jewish-Catholic Relations of Saint Joseph's University, Philadelphia. He is the author or editor of numerous publications on Christian-Jewish relations, including the coedited volume* Christ Jesus and the Jewish People Today: New Explorations of Theological Interrelationships.

Building a New Relationship: A Jewish Perspective

by Michael S. Kogan

The first thing many readers will note in examining the fourteen Jewish documents in this collection is that only one of them contains an official statement of any branch of the Jewish faith. This fact contrasts vividly with the large number of official statements issued by Christian denominations in the ongoing Christian-Jewish dialogue. There are a number of reasons for this discrepancy.

First of all, when Christians evaluate Judaism they are dealing with a reality that is, in their minds, in some ways intrinsic to their Christian faith. The Jewish holy scriptures, the saints and heroes of what they call the "Old Testament," the great historical saga of ancient Israel are all part of Christian salvation history. Jewish texts contain events, personalities, and religious ideas already familiar to every Christian Sunday school student and churchgoer. In dealing with this material a Christian is not asked to go beyond the borders of territory with which he or she is already well acquainted. What is asked of the Christian participant in the dialogue with Jews is the adoption of new attitudes toward the Jewish people, their faith, history, and sacred texts. Such a rethinking is no easy matter, but it is, at least, taking place in familiar territory.

By way of contrast, Jews in the dialogue are required to explore texts, history, and religious ideas beyond the borders of their own faith and culture. Christianity and Judaism may have common roots in ancient Israelite religion, but they have developed along very different and, at times, strongly divergent paths. Their patterns of thought, their theological and anthropological emphases, and their basic self-definitions seem, at least on the surface, to differ widely. Jews attempting to understand Christianity will find themselves in unfamiliar territory. And they will discover that many formerly held Christian attitudes have often been hostile to Jews and Judaism.

The result of this imbalance between what Christians and Jews are required to do in the dialogue is that Christians will be able more easily to adjust their views of Judaism than Jews will of Christianity. Moreover, the dialogue was initiated by Christians, not Jews. This is for the obvious reason that it was usually the Christians who persecuted Jews and not the other way around. The Jews, as the historically injured party, feel less compelled to reevaluate their former persecutors. The dialogue was started by Christians who saw in the Shoah the poisonous fruits of two millennia of the church's anti-Jewish and anti-semitic teaching. They determined that guilt must be acknowledged and a total change in direction undertaken. Those Jews who do not dismiss the whole exercise as too little and too late are eager to engage in the new dialogue, but are generally content simply to react, whether with approval or with disappointment, to the many statements of good will coming from the churches. Most of them do not feel called upon to reevaluate those who are reevaluating them.

Another reason for the near absence of Jewish denominational statements is the structure of the Jewish religious community. Ours is a congregational system. Our several branches—Orthodox, Conservative, Reform, Reconstructionist, Renewal—are not very strong organizationally. There is no true hierarchy of authority, no central committee that could ever agree on a united view of Christianity. For many the residual pain of persecution is too great; for others the complexities of Christian theology are too alien to evaluate. Hence only one denomination (Conservative) has ever produced an official document containing a statement on Judaism and other faiths (Document No. 90, *Emet ve'Emunah*). While this is a preliminary statement that cries out for further development, it is exceedingly clear and truly pluralistic in many ways. But, as of today, it continues to stand alone. (See my further comments on this document below.)

The result of the failure of our religious branches to develop a theological evaluation of Christianity is that the field has been left to Jewry's secular organizations (the Anti-Defamation League and the American Jewish Committee) to express the community's position in the dialogue. And as secular organizations, these groups have nothing to say of a theological nature. They restrict themselves mostly to monitoring and responding to Christian initiatives. Their focus is on the two great twentieth-century realities of Jewish history: the Shoah and the reborn state of Israel. With their oft-stated demands that

Christians engage in full and ongoing repentance for complicity in the Shoah while refraining from any and all criticism of Israeli government policy, these organizations have a political impact (not always positive), but they bring no religious insights or creative theological ideas to the dialogue. Such insights and ideas are to be found, rather, in the writings of individual Jewish theologians and biblical scholars who are developing new conceptions of Christianity and its relationship to Judaism and who have, in recent years, been formulating interesting and unprecedented Jewish evaluations of Jesus and the New Testament record.

The present collection of documents does not contain selections from individual Jewish theologians but focuses on public statements by rabbis and political leaders growing out of their encounters with Christian authorities, often at public events. A number of these statements (Documents 86–89 and 93) are polite responses to Catholic initiatives (papal visits, etc.) and do little to break new ground. However, several others (most notably Documents 90, 94, 95, 97, and 99) do advance the dialogue by expressing new Jewish conceptions of our Christian partner. They are worthy of serious study.

Overview of the Documents

In 1988, several organizations within the Conservative Movement of American Judaism published a significant statement entitled *Emet ve'Emunah* ("Truth and Faithfulness," Document 90). In its section "Relations with Other Faiths," the authors acknowledge the beneficial mutual influences flowing between Judaism and the other Abrahamic faiths among which Jews have lived. This has always been true and is especially so in North America where Jews live as free and accepted citizens, equal in every way to their fellows of other faiths. In such an atmosphere Jews can afford to abandon defensive postures and express full respect for "other ways of serving God." The document goes on to endorse Maimonides's view that Christianity and Islam have spread word of the true God and God's moral law across the globe. It even suggests that the same God Jews worship has entered into covenants with other religious communities. No religion—including our own—should hold exclusivist views that deny the truths to be found in other faiths. Xenophobic attitudes must be eschewed by us as well as by others.

This progressive statement culminates in the happy proclamation that "although we have but one God, God has more than one nation." We must learn from the truths treasured by others and be eager to share our truths with them. The heart of this statement is that we are one chosen people among others. This is healthy Jewish self-affirmation coupled with a humble self-transcendence in which we reach beyond our own borders to affirm the validity of the religious others. For a major branch of Judaism to officially express itself in these terms was a significant victory for Jewish theological pluralism.

Documents 91 and 92 are essentially responses to Catholic statements and papal initiatives. But they are more than the polite, pro-forma responses of Documents 86 through 89.

Document 91, issued in 1998 by the International Jewish Committee on Interreligious Consultations, finds fault with the Vatican document "We Remember: A Reflection on the Shoah." It expresses disappointment that the Vatican document does not go as far as a variety of statements issued by certain national Catholic bishops' conferences. In their pronouncements, these conferences (see Documents 58–60 in this volume) had fully acknowledged the guilt of the Church as an institution in fomenting anti-Jewish and antisemitic attitudes among the faithful. Popes and church councils, not simply individual Catholics, had been criticized in these statements for sinful teachings and actions against Jews and Judaism. But the Vatican statement distinguishes between "sons and daughters of the Church" who erred and "the Church as such," the mystical bride of Christ, which it apparently views as incapable of sin. The earlier Bishops' Conference statements had been able to hold together two paradoxical ideas—a holy Church and yet a sinful Church—but the Vatican statement refers only to the former. This failure to assume guilt on the part of the Church itself is coupled, the Jewish response notes, with an equal failure fully to connect Christian anti-Judaism with Nazi antisemitism. This very distinction is seen as invalid by these Jewish commentators, since Catholic teaching had long denounced Jews as a deicide people as well as Judaism as a faith.

The Jewish response goes on to criticize the Vatican document for understating historical church persecution of Jews and, once again, calls for a full investigation of the conduct of Pope Pius XII during the Nazi period.

This Jewish document is not meant to break new ground, but is reactive in nature. It expresses the fear that the Vatican is pulling back from the clear statements of the bishops by defending a mystical view of the Church that cannot acknowledge institutional sin on the part of a divinely conceived entity. It may be that Vatican documents are by nature more cautious than local or national Catholic statements or that the Vatican will always be more protective of Mother Church. Tensions will inevitably rise when moral demands are brought against entities conceived in supernatural terms. Unless or until the Church is willing to conceive of itself in more earthly categories, the tension will remain.

Document 92 expresses the other side of the Jewish attitude toward Catholic conduct in the dialogue. "Recognizing Bonds Between Jewish and Catholic Communities" is a joint statement of the Reform and Conservative movements. It comments formally on the changed Catholic attitudes toward Jews and Judaism. It affirms the growing bonds between the two faiths and praises Pope John Paul II for recognizing the irrevocable covenant between God and Israel, the sinfulness of antisemitism, the responsibility for Christianity to denounce her past sins against the Jews, and the need to cease all official Catholic efforts to convert Jews. This document is a response to the pope's visit to Israel and is as laudatory as the previous statement was critical.

By far the most important document in this collection is number 93, *Dabru Emet* ("Speak the Truth"). Significantly, this statement was not issued by any official branch of the Jewish faith, but by a small group of Jewish scholars convened by the Institute for Christian and Jewish Studies in Baltimore, itself a group of scholars of both faiths devoted to advancing the interfaith dialogue. Composed by its authors to be a Jewish response to "the efforts of Christians to honor Judaism" over the previous thirty-five years, this statement, issued in 2000, contains eight pronouncements on Christianity and its relationship to Judaism.

It begins by noting that Jews and Christians worship the same God and rejoices that Christianity has spread the worship of Israel's God and God's moral teachings to the ends of the earth. A number of medieval and modern Jewish authorities had said much the same thing, and yet the ongoing difficulties virtually all creeds have in dealing with the religious "other" makes it necessary to rekindle the light of universalism over and over in every generation. This is a good beginning.

The statement goes on to refer to the shared scriptures of both faiths (the Hebrew Bible) and the moral law that both observe. These are crucial points. Our relationship with Christianity is unique in part because we share a sacred text, but add different commentaries through which we interpret it. This situation is ideally structured to provide endless hours of fruitful discussion and debate over the meanings of the common scriptures. Now that both parties have transcended their initial project of triumphing over the rival "other," we can look forward to mutually enriching shared study of texts honored by both traditions.

Two paragraphs of *Dabru Emet* refer to the two great historical events of modern Jewish history: the Shoah and the rebirth of Zion. While recognizing that without two thousand years of Christian oppression of Jews in word and deed the Nazi propaganda could not have taken hold, the framers of the statement do not see Nazism as a Christian phenomenon. They applaud Christian efforts to put an end to all antisemitic teachings and actions. *Dabru Emet* is a Jewish response to those efforts.

Pointing out that the divine promise to give the land of Israel to the Israelites is found in the Bible honored by Christians as well as Jews, the framers call upon Christians to respect Jewish claims to the land. Such a call seems to Jews to be necessary to the dialogue since the link between Jewish people and Jewish homeland is essential to Jewish faith. Jewish historical experience that includes the Shoah but not the restoration of Zion would be as unthinkable as Christian faith with the crucifixion but without the resurrection of Christ. However, this having been said, there is no reason Jews should expect Christians to be bound to support all the policies of Israel's government. We are faced with a paradoxical situation in which Christians who are most eager to give up triumphalist Christologies and recognize the validity of Judaism are often the least willing to support Israeli policies vis-à-vis the Palestinians. At the same time, evangelical Christians who would delight to see all Jews converted to Christianity are often most supportive of all Israeli policies.

The political reality of Israel will continue to trouble a dialogue originally conceived as a religious and spiritual conversation. There is a legitimate conflict here and Jews would do well to recognize it. Religion calls for individual self-transcendence, nationalism for group self-affirmation. Christians must realize that nation states act far differently from spiritual communities. Jews conceive of themselves under both categories. This will make the dialogue an increasingly delicate project as both partners work to keep the entire enterprise from being hijacked by politics.

After affirming the commitment by Jews and Christians to the "sanctity and dignity of every human being," the statement recognizes that the two faiths serve God through differing traditions and symbol systems: Christ and the Church or Torah and the Jewish people. What is new here is that paragraph six goes on to hold that "Jews can respect Christians' faithfulness to their revelation."

This is, to my knowledge, the first time in the dialogue that a Jewish statement has explicitly held that Christianity is as much a revealed religion as is Judaism. This is crucial. If Christianity is based on a revelation, then God is as much its founder as God is the founder of Judaism. For Jews to say this is a proper response to the new Christian recognition that God continues to covenant with Israel through the Jewish faith. Christians have affirmed the ongoing activity of God in our religion. Are we to go on assuming that Judaism has a divine origin while all other faiths, including Christianity, originate in human thought? What a strange picture such thinking would portray. God would be actively involved in the doings of less than fifteen million people while remaining aloof from the spiritual lives of more than six billion. No, we can no longer insist that God is the founder of only one faith. *Dabru Emet* follows and develops the ideas of *Emet ve'Emunah* in expanding on the thought that "God has more than one nation." Christianity also originated in a divine revelation, and like Judaism is a holy vehicle for the establishment of God's reign in the human community. Once it had been published in leading newspapers, *Dabru Emet* was signed by hundreds of rabbis and Jewish scholars. It represents a great step forward in the developing dialogue.

Document 95, a rabbinical address to Pope Benedict XVI at the Vatican in 2008, rejoices that Jews and Catholics now commemorate the Shoah as partners in remembrance. But it soon expresses disappointment that a prayer for the conversion of the Jews has been reintroduced in the Good Friday liturgy when celebrated in its older form. This liturgical "regression" under a new pope was protested by Jews, only to be "clarified" by Cardinal Kasper. He stated that the hope for the Jewish recognition of Christ is "eschatological," pointing to the second coming of Christ, at which distant date everyone will receive him. In no way, he said, does it call for conversion of Jews during the present dispensation. Thus, the Church, while expecting that all will eventually join the Christian faith, is content to live as siblings with other faiths for the foreseeable future. Jews can live with that; it is pluralism in practice if not in ultimate theory.

The statements that follow (Documents 96–98) speak, among other things, of Christian-Jewish cooperation in preserving and protecting this earth, the home given to us by our God, to be loved and shared by all. Emphasis is placed on the common image of God we all reflect, as well as the universalist conception of our faiths as calling us to realize our common humanity.

The final document (Document 99) is of significance partly because it was issued by the Center for Jewish-Christian Understanding and Cooperation, an Orthodox Jewish center in Israel. The Orthodox branch of Judaism has traditionally been the most resistant to in-depth dialogue and has steered clear of theological exchanges with Christians.

The statement notes that a prominent strain in contemporary Christianity no longer seeks to displace Judaism but affirms the eternal covenant between God and Israel while seeing itself as a partner with Judaism in working for peace and redemption in God's world. Remarkably, it goes on to proclaim that the worldwide Christian community's role in spreading knowledge of the one God was precisely what "Abraham's seed" was called to do four thousand years ago. The great rabbis of the seventeenth, eighteenth, and nineteenth centuries are quoted to support this view of Christianity's Abrahamic mission. Thus Jews today can affirm that Christians and Jews are partners in the redemptive work. At the same time, each one can continue to hold the eschatological hope that the "other" will, at the end of days, come to recognize its truth claims. Meanwhile, we work side by side toward redemption.

Here, in a direct quote from *Dabru Emet*, Jews are called on to "respect Christian faithfulness to their revelation." For Orthodox Jews to recognize Christianity as a revealed religion is truly extraordinary and a world away from the days when Orthodox patriarch Rabbi Joseph B. Soleveitchik advised his peers to avoid all theological exchanges with Christians (see his essay, Document 67 in the first volume of *Bridges*). The reason for the change seems to be that these

Orthodox Jews, at least, have finally come to accept as genuine the Christian repudiation of triumphalist replacement attitudes toward Judaism. Now that Christians have truly changed their views of us, we can do the same of them.

This document sees Christianity as a relationship between a people and its God...the same God to whom Jews relate through Torah. Today these two peoples must witness together. The world needs them both. This remarkable statement ends with the observation that if these two communities, which have such a depressing history of mutual hostility, can become partners rather than antagonists, then any two peoples anywhere can do it. This promise is the ultimate gift Jews and Christians can offer a deeply conflicted world. "There is hope for your future, says the Lord" (Jer. 31:17).

Michael S. Kogan *is Professor of Religious Studies at Montclair State University, New Jersey. The author of* Opening the Covenant: A Jewish Theology of Christianity *as well as numerous journal articles, he lectures widely at churches, synagogues, and universities.*

PART ONE

Protestant Statements

1

A Theological Understanding of the Relationship between Christians and Jews

Prepared by a task force of the Council for Theology and Culture of the Presbyterian Church (U.S.A.) and submitted to the 99th General Assembly, meeting in Biloxi, Mississippi, in June 1987. The Assembly, after making revisions, voted to commend the statement to the church for study and reflection. The statement has an extensive Introduction that is abridged below.

INTRODUCTION

Christians and Jews live side by side in our pluralistic American society. We engage one another not only in personal and social ways but also at deeper levels where ultimate values are expressed and where a theological understanding of our relationship is required. The confessional documents of the Reformed tradition are largely silent on this matter. Hence this paper has been prepared by the church as a pastoral and teaching document to provide a basis for continuing discussion within the Presbyterian community in the United States and to offer guidance for the occasions in which Presbyterians and Jews converse, cooperate, and enter into dialogue. What is the relationship which God intends between Christians and Jews, between Christianity and Judaism? A theological understanding of this relationship is the subject which this paper addresses...

The following affirmations are offered to the church for our common edification and growth in obedience and faith. To God alone be the glory.

AFFIRMATIONS AND EXPLICATIONS

Affirmation

1. We affirm that the living God whom Christians worship is the same God who is worshiped and served by Jews. We bear witness that the God revealed in Jesus, a Jew, to be the Triune Lord of all, is the same one disclosed in the life and worship of Israel.

Explication

Christianity began in the context of Jewish faith and life. Jesus was a Jew, as were his earliest followers. Paul, the apostle of the Gentiles, referred to himself as a "Hebrew of the Hebrews." The life and liturgy of the Jews provided the language and thought forms through which the revelation in Jesus was first received and expressed. Jewish liturgical forms were decisive for the worship of the early church and are influential still, especially in churches of the Reformed tradition.

Yet the relationship of Christians to Jews is more than one of common history and ideas. The relationship is significant for our faith because Christians confess that the God of Abraham and Sarah and their descendants is the very One whom the apostles addressed as "the God and Father of our Lord Jesus Christ." The one God elected and entered into covenant with Israel to reveal the divine will and point to a future salvation in which all people will live in peace and righteousness. This expectation of the reign of God in a Messianic Age was described by the Hebrew prophets in different ways. The Scriptures speak of the expectation of a deliverer king anointed by God, of the appearing of a righteous teacher, of a suffering servant, or of a people enabled through God's grace to establish the Messianic Age. Early Christian preaching proclaimed that Jesus had become Messiah and Lord, God's anointed who has inaugurated the kingdom of peace and righteousness through his life, death, and resurrection. While some Jews accepted this message, the majority did not, choosing to adhere to the biblical revelation as interpreted by their teachers and continuing to await the fulfillment of the messianic promises given through the prophets, priests, and kings of Israel.

Thus the bond between the community of Jews and those who came to be called Christians was broken, and both have continued as vital but separate communities through the centuries. Nonetheless, there are ties which remain between Christians and Jews: the faith of both in the one God whose loving and just will is for the redemption of all humankind and the Jewishness of Jesus whom we confess to be the Christ of God.

In confessing Jesus as the Word of God incarnate, Christians are not rejecting the concrete existence of Jesus who lived by the faith of Israel. Rather, we are affirming the unique way in which Jesus, a Jew, is the being and power of God for the redemption of the world. In him, God is disclosed to be the Triune One who creates and reconciles all things. This is the way in which Christians affirm the reality of the one God who is sovereign over all.

Affirmation

2. We affirm that the church, elected in Jesus Christ, has been engrafted into the people of God established by the covenant with Abraham, Isaac, and Jacob. Therefore, Christians have not replaced Jews.

Explication

The church, especially in the Reformed tradition, understands itself to be in covenant with God through its election in Jesus Christ. Because the church affirms this covenant as fundamental to its existence, it has generally not sought nor felt any need to offer any positive interpretation of God's relationship with the Jews, lineal descendants of Abraham, Isaac, and Jacob, and Sarah, Rebekah, Rachel, and Leah, with whom God covenanted long ago. The emphasis has fallen on the new covenant established in Christ and the creation of the church.

Sometime during the second century of the Common Era, a view called "supersessionism," based on the reading of some biblical texts and nurtured in controversy, began to take shape. By the beginning of the third century, this teaching that the Christian church had superseded the Jews as God's chosen people became the orthodox understanding of God's relationship to the church. Such a view influenced the church's understanding of God's relationship with the Jews and allowed the church to regard Jews in an inferior light.

Supersessionism maintains that because the Jews refused to receive Jesus as Messiah, they were cursed by God, are no longer in covenant with God, and that the church alone is the "true Israel" or the "spiritual Israel." When Jews continue to assert, as they do, that they are the covenant people of God, they are looked upon by many Christians as impertinent intruders, claiming a right which is no longer theirs. The long and dolorous history of Christian imperialism, in which the church often justified anti-Jewish acts and attitudes in the name of Jesus, finds its theological base in this teaching.

We believe and testify that this theory of supersessionism or replacement is harmful and in need of reconsideration as the church seeks to proclaim God's saving activity with humankind. The scriptural and theological bases for this view are clear enough; but we are prompted to look again at our tradition by events in our own time and by an increasing number of theologians and biblical scholars who are calling for such a reappraisal. The pride and prejudice which have been justified by reference to this doctrine of replacement themselves seem reason enough for taking a hard look at this position.

For us, the teaching that the church has been engrafted by God's grace into the people of God finds as much support in Scripture as the view of supersessionism and is much more consistent with our Reformed understanding of the work of God in Jesus Christ. The emphasis is on the continuity and trustworthiness of God's commitments and God's grace. The issue for the early church concerned the inclusion of the Gentiles in God's saving work, not the exclusion of the Jews. Paul insists that God is God of both Jews and Gentiles and justifies God's redemption of both on the basis of faith (Rom 3:29–30). God's covenants are not broken. "God has not rejected his people whom he foreknew" (Rom 11:2). The church has not "replaced" the Jewish people. Quite the contrary! The church, being made up primarily of those who were once aliens and strangers to the covenants of promise, has been engrafted into the people of God by the covenant with Abraham (Rom 11:17–18).

The continued existence of the Jewish people and of the church as communities elected by God is, as the apostle Paul expressed it, a "mystery" (Rom 11:25). We do not claim to fathom this mystery but we cannot ignore it. At the same time we can never forget that we stand in a covenant established by Jesus Christ (Heb 8) and that faithfulness to that covenant requires us to call all women and men to faith in Jesus Christ. We ponder the work of God, including the wonder of Christ's atoning work for us.

Affirmation

3. We affirm that both the church and the Jewish people are elected by God for witness to the world and that the relationship of the church to contemporary Jews is based on that gracious and irrevocable election of both.

Explication

God chose a particular people, Israel, as a sign and foretaste of God's grace toward all people. It is for the sake of God's redemption of the world that Israel was elected. The promises of God, made to Abraham and Sarah and to their offspring after them, were given so that blessing might come upon "all families of the earth" (Rom 12:1–3). God continues that purpose through Christians and Jews. The church, like the Jews, is called to be a light to the nations (Acts 13:47). God's purpose embraces the whole creation.

In the electing of peoples, God takes the initiative. Election does not manifest human achievement but divine grace. Neither Jews nor Christians can claim to deserve this favor. Election is the way in which God creates freedom through the Holy Spirit for a people to be for God and for others. God, who is ever faithful to the word which has been spoken, does not take back the divine election. Whenever either the Jews or the church have rejected God's ways, God has judged but not rejected them. This is a sign of God's redeeming faithfulness toward the world.

Both Christians and Jews are elected to service for the life of the world. Despite profound theological differences separating Christians and Jews, we believe that God has bound us together in a unique relationship for the sake of God's love for the world. We testify to this election, but we cannot explain it. It is part of the purpose of God for the whole creation. Thus there is much common ground where Christians and Jews can and should act together.

Affirmation

4. We affirm that the reign of God is attested both by the continuing existence of the Jewish people and by the church's proclamation of the gospel of Jesus Christ. Hence, when speaking with Jews about matters of faith, we must always acknowledge that Jews are already in a covenantal relationship with God.

Explication

God, who acts in human history by the Word and Spirit, is not left without visible witnesses on the earth. God's sovereign and saving reign in the world is signified both by the continuing existence of and faithfulness within the Jewish people who, by all human reckoning, might be expected to have long since passed from the stage of history and by the life and witness of the church.

As the cross of Jesus has always been a stumbling block to Jews, so also the continued existence and faithfulness of the Jews is often a stumbling block to Christians. Our persuasion of the truth of God in Jesus Christ has sometimes led Christians to conclude that Judaism should no longer exist, now that Christ has come, and that all Jews ought properly to become baptized members of the church. Over the centuries, many afflictions have been visited on the Jews by Christians holding this belief—not least in our own time. We believe that the time has come for Christians to stop and take a new look at the Jewish people and at the relationship which God wills between Christian and Jew.

Such reappraisal cannot avoid the issue of evangelism. For Jews, this is a very sensitive issue. Proselytism by Christians seeking to persuade, even convert, Jews often implies a negative judgment on Jewish faith. Jewish reluctance to accept Christian claims is all the more understandable when it is realized that conversion is often seen by them as a threat to Jewish survival. Many Jews who unite with the church sever their bonds with their people. On the other hand, Christians are commissioned to witness to the whole world about the good news of Christ's atoning work for both Jew and Gentile. Difficulty arises when we acknowledge that the same Scripture which proclaims that atonement and which Christians claim as God's word clearly states that Jews are already in a covenant relationship with God who makes and keeps covenants.

For Christians, there is no easy answer to this matter. Faithful interpretation of the biblical record indicates that there are elements of God's covenant with Abraham that are unilateral and unconditional. However, there are also elements of the covenant which appear to predicate benefits upon faithfulness (see Gen 17:1ff.). Christians, historically, have proclaimed that true obedience is impossible for a sinful humanity and thus have been impelled to witness to the atoning work of Jesus of Nazareth, the promised Messiah, as the way to a right relationship with God. However, to the present day, many Jews have been unwilling to accept the Christian claim and have continued in their covenant tradition. In light of Scripture, which testifies to God's repeated offer of forgiveness to Israel, we do not presume to judge in God's place. Our commission is to witness to the saving work of Jesus Christ; to preach good news among all the "nations" (*ethne*).

Dialogue is the appropriate form of faithful conversation between Christians and Jews. Dialogue is not a cover for proselytism. Rather, as trust is established, not only questions and concerns can be shared but faith and commitments as well. Christians have no reason to be reluctant in sharing the good news of their faith with anyone. However, a militancy that seeks to impose one's own point of view on another is not only inappropriate but also counterproductive. In dialogue, partners are able to define their faith in their own terms, avoiding caricatures of one another, and are thus better able to obey the commandment, "Thou shalt not bear false witness against thy neighbor." Dialogue, especially in light of our shared history, should be entered into with a spirit of humility and a commitment to reconciliation. Such dialogue can be a witness that seeks also to heal that which has been broken. It is out of a mutual willingness to listen and to learn that faith deepens and a new and better relationship between Christians and Jews is enabled to grow.

Affirmation

5. We acknowledge in repentance the church's long and deep complicity in the proliferation of anti-Jewish attitudes and actions through its "teaching of contempt" for the Jews. Such teaching we now repudiate, together with the acts and attitudes which it generates.

Explication

Anti-Jewish sentiment and action by Christians began in New Testament times. The struggle between Christians and Jews in the first century of the Christian movement was often bitter and marked by mutual violence. The depth of hostility left its mark on early Christian and Jewish literature, including portions of the New Testament.

In subsequent centuries, after the occasions for the original hostility had long since passed, the church misused portions of the New Testament as proof texts to justify a heightened animosity toward Jews. For many centuries, it was the church's teaching to label Jews as "Christ-killers" and a "deicide race." This is known as the "teaching of contempt." Persecution of Jews was at times officially sanctioned and at other times indirectly encouraged or at least tolerated. Holy Week became a time of terror for the Jews.

To this day, the church's worship, preaching, and teaching often lend themselves, at times unwittingly, to a perpetuation of the "teaching of contempt." For example, the public reading of Scripture without explicating potentially misleading passages concerning "the Jews," preaching which uses Judaism as a negative example in order to commend Christianity, public prayer which assumes that only the prayers of Christians are pleasing to God, teaching in the church school which reiterates stereotypes and non-historical ideas about the Pharisees and Jewish leadership—all of these contribute, however subtly, to a continuation of the church's "teaching of contempt."

It is painful to realize how the teaching of the church has led individuals and groups to behavior that has tragic consequences. It is agonizing to discover that the church's "teaching of contempt" was a major ingredient that made possible the monstrous policy of annihilation of Jews by Nazi Germany. It is disturbing to have to admit that the churches of the West did little to challenge the policies of their governments, even in the face of the growing certainty that the Holocaust was taking place. Though many Christians in Europe acted heroically to shelter Jews, the record reveals that most churches as well as governments the world over largely ignored the pleas for sanctuary for Jews.

As the very embodiment of anti-Jewish attitudes and actions, the Holocaust is a sober reminder that such horrors are actually possible in this world and that they begin with apparently small acts of disdain or expedience. Hence, we pledge to be alert for all such acts of denigration from now on, so that they may be resisted. We also pledge resistance to any such actions perpetrated by anyone, anywhere.

The church's attitudes must be reviewed and changed as necessary, so that they never again fuel the fires of hatred. We must be willing to admit our church's complicity in wrongdoing in the past, even as we try to establish a new basis of trust and communication with Jews. We pledge, God helping us, never again to participate in, to contribute to, or (insofar as we are able) to allow the persecution or denigration of Jews or the belittling of Judaism.

Affirmation

6. We affirm the continuity of God's promise of land along with the obligations of that promise to the people Israel.

Explication

As the Church of Scotland's (1985) report says:

We are aware that in dealing with this matter we are entering a minefield of complexities across which is strung a barbed-wire entanglement of issues, theological, political and humanitarian.

However, a faithful explication of biblical material relating to the covenant with Abraham cannot avoid the reality of the promise of land. The question with which we must wrestle is how this promise is to be understood in the light of the existence of the modem political State of Israel which has taken its place among the nations of the world.

The record indicates that "the land of your sojournings" was promised to Abraham and his and Sarah's descendants. This promise, however, included the demand that "You shall keep my covenant..." (Gen 17:7–8). The implication is that the blessings of the promise were dependent upon fulfillment of covenant relationships. Disobedience could bring the loss of land, even while God's promise was not revoked. God's promises are always kept, but in God's own way and time.

The establishment of the State of Israel in our day has been seen by many devout Jews as the fulfillment of God's divine promise. Other

Jews are equally sure that it is not and regard the State of Israel as an unauthorized attempt to flee divinely imposed exile. Still other Jews interpret the State of Israel in purely secular terms. Christian opinion is equally diverse. As Reformed Christians, however, we believe that no government at any time can ever be the full expression of God's will. All, including the State of Israel, stand accountable to God. The State of Israel is a geopolitical entity and is not to be validated theologically.

God's promise of land bears with it obligation. Land is to be used as the focus of mission, the place where a people can live and be a light to the nations. Further, because land is God's to be given, it can never be fully possessed. The living out of God's covenant in the land brings with it not only opportunity but also temptation. The history of the people of Israel reveals the continual tension between sovereignty and stewardship, blessing and curse.

The Hebrew prophets made clear to the people of their own day as well, indeed, as any day, that those in possession of "land" have a responsibility and obligation to the disadvantaged, the oppressed, and the "strangers in their gates." God's justice, unlike ours, is consistently in favor of the powerless (Ps 103:6). Therefore we, whether Christian or Jew, who affirm the divine promise of land, however land is to be understood, dare not fail to uphold the divine right of the dispossessed. We have indeed been agents of the dispossession of others. In particular, we confess our complicity in the loss of land by Palestinians, and we join with those of our Jewish sisters and brothers who stand in solidarity with Palestinians as they cry for justice as the dispossessed.

We disavow any teaching which says that peace can be secured without justice through the exercise of violence and retribution. God's justice upholds those who cry out against the strong. God's peace comes to those who do justice and mercy on the earth. Hence we look with dismay at the violence and injustice occurring in the Middle East.

For three thousand years the covenant promise of land has been an essential element of the self-understanding of Jewish people. Through centuries of dispersion and exile, Jews have continued to understand themselves as a people in relation to the God they have known through the promise of land. However, to understand that promise solely in terms of a specific geographical entity on the eastern shore of the Mediterranean is, in our view, inadequate.

"Land" is understood as more than place or property; "land" is a biblical metaphor for sustainable life, prosperity, peace, and security.

We affirm the rights to these essentials for the Jewish people. At the same time, as bearers of the good news of the gospel of Jesus Christ, we affirm those same rights in the name of justice to all peoples. We are aware that those rights are not realized by all persons in our day. Thus we affirm our solidarity with all people to whom those rights of "land" are currently denied.

We disavow those views held by some dispensationalists and some Christian Zionists that see the formation of the State of Israel as a signal of the end time, which will bring the Last Judgment, a conflagration which only Christians will survive. These views ignore the word of Jesus against seeking to set the time or place of the consummation of world history.

We therefore call on all people of faith to engage in the work of reconciliation and peacemaking. We pray for and encourage those who would break the cycles of vengeance and violence, whether it be the violence of states or of resistance movements, of terror or of retaliation. We stand with those who work toward nonviolent solutions, including those who choose nonviolent resistance. We also urge nation-states and other political institutions to seek negotiated settlements of conflicting claims.

The seeking of justice is a sign of our faith in the reign of God.

Affirmation

7. We affirm that Jews and Christians are partners in waiting. Christians see in Christ the redemption not yet fully visible in the world, and Jews await the messianic redemption. Christians and Jews together await the final manifestation of God's promise of the peaceable kingdom.

Explication

Christian hope is continuous with Israel's hope and is unintelligible apart from it. New Testament teaching concerning the Kingdom of God was shaped by the messianic and apocalyptic vision of Judaism. That prophetic vision was proclaimed by John the Baptist, and the preaching of Jesus contained the same vision. Both Jews and Christians affirm that God reigns over all human destiny and has not abandoned the world to chaos and that, despite many appearances to the contrary, God is acting within history to establish righteousness and peace.

Jews still await the kingdom which the prophets foretold. Some look for a Messianic Age in which God's heavenly reign will be ushered in upon the earth. Christians proclaim the good news that in Christ "the Kingdom of God is at hand," yet we, too, wait in hope for the consummation of the redemption of all things in God. Though the waiting of Jews and Christians is significantly different on account of our differing perception of Jesus, nonetheless, we both wait with eager longing for the fulfillment of God's gracious reign upon the earth—the kingdom of righteousness and peace foretold by the prophets. We are in this sense partners in waiting.

Both Christians and Jews are called to wait and to hope in God. While we wait, Jews and Christians are called to the service of God in the world. However that service may differ, the vocation of each shares at least these elements: a striving to realize the word of the prophets, an attempt to remain sensitive to the dimension of the holy, an effort to encourage the life of the mind, and a ceaseless activity in the cause of justice and peace. These are far more than the ordinary requirements of our common humanity; they are elements of our common election by the God of Abraham, Isaac, and Jacob, and Sarah, Rebekah, Rachel, and Leah. Precisely because our election is not to privilege but to service, Christians and Jews are obligated to act together in these things. By so acting, we faithfully live out our partnership in waiting. By so doing, we believe that God is glorified.

2

The Relationship between the United Church of Christ and the Jewish Community

Adopted by the Sixteenth General Synod of the United Church of Christ, meeting in Ames, Iowa, in June/July 1987.

Historical Background and Theological Rationale

Christianity, developing its faith and identity, its life, and its creativity from a common heritage with Judaism, has a unique relationship to the Jewish people. The New Testament can only be adequately understood in the light of this common heritage with the Jewish people. The New Testament testifies to how painful was the historical process of separation of the Christian community from the Jewish people.

We in the United Church of Christ acknowledge that the Christian Church has, throughout much of its history, denied God's continuing covenantal relationship with the Jewish people expressed in the faith of Judaism. This denial has often led to outright rejection of the Jewish people and to theologically and humanly intolerable violence. The Church's frequent portrayal of the Jews as blind, recalcitrant, evil, and rejected by God has found expression in much Christian theology, liturgy, and education. Such a negative portrayal of the Jewish people and of Judaism has been a factor in the shaping of anti-Jewish attitudes of societies and the policies of governments. The most devastating lethal metastasis of this process occurred in our own century during the Holocaust.

Summary

Faced with this history from which we as Christians cannot, and must not, disassociate ourselves, we ask for God's forgiveness through our Lord Jesus Christ. We pray for divine grace that will enable us, more firmly than ever before, to turn from this path of rejection and persecution to affirm that Judaism has not been superseded by Christianity; that Christianity is not to be understood as the successor religion to Judaism; God's covenant with the Jewish people has not been abrogated. God has not rejected the Jewish people; God is faithful in keeping covenant.

Resolution

WHEREAS, the God we worship is the God of all creation; and

WHEREAS, the Christian communities of recent times have come more and more to recognize that God's covenant with the Jewish people stands inviolate (Rom 9–11); and

WHEREAS, the Christian Church also stands bound to the same God in covenant, the covenant affirmed and embodied in Jesus as the Christ; and

WHEREAS, the Christian Church has denied for too long the continuing validity of God's covenant with the Jewish people, with all the attendant evils that have followed upon such denial;

THEREFORE, the Sixteenth General Synod of the United Church of Christ affirms its recognition that God's covenant with the Jewish people has not been rescinded or abrogated by God, but remains in full force, inasmuch as "the gifts and the promise of God are irrevocable" (Rom 11:29).

FURTHER, the Sixteenth General Synod of the United Church of Christ expresses its determination to seek out and to affirm the consequences of this understanding of the continuing divine covenant with the Jewish people in the Church's theological statements, its liturgical practices, its hymnody, its educational work, and its witness before the world.

1. Calls upon those boards, and instrumentalities responsible for the development of our educational materials to:

– Examine and evaluate the image of Jews and Judaism presented in curriculum for use in local churches, seminary Church History courses, and other literature which is used to promote greater understanding of our tradition through the United Church of Christ, and:

– On the basis of the evaluation to develop guidelines and educational resources for suggested use in the local church and seminaries to enable the literature to be representative of the understanding of Judaism and the Jewish people as a continuing witness in Covenant to God's presence in the world.

2. Calls upon those boards, offices and instrumentalities responsible for the development of literature relating to worship in the United Church of Christ to examine the liturgical materials, and based on this evaluation to create guidelines which will reflect a sensitivity to the image of Jews and Judaism which is projected in our liturgical content.

3. Calls upon the Office for Church in Society to coordinate the work of the established Inter-agency Task Force on Jewish-Christian Relations, the Jewish-Christian Dialogue Project in the United Church of Christ, and other groups within the United Church of Christ locally and regionally and nationally who are presently engaged in dialogue with the Jewish community.

4. Calls upon all local congregations, and regional judicatories of the United Church of Christ actively to engage in dialogue with the Jewish community in order to establish relationships of trust and to participate in a joint witness against all injustice in our local communities and in the world.

3

Guidelines for
Christian-Jewish Relations
for Use in the Episcopal Church

Adopted by the 69th General Convention of the Episcopal Church in the United States of America, meeting in Detroit, Michigan, in July 1988.

Among Christian communities, the Episcopal Church has special gifts to bring to the Christian-Jewish dialogue (see General Convention Resolution on this, Convention Journal 1979, pp. C47–48). It has a tradition of respect for truth wherever found and a critical appreciation of Scripture and historical development. It is, therefore, in a position to make a significant contribution to Jewish-Christian relations.

Preface to the Guidelines

One of the functions of the Christian-Jewish dialogue is to allow participants to describe and witness to their faith in their own terms. This is of primary importance since self-serving descriptions of other people's faiths are among the roots of prejudice, stereotyping and condescension. Careful listening to each other's expression of faith enables Christians to obey better the commandment not to bear false witness against their neighbors. Partners in dialogue must recognize that any religion or ideology which claims universality will have its own interpretations of other religions and ideologies as part of its own self-understanding. Dialogue gives the opportunity for mutual questioning of those understandings. A reciprocal willingness to listen, learn and understand enables significant dialogue to grow.

I. Principles of Dialogue

The following principles are offered to aid and encourage the Episcopal Church to make an increasingly vital and substantive impact on the dialogue.

1. In all dialogue, recognition of marked cultural differences is important. The words employed in religious discussion are not innocent or neutral. Partners in dialogue may rightly question both the language and the definitions each uses in articulating religious matters.

2. In the case of Christian-Jewish dialogue, a historical and theological imbalance is obvious. While an understanding of Judaism in New Testament times is an indispensable part of any Christian theology, for Jews a "theological" understanding of Christianity is not of the same significance. Yet neither Judaism nor Christianity, at least in the Western world, has developed without interaction with the other.

3. The relations between Jews and Christians have unique characteristics, since Christianity historically emerged out of early Judaism. Christian understanding of that process constitutes a necessary part of the dialogue and gives urgency to the enterprise. As Christianity came to define its own identity in relation to Judaism, the Church developed interpretations, definitions and terms for those things it had inherited from Jewish traditions. It also developed its own understanding of the Scriptures common to Jews and Christians. In the process of defining itself, the Church produced its own definition of God's acts of salvation. It should not be surprising that Jews resent those scriptural and theological interpretations in which they are assigned negative roles. Tragically, such patterns of thought have led Christians to overt acts of condescension, prejudice and even violent acts of persecution. In the face of those acts, a profound sense of penitence is the necessary response.

4. Many Christians are convinced that they understand Judaism since they have the Hebrew Scriptures as part of their Bible. This attitude is often reinforced by a lack of knowledge about the history of Jewish life and thought through the nineteen hundred years since Christianity and Judaism parted ways.

5. There is, therefore, a special urgency for Christians to listen, through study and dialogue, to ways in which Jews understand their own history, their Scriptures, their traditions, their faith and their practice. Furthermore, a mutual listening to the way each is perceived

by the other can be a step toward understanding the hurts, overcoming the fears, and correcting the misunderstandings that have separated us throughout the centuries.

6. Both Judaism and Christianity contain a wide spectrum of opinions, theologies, and styles of life and service. Since generalizations often produce stereotyping, Jewish-Christian dialogue must try to be as inclusive of the variety of views within the two communities as possible.

II. The Necessity for Christians to Understand Jews and Judaism

1. Through dialogue with Jews, many, though yet too few, Christians have come to appreciate the richness and vitality of Jewish faith and life in the Covenant and have been enriched in their own understandings of Jesus and the divine will for all creatures.

2. In dialogue with Jews, Christians have learned that the actual history of Jewish faith and experience does not match the images of Judaism that have dominated a long history of Christian teaching and writing, images that have been spread by Western culture and literature into other parts of the world.

3. Jesus was a Jew, born into the Jewish tradition. He was nurtured by the Hebrew Scriptures of his day, which he accepted as authoritative and interpreted both in terms of the Judaism of his time and in fresh and powerful ways in his life and teaching, announcing that the Kingdom of God was at hand. In their experience of his resurrection, his followers confessed him as both Lord and Messiah.

4. Christians should remember that some of the controversies reported in the New Testament between Jesus and the "scribes and Pharisees" found parallels within Pharisaism itself and its heir, Rabbinic Judaism. The controversies generally arose in a Jewish context, but when the words of Jesus came to be used by Christians who did not identify with the Jewish people as Jesus did, such sayings often became weapons in anti-Jewish polemics and thereby their original intention was tragically distorted. An internal Christian debate has been taking place for some years now about how to understand and explain passages in the New Testament that contain anti-Jewish references.

5. From the early days of the Church, many Christian interpreters saw the Church replacing Israel as God's people. The destruction of

the Second Temple of Jerusalem was understood as a warrant for this claim. The Covenant of God with the people of Israel was seen only as a preparation for the coming of Jesus. As a consequence, the Covenant with Israel was considered to be abrogated.

6. This theological perspective has had fateful consequences. As Christians understood themselves to replace the Jews as God's people, they often denigrated the Judaism that survived as a fossilized religion of legalism. The Pharisees were thought to represent the height of that legalism; Jews and Jewish groups were portrayed as negative models; and the truth and beauty of Christianity were thought to be enhanced by setting up Judaism as false and ugly. Unfortunately, many of the early Church fathers defamed the Jewish people.

7. Through a renewed study of Judaism and in dialogue with Jews, Christians have become aware that Judaism in the time of Jesus was in but an early stage of its long life. Under the leadership of the Pharisees, the Jewish people began a spiritual revival of remarkable power, which gave them the vitality capable of surviving the catastrophe of the loss of the Temple. It gave birth to Rabbinic Judaism, which produced the Talmud, and built the structures for a strong and creative life through the centuries.

8. Judaism is more than the religion of the Scriptures of Israel (called by Christians the Old Testament and by Jews the Hebrew Scriptures or the Hebrew Bible). The Talmud and other later writings provide interpretations that for much of Judaism are central and authoritative with the Torah.

9. For Christians, the Bible (that is, the two Testaments) is also followed by traditions for interpretation, from the Church Fathers to the present time. Thus, both Judaism and Christianity are nurtured by their Scriptures, scriptural commentaries and living and developing traditions.

10. Christians as well as Jews look to the Hebrew Bible as the record of God's election of and covenant with God's people. For Jews, it is their own story in historical continuity with the present. Christians, mostly of gentile background since early in the life of the Church, believe themselves to have entered this Covenant by grace through Jesus Christ. The relationship between the two communities, both worshiping the God of ancient Israel, is a given historical fact, but how it is to be understood and explained theologically is a matter of internal discussion among Christians and Jews in dialogue.

11. What Jews and Christians have in common needs to be examined as carefully as their differences. Finding in the Scriptures the faith sufficient for salvation, the Christian Church shares Israel's trust in the One God, whom the Church knows in the Spirit as the God and Father of the Lord Jesus Christ. For Christians, Jesus Christ is acknowledged as the only begotten of the Father, through whom millions have come to share in the love of, and to adore, the God who first made covenant with the people of Israel. Knowing the One God in Jesus Christ through the Spirit, therefore, Christians worship One God with a trinitarian confession involving creation, incarnation, and pentecost. In so doing, the Church worships in a language that is strange to Jewish worship and sensitivities, yet full of meaning to Christians. Dialogue is a means to help clarify language and to lead to the grasp of what the participants are really saying.

12. Christians and Jews both believe that God has created men and women and has called them to be holy and to exercise stewardship over the creation in accountability to God. Jews and Christians are taught by their Scriptures and traditions to recognize their responsibility to their neighbors, especially the weak, the poor, and the oppressed. In various and distinct ways they look for the coming of the Kingdom of God. In dialogue with Jews, many Christians have come to a more profound appreciation of the Exodus hope of liberation, praying and working for the coming of justice and peace on earth.

13. Jews found ways of living in obedience to Torah both before and after the emergence of Christianity. They maintained and deepened their call to be a distinctive people in the midst of the nations. Jews historically were allowed to live with respect and acceptance in some of the cultures in which they resided. Here their life and values thrived and made a distinct contribution to their Christian and Muslim neighbors. It is a sad fact, however, that Jews living in Christian countries have not fared better than those in non-Christian countries.

14. The land of Israel and the city of Jerusalem have always been central to the Jewish people. "Next year in Jerusalem" is a constant theme of Jewish worship in the diaspora. The continued presence of Jews in that land and in Jerusalem is a focal point for Judaism and must be taken into account in dialogue.

15. Many Jews differ in their interpretations of the religious and secular meaning of the State of Israel. For almost all Jewish people, however, Israel is an integral part of their identity.

16. Jews, Christians and Muslims have all maintained a presence in that land for centuries. The land is holy to all three, though each may understand holiness in different ways.

17. The existence of the State of Israel is a fact of history (see General Convention Resolution affirming "the right of Israel to exist as a free state within secure borders," Convention Journal 1979, p. C-104). However, the quest for homeland status by Palestinians—Christian and Muslim—is a part of their search for identity also, and must be addressed together with the need for a just and lasting solution to the conflict in the Middle East.

III. Hatred and Persecution of Jews—A Continuing Concern

1. Christians need to be aware that hatred and persecution of Jews have a long, persistent history. This is particularly true in countries where Jews have been a minority presence among Christians. The tragic history of the persecution of Jews includes massacres by the Crusaders, the Inquisition, pogroms and the Holocaust. The World Council of Churches Assembly at its first meeting in Amsterdam in 1948 declared: "We call upon the churches we represent to denounce antisemitism, no matter what its origin, as absolutely irreconcilable with the profession and practice of the Christian faith. Antisemitism is sin against God and human life." This appeal has been reiterated many times. Those who live where there is a history of prejudice and persecution of the Jews can serve the whole Church by revealing that danger whenever it is recognized.

2. Teachings of contempt for Jews and Judaism in certain traditions have proved a spawning ground for such evils as the Nazi Holocaust. It has, in this country, helped to spawn the extremist activities of the Ku Klux Klan and the defacement of synagogues, and stimulates the more socially acceptable but often more pernicious discriminatory practices seen in housing patterns and in private clubs. The Church must learn to proclaim the Gospel without generating contempt for Judaism or the Jewish people. A Christian response to the Holocaust is a resolve that it will never happen again.

3. Discrimination and persecution of the Jewish people have not only deep-rooted theological but also social, economic, and political aspects. Religious differences are magnified to justify ethnic hatred in

support of vested interests. Similar manifestations are also evident in many interracial conflicts. Christians are called to oppose all religious prejudices through which Jews or any people are made scapegoats for the failures and problems of societies and political regimes.

IV. Authentic Christian Witness

1. Christians believe that God's self-revelation is given in history. In the Covenant with the Jewish people at Mt. Sinai, the sacred law became part of our religious heritage. Christians see that same God embodied in the person of Jesus Christ, to whom the Church must bear witness by word and deed among all peoples. It would be false to its deepest commitment if the Church were to deny this mission. The Christian witness toward Jews, however, has been distorted by coercive proselytism, conscious and unconscious, overt and subtle. The Joint Working Group of the Roman Catholic Church and the World Council of Churches has stated: "Proselytism embraces whatever violates the right of the human person, Christian or non-Christian, to be free from external coercion in religious matters" (*Ecumenical Review*, 1/1971, p. 11).

2. Dialogue can rightly be described as a mutual witness, for witness is a sharing of one's faith conviction without the intention of proselytizing. Participants are invited to hear each other in order to understand their faiths, hopes, insights and concerns. The goal of dialogue is to communicate truth as the participants perceive it within their own traditions. The spirit of dialogue is to be present to each other in full openness and human vulnerability.

V. Practical Recommendations

1. It is recommended that the relationship between Christians and Jews be observed liturgically each year. A fitting occasion would be on or near the observance of Yom HaShoah, the Holocaust remembrance, since Jews and Christians would then have a common, or approximately common, day of observance. Another such occasion for an annual observance might be the Feast of St. James of Jerusalem on October 23, or a Sunday before or after that date.

2. It is recommended that in the services of the Church and in church school teaching, careful explanations be made of the New Testament texts which appear to place all Jews in an unfavorable light, particularly the expression "the Jews" in the English translations of the Gospel of John and in other references (see General Convention Resolution on "Deicide and the Jews," *Journal* 1964, pp. 279–80).

3. It is recommended that each diocese of the Church not already having a Committee on Christian-Jewish Relations establish one at the first opportunity in order to coordinate efforts and help to avoid haphazard and unrelated activities.

4. It is recommended that each parish situated in an area with a significant Jewish population organize with proper care and oversight an ongoing dialogue with Jews. If the dialogue is to be thorough and productive, it must include basic local exchanges between Episcopal and Jewish congregations.

5. It is recommended that seminaries of the Church undertake programs for their students which promote a greater understanding and appreciation for our common heritage with the Jews as well as for living Judaism today, addressing in particular those matters which eliminate prejudice and the presuppositions that feed it.

6. It is recommended that cooperation with Jewish and interreligious organizations concerned with service and the common good, interreligious programs, cultural enrichment and social responsibility be continued and intensified.

4

A Statement on Relations between Jews and Christians

Presented by the Commission on Theology to the General Assembly of the Christian Church (Disciples of Christ), meeting in St. Louis, Missouri, in July 1993, and received by the Assembly.

Preface: The Enormity of the Problem

Why is it imperative that Christians in the late twentieth century take up the responsibility to rethink their understanding of the relation between the church and the Jewish people? Why is it urgent that Christians learn new ways of talking about and acting toward Jewish people? Answers to these questions will set the report from the Commission on Theology in context and enable Disciples to grasp the significance of the task which the General Assembly assigned to the Commission.

Since the first century, Jews and Christians have shared a common history. Jews know this history very well, Christians hardly at all. Although Jesus of Nazareth was a Jew among Jews, whose birth was proclaimed by Simeon as "a light for revelation to the Gentiles and for glory to your people Israel" (Luke 2:32), within a century his followers had begun to distance themselves from the people of Israel and to define themselves as the "new Israel." As the "new Israel," they claimed to have displaced the Jewish people (the "old Israel") in the covenant with God. This language of an "old" and "new" Israel is not in the New Testament and has no biblical warrant. The church talked of the people Israel as a people that should not and would not exist save for the willful "blindness" and "obstinacy" by which Jews avoid disappearing. An unremitting parody of evil was projected upon the people Israel. They have been viewed as everything old, carnal, ethnocentric, and disobedient that the new, spiritual, universal, obedient

74

Gentile church displaces, and Christians as everything good that Jews can never be.

Beginning in the fourth century, the church passed laws defining relations between Christians and Jews, and ensuring that the situation of Jews in the society and economy mirrored the image of them in rhetoric. Each of Hitler's laws found its precedent in a law passed by councils of the church. For example, the requirement that all Jews wear the Star of David found its antecedent in a law passed by an ecumenical council of the church in 1215 requiring all Jews to wear distinctive dress. Jews were barred from any significant role in the society, economy, government, and military, and forced into making a living by selling old clothes and lending money (illegal for Christians). Church and later state laws forced Jews to live in ghettoes. Regularly, Jews were offered a choice of baptism or forced expulsion from the country. All Jews were expelled from England in 1290, France in 1394, Spain in 1492, Portugal in 1497, Brazil in 1654 (when the first Jews came to America). Beginning in the eleventh century, we witness the outbreaks of incidents of mob violence and mass murder committed against Jews. These grew in magnitude, becoming ever more destructive, with Hitler's so-called "final solution" the most recent and deadly. One scholar estimates that of all the people who might be alive today as Jews, only about 20 percent are living; another says that about half the Jews born into the world in the last eight hundred years have been killed.[1]

Since the second Vatican Council issued its statement on relations between the church and the Jewish people in the 1960s [*Bridges*, Vol. 1, Document 30], the Holy Spirit has been leading the churches to a new understanding of themselves in relation to the Jewish people. We thank God for the new spirit of repentance and self-criticism among Christians. Because of the history of Christian mistreatment of Jews, because anti-Jewish acts continue and again seem to be on the increase, because the church can understand its own central affirmations properly only if it understands Judaism and the Jewish people in the purpose of God, we offer the following theological remarks.

Statement of Theological Foundations of Jewish/Christian Relations

1. At the heart of the faith of the Christian Church (Disciples of Christ) is the confession that God has acted and revealed God's self in

Jesus Christ as Lord and Savior of the world. We confess that the God who was present in Jesus Christ reconciling the world to God is none other than the God of Israel, maker of heaven and earth, and known through the law and the prophets.

2. While this confession has often been used as a pretext for Christians to contend that God has rejected Israel, canceled God's covenant with Israel, and replaced Israel with the church, it is clear that these past emphases and their practical, historical consequences of encouraging persecution of Jews by Christians represent a profound misunderstanding of God and Jesus Christ, Israel and the church. We confess and repent of the church's long and deep collusion in the spread of anti-Jewish attitudes and actions through its "teaching of contempt" for Jews and Judaism. We disclaim such teaching and the acts and attitudes which it reflects and reinforces.

3. God's presence in Jesus Christ for the redemption of the world is rooted in God's call and election of Israel. Thus, to affirm that presence is to join with Judaism in affirming God's election of Israel and God's purpose to bring blessing to all the families of the earth through Abraham (Gen 12:3). We confess that both the church and the Jewish people are elected by God for witness to the world and that the relation of the church and the Jewish people to each other is grounded on God's gracious election of each.

4. It is indispensable to an adequate and truthful understanding of God's action in Jesus Christ that it be seen in continuity with God's unsearchable and particular election and covenant with Israel. God is faithful to that covenant in the historical life of Israel, whether or not Israel is itself faithful, just as God is faithful to the church in spite of its sin and rebellion. The God who calls Israel and acts in Israel's life is the God who creates all things and has acted in Jesus Christ.

5. The distinctive work of God in Jesus Christ, which often has been seen by Christians as a sign of God's *rejection* of the Jews, is rather a sign of the continuing *affirmation* of God's election of Israel and the Jewish people. We confess that the covenant established by God's grace with the Jewish people has not been abrogated but remains valid, precisely because "the gifts and the call of God are irrevocable" (Rom 11:29).

6. The Jewishness of Jesus ties Christians to Jews both historically and theologically. Jesus was shaped by and lived in the midst of Jewish traditions and culture, and understood his life and ministry to be, at the

least, for and with the Jews. A "non-Jewish Jesus," or even an indifferently Jewish Jesus, is one of the most unhistorical and corrupting myths which later church theology and practice have perpetrated. The Jewishness of Jesus deepens the tragedy of Christian mistreatment of the Jewish people. In this regard, the church has historically blamed the Jewish people for the crime of "deicide" (the killing of God) in the crucifixion of Jesus. This we now declare to be a theological and historical error. Although the historical details surrounding Jesus' death are not fully clear, it is evident that Jesus died as a result of the Roman imperial system and with the collusion of some of his fellow Jews. At the same time, we must understand that the crucifying actions of Jesus' contemporaries are representative of humanity as such, and are not peculiarly Jewish or Roman. Certainly history has witnessed the same crucifying actions by Christians toward Jews. The primary point of the Christian understanding of Jesus' crucifixion is the acknowledgment of God's unsearchably loving presence and action in Jesus' death and thereby God's final redemptive presence in any human situation.

7. Still, in the heart of the confession is a profound sense that what God has done in Jesus Christ is a new event unintelligible apart from Israel's story, but not merely a repetition of that story. Christians affirm that this new event is the Good News of God's taking up the cause both of Israel and of all humanity, and fulfilling Israel's and humanity's call to love and do justice before God and neighbor. This God in Jesus Christ has radically declared an unfathomable grace and love for Israel and for all humanity, grace and love moving God's creative work and hope toward which all creation moves. This new event in Jesus of Nazareth does not cancel or reject Israel, even if most Jews then and now were either indifferent to Jesus or rejected the affirmations of lordship and divinity about Jesus.

8. Jews and Christians share a history, a body of scripture, a communal and ethical tradition, and a treasury of prayers, although each has its own distinctive literature—the New Testament for Christians, the Talmud and midrash for Jews. And for both, history under God continues, requiring a continuing reclaiming of the truth and power of God's revelation in every generation. Thus, the unending task of interpretation requires Christians to be attentive to God's ongoing work of redemption among Jews as well Christians.

9. Christians must acknowledge that the language of invective, condemnation, and rejection against Jews, vexing and difficult as it is

to understand, is present in the New Testament and throughout most traditions of the church. This language has all too often gone hand in hand with actions undertaken by Christians against Jews. The church has repeatedly forgotten that the grace and love of God evident in Jesus Christ is *for* Israel and all Jews and is not a blessing dependent for its ultimate efficacy on how righteous or faithful or "Christian" one might be. God does not bestow God's grace and love on the church because the church is righteous and faithful. Both Jews and Christians have standing before God because and only because of the grace of the God who ever justifies the *unrighteous.*

10. Although we do not want to say Judaism is for Jews and the church for Gentiles, we must acknowledge that the continued existence of Jewish people who do not confess the lordship of Jesus Christ and who see their Jewishness as incompatible with this confession is, as Paul the apostle declares, a mystery and witness to the church: "O the depth of the riches and wisdom and knowledge of God! How unsearchable are his judgments and how inscrutable his ways!" (Rom 11:33). The church must receive this mystery and witness as essential to its own identity and destiny.

11. While we want to propose more vigorous study and conversation between Christians and Jews, it is necessary to declare now, in the light of what we have affirmed above, that:

    a. The Christian faith is not against Jewish people or Judaism as such.

    b. Anti-Jewish teaching and practices by Christians must be stopped and eradicated.

    c. However much Christians may want to point to what God has done in Jesus Christ for Israel and all humanity, they cannot appropriately say that God's election of and covenant with Israel have been canceled.

    d. Christians today have an urgent responsibility to converse, to cooperate with, and to affirm Jewish people as the special kindred of Christians.

    e. In acknowledging God's covenant with Israel, Christians today must take seriously the meaning of land to Jewish people and the relation of land to the contemporary state of Israel.

Practical/Pastoral Dimensions of Jewish/Christian Relations

There are also pastoral and practical considerations on the relations of Jews and Christians, and there are practical steps that need to be taken at this time.

1. The Bible has on occasion been read as a story of Israel's failure and of God's turning to the church and away from the synagogue. Such a reading is wrong and reflects the church's traditional anti-Jewish exegesis described in chapter four of *The Church and the Jewish People: A Study Guide for the Christian Church (Disciples of Christ)* (St. Louis: Christian Board of Publication, 1993). The Bible's central testimony never allows human failure or faithlessness to "nullify the faithfulness of God" (Rom 3:3).

2. Study of Jewish history and thought should not stop with the first century. All Christians need to have some introduction to the great rabbinical heritage, to Jewish history and religion up to the present time, about Jesus and to the story of Christian persecution of the Jews. Such an introduction provides the groundwork for better relations with contemporary Jews in all their diversity. It enables Christians to express genuine sorrow for past actions and to be attentive to the danger of repeating those actions.

3. Study of the Holocaust and regular participation in acts of remembrance enable Christians to hold before the world and before themselves the culminating horror and tragedy of the persecution of the Jews.

4. Common witness, worship, and service are always appropriate. Interfaith occasions, Bible study by clergy and rabbis, and sessions on Jewish/Christian relations all help to promote understanding and genuine conversation.

A Call for Further Study

Both because of what is essential to Christian faith and to the church's proper self-understanding and because of the indefensibly cruel treatment of Jewish people by Christians, it is important for the Christian Church (Disciples of Christ) to pray, study, and engage in conversations with its Jewish neighbors. This dialogue will enable Christians and Jews to understand their own continuities and discontinuities with each other and ancient Israel. For its well-being the church must recover its rootage in Israel, repent of its grievous sins against Jewish people in the past and present, and acknowledge its own dependence on the unmerited grace of the God who creates all things, called Israel into covenant, and acted in Jesus Christ for the redemption of the whole world.

This study and conversation should be:

a. undertaken in earnest by all manifestations of the Christian Church (Disciples of Christ);

b. given oversight, coordination, and focus by the Council on Christian Unity;

c. further stimulated, nurtured, and perpetuated by the study guide, *The Church and the Jewish People*, from the Commission on Theology, that elaborates a wide range of theological issues and historical knowledge about relations between Christians and Jews, and provides practical guidance for the church's conduct in relation to Jewish people.

Commission on Theology

William R. Baird, Fort Worth, TX

Walter D. Bingham, Louisville, KY

Paul A. Crow, Jr., Indianapolis, IN

James O. Duke, Berkeley, CA

Wallace Ford, Albuquerque, NM

Jack Forstman, Nashville, TN, Chairperson

Richard L. Harrison, Jr., Nashville, TN

Kenneth Henry, Decatur, GA

Joe R. Jones, Indianapolis, IN

Michael Kinnamon, Lexington, KY

Vance Martin, Los Angeles, CA

Eleanor Scott Meyers, Kansas City, MO

Narka Ryan, Baltimore, MD

Clark Williamson, Indianapolis, IN

Note

1. See respectively Arthur Gilbert, *The Vatican Council and the Jews* (New York: World Publications, 1968), p. 51 and Irvin J. Borowsky, "Foreword," in *Jews and Christians*, ed. by J. H. Charlesworth (New York: Crossroad, 1990), p. 9.

5

Declaration of the Evangelical Lutheran Church in America to the Jewish Community

Adopted by the Church Council of the Evangelical Lutheran Church in America, meeting in Chicago, Illinois, in April 1994.

In the long history of Christianity there exists no more tragic development than the treatment accorded the Jewish people on the part of Christian believers. Very few Christian communities of faith were able to escape the contagion of anti-Judaism and its modern successor, antisemitism. Lutherans belonging to the Lutheran World Federation and the Evangelical Lutheran Church in America feel a special burden in this regard because of certain elements in the legacy of the reformer Martin Luther and the catastrophes, including the Holocaust of the twentieth century, suffered by Jews in places where the Lutheran churches were strongly represented.

The Lutheran communion of faith is linked by name and heritage to the memory of Martin Luther, teacher and reformer. Honoring his name in our own, we recall his bold stand for truth, his earthy and sublime words of wisdom, and above all his witness to God's saving Word. Luther proclaimed a gospel for people as we really are, bidding us to trust a grace sufficient to reach our deepest shames and address the most tragic truths.

In the spirit of that truth-telling, we who bear his name and heritage must with pain acknowledge also Luther's anti-Judaic diatribes and the violent recommendations of his later writings against the Jews. As did many of Luther's own companions in the sixteenth century, we reject this violent invective, and yet more do we express our deep and abiding sorrow over its tragic effects on subsequent generations. In concert with the Lutheran World Federation, we particularly deplore the appropriation of Luther's words by modern antisemites for the teaching of hatred toward Judaism or toward the Jewish people in our day.

Grieving the complicity of our own tradition within this history of hatred, moreover, we express our urgent desire to live out our faith in Jesus Christ with love and respect for the Jewish people. We recognize in antisemitism a contradiction and an affront to the Gospel, a violation of our hope and calling, and we pledge this church to oppose the deadly working of such bigotry, both within our own circles and in the society around us. Finally, we pray for the continued blessing of the Blessed One upon the increasing cooperation and understanding between Lutheran Christians and the Jewish community.

6

Building New Bridges in Hope

Statement of the United Methodist Church on Christian-Jewish Relations adopted by the General Conference of the United Methodist Church, meeting in Denver, Colorado, in April 1996.

While we are committed to the promotion of mutual respect and understanding among people of all living faiths, we as Christians recognize a special relationship between Christians and Jews because of our shared roots in biblical revelation.[1]

A Quest for New Understanding

What is the relationship that God intends between Christianity and Judaism, between Christians and Jews? In The United Methodist Church, a search for understanding and appropriate response to this important theological and relational question has been under way for some time. A significant step in the development of United Methodist understanding of and intention for Christian-Jewish relations was taken in 1972, when the General Conference adopted a position statement under the title *Bridge in Hope* [*Bridges*, Vol. 1, Document 13]. This denominational statement urged church members and congregations to undertake "serious new conversations" with Jews in order to promote "growth in mutual understanding."[2] As it has been studied and used, *Bridge in Hope* has served as a strong foundation for United Methodist–Jewish dialogue in many settings.

Since 1972, other Christian denominations, as well as ecumenical bodies in which The United Methodist Church participates, such as the World Council of Churches, have also made statements on Christian-Jewish relations. Those voices have contributed to our further knowledge, reflection, and understanding. At the same time, we have learned much from the many relationships and dialogues that have flourished between Jews and Christians locally, nationally, and internationally.

Especially crucial for Christians in our quest for understanding has been the struggle to recognize the horror of the Holocaust as the catastrophic culmination of a long history of anti-Jewish attitudes and actions in which Christians, and sometimes the church itself, have been deeply implicated. Dialogues with Jewish partners have been central for Christians in our process of learning of the scope of the Holocaust atrocities, acknowledgment of complicity, and responsibility, repentance, and commitment to work against antisemitism in all its forms in the future.

We are aware, however, that the Christian-Jewish bridge of understanding has only begun to be constructed. The United Methodist Church is committed to continuing clarification and expansion of our knowledge of Judaism and to strengthening our relationships with Jewish people. We seek mutual exploration of the common ground underlying Christianity and Judaism as well as that which makes each faith unique. This statement is an expression of the principles of that commitment.

Foundation for United Methodist Understandings of Christian-Jewish Relations

As expressed in its Constitution, The United Methodist Church has long been strongly committed to the unity of the church: "As part of the church universal, The United Methodist Church believes that the Lord of the church is calling Christians everywhere to strive toward unity..."[3] For many years, The United Methodist Church has devoted itself at all levels of church life to building partnerships with other Christian denominations in striving to reveal the reality of the one Body, the whole church of Jesus Christ. "We see the Holy Spirit at work in making the unity among us more visible."[4]

By its Book of Discipline, The United Methodist Church is also dedicated to "serious interfaith encounters and explorations between Christians and adherents of other living faiths in the world." We believe that "Scripture calls us to be both neighbors and witnesses to all peoples...In these encounters, our aim is not to reduce doctrinal differences to some lowest common denominator of religious agreement, but to raise all such relationships to the highest possible level of human fellowship and understanding."[5] In an interdependent world of increasing awareness of the vitality and challenges of religious pluralism, we are called to "labor together with the help of God toward the salvation, health, and peace of all people."[6]

As with all theological questions, United Methodists approach the issues of interfaith relationships, including Christian-Jewish dialogue, by seeking understanding of God's will in Scripture in the context of tradition, reason, and experience. In that spirit and with that intention, we affirm the following principles for continued study, discussion, and action within The United Methodist Church, with other Christians, and especially with Jews.

United Methodist Guiding Principles for Christian-Jewish Relations

In order to increase our understanding of and with peoples of other living faith traditions, of ourselves as followers of Jesus Christ, and of God and God's truth, The United Methodist Church encourages dialogue and experiences with those of other faiths. For important and unique reasons, including a treasury of shared Scripture and an ancient heritage that belong to us in common but which also contain our dividedness, we look particularly for such opportunities with Jews. United Methodist participation in Christian-Jewish dialogue and relationships is based on the following understandings:

1. There is one living God, in whom both Jews and Christians believe.

While the Jewish and Christian traditions understand and express their faith in the same God in significantly different ways, we believe with Paul that God, who was in Christ reconciling the world to God's own self (2 Cor 5:18–19), is none other than the God of Israel, maker of heaven and earth. Above all else, Christians and Jews are bonded in our joyful and faithful response to the one God, living our faith as each understands God's call.

2. Jesus was a devout Jew, as were many of his first followers.

We know that understanding our Christian faith begins by recognizing and appreciating this seminal fact. Neither the ministry of Jesus and his apostles nor the worship and thought of the early church can be understood apart from the Jewish tradition, culture, and worship of the first century. Further, we believe that God's revelation in Jesus Christ is unintelligible apart from the story of what God did in the life of the people of Israel.

Because Christianity is firmly rooted in biblical Judaism, we understand that knowledge of these roots is essential to our faith. As expressed in a statement from the Consultation on the Church and Jewish People of the World Council of Churches: "We give thanks to God for the spiritual treasure we share with the Jewish people: faith in the living God of Abraham, Isaac, and Jacob; knowledge of the name of God and of the commandments; the prophetic proclamation of judgment and grace; the Hebrew Scriptures; and the hope of the coming Kingdom. In all these, we find common roots in biblical revelation and see spiritual ties that bind us to the Jewish people."[7]

3. Judaism and Christianity are living and dynamic religious movements that have continued to evolve since the time of Jesus, often in interaction with each other and with God's continual self-disclosure in the world.

Christians often have little understanding of the history of Judaism as it has developed since the lifetime of Jesus. As a World Council of Churches publication points out: "Bible-reading and worshiping Christians often believe that they 'know Judaism' since they have the Old Testament, the records of Jesus' debates with Jewish teachers and the early Christian reflections on the Judaism of their times…This attitude is often reinforced by lack of knowledge about the history of Jewish life and thought through the 1,900 years since the parting of the ways of Judaism and Christianity."[8]

As Christians, it is important for us to recognize that Judaism went on to develop vital new traditions of its own after the time of Jesus, including the Rabbinic Judaism that is still vibrant today in shaping Jewish religious life. This evolving tradition has given the Jewish people profound spiritual resources for creative life through the centuries. We increase our understanding when we learn about the rich variety of contemporary Jewish faith practice, theological interpretation, and worship, and discover directly through dialogue how Jews understand their own history, tradition, and faithful living.

4. Christians and Jews are bound to God though biblical covenants that are eternally valid.

As Christians, we stand firm in our belief that Jesus was sent by God as the Christ to redeem all people, and that in Christ the biblical covenant has been made radically new. While church tradition has taught that Judaism has been superseded by Christianity as the "new Israel," we do not believe that earlier covenantal relationships have been invalidated or that God has abandoned Jewish partners in covenant.

We believe that just as God is steadfastly faithful to the biblical covenant in Jesus Christ, likewise God is steadfastly faithful to the biblical covenant with the Jewish people. The covenant God established with the Jewish people through Abraham, Moses, and others continues because it is an eternal covenant. Paul proclaims that the gift and call of God to the Jews is irrevocable (Rom 11:29). Thus, we believe that the Jewish people continue in covenantal relationship with God.

Both Jews and Christians are bound to God in covenant, with no covenantal relationship invalidated by any other. Though Christians and Jews have different understandings of the covenant of faith, we are mysteriously bound to one another through our covenantal relationships with the one God and Creator of us all.

5. As Christians, we are clearly called to witness to the gospel of Jesus Christ in every age and place. At the same time, we believe that God has continued, and continues today, to work through Judaism and the Jewish people.

Essential to the Christian faith is the call to proclaim the good news of Jesus Christ to all people. Through the announcement of the gospel in word and work comes the opportunity for others to glimpse the glory of God, which we have found through Jesus Christ. Yet we also understand that the issues of the evangelization of persons of other faiths, and of Jews in particular, are often sensitive and difficult. These issues call for continuing serious and respectful reflection and dialogue among Christians and with Jews.

While we as Christians respond faithfully to the call to proclaim the gospel in all places, we can never presume to know the full extent of God's work in the world, and we recognize the reality of God's activity outside the Christian church. It is central to our faith that salvation is accomplished not by human beings, but by God. We know that judgment as to the ultimate salvation of persons from any faith community, including Christianity and Judaism, belongs to God alone.

It is our belief that Jews and Christians are coworkers and companion pilgrims who have made the God of Israel known throughout the world. Through common service and action, we jointly proclaim the

God we know. Together through study and prayer, we can learn how the God we believe to be the same God speaks and calls us continually into closer relationship with one another, as well as with God.

6. As Christians, we are called into dialogue with our Jewish neighbors.

Christians and Jews hold a great deal of Scripture, history, and culture in common. And yet, we also share two thousand painful years of antisemitism and the persecution of Jews by Christians. These two apparently discordant facts move Christians to seek common experiences with Jews, and especially to invite them into dialogue to explore the meaning of our kinship and our differences. Our intention is to learn about the faith of one another and to build bridges of understanding.

While for Christians, dialogue will always include testimony to God's saving acts in Jesus Christ, it will include in equal measure listening to and respecting the understanding of Jews as they strive to live in obedience and faithfulness to God and as they understand the conditions of their faith.

Productive interfaith dialogue requires focused, sustained conversation based on willingness to recognize and probe genuine differences while also seeking that which is held in common. We are called to openness so that we may learn how God is speaking through our dialogue partners. As stated in the World Council of Churches' "Guidelines on Dialogue": "One of the functions of dialogue is to allow participants to describe and witness to their faith on their own terms...Participants seek to hear each other in order to better understand each other's faith, hopes, insights, and concerns."[9] Fruitful and respectful dialogue is centered in a mutual spirit of humility, trust, openness to new understanding, and commitment to reconciliation and the healing of the painful wounds of our history.

7. As followers of Jesus Christ, we deeply repent of the complicity of the church and the participation of many Christians in the long history of persecution of the Jewish people.

The Christian church has a profound obligation to correct historical and theological teachings that have led to false and pejorative perceptions of Judaism and contributed to persecution and hatred of Jews. It is our responsibility as Christians to oppose antisemitism whenever and wherever it occurs.

We recognize with profound sorrow that repeatedly and often in the last two thousand years the worship, preaching, and teaching of the

Christian church has allowed and sometimes even incited and directed persecution against Jews.

The church today carries grave responsibility to counter the evil done by Christians to Jews in the Crusades, the Inquisition, and the pogroms of Eastern Europe and elsewhere, carried out in the name of Jesus Christ. In the twentieth century there is the particular shame in the failure of most of the church to challenge the policies of governments that were responsible for the unspeakable atrocities of the Holocaust.

Historically and today, both the selective use and the misuse of Scripture have fostered negative attitudes toward and actions against Jews. Use of New Testament passages that blame "the Jews" for the crucifixion of Jesus has throughout history been the basis of many acts of discrimination against Jews, frequently involving physical violence. There is no doubt that traditional and often officially sanctioned and promulgated Christian teachings, including the uncritical use of anti-Jewish New Testament writings, have caused untold misery and form the basis of modern antisemitism.

Misinterpretations and misunderstanding of historical and contemporary Judaism continue, including the mistaken belief that Judaism is a religion solely of law and judgment while Christianity is a religion of love and grace. The characterizations of God in the Hebrew Bible (called the Old Testament by Christians) are rich and diverse; strong images of a caring, compassionate, and loving deity are dominant for Jews as well as for Christians. Further, there are parallels between New Testament Christian understandings of the "spirit of the law" and contemporaneous theological developments in first-century Jewish theology.

The church has an obligation to correct erroneous and harmful past teachings and to ensure that the use of Scripture, as well as the preparation, selection, and use of liturgical and educational resources, does not perpetuate misleading interpretations and misunderstanding of Judaism.

It is also essential for Christians to oppose forcefully anti-Jewish acts and rhetoric that persist in the present time in many places. We must be zealous in challenging overt and subtle antisemitic stereotypes and bigoted attitudes that ultimately made the Holocaust possible, and which stubbornly and insidiously continue today. These lingering patterns are a call to Christians for ever-new educational efforts and continued vigilance, so that we, remembering and honoring the cries of the tortured and the dead, can claim with Jews around the world to be faithful to the post-Holocaust cry of "Never Again."

8. As Christians, we share a call with Jews to work for justice, compassion, and peace in the world in anticipation of the fulfillment of God's reign.

Together, Jews and Christians honor the commandment to love God with all our heart, soul, and might. It is our task to join in common opposition to those forces—nation, race, power, money—that clamor for ultimate allegiance. Together, we honor the commandment to love neighbor as self. It is our task to work in common for those things that are part of God's work of reconciliation. Together, we affirm the sacredness of all persons and the obligation of stewardship for all God has created.

Jews still await the messianic reign of God foretold by the prophets. Christians proclaim the good news that in Jesus Christ, "the kingdom of God is at hand"; yet we, as Christians, also wait in hope for the consummation of God's redemptive work. Together, Jews and Christians long for and anticipate the fulfillment of God's reign. Together, we are "partners in waiting." In our waiting, we are called to witness and to work for God's reign together.

9. As United Methodist Christians, we are deeply affected by the anguish and suffering that continue for many people who live in the Middle East region that includes modern Israel.

We commit ourselves through prayer and advocacy to bring about justice and peace for those of every faith.

Within The United Methodist Church, we struggle with our understanding of the complexity and the painfulness of the controversies in which Christians, Jews, and Muslims are involved in the Middle East. The issues include disputed political questions of sovereignty and control, and concerns over human rights and justice. We recognize the theological significance of the Holy Land as central to the worship, historical traditions, hope, and identity of the Jewish people. We are mindful of this land's historic and contemporary importance for Christians and Muslims. We are committed to the security, safety, and well-being of Jews and Palestinians in the Middle East, to respect for the legitimacy of the state of Israel, to justice and sovereignty for the Palestinian people, and to peace for all who live in the region.

As we join with others of many religious communities in wrestling with these issues and searching for solutions, we seek to work together

with other Christians, Jews, and Muslims to honor the religious significance of this land and to bring about healthy, sustainable life, justice,
and peace for all.

New Bridges to Christian-Jewish Understanding

The above statements of principle and affirmation offer a foundation for theological reflection within The United Methodist Church
and with other Christians on our understanding of our relationships
with the Jewish people. They are meant to be the basis of study, discussion, and action as we strive for greater discernment within the church.

Further, we hope that the statements of guiding principle will be
important as bases of cooperative efforts, and especially for dialogue
between United Methodists (sometimes in the company of other
Christians) and Jewish communities, as we mutually explore the meaning of our kinship and our differences.

Using the foregoing foundation and principles, The United
Methodist Church encourages dialogue with Jews at all levels of the
church, including and especially local congregations. It is also hoped
that there will be many other concrete expressions of Jewish-Christian
relationships, such as participating in special occasions of interfaith
observance, and joint acts of common service and programs of social
transformation. These offer great opportunity to Christians and Jews to
build relationships and together work for justice and peace (shalom) in
our communities and in the world, serving humanity as God intends.

We dare to believe that such conversations and acts will build new
bridges in hope between Christians and Jews, and that they will be
among the signs and first fruits of our sibling relationship under our
parent God. Together, we await and strive for the fulfillment of God's
reign.

Notes

1. "The Churches and the Jewish People, Towards a New Understanding," adopted at Sigtuna, Sweden, by the Consultation on the Church and
the Jewish People, sponsored by the World Council of Churches, 1988
[Document 67 below].

2. "Bridge in Hope: Jewish-Christian Dialogue," adopted by the General Conference of The United Methodist Church, 1972 [*Bridges*, Vol. 1, Document 13].

3. *The Book of Discipline of The United Methodist Church*, 1992, Constitution, Division One, Article 5; page 22.

4. *Book of Discipline*, Doctrinal Standards, Our Theological Task; page 84.

5. Ibid.

6. Ibid.

7. "The Churches and the Jewish People..."

8. "Ecumenical Considerations on Jewish-Christian Dialogue," 1982, World Council of Churches [*Bridges*, Vol. 1, Document 51], paragraph 1.6.

9. "Guidelines on Dialogue," adopted at London Colney, England, by the Consultation on the Church and the Jewish People of the Unit on Dialogue with People of Living Faiths and Ideologies, World Council of Churches, 1981 [cf. *Bridges*, Vol. 1, Document 51], paragraph 3.4.

7

Guidelines on
Lutheran-Jewish Relations

Adopted by the Church Council of the Evangelical Lutheran Church in America, meeting in Chicago, Illinois, in November 1998.

The following suggestions for fostering Lutheran-Jewish dialogue and cooperation were drafted by the Consultative Panel on Lutheran-Jewish Relations of the ELCA Department for Ecumenical Affairs, and were adopted by the ELCA Church Council at its meeting on November 16, 1998. These guidelines are an outgrowth of the ELCA's April 1994 "Declaration to the Jewish Community" [Document 5 above], which repudiated the anti-Jewish writings of Martin Luther and expressed "our urgent desire to live out our faith in Jesus Christ with love and respect for the Jewish people."

The Evangelical Lutheran Church in America hopes also to issue guidelines for relations with members of other faith communities in the United States.

As Lutherans, we seek to renew and enhance our relationship with the Jewish people, a relationship long distorted by misunderstanding and prejudice. In its 1994 Declaration to the Jewish Community, the Evangelical Lutheran Church in America publicly repudiated the anti-Jewish views of Martin Luther, expressed repentance for Christian complicity in hatred and violence against the Jews through the centuries, and committed itself to building a relationship with the Jewish people based on love and respect. For Lutherans to read, understand, and acknowledge this Declaration can be a first step in renewing our relationship with the Jewish community. Reconciliation always begins with an understanding of the offense and a willingness to repent and amend one's ways. Only then can further steps be taken to forge a new relationship.

We as Christians share deep and common roots with Jews, not least books of Scripture revered by both communities. There is much to be gained in exploring those common roots, as well as the reasons for the "parting of the ways" during the first generations of the followers of Jesus. New Testament texts reflect at many points the hostility between the two communities, but also point to ways in which a new spirit of mutual respect and understanding can be achieved.

We as Christians also need to learn of the rich and varied history of Judaism since New Testament times, and of the Jewish people as a diverse, living community of faith today. Such an encounter with living and faithful Judaism can be profoundly enriching for Christian self-understanding. It is to nurture this blessing that we offer these guidelines for honest and faithful conversation and cooperation between Lutherans and Jews.

1. Lutherans are urged to take the initiative in fostering Lutheran-Jewish dialogue. In many cases, it will be helpful to cooperate with other Christians in organizing and sustaining such conversations.

2. Meetings should be jointly planned so as to ensure sensitivity toward and accurate information about the other group. For example, Lutherans need to remember the importance of the Sabbath and other holy days and of dietary observance for their Jewish partners in dialogue.

3. Because time is needed to cultivate relationships and build mutual understanding, planners of such dialogues should anticipate the need for a series of sessions.

4. On both sides, living communities of faith and worship are involved. Because of strong commitments and painful memories, emotions may run deep. Participants should be prepared to hear one another out and to help all move toward healing.

5. It should be understood that the aim of such conversations is not shallow tolerance or mere surface agreement, but greater self-understanding and mutual enrichment. Honest differences will remain, even as broad areas of commonality are discovered.

6. On the basis of new understandings reached through dialogue, plans can be made for cooperation in spiritual and social concerns, struggling against those forces that deny or degrade the divine image in humankind. Among such issues of common concern are questions of church-state relations, religious freedom, and social justice.

7. Joint activities such as the following can be planned:
   a. Visits to one another's houses of worship, either at regular services or at specially arranged open houses, accompanied by explanation and discussion. Such visits are appropriate both for adults and for youth groups and confirmation or Bar/Bat Mitzvah classes. Lutherans should consider, however, that Christians may be able more easily to share in a typical weekly Jewish worship service than Jews can in a typical Christian service, since the latter includes prayers and blessings which presume faith in Jesus and the Trinity.
   b. Informal discussions in homes, using materials designed for interreligious study. Participants may be drawn from one church and one synagogue or several congregations.
   c. Joint trips and study tours to places of historical and religious significance to each tradition.
   d. Lectures and discussions on topics of mutual interest. These may include biblical, historical, theological, and ethical topics or interfaith Bible study for laity and clergy.
   e. Joint clergy and/or lay retreats.

8. Attendance by Lutherans at Bar and Bat Mitzvahs, Seders (Passover meals) in Jewish homes or synagogues, and Yom HaShoah (Holocaust Remembrance Day) observances can be of great educational and spiritual value. Likewise, Lutherans should welcome Jews at our occasions and ceremonies.

9. Although attendance at Seders in Jewish homes or synagogues is to be preferred, "demonstration Seders" have been held rather widely in Christian churches and can serve a useful educational purpose, in which both common roots and significant differences can be learned. This should be approached with caution, however, and with the awareness that this might be considered "trampling on the

other's holy ground." If such demonstrations are done, they should be done carefully, preferably in consultation with, or hosted by, a local rabbi.

10. Lutherans may be invited to offer prayer in civic settings such as legislative assemblies or public school baccalaureates. Compromising essentials of our faith to American civil religion is always a clear danger. Such occasions, however, can be regarded as times when our common faith in God finds expression, as indeed it does in the prayer that Jesus himself gave us. On some occasions, when persons of several faiths offer prayer, it may be possible by way of introduction to note that each will pray in language fully reflecting each tradition. In such settings Lutherans will want to witness to our tradition of Trinitarian prayer offered "in the name of Jesus" or "through Jesus Christ our Lord."

11. Groups such as "Jews for Jesus" or "Messianic Jews" consist of persons from a Jewish background who have converted to Christianity and who wish to retain their Jewish heritage and identity. Lutherans should be aware that most Jews regard such persons as having forsaken Judaism, and consider efforts to maintain otherwise to be deceptive.

12. Lutherans need to understand the depth of Jewish concern for communal survival, a concern shaped not only by the Holocaust but by centuries of Christian antipathy toward Judaism. Jews will thus feel strongly about topics such as the security of the State of Israel, intermarriage, and conversion, in which Jewish survival is seen to be at stake. Lutherans are not obligated to adopt the same perspective on these matters, but it is vital for us to understand and respect our neighbors' concerns.

13. Lutheran pastors should make it clear in their preaching and teaching that although the New Testament reflects early conflicts, it must not be used as justification for hostility toward present-day Jews. Blame for the death of Jesus should not be attributed to Judaism or the Jewish people, and stereotypes of Judaism as a legalistic religion should be avoided. Lutheran curricular materials should exercise the same care.

14. Topics pertaining to Christian-Jewish relations should be included in educational events at synod assemblies and professional leadership conferences and should be addressed in Lutheran seminary education. In addition, comment may be sought from Jewish scholars and leaders on issues under discussion and debate by Lutherans.

15. Student and faculty exchanges between Lutheran and Jewish theological schools and other educational institutions can be invaluable in preparing the next generation for greater interfaith understanding and cooperation.

These guidelines have been issued so that those who desire to engage in interfaith dialogue might benefit from the experience of those who have gone before. They are intended to provide practical assistance as well as the encouragement needed for a rewarding journey.

8

A Statement on Jewish-Christian Relations

Adopted at the 2003 Convocation of the Alliance of Baptists, meeting in Vienna, Virginia, in April 2003. This is a revision of a similar statement adopted at the 1995 Convocation.

As Baptist Christians we are the inheritors of and, in our turn, have been the transmitters of a theology which lays the blame for the death of Jesus at the feet of the Jews; a theology which has taken the anti-Jewish polemic of the Christian Scriptures out of its first-century context and has usurped for the Church the biblical promises and prerogatives given by God to the Jews; a theology which ignores nineteen centuries of Jewish development by viewing contemporary Jews as modern versions of their first century co-religionists; a theology which views the Jewish people and Jewish nationhood merely as pieces in an eschatological chess game; a theology which has valued conversion over dialogue, invective over understanding, and prejudice over knowledge; a theology which does not acknowledge the vibrancy, vitality, and efficacy of the Jewish faith.

The madness, the hatred, the dehumanizing attitudes which led to the events known collectively as the Holocaust did not occur overnight or within the span of a few years, but were the culmination of centuries of such Christian theology, teaching and church-sanctioned action directed against the Jews simply because they were Jews. In spite of the evidence of humankind's inhumanity to its own bolstered by religious prejudice, most Christians have done little or nothing to correct the theology which nurtures such hatred or develop avenues of understanding which counter the centuries of prejudice. While some notable strides have been made in post-Holocaust theology which provide new ways of reading the biblical text, especially the Johannine and Pauline texts, we have done little to utilize those understandings in the preaching and teaching ministries of our churches.

It is in recognition of a past and present among Baptists that are complicit in perpetuating negative stereotypes and myths concerning Jews, that we, the Alliance of Baptists, meeting in convocation on April 25, 2003, at Vienna, Virginia, adopt as an Institutional Understanding for Jewish-Christian Relations the following confessions and affirmations which were first adopted as a Resolution by those meeting in convocation at Vienna Baptist Church, Vienna, Virginia, March 4, 1995:

As individual members and churches of the Alliance of Baptists, we:
- Confess our sin of complicity
- Confess our sin of silence
- Confess our sin of interpreting our sacred writings in such a way that we have created enemies of the Jewish people
- Confess our sins of indifference and inaction to the horrors of the Holocaust
- Confess our sin against the Jewish people, and
- Offer this confession with humility and with hope for reconciliation between Christians and Jews toward which end we will work.

As the Alliance of Baptists, institutionally, and as individual members and churches, we:
- Affirm the teaching of the Christian Scriptures that God has not rejected the community of Israel, God's covenant people (Rom 11:1–2), since the gifts and calling of God are irrevocable (Rom 11:29)
- Renounce interpretations of Scripture which foster religious stereotyping and prejudice against the Jewish people and their faith
- Seek genuine dialogue with the broader Jewish community, a dialogue built on mutual respect and the integrity of each other's faith
- Lift our voices quickly and boldly against all expressions of anti-semitism
- Educate ourselves and others on the history of Jewish-Christian relations from the first century to the present, so as to understand our present by learning from our past, and
- Commit ourselves to rigorous consideration of appropriate forms of Christian witness for our time.

9

Bearing Faithful Witness: United Church–Jewish Relations Today

Approved by the 38th General Council of the United Church of Canada, meeting in Wolfville, Nova Scotia, in August 2003. The statement was accompanied by extensive study materials.

The United Church of Canada is called to be faithful to Jesus Christ in worship, prayer, word and action in the midst of our neighbors and in the world. Accordingly, the 36th General Council, meeting in Camrose, Alberta in 1997, authorized for the whole church a study of the document "Bearing Faithful Witness: United Church–Jewish Relations Today."

People of the United Church have responded thoughtfully and prayerfully to the study document and to the proposed policy statement. This statement encompasses that response, and seeks to be a faithful expression of our understanding of United Church/Jewish relations.

We believe this statement reflects our faith in Christ and is consistent with our historic witness as part of the Body of Christ. We believe that the God whom we know in Jesus Christ is the One who called Sarah and Abraham, gave the Torah to Moses, and put passion for justice into the hearts of the prophets. We believe, above all, in the faithfulness of God.

Holy Scripture teaches that the eternal Word became flesh in the person of Jesus, a Jew. The One who is "our judge and our hope" lives as a Jew, dies as a Jew and is raised as a Jew. In making these affirmations we seek to bear faithful witness to the Jewishness of Jesus.

We believe that the Holy Spirit calls us to bear faithful witness concerning God's reconciling mission in Jesus Christ. In Jesus Christ, God has opened the door in a new way to those previously outside the covenant. Our understanding of the faithfulness of God would be at risk if we were to say that God had abandoned the covenant with the Jewish people. As Paul says in Romans 9–11, the covenant is irrevocable because God is faithful.

We believe that our faith issues in action. Jesus commands us to love our neighbors, but all too often Christians have treated Jews, our sisters and brothers, as enemies. We believe that our faith calls us to repent when the church has been unfaithful in its witness by not loving Jews as neighbors.

Therefore, as an act of repentance and in faithfulness to the commandment that we should not bear false witness against our neighbors, The United Church of Canada...

a) ACKNOWLEDGES:
- a history of anti-Judaism and antisemitism within Christianity as a whole, including the United Church of Canada
- a history of interpretation of New Testament texts which has often failed to appreciate the context within Judaism from which these texts emerged, resulting in deeply rooted anti-Jewish misinterpretation
- a history of insensitivity with respect to the importance of the Shoah[1] for Jews
- antisemitism and anti-Judaism as affronts to the gospel of Jesus Christ.

b) REJECTS:
- all teaching of a theology of contempt toward Jews and Judaism
- the belief that God has abolished the covenant with the Jewish people[2]
- supersessionism, the belief that Christians have replaced Jews in the love and purpose of God
- proselytism which targets Jews for conversion to Christianity.

c) AFFIRMS:
- the significance of Judaism as at once a religion, a people, and a covenant community
- that Judaism, both historically and currently, cannot be understood from knowledge of the Old Testament alone

- that the gifts and calling of God to the Jewish people are irrevocable
- the uniqueness for Christianity of the relationship with Judaism
- that both Judaism and Christianity, as living faiths, have developed significantly from a common root
- that the love of God is expressed in the giving of both Torah and Gospel
- that the State of Israel has the right to exist in peace and security[3]
- our common calling with Jews and others to align ourselves with God's world-mending work
- the opportunity for growth in Christian self-understanding that exists through closer dialogue with, openness to, and respect for Judaism.

d) ENCOURAGES members, congregations, presbyteries, conferences and the General Council:
- to seek opportunities to meet with Jews and to learn about modern Judaism
- to continue to study the issues raised by the study document, "Bearing Faithful Witness," along with other issues of significance within the Jewish-Christian relationship
- to be vigilant in resisting antisemitism and anti-Judaism in church and society
- to create ongoing worship opportunities within the church for highlighting the importance of the Jewish-Christian relationship, such as at the time of Shoah Remembrance in April, or the high Jewish Holy Days in September/October, or Kristallnacht in November or Brotherhood/Sisterhood Week in February.

Notes

1. Shoah, which is a Hebrew term meaning "catastrophic destruction" is often the preferred term over the more-familiar "Holocaust." This is because the word "holocaust" comes from a Greek term which is used in the Septuagint to signify the Hebrew term for "burnt offering." Many do not consider it helpful or appropriate to refer to the destruction of most of European

Jewry as an "offering." The usage of these terms is not yet a completely set-tled question.

2. The biblical covenant with the Jewish people includes the promise of land. Whether that means exclusive occupation and control is disputed.

3. The United Church of Canada strongly affirms the right of the State of Israel to exist in peace and in secure boundaries and the right of Palestinians to a homeland state. United Church of Canada support of specific United Nations resolutions implies support for the boundaries of Israel and the Palestinian state being approximately represented by the pre-1967 borders of Israel and the West Bank and Gaza, subject to mutually agreed negotiations on the transfer of land.

10

Our Relationship
with the Jewish People

Adopted by the 137th General Assembly of the Presbyterian Church in Canada, meeting in London, Ontario, in June 2011.

The Statement of The Presbyterian Church in Canada on Our Relationship with the Jewish People is a summary of conclusions on the specific topic of the relationship between the church, specifically The Presbyterian Church in Canada, and the Jewish community. We recognize this topic exists within a broader framework of concerns, such as the relationship between Palestinians and the State of Israel. Those concerns have been addressed in other church study documents. The background and rationale for this statement are contained primarily in the study document, "One Covenant of Grace" (A&P [*Acts & Proceedings*] 2010, pp. 291–355). Other documents, such as, "A Reaffirmation of the Uniqueness and Finality of Jesus Christ and its Relevance for Inter-faith Dialogue Today" (A&P 2009, pp. 254–59) and General Assembly actions affirming UN Security resolutions re: Palestine and Israel (such as A&P 1983, p. 374 and A&P 1990, pp. 395–400, 62–63), as well as our subordinate standards, address broader concerns.

In stating our relationship with the Jewish people we reaffirm a central tenet of our Reformed faith expressed in the Westminster Confession of Faith, that there is one covenant of grace embracing Jews and Gentiles and therefore, not "two covenants of grace differing in substance, but one and the same under various dispensations" (VII, 6).

Accordingly, we affirm that the Jewish people have a unique role in God's economy of salvation and healing for our world. Jesus himself taught that "salvation is from the Jews" (John 4:22) and the Apostle Paul stated: "to them belong the sonship, the glory, the covenants, the giving of the law, the worship and the promises; to them belong the patriarchs, and of their race, according to the flesh, is the Christ, God who is over all be blessed forever. Amen" (Rom 9:4–5). The Jewish people have a pre-eminent place in God's covenant, John Calvin finely said, for they are "the firstborn in God's family."

We affirm that God has graciously included Gentile Christians, rightly called "posthumous children of Abraham" (J. Calvin), by engrafting them into the one people of God established by God's covenant with Abraham. This means that Jews have not been supplanted and replaced by Christians in the one covenant. As Paul teaches, God has not rejected or abandoned them: "I ask, then has God rejected his people? By no means!" (Rom 11:1).

We believe that the Triune God who is revealed in Jesus Christ is the same God who chose and made himself known to the people of Israel. We believe that both Christians and Jews worship and serve the One Living God.

We confess God's grace, mercy and faithfulness in the miracle of Jewish survival and the continuing existence and witness of the Jewish people. We are grateful that the State of Israel is a place the Jewish people can call home and we express our commitment as The Presbyterian Church in Canada to their right to live in peace, both in the Middle East and throughout the world. We also commit ourselves to pray for the peace of Jerusalem so all the children of Abraham may freely worship and live in a place they call holy.

It is always good for us to confess our sins to God. We acknowledge with shame and penitence the Church's long complicity in the persecution, exclusion and expulsions of the Jews through the "teaching of contempt," beginning in the first centuries of the Christian era, gathering strength during the Crusades and culminating in the Shoah or Holocaust. As Christians we have failed to demonstrate to the Jewish community and to individual Jews that love which Jesus Christ commanded us to show. Of this lack of love and teaching of contempt and the attitudes and acts which proceeded from it, we humbly repent.

It is also, however, a matter of historical record that countries in which the Reformed tradition and its "one covenant of grace" theology took root have provided refuge for this persecuted people. The Spanish and Portuguese Jewish community has lived in the Netherlands (and Dutch colonies like Curacao) with full citizenship rights since the seventeenth century. There were no pogroms in

Scotland. During the Puritan Commonwealth Jews were readmitted to England and have flourished as a community both there and in what became the United States. We are thankful for Christians, of all traditions throughout the ages, who have stood in solidarity with Jews. We call upon our people to eschew the use of language and innuendo which may disparage, slander and harm Jews and we urge Christians to show solidarity with Jews when acts of hatred, such as the desecration of graves, synagogues and schools are perpetrated against them.

We affirm the uniqueness, finality and unsurpassability of Jesus Christ the sole mediator of the one covenant of grace and acknowledge our commission to bear witness to our Lord to all peoples, without distinction, remembering as Living Faith reminds us: "We should not address others in a spirit of arrogance implying that we are better than they. But rather in the spirit of humility, as beggars telling others where food is to be found, we point to Christ" (9.2.1). We confess we have not always borne witness to Jesus Christ in ways that have been faithful to our Lord and sensitive to our neighbors, including—and perhaps especially—our Jewish brothers and sisters.

Both Christians and Jews look forward in hope to God's full redemption which Christians believe will occur in the Second Advent when Jesus Christ returns, a hope which includes the Jews, for as Paul teaches in Romans 9–11, in Jesus Christ there will be an ingathering of people, whether of Jewish or Gentile background: "so all Israel will be saved" (Rom 11:26).

The Presbyterian Church in Canada has sought to serve Jewish people in Canada in the name of our Lord through specific mission efforts in Montreal, Toronto and Winnipeg. The most well known of those was the Christian Synagogue in Toronto which evolved into the Scott Mission.

Finally we encourage our congregations and people to take the initiative and to reach out in friendship and hospitality to neighboring synagogues and Jewish people and where they can, to engage in Jewish-Christian dialogue to promote better mutual understanding and to pursue and ensure the establishment of peace and justice and the good and betterment of the wider community.

11

Statement on the Fiftieth Anniversary of the Pogrom in November 1938

Issued in Berlin in May 1988 by the Federation of Protestant Churches in the German Democratic Republic (Bund der Evangelischen Kirchen in der DDR) and the Protestant Church in [West] Germany (Evangelische Kirche in Deutschland).

November 9, 1988 marks fifty years since in the then German Reich, at the order of the National Socialist authorities, the synagogues were set on fire. Jewish places of worship were desecrated; Jewish shops and homes were pillaged; Jewish fellow-citizens were mistreated, displaced, beaten to death.

What happened in November 1988 was carried out in public; it took place before the eyes of everyone. The persecution was directed against all Jews. Racist insanity displayed its humanity-despising cruelty. No one could say that he or she knew nothing about it. Those who planned and carried out these crimes were able to count on the majority of our people either being in agreement with what was done, looking the other way out of indifference, or remaining silent out of fear. Christians too—with a few exceptions—kept silent.

How was it possible that such injustice could occur in a country where people demanded, above all, law and order? In organizing the November pogrom, the National Socialist leadership focused on two objectives:

German Jews were to be humiliated in a public act. The aim was to isolate them, to intimidate them, and where possible, to force them to emigrate—while leaving their possessions behind. The term "Reichskristallnacht" (Reich Crystal Night) minimizes what the day of the destruction of the synagogues really meant. It was a further step on the fateful road which eventually led to the murder of millions in Auschwitz and other extermination sites.

In addition, the brutal treatment of the Jews served to intimidate the entire German population. The absence of any serious protest demonstrated how powerful the dictatorship had already become at that point in time. From then on, the authorities knew to what extent they could allow injustice and violence without encountering resistance from the public. This is how November 9, 1938 paved the way for the so-called "Final Solution of the Jewish Question," propelled by racist insanity. It also accelerated the plunge into the catastrophe of the Second World War. The burning synagogues were a flaming signal. Soon German cities and their churches were also burning.

When we today evoke the memory of the events of November 1938, we do not do so in order to stand as accusers before the generation of those involved at the time. Rather we do so in the awareness that the guilt of that period retains its potency if we keep it secret or suppress it. Even if some who were involved at the time have atoned for their acts, even though others have died and a new generation has grown up, we are all responsible for the consequences of this guilt-ridden past. In acknowledging this bitter truth, we are cognizant of the fact that both theology and the church were complicit in the long history of alienation and hostility toward the Jews. The church failed to see the deep inner bond between Judaism and Christianity. It viewed the synagogue as having been rejected by God, rather than as the people whom God first loved and chose. The Jews experienced the cross to a large extent only as a sign of persecution.

In recent years theological and historical research has opened our minds anew to that which is unifying and common in the faith of Christians and Jews. We are aware of what it means that the Father of Jesus Christ is the One God testified to by the Bible, who freed his people from slavery, who is faithful to them and has never revoked his covenant with Israel.

Therefore our thinking, speaking, and acting must never contribute to fostering animosity toward Jews. We must strive to rid ourselves, in our everyday language, of all expressions that are hurtful to Jews. The same applies to the language of preaching. But above all we have the duty to disseminate and to deepen—in particular for the younger generation—accurate information about the Jewish people and Jewish religion, history, and culture, as well as the Jewish state. Christian-Jewish dialogue about central questions of our faith deserves encouragement and support at all levels. We are grateful for the existence of various working groups and study circles that for years have dealt with the theme of "The Church and Judaism." We urge everyone not to weaken in their efforts to seek understanding between Christians and Jews. We ask our congregations to give vigorous support to this important task and to seek out opportunities for encounter between Christians and Jews.

Recognition should also be given to efforts to preserve and give proper care to whatever bears witness to the rich heritage of the Jewish-German past.

We would like to assure the Jews who live among us despite the calamitous past that they have a homeland here. We also support the efforts of the State of Israel to find a secure peace with its neighbors within just borders.

Fifty years after the day of the destruction of the synagogues, we pray to God that Jews and Christians may be able to walk together toward the future under his loving-kindness. May God fulfill his promise with us all—Jews and Christians.

Berlin, May 26, 1988

Federation of Protestant Churches in the German Democratic Republic
Dr. Werner Leich
Bishop
Chair, Leadership Conference of Protestant Churches

Protestant Church in Germany
Dr. Martin Kruse
Bishop
Chair of the Council

12

The Church and the Jewish People

Adopted by the Synod of the Protestant Church of the Palatinate (Evangelisch Kirche der Pfalz), Germany, in May 1990.

I

HISTORICAL RETROSPECT

For centuries the Rhine-Palatinate was a settlement center of Jews in Central Europe. Christians and Jews lived side by side in our area. We are reminded of this fact by the Yiddish language, which originated in the area of the Rhine-Palatinate and Hesse. Many words of the Palatine dialect, down to the present day, testify to this. In general, the Jews were only tolerated at best. They had to suffer from discrimination, expulsion, and pogroms. However, there were also times when, in some places, living side by side turned into a genuine living with each other, with a certain intimacy and a sense of being good neighbors to one another. Seen in a broad historical context, however, it can be said that Christians' sense of superiority prevented them from taking notice of the Jewish faith at all. Therefore, one could not become aware of the many things they in fact had in common.

Instead, an anti-Jewish body of thought was passed on from generation to generation. It was in this way that Christian anti-Judaism could be assimilated into racial and economic antisemitism, and even provide ideological undergirding for it. With this state of mind, wide segments of our church believed they could serve the German people while adhering to the tradition of support for an authoritarian state. In the time of National Socialism, the church, apart from individual instances, did not stand by the dishonored and threatened Jews, and did not oppose their annihilation. When fifty years ago, on October 22, 1940, the remaining Jews of the Palatinate were deported to Gurs

110

in Southern France, no voice of protest rose from our church. After war and defeat, when the vast scale of the crimes and guilt became known, the majority avoided coming to terms with what Germans had inflicted upon other nations, upon dissenters, weak and sick persons, and above all, upon the Jewish people.

It is, therefore, all the more significant for us today that immediately after the war, the initiative for a new start of the Christian-Jewish dialogue came from the Jewish side. It is a sign of hope that this dialogue is being continued in our area and in other countries, not least in Israel.

II

INSIGHTS AND AGREEMENTS OF THE CHRISTIAN-JEWISH DIALOGUE THAT WE WANT TO AFFIRM

The Holocaust as a crisis of our faith

1. *The Holocaust, and that for which this word stands, deeply shakes our Christian self-understanding.*

Our request for pardon of our guilt (fifth petition of the Lord's Prayer) includes our guilt toward the Jews all over the world, the people of Israel.

The complicity of the church in the persecution and annihilation of the Jews, grown out of centuries-old disregard of Israel and enmity against Israel, demands of us that we grapple with our own faith history on all levels (research, doctrine, congregational work).

Learning from the faith example of Israel

2. *By its life as a chosen people and through faithfulness to its God, Israel has witnessed to God even in martyrdom.*

Many Jews went to their deaths with the mourners' prayer (the *Kaddish*: sanctified be your name) and with the confession "Hear Israel, the Lord is our God, the Lord is one." In this way they were, in an age of the "eclipse of God," witnesses to the God of Israel, who is also our God.

The dying Jesus identifies himself with Israel's tradition of suffering with the words of Psalm 22 (Mk 15).

Israel remains God's first love

3. *Israel's permanent election means that the church cannot put Israel in the same category as the gentiles.*

The missionary command in Matthew 28:19, "Go therefore and make disciples of all nations, baptizing them in the name of the Father and of the Son and of the Holy Spirit," is misunderstood if Israel is counted among the "nations."

The witness required of us Christians in relation to Israel is discipleship to Jesus. This includes always remembering that Jesus was a Jew. As we cling to Jesus, so at the same time we cling to Israel (cf. thesis 5 below).

The significance of the Jewish "No" to Jesus Christ

4. *The "No" of a large part of Israel to Jesus Christ is meaningful for Christians in several ways and has to be received and understood differently from the "No" of the rest of the world.*

- The "No" to Jesus Christ as Messiah is the expression of the people of Israel's messianic hope for the still expected kingdom of God, and of Israel's faithfulness to the biblical God.
- The "No" to Jesus Christ is also the result of the church's failure toward Israel. It challenges the church to witness to Jesus Christ in credible action toward Israel.
- Finally, the "No" of Israel to Jesus Christ has, according to Paul, "happened for our salvation" (Rom 11:11ff.).

Our "Yes" to Jesus Christ has to prove itself always anew in the face of Israel's "No."

Jesus belongs to his people

5. *Jesus was a Jew. Therefore, we must not separate him from his people or put him in opposition to his people.*

Many biblical testimonies stress Jesus' attachment to his people: Matthew 10:5, Matthew 15:24, Luke 15:31, and others. According to Luke 2:30–32, Simeon speaks these words at the circumcision of Jesus: "My eyes have seen your salvation, which you have prepared in the presence of all peoples, a light for revelation to the Gentiles and for glory to your people Israel."

When we as the church, contrary to the biblical witness, have separated Jesus Christ again and again from his people, we have at the same time set ourselves up against our Lord, who saw himself first of all sent to Israel (Matt 15:24) and who identified with his people until death.

Through Jesus Christ we again discover the Torah

6. *Torah is, according to Old Testament and Jewish understanding, the sum of the God of Israel's gracious expression of his will and his instructions for his chosen people.*

Jesus is to be presented as the fulfillment and the living interpretation of the Torah (the "law"), and not as a witness against the Torah.

As little as Jesus can be separated from his people, so little can he be presented as if he stood against the Old Testament, that is, the Torah. The Christian rejection of the Torah as "law" is by no means supported by the New Testament, not even by Paul. Paul shares with his fellow believers the conviction that God has revealed himself to the Jewish people in the Torah. In the Torah, God himself is present in his word. It is not the Torah Paul rejects—it is rather, according to Romans 7:12, "holy, just and good"—but an inappropriate use of it. Therefore, Paul speaks critically not of the Torah, but of "the works of Torah." It is this that he sets over against "faith." While the works of the law miss the Torah as gift of God's grace, faith gives the Torah validity. Thus love is the fulfillment of the "law" (Rom 13:8).

Jesus himself, in his adherence to the Torah in faithfulness to God (Matt 5:17ff.), witnesses to the possibility of genuine discipleship. Jesus himself, in his faithfulness to Torah, has for Christians, therefore, become the authoritative and vivid living interpretation of the Torah.

Just at this point, Christian theology has to learn a new understanding of Torah, which must not be limited to the correction of a wrong and non-biblical view of the Pharisees. The rethinking has to go much deeper, working toward a new discovery of Torah for us Christians, according to the living Torah interpretation, through Jesus Christ himself. In this way, we remain dependent, in our faith practice, on the Jewish root.

Our faith remains dependent on the Old Testament

7. *Without reference to the Old Testament and the Jewish faith tradition, central contents of our faith and liturgy remain sealed to us.*

In our dealings with the Bible we must therefore learn that the New Testament has to be understood in light of the Old (the Hebrew Bible). So also Jesus has to be understood in light of the Old Testament, God's revelation to Israel. The interpretation of the New Testament in terms of the horizon of Israel's faith history takes account of the irrefutable insight that Jesus was a Jew and that he stood with his people.

Traditional Israel-blindness or return to the Jewish root

8. *The Holocaust has shown in a frightful manner where Israel-oblivion has led us. The right relationship of Christians to the Jewish people is therefore of decisive significance for our faith and for our whole theology.*

Our relationship to Judaism is not a topic among or in addition to others. Rather, our faith and our theology stand or fall with the question of whether we have an eye for this central Israel-related dimension of our faith in all significant faith questions and church decisions, especially with regard to the current discussion of "justice, peace and responsibility for the creation." It is in this context that it will be decided whether we continue to practice our Israel-oblivion and Israel-blindness and pass it on to the next generation, or are ready for repentance. "Christian faith is Christian only as long as it carries the Jewish faith in its heart," wrote Ernst Lohmeyer in a 1933 letter to Martin Buber.

III

OPEN QUESTIONS AND PERSPECTIVES

1. The Trinity

When we begin our liturgy "in the name of the Father, the Son and the Holy Spirit," we profess the triune God. Christian acting and speaking about God has, from the very beginning, involved the God of Israel, the coming, suffering, and dying of Jesus, and the work of the Holy Spirit. To what extent do we thereby differentiate ourselves from the Jewish understanding of God? How can we talk appropriately of God and allow our thinking about God to be enriched by Jewish theology?

2. The State of Israel

The clarification of our relationship to the State of Israel we see as a task for the future, because we are aware of the special significance of this topic for our Jewish brothers and sisters. We will have to consider, in this connection, the following questions, among others:

- Is the State of Israel for us a purely political entity, or do we also have to say something about it on a theological basis?
- How can we cope with our special responsibility to help Jews and Palestinians to find a lasting solution of their conflict?

3. The concept of the law

The question of the meaning of law in Paul needs further discussion.

4. Eschatology

We have to reflect further on the coming/second coming of Christ and the incompleteness of redemption. This task is set before us with special urgency by the Jewish expectation of the Messiah.

IV

IMPLICATIONS FOR OUR TERRITORIAL CHURCH

God in his love turns to humanity and in so doing frees and renews us for service to and in this world. We share this faith with one another: both Jews and Christians are witnesses against despair about the fate of the world. They ought to and can work together in supporting what in Hebrew is called "Shalom." Therefore, we want to endeavor to witness also in common action to what unites us in faith. We realize that we stand at the very beginning of this conversation. We rejoice that in many areas of our church work is already being done to put into practical action the results of the Christian-Jewish dialogue. We encourage all to continue this work.

We ask
- our congregations to continue to concern themselves with the questions of the Christian-Jewish relationship; to assist in the preservation of the testimonies of the rich and long history of Palatine Judaism in our region; to seek dialogue with Jews who live among us; to oppose impulses and expressions of anti-semitism in our society and to stand in solidarity with those who are threatened
- all who preach and teach to continue to educate themselves in the questions of the Christian-Jewish dialogue
- that the findings of the Christian-Jewish dialogue be included in sermons and Bible study.

We instruct
- all who are engaged in education, continuing education, adult education, religious instruction and confirmation classes on all levels of the church's work
  - to provide appropriate information about Judaism and to emphasize the significance for us as Christians of the topics dealt with in the manual "Church and Israel"
  - to check whether the curricula consider the results of Christian-Jewish dialogue in an appropriate manner
  - to include examples of Jewish biblical interpretation in the homiletic training of theologians

- in confirmation classes, to include, in dealing with the main parts of the Christian faith (the Creed, the Ten Commandments, the Lord's Prayer, Lord's Supper), the connection between Judaism and Christianity and common characteristics (in this regard, Peter von der Osten-Sacken's *Catechism and Siddur* can be helpful);
- the Church and Judaism working group
  - to consider again the problematic nature of Israel Sunday (tenth Sunday after Trinity) and to submit proposals as to how our bond with Israel can be expressed in the liturgy
  - to consider, in cooperation with the Territorial Church Council, how the bond with Israel can be anchored in our territorial church's constitution, and to propose formulations to this end;
- the Territorial Church Council
  - to support the endeavors to arrange Christian-Jewish conversations and cooperation in the Frank Löbschen House in Landau and if need be, also to support it financially.

13

Statement of the Reformed Church in Hungary on Its Relations with the Jews

Adopted at the General Synod meeting in Budapest in June 1990. Reaffirmed in 2007.

"Always be prepared to give an answer to everyone who asks you to give the reason for the hope that you have" (1 Pet 3:15). This hope obliges us to clarify our relations with the Jewish people, and believe in the roots onto which we, as Christians, were grafted. Some aspects of the current situation necessitate our opinion: the suppressed emotions of recent times and the specters once thought disappeared are re-emerging, pushing nationalism and racial hatred into the forefront and requiring that the fight be taken up against the portrayal of the Jews as the enemy. Our society is polarizing to a substantial extent, and the worrying malaise often fuels antisemitism. We were shocked by the antisemitic desecrations of graves and other acts of vandalism, which we resolutely condemn. The greater freedom afforded during the process of democratization brought many emotions to the surface, whose significance should not be either exaggerated or belittled. We are aware that the increase in economic difficulties can lead to the search for scapegoats in certain circles. We want to make people aware of these phenomena and use our own resources to fight against them; by means of our theological stances and by applying all other means, we wish to achieve social and religious peace.

Seeking a relationship between the Jews and the Christians is not a new endeavor within our church; in fact, it has a long-standing tradition: the history of the Hungarian people and the fate of our church bring us particularly close to our Jewish brothers. The church which set off down the reformation path in the sixteenth century has often compared itself to the Jewish people, and its historical ordeals with the fate of the chosen people. The awareness of the close affinity between the Jews and the Hungarian people led to our church being the first, in 1881, to propose that the Jewish people be declared an equal denomination. Outstanding reformed theologians enriched the religious life of our church by means of such comparisons with the Jews, particularly Mór Ballagi during the last century. We recommend that this special tradition be studied.

We were even more saddened by the persecution of Jews that took place in the twentieth century, which peaked with the Holocaust during the Second World War: an attempt made to systematically eradicate the Jews. The Reformed Church in Hungary today still examines its own conscience before Almighty God, when it recalls this stigma of Europe that led to the horrifying consequence of six million murdered Jews (including 600,000 Hungarian Jews). In these critical times, our church proved to be weak in its faith and deeds, and was unable to prevent this genocide. Although the evangelical work of the Good Shepherd Mission and the Budapest Scottish Mission in saving the Jews shone some light in these dark times, our church nevertheless has to confess that like Cain it shirked the question of the Lord: "Where is your brother?" (Gen 4:9). This voice of repentance spoke in the resolution of the General Synod Council in 1946, which was followed by a statement from the National Reformed Church Free Council: "Under the weight of responsibility and in light of the negligence and crimes committed against the Jewish people…we ask, albeit belatedly, for forgiveness before God from the Jews in Hungary" (Bp., 1949. 73. 1). We have to emphasize these themes of responsibility and remorse again and again, whenever we are dealing with Jewish-Christian relations. We are grateful that there are now more opportunities to do so, particularly with the establishment of the Hungarian Ecumenical Council, of which our church was one of the main initiators.

In the course of dialogue between Jews and Christians, we want first to prevent waking the memories of bitter past experience in our Jewish brothers. We fundamentally believe that true dialogue and cooperation is only possible if both parties preserve and indeed strengthen their own identity. One cannot ask Christians not to believe in the faith underlying the New Testament: "Jesus Christ is Lord" (Phil 2:11), and not to consider him the Son of God, the Savior of the world. Nor can we ask of Jews to deny the principles of their faith. We can only hope together with Paul the Apostle for the circumcision of all believers' hearts (Rom 2:29), and that we do not become cursed and cut off from each other forever (cf. Rom 9:3). Our reformed church predecessors identified this duality and this is why they emphasized that the peoples of the Old and New Testament are both part of God's redeeming covenant, and this is why they should consider not only themselves but also the other the people of God, the Creator and the one Eternal Lord. The grace and covenant of God links us with our Jewish brothers.

To reinforce this faith within ourselves, we need to ward off the temptations of so-called Christian antisemitism, whose most dangerous manifestations are the references to allegedly antisemitic biblical passages. The texts can only be interpreted in their context, and any presumedly damning passage expressed in a given situation cannot be applied universally and eternally. Otherwise, this may give rise to a similar impasse as when the Jews were accused of murdering Jesus Christ. Although this absurd thesis has never been professed by any Christian church, its use to justify antisemitic interests rears its head again and again throughout history. To counter this we deem it necessary to profess our faith again and again, according to which the outcome of Jesus' crucifixion was that he achieved peace and "made the two one and destroyed the barrier, the dividing wall of hostility" (Eph 2:14).

In light of the above, we must solemnly emphasize four things:

1. Let there be peace in the Holy Land between the faiths accepting the Old Testament as Holy Scripture.
2. We express our joy that our country has established diplomatic relations with Israel, thus declaring the high regard in which we hold the national independence of the Jewish state.
3. With our Christian conscience we declare that we stand beside the Jewish people living in Hungary, and are ready to support them in their troubles and cooperate with them.
4. We resolutely condemn the desecration of graves and the latent or open manifestations of antisemitism.

Our faith in Jesus Christ obliges us to sort out our relations with the Jewish people in this spirit. And although when determining the principles of dialogue we primarily bear the current situation of our country and society in mind, we are nevertheless convinced that doing so will also exert an impact internationally and ecumenically. We hope that the work of the Ecumenical Council will be integrated into the activities of international organizations; we believe that our work can serve as an example to resolve other conflicts—discord between Israelis and Palestinians, Jews and Muslims. We are convinced that in this way our God will bless his people, Jews and Christians alike: "You have enlarged the nation and increased their joy; they rejoice before you as people rejoice at the harvest" (Isa 9:3).

14

Declaration on the Relationship of Lutheran Christians and Jews

Adopted by the European Lutheran Commission on the Church and the Jewish People (LEKKJ) at its meeting in Driebergen, The Netherlands, in May 1990. The Commission represents Lutheran church bodies and church-related organizations in Austria, Denmark, Finland, France, Germany, Great Britain, Hungary, Ireland, Italy, The Netherlands, Norway, Poland, and Sweden.

The European Lutheran Commission on the Church and the Jewish People—a cooperative undertaking of Evangelical Lutheran churches and organizations from all parts of Europe—at its meetings in Birmingham 1986, Budapest 1987, Vienna 1988, Ustron 1989, and Driebergen 1990, has sought to formulate what Lutheran Christians from the various countries of Europe could say in common, out of their current experience and knowledge, about their attitude toward the Jews and Judaism. In this process it became increasingly clearer to what extent Christians, even after the Holocaust, still have to change their preaching and teaching and their whole practice. The churches as a whole, their organizations, their parishes, and all their coworkers in preaching and teaching are facing great learning challenges.

We have come to realize anew the extent to which theological assertions—then and now—affect society and politics, and we have become aware of the great responsibility the church has in this regard. The reappraisal of history, especially that of theology, is imperative if we want to attain credibility for the church and to reform our common life in Europe.

As Evangelical Lutheran Christians, we address the following assertions to Christians within and outside the churches we represent. It is our hope that they will help to renew the relationship between Christians and Jews.

I. Fundamental Points

1. Since Jesus comes from the Jewish people and did not dissociate himself from them, and since the Old Testament was the Bible of Jesus and the early church, Christians, by professing Jesus Christ, have a unique relationship to Jews and their faith which differs essentially from their relationship to other religions.

2. This relationship between Christians and Jews is rooted in the witness to the One God and his covenant faithfulness, as handed down to us in the Scriptures of the Old Testament, which we have in common. In these Scriptures we read the same words, although we interpret and pass them on differently, Jews through the Talmud and Christians through the New Testament.

3. God has chosen Israel as His people. This assertion has not been revoked; rather, it has been renewed and confirmed in the New Testament's confession of Jesus as the Messiah already come. Israel is not replaced by the church.

4. We believe that God in his faithfulness has led his people Israel through history and has preserved them as a people through the Jewish tradition of faith. We consider their return to the country of their fathers to be a sign of God's faithfulness to his covenant.

5. The Christian community originated within the Jewish people and needs, therefore, a relationship to Judaism for defining its own identity. From its beginning, the church consisted of Jewish people as well as people of other nations. Jewish Christians can contribute to the church's new and lasting consciousness of its Jewish roots. They can also make a special contribution to the encounter between Jews and Christians.

II. The Shoah (Holocaust) and Its Implications

1. The Shoah (the Holocaust) and the whole history of enmity toward Jews present a far-reaching challenge to Christian teaching and practice. In interpreting the Holy Scriptures, anti-Jewish motifs and patterns of interpretation have to be identified and overcome in teaching and preaching. Although from a historical point of view Christianity and Judaism have developed in mutual conflict, anti-Judaism is not part of the doctrine of the church, nor can it be part of Christian teaching and practice.

2. Christian triumphalism, which has long weighed heavily on the relationship between Christians and Jews, is incompatible with a serious encounter and an honest witness. Therefore, rethinking is necessary within the churches with regard to theology and behavior. Triumphalism means a feeling of superiority that compares the ideals of one's own religious tradition with the historical reality of that of others. Christian triumphalism—an expression of a *theologia gloriae* that disregards the cross of Christ—falsely converts affirmations about Jesus into affirmations about the reality of the church. In this connection, Judaism at the time of Jesus is shown as a dark background against which the church then and now can shine the brighter. This approach has often been used to justify oppression and persecution.

3. In order to find a new relationship with Jews, we as a church must learn to repent.

4. Jews and Christians are in search of salvation and redemption and find different answers. According to the New Testament, salvation is revealed in Jesus Christ, who is proclaimed as the way of salvation for Jews and Gentiles. All the more, we Christians need to meet our Jewish partners with humility, love, and respect. We must listen to their expression of faith concerning reconciliation and redemption and must take it seriously. The last judgment on humanity will be passed by God and remains his mystery.

III. Forms of Encounter

1. For many centuries, the relationship of Jews with Christians has been heavily burdened by the fact that the Jews, as a mostly small minority, found themselves standing over against a large majority of Christians. Jews have had to suffer from this situation in various ways. They are therefore rightly very sensitive regarding any use of power by Christians. We reaffirm our conviction that particularly the encounter between Christians and Jews must be free of any kind of pressure or exploitation of the other's situation of need. Such attitudes are not justified even if they have conversion as their goal. Organizations that make use of such methods (proselytism) should not exist among Christians.

2. The readiness of Christians to listen to the witness of Jews, to learn from their experience of faith and life, and thus to become aware

of new aspects of the biblical tradition, is an indispensable precondition of our encounter. Jews and Christians have much to say to each other in this encounter and can together rediscover God's reality.

3. Such encounters, however, also challenge our own Christian witness. It must not only consist of words, but must prove itself in our practical dealings with each other. Christians must be aware of the fact that their history of anti-Judaism frequently witnesses against their words. The encounter also includes the possibility for both partners to be persuaded by the witness of the other.

4. Any encounter between Christians and Jews must be based on the understanding that God himself is the one who sends out—who is the missionary. This insight into the *missio dei* helps us understand our own possibilities and tasks. God empowers us to mutually witness to our faith, trusting in the free working of the Holy Spirit. For it is God alone who decides what effect our witness will have; and it is his decision with regard to the eternal salvation of all mankind. He frees us from the pressure of having to accomplish everything ourselves. This insight places Christians under the obligation to give witness and render service with due respect for the convictions and the faith of their Jewish partners.

5. Churches and organizations that are open to encounter in such a way are doing a service to the renewal of the relationship between Christians and Jews.

IV. Consequences

1. We hope that, on the basis of these assertions, a clarification and intensification of the encounter between Lutherans and Jews can be brought about. We declare our readiness to take an active part in promoting this aim within the possibilities of our Commission.

In this context it is indispensable:

- to think through in historical-critical terms the origin of tensions between Christians and Jews, as already seen in the Holy Scriptures
- to refrain from comparing ideals on the one side with everyday reality on the other
- to find a common ground of language. The encounter between Jews and Christians is frequently made more difficult

by the fact that the same biblical concepts have developed differently. In order to avoid misunderstandings, it is necessary to use a descriptive, instrumental language in order to clarify the meaning of such concepts.

• to take into account the historical and other context when interpreting contemporary events

2. We strongly urge that, within the Lutheran Churches, the anti-Jewish attacks in Luther's later works and their disastrous consequences be worked on as was done in the Stockholm statement of 1983.[1] We also urge that fundamental patterns of Lutheran theology and teaching such as "law and gospel," "faith and works," "promise and fulfillment," and the "two kingdoms/realms" be reconsidered in view of their effects on the relationship between Christians and Jews. Joint theological work with Jews especially in the field of biblical interpretation can be important in this respect.

3. We encourage that Christians be taught about Judaism in order to help them gain a positive, undistorted attitude toward contemporary Judaism and thus to overcome secular antisemitism as well as the anti-Judaism which has been handed down to us within the churches.

4. We ask that the Jewish people, its salvation, and its peace be included in the prayers of intercession. We feel solidarity with all who see in the State of Israel their home, their refuge, and their hope.

Note

1. See Jean Halperin/Arne Sovik (eds.), *Luther, Lutheranism and the Jews.* A record of the Second Consultation between Representatives of the International Jewish Committee for Interreligious Consultations and the Lutheran World Federation, held in Stockholm, Sweden, July 1983. LWF-Studies, Geneva, 1984. [*Bridges*, Vol. 1, Document 63.]

15

Message on the Fiftieth Anniversary of the End of the Second World War and the Fiftieth Anniversary of the Liberation of the Concentration Camp at Auschwitz

Issued in May 1995 by the Synod of the Evangelical Reformed Church in Poland.

The recent Synod of the Evangelical Reformed Church in Poland met only a few days after the celebration of the fiftieth anniversary of the end of the Second World War in Europe. This time of celebration has provoked us as Christians and as Poles to a deeper reflection about the past.

It is the duty of the church, for the sake of the next generation, to recall and to give a faithful and truthful witness to the terrible events of that time. The present and the future of the world, of our continent, and of our homeland depend in great measure on how people today view and evaluate this history, and what conclusions they draw from it for today and tomorrow.

It is also the duty of the church to be on the alert for symptoms and systems in today's world like those that lay at the root of the evil of both totalitarianisms—the brown and the red. This evil led to the enslavement of the human spirit and soul and to the cruel annihilation of many millions of human beings, wreaking disaster upon the whole Jewish people, as well as many Gypsies, in the name of a demonic racist, nationalistic, and socialist ideology.

Christians who base their lives on the gospel, as well as other people of good will who stand ready to protect the dignity and life of human beings as the highest value, must act together to warn of such evil when it lies in wait, to prevent it, and to confront it wherever it arises.

If we remain passive or indifferent at the first signs of such evil, we thereby open the way for usurpers motivated by a burning lust for power and insane ideas of "leadership" to occupy, sooner or later, the place that belongs solely to the living God.

We Poles, as a nation and as individuals, have paid a very high price for opposition to two totalitarianisms. In honoring today the soldiers who fought on all fronts of the Second World War, as well as the civilian victims of the war, we reflect—not without bitterness—on how we stood alone in September 1939 and in August 1944, and on the way the fate of our country was determined in the post-war decades. We think with heartfelt sorrow of the martyrdom of fellow Poles who in the aftermath of the war lost their lives, often at the hands of their fellow citizens, or whose lives were turned into a living hell.

We remember with deepest sorrow the slaughtered Jewish people who met their fate on the soil of our homeland. Auschwitz has become the symbol of this disaster.

The tragedy of the Jewish people affects us in a twofold way: as Poles, and as Christians. During the war many Poles, at great risk to their own lives, sheltered Jews from the Germans and rescued them. However, there were also some—and not as few as is often maintained—who handed over Jews to certain death. And the greater part of the population remained indifferent to the fate of the Jews. In remembering this today, we acknowledge that indifference as guilt and sin. Antisemitism was a common phenomenon in Europe before the Holocaust. For centuries, the Christian churches in Europe had turned away from Jews. They were anti-Jewish in their theology and they burdened every Jew with blame for the death of Christ. Among the exceptions to this was the thinking and the attitude of John Calvin, the great reformer of the church in the sixteenth century. He wrote, among other things:

> How can the Jews be separated from Christ? For a covenant was made with them whose sole foundation is Christ.

> How can they be cast out from the unmerited salvation of the redemption? For the Jews knew justification by faith from their own experience.

The stereotype "Jew 'God-murderer'" is something that is still in the consciousness of many Christians, even though in Christian Europe since the Holocaust the churches' official teachings about their relation to the Jewish people have been radically changed. Despite this, anti-semitism still exists, even though the Holocaust showed that *every* form of antisemitism is *criminal*. Christians must confess this sin, express repentance for all antisemitic crimes, and unceasingly beseech our sisters and brothers of the chosen people—Israel—for forgiveness.

16

Origin and Goal of
the Christian Journey with Judaism

Adopted by the Council of the Federation of Swiss Protestant Churches at its meeting in Bern, Switzerland, in June 1997.

The Council of the Federation of Swiss Protestant Churches (F.E.P.S.) recommends that its member churches and their parishes organize, in September 1997, a Day of Encounter and Discovery to emphasize and illuminate the unique and enduring relation between the church and the Jewish people. The reflections that follow will foster a better understanding of the origin and goal of the Christian journey with Judaism. The theme chosen this year is "Reconciliation." The F.E.P.S. Council thanks the Dialogue Commission jointly mandated by the Federation of Jewish Communities of Switzerland and the F.E.P.S. for the preparation of this document.

1. Introduction

The churches and Christian communities today must—in theology, in proclamation, and in action—regain awareness of their original and inalienable relation with the Jewish people. The church and Israel have in common the faith that the world is the creation of God in the expectation of its fulfillment. The path of the Jews, the first chosen people, is different from that of Christians. The latter have been called, as the people chosen in Jesus Christ, to enter into the covenant with Israel. All those who raise their eyes to the God who has called them go forward together on their respective paths. For centuries the Christian church has forgotten Israel and anti-Judaic enmity has raged, culminating in the incomprehensible atrocity of the Shoah. It was not until after 1945 that a process of recognition of faults, a will to drastic change, and a search for reconciliation have become widespread in our country and elsewhere. This movement of change needs a constant renewal, because it never proceeds automatically.

With regard to the responsibilities that the Protestant churches have today in a multicultural society, the reconciliation between the church and the Jewish people is of the greatest importance. In order to be credible in their commitment to cultural and social peace, the churches must foster reconciliation with their first partner. In order to be able to preach reconciliation, the movement of the faithful to God must have as its corollary the movement toward the victims of a Christian anti-Judaic theology. Obviously the past cannot be wiped out, but its evil effects can be reduced. Theological thought must be renewed. Therefore the Council of the F.E.P.S. invites its member churches and their congregations to start on the pathway of learning to meet "under the arch of the one covenant."

2. "For after I had turned away I repented" [Jer. 31:19]

According to Jewish and Christian faith, God has created the world for justice and peace. The Bible and the Jewish tradition regard humanity as God's partner in this project. In spite of our imperfections, we can assume this task because, since the beginning, God has given us a precious gift: the faculty of retracing our steps, of doing *teshuvah*, that is, of recognizing our wrong choices and our faults and committing ourselves, from that moment on, toward a new direction. This gift allows humanity to remain on the path of perfection. To make peace, to engage in acts of reconciliation, is the prerequisite for true reconciliation not only among humans but also between God and humans. Thus a Talmudic source states: "Sins against God are atoned for on the Day of Atonement. Sins against one's neighbor can be atoned for on the Day of Atonement only if one has made peace with one's neighbor."

Such inner change is a dynamic event that goes beyond the recognition of particular faults and that does not end as long as human beings carry responsibility toward their fellow humans and toward all creation. This Jewish spirituality retains all its value in today's world. Among the steps of such a change that open new perspectives on relations with other people and with God, one finds, according to Psalm

34:15, the decision to abandon evil, the emotional and intellectual awareness of the roots of evil, and the search for new relationships that foster justice and peace. The healing of wounds received as well as inflicted is not possible unless the first step of one toward the other is followed by many joint steps, in a process of shared suffering and of growing reconciliation, looking toward a new future. In order to receive God's healing, we await together the kingdom of God while we work like those who "serve him with one accord" (Zeph 3:9).

3. God's precious gift: peace and reconciliation

Reconciliation is at the beginning and reconciliation is at the end. According to the Christian view, God created the world and God reconciled all things with himself through Jesus Christ (Col 1:19–20). God made humanity in God's own image in hope (Ps 8), with the mandate of communicating God's work of reconciliation to all humankind (2 Cor 5:18).

Our broken and violated world, our divided churches, and the impaired relations between Christians and their Jewish counterparts give evidence of the sorrow that is always connected with the Christian calling. Too often, the churches have poorly understood the reconciliation accomplished in Christ; they have not realized that life in Christ is to be expressed in inner change, repentance, and forgiveness. It is not a substitute for the latter, but on the contrary, makes them possible. Too often Christians have managed to forget that the path of changes and repentance, with, at the end, a total and complete reconciliation, is generally very long.

The freedom granted to human beings makes them responsible for determining their own path. Only those who are reconciled with their neighbors and who have arrived at peace will dare to present themselves before God to say, "Forgive us our trespasses" (Matt 5:23–24, Luke 11:4).

The conviction that God has reconciled all creation with himself through Jesus Christ not only engages Christians in repentance and inner change but also allows them to pursue God's work of reconciliation. Such a change becomes a new beginning for all creation and a meeting on the path of justice and peace. In order for Jews and Christians to pursue this path together, it must be acknowledged that the Jewish people remain the witness to God's irrevocable covenant (Rom 9–11).

17

Declaration on Ecumenical and Interreligious Dialogue (excerpt)

Sections 51–56 of the above-titled document, as adopted by the Synod of the Waldensian Protestant Church in Italy, meeting in Torre Pellice, Italy, in August 1998.

Relations to Judaism

51. **The burden of the past.** The decades following the Second World War saw the beginning and development throughout the Christian world of a process of reconsideration of the relations between the churches and Judaism.

Reflection on the Shoah[1] led, first of all, to the recognition and confession of the co-responsibility that Christians bore, by their direct participation or their acquiescence, in the persecution and the extermination of the Jews carried out by the Nazis—even if there were Christians who sought dialogue and acted in support of persecuted Jews. Later on, awareness grew of the role that anti-Jewish bias has had throughout the centuries, and up to the Shoah, in the theology, preaching, catechesis, and practice of the Christian churches. Clearly, the guilt of the churches during the Shoah is connected to the centuries-old "teaching of contempt"; in the latter lies one of the principal sources of modern antisemitism. Reflection on the Shoah has thus started a process of denouncing and overcoming anti-Jewish tendencies not only in practice but also in theology and Christian teaching.

52. Also realized anew was a dimension that for centuries had been "lost," or rather denied: the deep link that unites Christianity and Judaism on more than the historical level. A major reconsideration of issues including the relationship between the two parts of the Christian canon, the Jewishness of Jesus, and the Pauline argument in Romans 9–11 has led to a rethinking of the relation between the church and

Judaism, as well as to a reaffirmation of the high value placed on the
Old Testament that has been characteristic of Reformed Protestantism.

For centuries, Christianity defined and labeled Judaism from the
standpoint of polemical opposition. Judaism was a poorly known reality,
indeed for the most part an unknown one. Today the churches realize the
need to understand Israel also in terms of the Jews' own self-understanding (for example, of God, people, land) in all its rich complexity. This can
already be seen in the various meanings that the term "Israel" can have:
the chosen people in the theological sense; the Jewish state in a political
sense; the people that expresses itself religiously in the various currents
and communities found today in Israel and in the diaspora; and so forth.
Stereotypical definitions and caricatures based on a schematic and ideological interpretation of the critical or polemical pages of the New
Testament have gradually been replaced by an interest in the study of
Judaism and in dialogue with Jews and their tradition.

An awareness has grown that in the light of the biblical witness, the
relation between the church and Israel is on a different plane than the
church's relation to other religions.

53. **Toward a new Christian understanding of Israel.** The path
established by the successive phases of reflection on the Shoah is only
at its beginnings. It appears to be a true and real change of direction,
destined to have a profound effect on praxis and on theology. If the
positions from which it is necessary to keep a decided distance are clear
enough, the formulations with which the relation between the church
and Israel is to be expressed in a new way have only been sketched out.

In their reflections, the individual churches do not proceed in isolation; rather, each can make use of the contributions of the others. We
think particularly of the numerous documents of sister churches[2] and
of those related to the World Council of Churches.[3]

54. In the path traversed so far by the ecumenical world, in particular the Protestant world, the following affirmations can be said to
express the contemporary Protestant point of view on the relations
between the church and Israel, as it appears in the above-mentioned
documents.

> (a) The God of Jesus is the God of Israel, from Abraham to
> today. Jews and Christians speak of the same one God. To set
> "the God of Israel" (or of the Old Testament, or of "judg-
> ment") in opposition to "the God of Jesus" (or of the New
> Testament, or of "compassion") has no biblical foundation.

(b) Jews find in the rabbinical tradition (in particular the Talmud) and Christians in the New Testament, respectively, the roots of their faith as well as their own approach to the Scriptures of Israel, the Old Testament in the Christian canon. The comparison of readings from different periods, provided they are not put in polemical opposition, is spiritually fertile because it can deepen the understanding of our common Scriptures.

(c) The idea that the election of the church has annulled the election of Israel must be rejected. The church, chosen by Jesus Christ, has been incorporated into the covenant of God with his people. Therefore, it must not be said that the church has replaced Israel as the people of God.

(d) Over against the point of view that Israel has been rejected by God is the acknowledgment that Israel continues to live with the covenant (promise and calling) established by God with the patriarchs and never revoked. The continuing existence of the people of Israel appears in this perspective as a sign of God's faithfulness to his promises.

(e) The church, confessing Jesus Christ as the Messiah of Israel and Savior of the world, recognizes in him the one who unites the peoples of the world with the people of God. Faith in Jesus as the Savior of the peoples, biblically understood, does not divide us from Israel and is not opposed to it, because no hostility against the Jewish people can be associated with the name of Jesus.

(f) Both the church and the people of Israel are called, each according to its proper vocation, to believe in one God, to serve him, and to give witness to him in the world. By accepting their respective vocations and having overcome, on the Christian side, the traditional polemical—if not denigrating—attitude, the church and Israel can discover the possibility of dialogue, common prayer, and fraternal comparison. In the Protestant ecumenical world, there is a discussion of how to conceive of the witness vis-à-vis Israel, whether as dialogue in solidarity or as proclamation. In any case, all are agreed that the relation between the church and Israel is a unique reality, different from the relation with religions and cultures in general.

(g) The church recognizes that it shares with Israel the expectation of the Kingdom of God and the hope that grounds and shapes, for both Christians and Jews, their commitment to justice and peace.

55. **Open questions.** The process of rethinking these matters and the dialogue must be developed in two directions. On the one hand, the churches have the task of spreading within their membership, and establishing at all levels (theology, catechesis, and preaching) the gains that are the fruit of a dialogue that is now several decades old. The critique of the anti-Jewishness of the past and the quest for a new relation with Israel cannot remain limited to a small elite, but must be a part of the common Christian consciousness. On the other hand, many theological questions must still be explored more deeply. It is not enough to denounce the views that today are no longer acceptable; one must reach convincing positive formulations.

By way of example, the following points can be mentioned, on which different positions are taken also within the Protestant world:

(a) What is the relation between the "covenant not revoked" with Israel and the covenant in Christ?

(b) What is the value, the significance, and the role of "law" for Jews and Christians?

(c) What is today a "Christian" reading of those Scriptures that the church and Israel have in common? How can one give proper attention to the specificity of the Old Testament and at the same time confess that the work of Christ is "according to the Scriptures"?

(d) What is the significance of the biblical promises to Israel, in particular the promise of the land, and what is its relation to the return of the Jews to their land and the establishment of the State of Israel?

(e) What is the relation between the confession of the Trinitarian faith in one God, Father, Son, and Holy Spirit, and Jewish monotheism?

(f) What is the relation between the Jewish and Christian concepts of the human condition and of salvation? Faith and works, human freedom and God's initiative, grace and merit, sin and free will are some of the terms in which the comparison between the respective positions has traditionally been expressed.

(g) How can one deal with Christology in dialogue with Israel without having to attenuate the confession of our faith in Jesus as savior of all?

56. In the specific Italian situation, we need to revisit the parallel histories of the Jewish and Protestant minorities, characterized by very similar sensibilities, by episodes of dialogue, solidarity, and a common commitment to freedom, especially religious freedom. In this past there are significant roots for the dialogue today.

Notes

1. We use, to designate the extermination of six million Jews carried out by the Nazis, the Jewish term "Shoah" (catastrophe), which is preferable to the widespread term "Holocaust." The latter expresses the idea of a total annihilation (which was exactly the Nazi intent), and runs the risk of introducing a sacrificial motif [since "holocaust" means "burnt offering"], which is very misleading.

2. For example, those of the Reformed Church of the Netherlands of 1970 on "Israel: People, Land, and State," or of the Protestant Church of the Rhineland of 1980, or of the 119th General Assembly of the Presbyterian Church (U.S.A.) of 1987.

3. For example, "The Church and the Jewish People," issued by the Faith and Order Commission of the World Council of Churches in 1967, or "Ecumenical Considerations on Christian-Jewish Dialogue," issued by the WCC Executive Committee in 1982.

18

Time to Turn: The Protestant Churches in Austria and the Jews

Adopted by the General Synod of the Protestant Church of the Augsburg and Helvetic Confessions in Austria, meeting in Vienna in November 1998.

I

November 9th of this year will see the sixtieth anniversary of the 1938 pogrom against Jews. This event prompts us Protestant Christians and churches in Austria to again grapple with this century's dreadful history of the deliberate attempt to annihilate Europe's Jews. The part played by Christians and churches and their shared responsibility for the suffering and misery of Jews can no longer be denied. The word of the General Synod of 1965 and the "Declaration of Principle" of the Evangelical Church of the Helvetic Confession of 1996 are to be remembered.

II

We realize with shame that our churches showed themselves to be indifferent to the fate of the Jews and countless other victims of persecution. This is all the more incomprehensible because Protestant Christians in their own history, especially during the Counter-Reformation, were themselves discriminated against and persecuted. The churches did not protest against visible injustice; they were silent and looked away. They did not "throw themselves into the spokes of the wheel" (Bonhoeffer).

Therefore, not only individual Christians but also our churches share in the guilt of the Holocaust/Shoah.

We remember with grief all victims of persecution who were divested of their civil rights and their human dignity, abandoned to an unrelenting pursuit and murdered in concentration camps.

III

The General Synod asks the Jewish congregations and the Jews in Austria to receive the following assurances:

- The Protestant churches know themselves obliged to always keep alive the memory of the Jewish people's history of suffering and the Shoah.
- The Protestant churches know themselves obliged to check the teaching, preaching, instruction, liturgy, and practice of the church for any antisemitism. and to also, through their media, stand up against prejudice.
- The Protestant churches know themselves obliged to fight against every form of social and personal antisemitism.
- The Protestant churches want, in their relations to Jews and Jewish congregations, to walk a common way into a new future.

Therefore, we make an effort to reconsider and shape the relationship of Protestant Christians and Jews accordingly.

IV

The development of antisemitism into the Shoah represents for us as Protestant churches and Protestant Christians a challenge that reaches down into the roots of our faith. The God of Christians is no other than the God of Israel who called Abraham to faith and chose the enslaved Israelites to be his people. We affirm the permanent election of Israel as God's people. "God has not terminated this covenant" (Martin Buber). It exists to the end of time.

We read God's word in John's Gospel: "Salvation is from the Jews" (John 4:22). God himself is the salvation which he gave to his people and which he extends to everyone in the Jew Jesus, whom we confess as the Christ. God "desires everyone to be saved and to come to the knowledge of the truth" (1 Tim 2:4).

The disputes in the New Testament about the meaning of Jesus and the gospel must not be misused in anti-Jewish ways. The fact that these were arguments within the Jewish community was suppressed by the gentile Christian community. The church felt itself chosen alone to be the people of God and claimed that Israel had been rejected. Since then anti-Jewish excesses have run all the way through the entire history of the church.

In this regard we as Protestant Christians are burdened by the late writings of Luther and their demand for expulsion and persecution of the Jews. We reject the contents of these writings.

The biological and political racism of the nineteenth and twentieth centuries was able to make use of Christian anti-Judaism for its religious-ideological confirmation. Against this there was hardly any resistance in our churches. Rather, Protestant Christians and pastors also involved themselves in antisemitic propaganda. If the churches looked after persecuted Jews, it looked mainly after those who were baptized.

This, our burdened past, demands an about-turn which includes the church's interpretation of the Holy Scriptures, its theology, teaching, and practice.

V

When we Christians read the Bible of both testaments as a unified whole, we have to listen carefully to the Jewish interpretation of the Hebrew Bible—of our Old Testament—knowing well that for Jews the New Testament is not Holy Scripture.

Differences in the understanding of Scripture can be tolerated in mutual respect. "The Biblical symbols of hope are an impulse for the common effort for the formation of a world of justice and peace" (Ecumenical Assembly, Erfurt, 1996).

It is to be considered that the New Testament—which proclaims Jesus Christ as the redeemer of the world—was written mainly by Jews.

Our Lord Jesus Christ was, according to origin, education, and his faith in God, a Jew and has to be understood as a Jew.

According to the resolution of the Ecumenical Assembly in Erfurt, 1996, the Christian proclamation must learn "to recognize Judaism as a living and diverse entity that existed already before Christianity and has existed simultaneously with it." That forbids any triumphalist arrogance.

The "Declaration on the Relationship of Lutheran Christians and Jews" of 1990 [Document 14 above] calls for the realization that God himself sends his people. This *missio dei* teaches one to understand one's own possibilities and tasks. "God empowers us to mutually witness to our faith, trusting in the free working of the Holy Spirit. For it is God alone who decides what effect our witness will have; and it is his decision with regard to the eternal salvation of all mankind. He frees one from the pressure of having to do everything ourselves. This insight places Christians under the obligation to give witness and render service with due respect for the convictions and the faith of their Jewish dialogue partners."

Because the covenant of God with his people Israel exists in nothing but grace to the end of time, mission among Jews is theologically not justifiable and must be rejected as a church program.

The dialogue of Christians with Judaism, in which they are rooted, is to be fundamentally distinguished from a dialogue of Christians with other religions.

VI

Fifty years ago the State of Israel was founded. We wish it justice and peace. We hope and pray that this state finds a secure peace with its neighbors—in particular with the Palestinian people—in mutual respect of the right of residence, so that Jews, Christians, and Muslims can live together peacefully.

We endorse the recommendation of the Ecumenical Council of Churches in Austria to observe the 17th of January, the day before the beginning of the World Week of Prayer for Christian Unity, as a day of solidarity with Judaism and to include the Jewish people in the prayers of intercession.

19

Christians and Jews: A Manifesto Fifty Years after the Weissensee Declaration

A declaration by Ninth Synod of the Protestant Church in Germany (Evangelische Kirche in Deutschland), meeting in Braunschweig, Germany, in November 2000.

Fifty years ago, at its second session in Berlin-Weissensee, the Synod of the Protestant Church in Germany declared:

> *We believe in the Lord and Savior, whose human origin was as a member of the people of Israel.*

> *We confess our belief in the church as one body, composed of Jewish and Gentile Christians, whose peace is Jesus Christ.*

> *We believe that God's promise to his people Israel has remained in force also after the crucifixion of Christ.*[1]

This was the first time that a Protestant synod contradicted the view, which is widespread in the Protestant Church, that the people of Israel were rejected by God and replaced by the church as the true Israel. Over against this it set its conviction that God's promise to the chosen people has remained in force.

At the same time the synod declared:

> *We state clearly that through omission and silence, we too are guilty before the Merciful God of the outrage perpetrated against the Jews by members of our people.*

The Synod thereby admitted the church's complicity in the persecution and murder of European Jewry. At the same time it added a warning "against any notion of an equivalency between what has befallen us Germans as God's judgment and what we have done to the Jews."

We reject all attempts to close the book on our German history before 1945.

On the basis of the studies on "Christians and Jews" issued by the Council of the Evangelical Church in Germany (I, 1975; II, 1991; III, 2000) as well as the synodical declarations of many member churches and church-related associations concerning a new approach in the church's relationship to Israel, we extend the declaration of 1950:

It is not only through "omission and silence" that the church has become guilty. It is rather through the disastrous tradition of estrangement from the Jews and enmity toward them that it has been implicated in the systematic destruction of European Jewry. It is this theological tradition that since 1945 has burdened and delayed all endeavors toward a new approach in the church's relations to the Jewish people.

Today we can state explicitly:

1. We believe that God the Creator and Lord of the universe, in Jesus Christ, "our Father," has chosen Israel as his people. He has bound himself to Israel forever and remains faithful to it in the continuity from biblical Israel to the Jewish people. Jews are witnesses to us of God's faithfulness.

2. We confess our belief in Israel's Holy Scripture, the Bible of Jesus and primitive Christianity and our Old Testament. The New Testament witness to Christ is the center and source of our Christian faith. The two testaments form a unity of reciprocal interpretation. They are the foundation and guideline for a new approach in our relations to the Jewish people. We are grateful that Jews through their interpretation help us to a deeper understanding of the Bible.

3. We believe in Jesus Christ, Son of God and member of his people. In him, Israel's God became human and reconciled the world to himself.

4. We give witness to our participation in God's history with his people. Our election in Christ is election through the same God who chose his people Israel.

5. The New Testament testifies to the one church of Jewish and Gentile Christians. We see our Christian sisters and brothers of Jewish descent as witnesses to our indissoluble bond with God's permanently chosen people Israel.

6. Despite all differences, we acknowledge that we have in common:
- belief in the One God—for us Christians, in the unity of Father, Son, and Holy Spirit
- the hearing and following of God's commandments—for us Christians, in discipleship to Jesus
- the expectation of the last judgment and the hope for a new heaven and a new earth—for us Christians, associated with the second coming of Christ.

Dialogue about faith includes respect for the identity of the other. The endeavors toward a brotherly and sisterly relationship between Christians and Jews are a basic challenge and a permanent task for the church and for theology.

Note

1. See *Bridges*, Vol. 1, Document 5. The above citations from the 1950 document are freshly translated from the original text.—Ed.

20

Statement on Antisemitism and Anti-Zionism

Adopted by the European Lutheran Commission on the Church and the Jewish People (LEKKJ) at its meeting in Kluj/Klausenberg, Romania, in May 2004.

We view with deep concern various expressions of animosity toward Jews in our countries. Jewish dialogue partners describe an increase in antisemitism, which has taken many forms: graffiti on synagogues and Jewish cemeteries, verbal abuse, telephone threats, and even physical violence.

Reports such as the study of the European Union Monitoring Centre on Racism and Xenophopia ("Manifestations of Antisemitism in the EU 2002–2003") confirm this increase of antisemitism and call for measures to combat it: "Europe's political leaders must make it very clear that they do not accept antisemitism and racism by taking a strong leadership position on the issue" (EUMC media release, 3-31-04).

We expect an equally strong attitude from church leaders and from all church members, since from a theological point of view, "antisemitism is sin against God and humanity" (First Assembly of the World Council of Churches, Amsterdam, 1948, "The Christian Approach to the Jews" [*Bridges*, Vol. 1, Document 4]). Likewise the Charta Oecumenica "Guidelines for the Growing Cooperation among the Churches in Europe" (Conference of European Churches and Council of European Bishops Conferences) [cf. Document 72 below] states: "We commit ourselves to oppose all forms of antisemitism and anti-Judaism in the church and in society; to seek and intensify dialogue with our Jewish sisters and brothers at all levels."

As Lutherans we bear a special responsibility in light of anti-Jewish elements in the Lutheran tradition. This has been an issue at LEKKJ Conferences for years, indeed decades. For example, the

LEKKJ Declaration of Driebergen, The Netherlands (1990) [Document 14 above] states: "We strongly urge that, within the Lutheran Churches, the anti-Jewish attacks in Luther's later words and their disastrous consequences be worked on as has been done in the Stockholm statement of 1983. We also urge that the fundamental patterns of Lutheran theology and teaching…be reconsidered in view of their effects on the relationship between Christians and Jews." We regret that these commitments are not yet shared by all church members. This challenge is still an acute problem.

Today we see antisemitism showing itself in the form of anti-Zionism. As churches we have close and lasting ties with the Jewish people and with the State of Israel. Our faith also gives us an inherent relationship with Palestinian Christians. Despite efforts to achieve a balanced position, we often see an unbalance favoring the Palestinian point of view within our churches.

In the public debate about these issues, we often note antisemitic allusions, as expressed, for example, in the intolerable equation of the Israeli government's present policies with the National Socialist policy of annihilation. To criticize the policies of the State of Israel is not per se antisemitic. But it becomes so when the very existence of the State of Israel is called into question. In public discussions, anti-Jewish clichés such as "retribution" and "an eye for an eye, a tooth for a tooth" occur repeatedly. We must state emphatically that political disagreements do not justify attacks on Jews. We further assert: The State of Israel has the right and the obligation to protect itself and its citizens from terror.

21

Statement on the Sixtieth Anniversary of the End of the Second World War

Issued jointly in May 2005 by the Community of Seventh Day Adventists in Germany and the Seventh Day Adventist Church in Austria.

Foreword

We are presently observing the sixtieth anniversary of the end of the Second World War. Our fathers and mothers experienced and suffered under what happened at that time. Their experiences and memories have become part of our history. Their texts and documents do not only lie in our archives; they are part of our awareness and our memory.

Conscious of our responsibility for our thoughts and actions here and now as well as with a view to the past and the future, we feel called to address the events of that time with openness and humility.

I. We deeply lament...

...that this fearsome war, which brought immeasurable suffering to humanity, was initiated by our countries—and that also Seventh-Day Adventists were participants.

...that the character of the National Socialist dictatorship was not recognized clearly and in a timely fashion and that the ungodly nature of the Nazi ideology was not understood.

...that expressions can be found in some of our own publications or in ones circulated by us that gave homage to Adolf Hitler and gave expression to the racist ideology of antisemitism in a way that is incomprehensible today.

...that our peoples were complicit in a racial mania that in just a few years cost six million Jews and other minorities in the whole of Europe their freedom and their lives—and that also many Seventh-Day Adventists ignored the needs and the suffering of their Jewish fellow citizens.

...that fellow citizens of Jewish heritage were ostracized and excluded, left to their own devices, and handed over to imprisonment, expulsion, or death.

II. We sincerely confess...

...that we, through our failure, have become guilty toward the Jewish people and toward all who were persecuted and affected by war and also toward Adventists in other countries. We therefore humbly ask God and the surviving victims for forgiveness.

...that we as Seventh-Day Adventists, despite our knowledge of Scripture and the prophetic word, did not act more courageously and consistently in that fateful time, and thus failed in imitation of our Lord. We did not follow bravely and resolutely enough those in our ranks who courageously resisted the Nazi dictatorship and neither bent to its demands nor made common cause with it.

... that neither the time that has elapsed nor the great desperation and distress of those days can justify or make good the evil that was done; God alone, in his grace, can grant forgiveness for failure and sin.

III. We want to strongly advocate...

...that never again shall a war against other peoples originate in Germany or Austria, and that no one be ostracized or disadvantaged because of race, religion, nationality, or gender.

...that the past not be forgotten, but stand before our eyes today as a lasting memorial.

...that the obedience we owe to civil authority never lead to surrender of our biblical convictions and values.

...that we stand ready to "discern the spirits" and to confess our faith courageously and live it out consistently, should we in our own time come into the hour of temptation.

Conclusion

We do not wish, in making this statement, to put ourselves forward as superior to those who lived and believed at that time. It is not our role to judge our fathers and mothers—God alone is the Judge. Neither is it our role to acquit others of their sins—God alone acquits.

We do wish, however, to advocate emphatically in our own time for lawfulness and justice for all human beings. We lay our sincere prayers for success in such efforts before God, who alone, out of his grace, can bestow the power both "to will and to work."

22

An Appeal against Antisemitism and Racism

Adopted by the European Lutheran Commission on the Church and the Jewish People (LEKKJ) at its meeting in Budapest, Hungary, in July 2010.

We note with great concern a new wave of antisemitism spreading across Europe. We are alarmed by the following that the extreme right Jobbik party has gained here in Hungary, the site of our meeting this year. We are aware of the anxiety and uncertainty in Hungarian society.

We appeal to the leaders of our churches and to all Christians to take a clear position against antisemitism and racism. We remember the World Council of Churches' declaration in 1948 that "antisemitism is sin against God and man."

We call also for a stand on behalf of all persons who are threatened and persecuted. In Middle and Eastern Europe this includes, above all, Jews and Gypsies. We ask all social and political authorities, and particularly the churches, to collaborate in struggling against racism and antisemitism. The following aspects seem to us of particular importance:

- Carrying out educational work in churches, schools, and communities
- Demanding and exemplifying a culture of respect and trust
- Building networks to connect political and church initiatives
- Documenting antisemitic incidents and crimes

In addition to church leaders, political parties, and the criminal justice system, every individual has a responsibility in this regard. Lutheran Christians in Hungary have provided an outstanding example of this in an initiative with the motto *cinkos, aki nema* ("One who remains silent becomes a collaborator," from the poet Mihály Babits) that offers programs aimed at supporting people in threatening situations and providing options for them.

We join the Protestant Churches in Austria (Evangelische Kirchen in Austria) in urging: "Don't look away when lawless actions occur in your community; resist them. Become active whenever people become victims of prejudice and intolerance."

23

Lutherans and the Jews

A statement by the Council of Presidents of the Lutheran Church of Australia adopted in September 1996.

This statement by the Council of Presidents of the Lutheran Church of Australia on Lutherans and Jews is in keeping with similar approaches in other Lutheran churches overseas, recognizing the need to address the prejudices inherited from the past. The statement is presented by the Presidents in their pastoral concern for the well-being of the church including its attitudes toward others.

Judaism, like Christianity, is one of the world's living religions. Although Jewish people have settled around the world, the State of Israel and the city of Jerusalem still hold a central place in the faith and the life of most Jews. Jewish people have lived in Australia from the earliest times of European settlement, as have Lutheran Christians.

We need to recognize that Christians over the centuries have often mistreated and persecuted the followers of Judaism and so have failed to live by the faith they profess. We Lutherans must also acknowledge that the anti-Jewish writings of Martin Luther were used by persecutors of Jews to justify their position and practices, and could be used by anti-Jewish extremists by tearing them out of their historical context.

Here in Australia, Lutherans have often been unaware of Luther's anti-Jewish writings and of their impact. Fortunately, perhaps because of greater tolerance under the "mateship" banner, and perhaps because both Lutherans and Jews were minority groups, there have been very few occurrences of direct confrontation between Lutherans and the Australian Jewish community.

It is true, however, that before and during World War II, our Lutheran church papers naively and uncritically published German propaganda against the Jews. It is also true that the stress in Australian

Lutheranism on the doctrinal gulf between Judaism and Christianity has led to instances of unloving attitudes by Lutherans toward Jewish people here. Unfortunately there are still some Lutherans who, through ignorance, envy or fear accept bigoted information put out by extreme right-wing groups about Jews; for example, that Jews control the international finance markets, or that there is a conspiracy among leading Jews to take over the world through a one-world government.

We declare that all forms of antisemitism are contrary to the Christian way of life. We urge the members of the Lutheran Church of Australia to repent of and to confess our silence over the Holocaust and other such attacks on Jews, and our sins of prejudice against and misunderstanding of the Jewish people. We also thank God for those of both faiths in Australia who have modeled the way of peace, love and friendship in the past.

We call on members of the Lutheran Church of Australia to make the following commitments:

- to respect and defend the rights of the Jewish community to observe the faith of their ancestors;
- to live out their Christian faith by showing love and understanding toward Jewish people;
- to engage in open and honest dialogue with Jewish people about our common Old Testament heritage and our distinctive religious beliefs; and
- to oppose in word and action religious bigotry of whatever form both within the church and in the wider community, and to join with members of other faiths in working for harmony and tolerance in Australian society.

At the same time, since we believe that Jesus is the savior of all people, let us all continue to confess him publicly as God's promised Messiah.

24

Jews and Judaism: A Statement by the Uniting Church in Australia

Adopted by the 12th Triennial Assembly of the Uniting Church in Australia, meeting in Sydney in July 2009.

The Uniting Church acknowledges:

1. that Jesus of Nazareth cannot be understood apart from the Judaism of his time as he was born, lived and died a faithful Jew, looking to the establishment of God's kingdom as the fulfillment of God's promises

2. that Judaism is a living faith today, and was at the time of Jesus, possessed of its own integrity and vitality within its own developing traditions

3. that historically, understandings of Judaism have been imposed from without, and that Judaism should be understood on its own terms

4. that both Torah and Gospel are expressions of God's grace, calling forth a response of thankful obedience;

5. that Christianity stands in a unique relationship with Judaism because:

   a. Christianity emerged from Judaism of the first century and cannot be understood apart from it

   b. Judaism and Christianity, as living faiths today, have developed significantly from this common root

   c. Christians and Jews share a common heritage in the unique testimony of the Hebrew Scriptures (Old Testament) to the One God

6. that Judaism, both historically and currently, cannot be understood from knowledge of the Hebrew Scriptures alone, or from references to Judaism in the New Testament alone

7. that many of the early Christian writings collected in the New Testament were written in a context of controversy and polemic between the Church and Synagogue

8. that antisemitism in all its expressions is an affront to the gospel of Jesus Christ.

The Uniting Church acknowledges with repentance:

9. a history of interpretation of New Testament texts which has often failed to appreciate the context from which these texts emerged, namely, the growing separation of Christianity and Judaism with attendant bitterness and antagonism, resulting in deeply rooted anti-Jewish misunderstandings

10. an anti-Judaism which developed in Christianity creating fertile ground for the spread of antisemitism culminating in the Shoah (Holocaust), and a history of insensitivity with respect to the importance of the Shoah for Jews.

The Uniting Church affirms:

11. that Christians in their lives and by their words bear witness to God as known to them through Jesus Christ whom they confess as Lord

12. that the gifts and calling of God to the Jewish people are irrevocable

13. that Christians and Jews have kindred ethical frameworks, grounded in the Hebrew Scriptures (Old Testament), which impel them to work together for the achievement of a just and responsible society

14. that Christian self-understanding is enhanced through closer dialogue with, and openness to, Judaism; such dialogue does not preclude opportunities for mutual faith sharing

15. that the State of Israel and a Palestinian State each have the right to live side by side in peace and security.

The Uniting Church does not accept:

16. Christian teaching that is derogatory toward Jews and Judaism

17. the belief that God has abolished the covenant with the Jewish people

18. supersessionism, the belief that Christians have replaced Jews in the love and purpose of God

19. forms of relationships with Jews that require them to become Christian, including coercion and manipulation that violate their humanity, dignity and freedom.

The Uniting Church encourages its members and Councils:

20. to seek opportunities to meet with Jews and to learn about modern Judaism (this might include, wherever possible, receiving hospitality in synagogue worship, inviting a rabbi to speak during a worship service or other gatherings, joining a Council of Christians and Jews)

21. to continue to study the Council of Christians and Jews (Victoria) documents "Rightly Explaining the Word of Truth" and "Re-reading Paul" along with the study of other writings of significance to the Christian-Jewish relationship

22. to respect the integrity of Jewish festivals, such as by refraining from use of a Passover Seder in Holy Week worship

23. to be vigilant in resisting antisemitism and anti-Judaism in church and society

24. to pray and work for a just and lasting peace for both Israelis and Palestinians.

25

Jews, Christians and Muslims:
The Way of Dialogue

Received by the Lambeth Conference, the decennial assembly of bishops of the Anglican Communion, meeting in Canterbury, England, in August 1988, and commended to the Churches of the Anglican Communion for study and as a basis for dialogue with Jews and Muslims.

1. While dialogue with all faiths is highly desirable, we recognize a special relationship between Christianity, Judaism and Islam. All three of these religions see themselves in a common relationship to Abraham, the father of the faithful, the friend of God. Moreover these faiths, which at times have been fiercely antagonistic to one another, have a particular responsibility for bringing about a fresh, constructive relationship which can contribute to the well-being of the human family, and the peace of the world, particularly in the Middle East. Dialogue is the work of patient love and an expression of the ministry of reconciliation. It involves understanding, affirmation and sharing.

The Way of Understanding

2. The essential condition of any true dialogue is a willingness to listen to the partner; to try to see with their eyes and feel with their heart. For understanding is more than intellectual apprehension. It involves the imagination and results in a sensitivity to the fears and hopes of the other. Understanding another means allowing them to define themselves in their terms rather than ours, and certainly not in terms of our inherited stereotypes. This means that in dialogue we may have to face some very different understandings of religion.

3. In relation to Judaism this means, first of all, recognizing that Judaism is still a living religion, to be respected in its own right. The

Judaism of today is not that of any one of the sects of first-century Palestine, and certainly not that of the plain text of the Hebrew scriptures. Its definitive works, such as the Mishnah and the Talmud, as well as its current liturgy, were produced by the post-Pharisee rabbis in the same period, the first to fifth centuries, within which the fathers of the church were defining the meaning of Christianity. Great care should be taken not to misrepresent Judaism by imputing to it, for example, the literal implementation of "an eye for an eye," which was repudiated by the rabbis, or the denial of life after death. This is also true of the long-standing stereotype of Judaism as a religion of works, completely ignoring the deep Jewish sense of the grace of God. Judaism is a living and still developing religion, which has shown spiritual and intellectual vitality throughout the medieval and modern periods despite its history of being maligned and persecuted. The Middle Ages saw great Jewish philosophers such as Maimonides, Bible commentators such as Rashi and the ibn Ezras, poets and mystics, as well as scientists and interpreters of the law. Our modern world is inconceivable without the contribution of Jewish thinkers from Spinoza to Buber, scientists such as Freud and Einstein, as well as musicians, artists and others who have helped shape our cultural life; we are, to our loss, less knowledgeable of the creative vitality of such Jewish spiritual movements of recent times as Hasidism and Musar.

4. Secondly, Judaism is not only a religion, as many Christians understand the word but a people and a civilization. Jews know and define themselves as Jews even when they do not fully share the religious beliefs of Judaism. It is against this background, at once secular and religious, that the importance of the land of Israel to the majority of Jews throughout the world needs to be understood.

5. Thirdly, it is necessary for Christians, as well as Jews, to understand the profound changes and potential for good in modern scholarly understanding of the Bible. Modern biblical scholarship is increasingly becoming a joint enterprise between Jews and Christians. Recent Jewish research has shed much light on the complex and varied religious and social situations in Palestine during the first century of the Common Era (i.e., the era common to Jews and Christians). Some Jews have become very aware of Jesus as part of their own history, and their writings have brought home to Christians his Jewishness. Renewed study of Jewish sources by Christian scholars has led them to see first-century Judaism in a new and more positive light, and to rec-

ognize that the predominantly negative assessment of Judaism in the early church is far from being the whole story. There were many different groups within Judaism at the time of Jesus and "the scribes and Pharisees" reported in the New Testament should be seen as part of a wider discussion within Judaism. The New Testament picture of Judaism needs to be supplemented by expressions of faith by Jews of the time if first-century Judaism is to be properly understood.

6. We now have a far better appreciation than ever before of first-century Judaism, and not least of political factors which led events to take the course they did. The trial and execution of Jesus are now recognized by many scholars to have been brought about to serve the political interests of the Roman occupation forces and those Jews who collaborated with them. It was Rome, too, by its destruction of Jerusalem at the end of the Jewish War in 70 CE which forced a reconstruction of Judaism along much narrower and more rigorous lines than had prevailed earlier.

7. This new understanding of events is leading both Jews and Christians also to look at the way in which Judaism and Christianity came to part company and go their separate ways. Since many of the factors in this split were contingent on specific historical developments, and events need not necessarily have turned out the way they did, there would seem to be no reason why a new understanding should not develop, based on a reconsideration of what originally drove Christianity and Judaism apart.

8. Islam, like Christianity, is a living, world religion. Dialogue with Muslims needs to take into account the fact that it has taken root in and shaped a wide range of countries and cultures. Contrary to popular opinion, for example, the largest Muslim country in the world is not in the Middle East. It is Indonesia in Southeast Asia. Over the last fourteen centuries, Muslims have developed a rich and varied mosaic of cultural patterns, theological schools, mystics and philosophers. Islam's impact on the development of both Jewish and Christian thought and civilization has been profound. Medieval Jewish thinkers like Maimonides and Saadia wrote many of their most influential works in Arabic. The philosophy of Aristotle and the Neo-Platonists came to Western Europe largely in translations from Arabic, the translators being in many cases Christians living in the Muslim world. If geometry is a Greek word, algebra, alchemy and chemistry are Arabic. We call our number system Arabic because the Arabs brought it to us from

India. The astrolabe and the architectural arch both came from
Muslim scientists. We are sadly unaware of much of Islamic history and
thought. So rich and varied is it, that many Muslims are not familiar
themselves with some of the thinkers and movements which are historically, geographically or theologically remote from their own experience: just as many Western Christians are unaware of Byzantine
Orthodox thought or of the life of the Oriental Churches and vice
versa. One of the values of an informed dialogue is that it can help both
partners become more aware of some of the riches of their own respective traditions.

9. In understanding Islam it is necessary for Christians to grasp the
central place of Islamic law in Muslim life. Islamic Law, shari'ah, is
based on the belief that God has, as a gracious act of mercy, revealed
to humanity basic guidelines to live both individually and in society.
Whereas Christians today tend to think of Christian faith as a personal
commitment which can be expressed quite happily in a secular society,
many Muslims believe that God has revealed his will on how the whole
of society is to be ordered, from details of banking to matters of public health. Although based on the Qur'an, the sources of Islamic law are
much wider. The picture becomes even more complex if one attempts
to include the Shiite who are the majority in Iran. A long development
independent from the majority Muslim community (Sunni) has
resulted in a very different ethos and theology, making blanket statements about Islam almost impossible when Iranian and other Shiite
thinkers are taken into account. Some non-Muslim communities living
under Islamic rule experience the application of Shari'ah law as oppressive and inhumane. Another aspect of Shari'ah law which causes some
distress is the treatment of women. We note that in many respects
Islamic law has pioneered the rights of women. For example, under
Islamic law married women had the right to own property and conduct
business in their own names thirteen centuries before these rights were
granted in many Western countries. It is hoped that Christians and
Muslims may search together for ways in which the position of women
may continue to be improved for the benefit of society as a whole. We
also need to remember that classical Islamic law provides safeguards
for the rights of religious minorities which are not actually being
enforced today. Further, in judging, we must always be careful to compare like with like. We must compare the highest and most humane

ideals of Islam with the highest and most humane ideals of Christianity and the misuse of power at the hands of Muslims with the misuse of power at the hands of those who call themselves Christians.

10. Islam, no less than Judaism, has suffered from Christian stereotyping. This is especially true of the notion that Islam is a religion committed to spreading its faith by the sword. History shows a much more complex pattern. It is true that the communities of the Middle East, North Africa and the northern half of the Indian subcontinent were originally brought under Islamic rule by military expansion. On the other hand, much of the part of the world which is now predominantly Muslim did not receive its Islam through military conquest. In fact, the majority of the territory won by Islam in its early advance was taken from it by the Mongols, who already numbered Christians among them. Yet Islam converted its Mongol conquerors and central Asia remains Islamic to this day.

11. In fact, ji'had, usually mistranslated "holy war," is a complex notion that needs to be seriously explored by Christians in dialogue with Muslims. The word actually means struggle and encompasses everything from spiritual struggle to armed struggle as sanctioned by Islamic law. Although Muslims have, in the course of history, sanctioned aggressive wars in this way, it is important to realize that there are many Muslim views of what kind of warfare is legal under Islamic law. The existence of such divergent views might be a constructive point of dialogue.

The Way of Affirmation

12. If Christians wish their own faith to be affirmed by others they themselves must be open to the full force of the attraction of the partner in the dialogue and be willing to affirm all they can affirm, especially when it resonates to the Gospel.

13. For Christians, Judaism can never be one religion among others. It has a special bond and affinity with Christianity. Jesus, our Lord and the Christ, was a Jew and the scriptures which informed and guided his life were the books of the Hebrew Bible. These still form part of the Christian scriptures. The God in whom Jesus believed, to whom he totally gave himself, and in whom we believe is "The God of Abraham,

Isaac and Jacob." A right understanding of the relationship with Judaism is, therefore, fundamental to Christianity's own self-understanding.

14. Christians and Jews share one hope, which is for the realization of God's Kingdom on earth. Together they wait for it, pray for it and prepare for it. This Kingdom is nothing less than human life and society transformed, transfigured and transparent to the glory of God. Christians believe that this glory has already shone in the face of Jesus Christ. In His life, death and resurrection the Kingdom of God, God's just rule, has already broken into the affairs of this world. Judaism is not able to accept this. However, both Jews and Christians share a common frame of reference, in which Christian belief in Jesus Christ is set. For it is as a result of incorporation into Jesus Christ that Christians share the Jewish hope for the coming of God's Kingdom.

15. Christian faith focuses quite naturally on Jesus the Christ and his church. However, both these realities can and should be seen within the hope for, and the horizon of, the Kingdom of God. The presence and the hope for the Kingdom of God were central to the preaching and mission of Jesus. Moreover, Christians continue to pray daily "thy Kingdom come." Christians and Jews share a common hope for the consummation of God's Kingdom which, for Christians, was inaugurated in the life, death and resurrection of Jesus the Christ. Thus, it is through incorporation into Christ, through membership in the Christian Church that Christians come to share in the hope for the Kingdom. We believe that if this hope for God's Kingdom were given its central place by both Jews and Christians this would transform their relationship with one another.

16. Christians and Jews share a passionate belief in a God of loving kindness who has called us into relationship with himself. God is faithful and he does not abandon those he calls. We firmly reject any view of Judaism which sees it as a living fossil, simply superseded by Christianity. When Paul reflects on the mystery of the continued existence of the Jewish people (Rom 9–11) a full half of his message is the unequivocal proclamation of God's abiding love for those whom he first called. Thus he wrote: "God's choice stands and they are his friends for the sake of the patriarchs. For the gracious gifts of God and his calling are irrevocable" (Rom 11:28–29).

17. However, with some honorable exceptions their relationship has too often been marked by antagonism. Discrimination and perse-

cution of the Jews led to the "teaching of contempt," the systematic dissemination of anti-Jewish propaganda by church leaders, teachers and preachers. Through catechism, teaching of school children, and Christian preaching, the Jewish people have been misrepresented and caricatured. Even the Gospels have, at times, been used to malign and denigrate the Jewish people. Anti-Jewish prejudice promulgated by leaders of Church and State has led to persecution, pogrom and finally, provided the soil in which the evil weed of Nazism was able to take root and spread its poison. The Nazis were driven by a pagan philosophy, which had as its ultimate aim the destruction of Christianity itself. But how did it take hold? The systematic extermination of six million Jews and the wiping out of a whole culture must bring about in Christianity a profound and painful re-examination of its relationship with Judaism. In order to combat centuries of anti-Jewish teaching and practice, Christians must develop programs of teaching, preaching, and common social action which eradicate prejudice and promote dialogue.

18. Many Christians would also affirm Islamic monotheism and speak approvingly of Islamic devotion to Jesus and to Mary, his virgin mother. Islam stands in a particular relationship to Christianity because of its acceptance of Jesus as the promised Messiah of Hebrew scripture. At the same time, however, we note that Muslims do not understand this affirmation to imply a doctrine of the person and work of Jesus as the Messiah which would be acceptable to most Christians. Nonetheless this affirmation of Jesus as the fulfillment of the Messianic promise is unique to Christians and Muslims. The same is true of the Islamic affirmation of Jesus as the "Word of God," although Islamic Christology does not accept this as implying the Christian doctrine of the Incarnation. Many Muslims, though not all, would confine its significance to reference to the miraculous events surrounding Jesus' conception and birth. At the same time, Islam affirms the Hebrew Scriptures and the special relationship which God had established with the Jewish people "to whom he had shown his special favor." While it is currently the majority view among Muslims that the whole Bible has been textually corrupted and is therefore no longer valid, this is not the only view found in either classical or contemporary Islamic thought. Some of Islam's greatest scholars have argued that the "corruption" of Jewish and Christian scriptures

referred to in the Qur'an is a corruption, not of text, but of interpretation only. Christians in dialogue ought to know the classical Islamic sources which have argued strongly for this view of the Bible.

19. On the other hand, it has been the almost unanimous Islamic tradition to reject the crucifixion of Jesus as either historical fact or as theologically significant. The Qur'anic material relating to the crucifixion is highly ambiguous and there is the possibility of theological dialogue with Muslims on the interpretation and significance of the Qur'anic material on Jesus. We need not, however, totally reject the Islamic affirmation of Jesus, even as we challenge it in its rejection of his atoning work upon the cross. It is important to note that the Islamic rejection of the crucifixion is not ultimately based on a rejection of the concept of the suffering of God's righteous prophets. God's power is not perceived in Islam as a magic charm against unjust suffering and persecution. The Qur'an often refers, as does the New Testament, to prophets of God who have been killed at various times in history. It accepts not only the possibility but the fact of prophets' death at the hands of the wicked. Nor can we say that Islam automatically rejects the positive value of suffering for others or in the cause of God. This it affirms strongly and in the Shiite tradition the concept of vicarious suffering is of fundamental importance.

20. Many Christians can also affirm the Islamic struggle to be faithful to the example of Abraham. Islamic tradition traces the descent of the Arabs, and so of Muhammad, to Abraham through Ishmael. Many Christians, among them John of Damascus and the Arab apologist Ishaq 'abd al-Masih al-Kindi, accept this genealogy. This is important for Muslims in their understanding of the prophetic mission of Muhammad and of their relationship with Judaism and Christianity as religions which also have a special connection with the faith of Abraham. Even though most Muslims today are not Arabs, they feel, like Christians, that they are children of Abraham by faith because of the message of Muhammad, descendant of Ishmael, son of Abraham.

21. Although Luther had already spoken positively about the faith of Ishmael, few Christians have given much thought to this child of Abraham, about whom the Bible says "God was with the lad and he grew up" (Gen 21:20). Although rejected from the line of the covenant, there is no biblical evidence that this child, miraculously saved by God in the wilderness, ever abandoned his faith in the God of his father Abraham. The figure of Ishmael is theologically challenging for, although rejected from the covenant, he and his mother were the

object of particular and miraculous attention on the part of God. Perhaps we need to challenge the negative assumptions that surround our reaction to this biblical character.

22. Many Christians also often feel challenged to affirm the religious devotion which Muslims display in their prayers. This is clear not only in their ritual prayers but in their own personal prayers such as have been gathered together with Christian prayers by Kenneth Cragg, former Anglican Bishop in Cairo in his book *Alive to God.*

23. Christians would also affirm the sense of fellowship which Muslims often show to each other, regardless of language, race or national origin. They can also affirm early Islamic ideals of religious tolerance. At the same time they would want to challenge Muslims to develop those aspects of their tradition which imply a broader understanding of the unity of all people.

24. Christians would also want to affirm the deep Islamic reliance on the grace and mercy of God. Although often misunderstood and misrepresented by Christian theologians as teaching salvation by works, all schools of Islamic thought are marked by a deep sense of the gratuitous mercy of God. This mercy cannot be earned by anyone because, in Islamic thought, no one can have any claims against God. All that God gives he gives not because we deserve it but gratuitously. This emphasis on the gratuitousness of God's gift has led Islamic theology to abandon the doctrine of the atonement as understood in Christianity, although both the word (*kaffarah*) and the concept are known and used in more restricted senses. Islamic theology argues that God needs no sacrifice or atonement in order to freely forgive human sin and alienation. This he may do simply because he is God almighty. And yet, Islamic thought does not reject the importance of human cooperation with God in working his revealed will here on earth. In this respect the Qur'an speaks of humanity as God's vice regent (*khalifah*) on earth, and this line of thought is developed by many Islamic thinkers. Although some forms of popular Islam may seem to have degenerated into legalism and fatalism, the normative Islamic emphasis on grace and human co-operation should always be borne in mind.

The Way of Sharing

25. Dialogue does not require people to relinquish or alter their beliefs before entering into it; on the contrary, genuine dialogue

demands that each partner brings to it the fullness of themselves and the tradition in which they stand. As they grow in mutual understanding they will be able to share more and more of what they bring with the other. Inevitably, both partners to the dialogue will be affected and changed by this process, for it is a mutual sharing.

26. Within this sharing there are a variety of attitudes toward Judaism within Christianity today. At one pole, there are those Christians whose prayer is that Jews, without giving up their Jewishness, will find their fulfillment in Jesus the Messiah. Indeed some regard it as their particular vocation and responsibility to share their faith with Jews, while at the same time urging them to discover the spiritual riches which God has given them through the Jewish faith. Other Christians, however, believe that in fulfilling the law and the prophets, Jesus validated the Jewish relationship with God, while opening this way up for gentiles through his own person. For others, the holocaust has changed their perception, so that until Christian lives bear a truer witness, they feel a divine obligation to affirm the Jews in their worship and sense of the God and father of Jesus. All these approaches recognize that Christians today are being called into a fresh, more fruitful relationship with Judaism. We urge that further thought and prayer, in the light of scripture and the facts of history, be given to the nature of this relationship.

27. Both these approaches, however, share a common concern to be sensitive to Judaism, to reject all proselytizing, that is, aggressive and manipulative attempts to convert, and of course, any hint of anti-semitism. Further, Jews, Muslims and Christians have a common mission. They share a mission to the world that God's name may be honored: "Hallowed be your name." They share a common obligation to love God with their whole being and their neighbors as themselves. "Your Kingdom come on earth as it is in heaven." And in the dialogue there will be mutual witness. Through learning from one another each will enter more deeply into their own inheritance. Each will recall the other to God, to trust him more fully and obey him more profoundly. This will be a mutual witness between equal partners.

28. Genuine sharing requires of Christians that they correct all distorted images of Judaism and Islam as it requires of Jews and Muslims that they correct distorted images of Christian faith. For Christians this will include careful use and explanation of biblical passages, particularly during Holy Week.

29. In this process it is important to remember also the damage that has been done to Christian-Muslim relations by a distorted view of Islam and by outright animosity. Both Jews and Muslims often shared a common fate at the hands of Christians in the Middle Ages and the centuries of warfare against the Muslims, although both Jews and Eastern Christians shared in the suffering inflicted by the Western Christian armies as they advanced to and through the Middle East. Christians have upon occasion seen Islam as a Christian heresy and at other times as the mere product of human imagination. Scholars have always stressed the influence of Jewish-Christian monotheism on Islam, for it was born in an area where both Judaism and Christianity were practiced. We should always be careful about how we characterize another person's faith and try to avoid hurtful language. This is especially the case when, as with both Judaism and Islam, the negative characterizations of the past have resulted in much pain and suffering inflicted by Christians in the name of religion or where it has left a legacy of bitterness and division, a legacy which continues to cause much suffering to innocent Christian communities today through an undiscriminating attitude on the part of others which unjustly associates them with events for which they bear no responsibility. Many Christians, for example, justly point out that their histories do not overlap the European experience of holocaust and pogrom at all or that they themselves fought against the Crusader armies of Western Europe.

30. There is also much in the way of common action that Jews, Christians and Muslims can join in; for example:
- the struggle against racism, apartheid and anti-semitism
- the work for human rights, particularly,
- the right of people to practice and teach their religion.

There is a common witness to God and the dignity of human beings in a world always in danger of becoming godless and dehumanized.

31. Understanding and affirming are already ways of sharing. However, if we are truly to share our faith we must not only affirm what we can but share our own deep convictions, even when these appear irreconcilably opposed to our partner's faith and practice. In the case of Islam particularly, Christians must first understand Islam if this witness is to be effective. Islam is a missionary religion that is fast gaining many adherents in many parts of the world. This missionary zeal is

not confined to the Middle East but is fervent in Africa, Southeast Asia and is apparent in the intellectual centers of the West. Muslims are often confidently superior to Christians in much the same way that Christians have often been toward Jews. Many Muslims would simply dismiss views which diverge from Islamic faith and practice with the conviction that if their partner only understood Islam he or she would be a Muslim. Christianity will only get a hearing by informed Muslims when it is clear that the Christian who is speaking understands Islam and yet remains a Christian by choice, not, as it were by default.

32. Many Muslims feel that Islam has superseded Christianity the way many Christians have traditionally felt that Christianity superseded Judaism (a view which the same Muslims would share). Just as Christian polemicists have often seized upon the writings of Jewish scholars to try to undermine the faith of the Jewish community, some Muslim intellectuals and propagandists rejoice when they feel able to use some pronouncement of a Western theologian to undermine Christianity and underscore the truth of Islam. Such pronouncements, designed to witness to and explain the Christian faith in liberal societies, are pounced upon and used to damage small Christian churches in Islamic societies.

33. One pressing concern that Christians will want to share with Muslims is the need for clear, strong safeguards for adherents of minority religions in Muslim societies. Any interpretation of Islamic law that seems to deny basic human rights, including the right of people to practice and teach their own faith, must be challenged. We recognize that here there is positive ground for dialogue because Muslim thinkers of the Middle Ages were among the first to actually incorporate ideas of tolerance and safeguards for minorities within their legal systems, centuries before such ideas were advocated by the European Enlightenment. However, Muslim thinkers of today must be challenged to develop even more positive understandings of the role of minorities in society. In particular, the law of apostasy is undergoing considerable discussion today by Muslim thinkers and jurists and is an area where Christians versed in Islamic law must enter into dialogue with Muslims. In matters such as this the sometimes tiny, struggling churches set in Islamic societies need the support of the wider church.

34. It is quite clear that there can be no genuine understanding, affirmation or sharing with Islam without quite detailed study by at least some experts. In this respect Jewish-Christian dialogue is better

served. Most of the important works of traditional and contemporary Jewish thought are available in English, French, Spanish or German translations (if indeed these are not the language of the original). Most of the basic works of traditional Islamic thought have not been translated into these languages and are accessible only to those with a knowledge of Arabic. Even today, although more Muslims are writing in these languages, most of the contemporary intellectual activity within the world of Islam is being conducted in Arabic, Urdu, Persian and Bahasa Malaysia/Indonesia. Valuable work is being done by Christian institutions, in which Anglicans play a part, such as the Centre for the Study of Islam and Christian-Muslim Relations at the Selly Oak Colleges (Birmingham, U.K.), the Henry Martin Institute (Hyderabad, India), the Duncan Black MacDonald Center (Hartford, U.S.A.) and the Christian-Muslim Study Centre (Rawalpindi, Pakistan). There is also the new study center recently established in the Gulf by the Bishop of Cyprus. Such work needs to be extended and supported by the Churches of the Anglican Communion.

26

Antisemitism and Anti-Judaism Today

Message of a Consultation of the Lutheran World Federation held at Dobogokö, Hungary, in September 2001.

Over a three-day period, we representatives of Lutheran World Federation member churches have met with members of the Jewish community from fifteen countries in a consultation on Antisemitism and Anti-Judaism Today: A Lutheran Contribution to the Jewish-Christian Dialogue, held September 9–13, 2001, at Dobogokö near Budapest, Hungary. Our encounter has been intensive, mutually respectful and mutually enriching. On the basis of our encounter, and in consultation with our Jewish colleagues and ecumenical observers, we wish to express our gratitude to those who have preceded us in establishing the Jewish-Lutheran dialogue and exploring the issues raised by and in it. We have gathered to assess the status of dialogue in these member churches of the Lutheran World Federation and to explore the directions in which our response to antisemitism and anti-Judaism must move from now on in the light of new and continuing challenges.

We use "anti-Judaism" to name specifically theological formulations that denigrate Jews and their faith. Looking at the roots of anti-Judaism in Christian theology, it can be understood as a phenomenon of the separation of the church from Judaism. Later on, other motives (social, political, economic, racist) became dominant and led to exclusion and persecution of Jews through centuries. In "antisemitism," we refer to a broader reality: the hatred of and hostility toward Jews, in reality and in rhetoric, that denies them legitimacy among the peoples of the world. This hatred and hostility is to be understood within the larger issues of racism and is countered by the affirmation of human rights that has been part of our heritage for more than fifty years.

Today we can see that in many countries Jews and Christians work together for social justice and respect for human rights and engage in dialogue on theological matters. Our consultation has been an example of this. Christians have increasingly started to seek the Jewish roots of Christianity and understand the Jewishness of Jesus and of the apostles. It has become clear that our common heritage, all that unites Jews and Christians, is a fruitful point of departure for our dialogue. In this dialogue antisemitism and anti-Judaism are key issues. The LWF and the WCC have repudiated all forms and expressions of these attitudes.

Antisemitism and anti-Judaism are present in every church and society represented in this consultation. The expressions are many, and the roots are several. Intolerance of difference and the absence of respect for the dignity of others are essential to these expressions and are the soil in which these sins take root. We therefore encourage member churches of the Lutheran World Federation to undertake appropriate action and education to protect the rights of all people, especially minorities, to build appreciation for difference, and to teach and guard respect for the dignity of others.

Such action and education will take different forms and have different goals in the various member churches. The religious, political and social circumstances of each church, together with its own experience, will shape the responses that are possible. Within the communion of the LWF, each member church retains the autonomy for addressing these concerns in accordance with its own discernment of the gospel in its particular context.

Yet all share in the heritage of biblical Israel that establishes the churches' bond to modern Jews and Judaism. In faithfulness to their calling in the gospel, the churches will seek to discern the significance of this bond for the life and mission of the church. What we affirm is the validity of God's covenant with the Jewish people which has never been superseded.

We acknowledge the importance of the land of Israel to the Jewish people and its central place in the promises of God. We therefore affirm that the connection of the Jewish people to the land is not a racist ideology but a central element of Jewish faith. In solidarity with the Jewish people, and in the spirit of the biblical prophets, the church will seek to understand the proper role and calling of the State of Israel among the nations of the world.

We are deeply concerned about the ongoing conflict in the Middle East and the sufferings of the Israelis and the Palestinians, including the members of the Evangelical Lutheran Church in Jordan. We urge the State of Israel and the Palestinian leadership to seek all possible ways to end the violence and to resume negotiations seeking a just agreement between these two peoples.

We affirm the legacy of the dialogue that is already ours in research, statements, and insights, and encourage the member churches and the Lutheran World Federation to build on this legacy to produce materials that counter anti-Judaism in the church's theology and liturgy. These materials should be addressed to every arena of the church's life: lay and theological education, worship, mission, service and organization. We call on the individual member churches to inform the LWF of any such materials that they may produce, so that these can be shared with other LWF member churches and other ecumenical partners.

We encourage the member churches to create and support opportunities for their members to learn about Jews and Judaism, and the church's shared heritage with them, from the youngest age and in face-to-face encounter, building trust and common understanding.

We encourage the member churches to advocate for adequate legal proscriptions and remedies against racist and antisemitic activities, deploying the legal tools of human rights in the effort.

We encourage the member churches to raise their voices against antisemitism and anti-Judaism wherever they appear and to actively support Jewish communities in maintaining their traditional observances.

We affirm the cooperation that has grown between Jews and Lutherans in work for peace and justice, social relief and community development, and we encourage all who are engaged in such work to continue and thrive in it.

We encourage the Lutheran World Federation to continue its support of Jewish-Lutheran dialogue in the member churches. We especially encourage the engagement of younger leadership in the dialogue, to help assure its continuation and its relevance to contemporary culture.

We encourage the Lutheran World Federation and member churches to convene theological consultations to pursue the theological, exegetical, missiological and pastoral issues that have been raised in and by the dialogue and our own plenary sessions.

We express our gratitude to the Lutheran World Federation for its leadership in this consultation and in the promotion of Jewish-Lutheran understanding. We call for patience and perseverance by all who share this goal, until the long-term process of change on which we have embarked is brought to fruition by the one God of Jews and Christians.

PART TWO

Roman Catholic Statements

27

Address at the Great Synagogue
of Rome

Pope John Paul II, Rome, April 13, 1986

Dear Chief Rabbi of the Jewish community in Rome,
Dear President of the Union of Italian Jewish communities,
Dear President of the Community in Rome,
Dear Rabbis,
Dear Jewish and Christian friends and brethren taking part in this
   historic celebration:

1.

First of all, I would like, together with you, to give thanks and praise
to the Lord who stretched out the heavens and laid the foundations of
the earth (cf. Isa 51:16) and who chose Abraham in order to make him
father of a multitude of children, as numerous "as the stars of heaven
and as the sand which is on the seashore" (Gen 22:17; cf. Isa 15:5)—to
give thanks and praise to Him because it has been His good pleasure, in
the mystery of His Providence, that this evening there should be a
meeting in this your Great Synagogue between the Jewish community
that has been living in this city since the times of the ancient Romans
and the Bishop of Rome and universal Pastor of the Catholic Church.
   I likewise feel it is my duty to thank the Chief Rabbi, Professor
Elio Toaff, who from the first moment accepted with joy the idea that
I should make this visit, and who is now receiving me with great openness of heart and a profound sense of hospitality; and in addition to
him I also thank all those members of the Jewish community in Rome
who have made this meeting possible and who is so many ways have

worked to ensure that it should be at one and the same time a reality
and a symbol.

Many thanks therefore to you all. *Todâ rabbâ* (Many thanks).

2.

In the light of the Word of God that has just been proclaimed and
that lives forever (cf. Isa 30:8), I would like us to reflect together, in the
presence of the Holy One—may He be blessed! (as your liturgy says)—
on the fact and the significance of this meeting between the Bishop of
Rome, the Pope, and the Jewish community that lives and works in this
city which is so dear to you and to me. I had been thinking of this visit
for a long time. In fact, the Chief Rabbi was kind enough to come and
see me, in February 1981, when I paid a pastoral visit to the nearby
Parish of San Carlo ai Catenari. In addition, a number of you have been
more than once to the Vatican, on the occasion of the numerous audi-
ences that I have been able to have with representatives of Italian and
world Jewry, and still earlier, in the time of my predecessors Paul VI,
John XXIII, and Pius XII. I am likewise well aware that the Chief Rabbi,
on the night before the death of Pope John, did not hesitate to go to
Saint Peter's Square; and accompanied by members of the Jewish faithful, he mingled with the crowd of Catholics and other Christians, in
order to pray and keep vigil, as it were bearing witness, in a silent but
very effective way, to the greatness of soul of that pontiff, who was open
to all people without distinction, and in particular to the Jewish brethren.
The heritage that I would now like to take up is precisely that of Pope
John, who on one occasion, as he passed by here—as the Chief Rabbi has
just mentioned—stopped the car so that he could bless the crowd of Jews
who were coming out of this very Temple. And I would like to take up
his heritage at this very moment, when I find myself not just outside, but,
thanks to your generous hospitality, inside the Synagogue of Rome.

3.

This gathering in a way brings to a close, after the pontificate of
John XXIII and the Second Vatican Council, a long period which we
must not tire of reflecting upon in order to draw from it the appropriate

lessons. Certainly, we cannot and should not forget that the historical circumstances of the past were very different from those that have laboriously matured over the centuries. The general acceptance of a legitimate plurality on the social, civil and religious levels has been arrived at with great difficulty. Nevertheless, a consideration of centuries-long cultural conditioning could not prevent us from recognizing that the acts of discrimination, unjustified limitation of religion freedom, oppression also on the level of civil freedom in regard to the Jews were, from an objective point of view, gravely deplorable manifestations. Yes, once again, through myself, the Church, in the words of the well-known declaration *Nostra Aetate* (no. 4) [*Bridges,* Vol. 1, Document 30], "deplores the hatred, persecutions and displays of antisemitism directed against the Jews at any time and by anyone"; I repeat: "by anyone."

I would like once more to express a word of abhorrence for the genocide decreed against the Jewish people during the last war, which led to the holocaust of millions of innocent victims.

When I visited on June 7, 1979 the concentration camp at Auschwitz and prayed for the many victims from various nations, I paused in particular before the memorial stone with the inscription in Hebrew and thus manifested the sentiments of my heart: "This inscription stirs the memory of the People whose sons and daughters were destined to total extermination. This People has its origin in Abraham, who is our father in faith" (cf. Rom 4:12), as Paul of Tarsus expressed it. Precisely this people, which received from God the commandment: "Thou shalt not kill," has experienced in itself to a particular degree what killing means. Before this inscription it is not permissible for anyone to pass by with indifference" (*Insegnamenti,* 1979, p. 1484). The Jewish community of Rome too paid a high price in blood. And it was surely a significant gesture that in those dark years of racial persecution the doors of our religious houses, of our churches, of the Roman Seminary, of buildings belonging to the Holy See and of Vatican City itself were thrown open to offer refuge and safety to so many Jews of Rome being hunted by their persecutors.

4.

Today's visit is meant to make a decisive contribution to the consolidation of the good relations between our two communities, in imitation of the example of so many men and women who have worked and who are still working today, on both sides, to overcome old prejudices and to secure ever wider and fuller recognition of that "bond" and that "common spiritual patrimony" that exists between Jews and Christians.

This is the hope expressed in the fourth paragraph of the Council's declaration *Nostra Aetate*, which I have just mentioned, on the relationship of the Church to non-Christian religions. The decisive turning-point in relations between the Catholic Church and Judaism, and with individual Jews, was occasioned by this brief but incisive paragraph.

We are all aware that, among the riches of this paragraph number 4 of *Nostra Aetate*, three points are especially relevant. I would like to underline them here, before you, in this truly unique circumstance. The first is that the Church of Christ discovers her "bond" with Judaism by "searching into her own mystery" (cf. *Nostra Aetate*, ibid.) The Jewish religion is not "extrinsic" to us, but in a certain way is "intrinsic" to our own religion. With Judaism therefore we have a relationship which we do not have with any other religion. You are our dearly beloved brothers and, in a certain way, it could be said that you are our elder brothers.

The second point noted by the Council is that no ancestral or collective blame can be imputed to the Jews as a people for "what happened in Christ's passion" (cf. *Nostra Aetate*, ibid.) Not indiscriminately to the Jews of that time, nor to those who came afterwards, nor to those of today. So any alleged theological justification for discriminatory measures or, worse still, for acts of persecution is unfounded. The Lord will judge each one "according to his own works," Jews and Christians alike (cf. Rom 2:6).

The third point that I would like to emphasize in the Council's declaration is a consequence of the second. Notwithstanding the Church's awareness of her own identity, it is not lawful to say that the Jews are "repudiated or cursed," as if this were taught or could be deduced from the Sacred Scriptures of the Old or the New Testament (cf. *Nostra Aetate*, ibid.). Indeed, the Council had already said in this same text of *Nostra Aetate*, but also in the dogmatic constitution *Lumen Gentium*, number 16, referring to Saint Paul in the Letter to the Romans (11:28–29), that the Jews are beloved of God, who has called them with an irrevocable calling.

5.

On these convictions rest our present relations. On the occasion of this visit to your Synagogue, I wish to reaffirm them and to proclaim them in their perennial value. For this is the meaning which is to be attributed to my visit to you, to the Jews of Rome. It is not of course because the differences between us have now been overcome that I have come among you. We know well that this is not so. First of all, each of our religions, in the full awareness of the many bonds which unite them to each other, and in the first place that "bond" which the Council spoke of, wishes to be recognized and respected in its own identity, beyond any syncretism and any ambiguous appropriation.

Furthermore, it is necessary to say that the path undertaken is still at the beginning, and therefore a considerable amount of time will still be needed, notwithstanding the great efforts already made on both sides, to remove all forms of prejudice, even subtle ones, to readjust every manner of self-expression and therefore to present always and everywhere, to ourselves and to others, the true face of the Jews and of Judaism, as likewise of Christians and of Christianity, and this at every level of outlook, teaching and communication. In this regard, I would like to remind my brothers and sisters of the Catholic Church, also those living in Rome, of the fact that the guidelines for implementing the Council in this precise field are already available to everyone in the two documents published respectively in 1974 and in 1985 by the Holy See's Commission for Religious Relations with the Jews [*Bridges*, Vol. 1, Documents 38 and 39]. It is only a question of studying them carefully, of immersing oneself in their teachings and of putting them into practice.

Perhaps there still remain between us difficulties of the practical order waiting to be overcome on the level of fraternal relations: these are the result of centuries of mutual misunderstanding, and also of different positions and attitudes, not easily settled, in complex and important matters.

No one is unaware that the fundamental difference from the very beginning has been the attachment of us Catholics to the person and teaching of Jesus of Nazareth, a son of your People, from which were also born the Virgin Mary, the Apostles who were the "foundations and pillars of the Church" and the greater part of the first Christian community. But this attachment is located in the order of faith, that is to say in the free assent of the mind and heart guided by the Spirit, and it can never be the object of exterior pressure, in one sense or the other.

This is the reason why we wish to deepen dialogue in loyalty and friendship, in respect for one another's intimate convictions, taking as a fundamental basis the elements of the Revelation which we have in common, as a "great spiritual patrimony" (cf. *Nostra Aetate*, 4).

6.

It must be said, then, that the ways opened for our collaboration, in the light of our common heritage drawn from the Law and Prophets, are various and important. We wish to recall first of all a collaboration in favor of man, his life from conception until natural death, his dignity, his freedom, his rights, his self-development in a society which is not hostile but friendly and favorable, where justice reigns and where, in this nation, on the various continents and throughout the world, it is peace that rules, the shalom hoped for by the lawmakers, prophets and wise men of Israel.

More in general, there is the problem of morality, the great field of individual and social ethics. We are all aware of how acute the crisis is on this point in the age in which we are living. In a society which is often lost in agnosticism and individualism and which is suffering the bitter consequences of selfishness and violence, Jews and Christians are the trustees and witnesses of an ethic marked by the Ten Commandments, in the observance of which man finds his truth and freedom. To promote a common reflection and collaboration on this point is one of the great duties of the hour.

And finally I wish to address a thought to this city in which there live side by side the Catholic community with its Bishops, and the Jewish community with its authorities and its Chief Rabbi. Let this not be a mere "co-existence," a kind of juxtaposition, interspersed with limited and occasional meetings, but let it be animated by fraternal love.

7.

The problems of Rome are many. You know this well. Each one of us, in the light of that blessed heritage to which I alluded earlier, is conscious of an obligation to work together, at least to some degree, for their solution. Let us seek, as far as possible, to do so together; from this visit of mine and from the harmony and serenity which we have attained may there flow forth a fresh and health-giving spring like the river that Ezekiel saw gushing from the eastern gate of the Temple of Jerusalem (cf. Ezek 47:1ff.), which will help to heal the wounds from which Rome is suffering.

In doing this, I venture to say, we shall each be faithful to our most sacred commitments, and also to that which most profoundly unites and gathers us together: faith in the One God who "loves strangers" and "renders justice to the orphan and the widow" (cf. Deut 10:18), commanding us too to love and help them (cf. ibid., and Lev 19:18:34). Christians have learned this desire of the Lord from the Torah, which you here venerate, and from Jesus, who took to its extreme consequences the love demanded by the Torah.

8.

All that remains for me now, as at the beginning of my address, is to turn my eyes and my mind to the Lord, to thank Him and praise Him for this joyful meeting and for the good things which are already flowing from it, for the rediscovered brotherhood and for the new and more profound understanding between us here in Rome, and between the Church and Judaism everywhere, in every country, for the benefit of all.

Therefore I would like to say with the Psalmist, in his original language which is also your own inheritance:

hodû la-Adonai ki tob
ki le-olam hasdô
yomar-na Yisrael
ki le-olam hasdô
yomerû-na yir'è Adonai
ki le-olam hasdô (Ps 118:1, 2–4).

O give thanks to the Lord for He is good,
His steadfast love endures for ever!
Let Israel say,
"His steadfast love endures for ever!"
Let those who fear the Lord say,
"His steadfast love endures for ever!"

Amen.

28

Address to the Australian Jewish Community (excerpt)

Pope John Paul II, Sydney, November 26, 1986

3.

My hope for this meeting is that it will help to consolidate and extend the improved relations you [Australian Jews] already have with members of the Catholic community in this country. I know that there are men and women throughout Australia, Jews and Catholics alike, who are working, as I stated at the synagogue in Rome, "to overcome old prejudices and to secure ever wider and fuller recognition of that 'bond' and that 'common spiritual patrimony' that exists between Jews and Christians." I give thanks to God for this.

4.

Where Catholics are concerned, it will continue to be an explicit and very important part of my mission to repeat and emphasize that our attitude to the Jewish religion should be one of the greatest respect, since the Catholic faith is rooted in the eternal truths contained in the Hebrew Scriptures, and in the irrevocable covenant made with Abraham. We, too, gratefully hold these same truths of our Jewish heritage and look upon you as our brothers and sisters in the Lord.

For the Jewish people themselves, Catholics should have not only respect but also great fraternal love for it is the teaching of both the Hebrew and Christian Scriptures that the Jews are beloved of God, who has called them with an irrevocable calling. No valid theological justification could ever be found for acts of discrimination or persecution against Jews. In fact, such acts must be held to be sinful.

5.

In order to be frank and sincere we must recognize the fact that there are still obvious differences between us in religious belief and practice. The most fundamental difference is in our respective views on the person and work of Jesus of Nazareth. Nothing, however, prevents us from true and fraternal cooperation in many worthy enterprises, such as biblical studies and numerous works of justice and charity. Such combined undertakings can bring us ever closer together in friendship and trust.

29

Address to Jewish Leaders in Warsaw

Pope John Paul II, Warsaw, June 14, 1987

I should like above all to thank you for this meeting which has found its place in my program. It recalls much to my memory, many experiences of my youth—and certainly not of my youth alone. Memories and experiences were good, and then terrible, terrible. Be sure, dear brothers, that the Poles, this Polish Church, is in a spirit of profound solidarity with you when she looks closely at the terrible reality of the extermination—the unconditional extermination—of your nation, an extermination carried out with premeditation.

The threat against you was also a threat against us; this latter was not realized to the same extent, because it did not have the time to be realized to the same extent. It was you who suffered this terrible sacrifice of extermination: One might say that you suffered it also on behalf of those who were meant for extermination like you. We believe in the purifying power of suffering. The more atrocious the suffering, the greater the purification. The more painful the experiences, the greater the hope.

I think that today the nation of Israel, perhaps more than ever before, finds itself at the center of the attention of the nations of the world, above all because of this terrible experience, through which you have become a loud warning voice for all humanity, for all nations, all the powers of this world, all systems and every person. More than anyone else, it is precisely you who have become this saving warning. I think that in this sense you continue your particular vocation, showing yourselves to be still the heirs of that election to which God is faithful.

This is your mission in the contemporary world before the peoples, the nations, all of humanity, the Church. And in this Church all peoples and nations feel united to you in this mission. Certainly they give great prominence to your nation and its sufferings, its Holocaust, when they wish to speak a warning to individuals and to nations; in your name, the pope, too, lifts up his voice in this warning. The Polish pope has a particular relationship with all this, because, along with you, he has in a certain sense lived all this here, in this land.

This is just one thought that I wished to put before you, thanking you for coming here, thanking you for this meeting. There have been many meetings with your brothers in various countries of the world. I cannot forget the visit last year, the first visit after very many centuries, to the Synagogue of Rome. I value this meeting in Poland in a particular way; it is especially meaningful for me, and I think that it will also be particularly fruitful. It helps me and all the Church to become even more aware of what unites us in the disposition of the Divine Covenant, as your spokesman has just said. This is what unites us in today's world, in face of the great tasks which this world sets you and the Church in the field of justice and of peace among the nations, in accordance with your biblical word *shalom*.

I thank you for the words spoken in the spirit of faith, of the faith in the same God who is your God and our God: the God of Abraham. I extend the greeting of peace and my respectful sentiments to the few heirs of the great Israelite community which existed in Poland, perhaps the largest community in the world. *Shalom*!

30

Address to the New Ambassador of the Federal Republic of Germany to the Holy See (excerpt)

Pope John Paul II, Vatican City, November 8, 1990

...Our first meeting today, as you yourself mentioned, takes place under the influence of the political events of recent months and the completion of German unity on October 3 of this year; it was achieved not least of all through the collaboration of the churches in your country...

...It was really the Second World War which came to an end on October 3 and made many people aware of what fate and guilt mean to all peoples and individuals. We think of the millions of people, most of them totally innocent, who died in that war: soldiers, civilians, women, the elderly and children, people of different nationalities and religions.

In this context we should also mention the tragedy of the Jews. For Christians the heavy burden of guilt for the murder of the Jewish people must be an enduring call to repentance; thereby we can overcome every form of antisemitism and establish a new relationship with our kindred nation of the Old Covenant. The Church, "mindful of her common patrimony with the Jews, and motivated by the Gospels' spiritual love and by no political considerations,...deplores the hatred, persecutions, and displays of antisemitism directed against the Jews at any time and from any source" [Second Vatican Council, declaration *Nostra Aetate*, 4; *Bridges*, Vol. 1, Document 30]. Guilt should not oppress and lead to self-agonizing thoughts, but must always be the point of departure for conversion.

31

Address on the Fiftieth Anniversary of the Warsaw Ghetto Uprising

Pope John Paul II, Vatican City, April 6, 1993

As the fiftieth anniversary of the Warsaw Ghetto uprising approaches, together with the whole Church, I wish to remember those terrible days of World War II, days of contempt for the human person, manifested in the horror of the sufferings endured at that time by so many of our Jewish brothers and sisters.

It is with profound grief that we call to mind what happened then, and indeed all that happened then, and indeed all that happened in the long black night of the Shoah. We remember, and we need to remember, but we need to remember with renewed trust in God and in his all-healing blessing.

In their pastoral letter of November 30, 1990 [Document 59 below], the Polish bishops wrote about what took place in Poland then, but also about the present-day responsibility of Christians and Jews: "The mutual loss of life, a sea of terrible suffering and of wrongs endured should not divide but unite us. The places of execution, and in many cases, the common graves, call for this unity."

As Christians and Jews, following the example of the faith of Abraham, we are called to be a blessing for the world [cf. Gen 12:2ff]. This is the common task awaiting us. It is therefore necessary for us, Christians and Jews, to be first a blessing to one another. This will effectively occur if we are united in the face of the evils that are still threatening: indifference and prejudice, as well as displays of antisemitism.

For what has already been achieved by Catholics and Jews through dialogue and cooperation I give thanks with you to God; for what we are still called to do I offer my ardent prayers. May God further guide us along the paths of his sovereign and loving will for the human family.

32

Address to the Pontifical Biblical Commission

Pope John Paul II, Vatican City, April 11, 1997*

1.

Your Eminence, I cordially thank you for the sentiments you have just expressed in presenting to me the Pontifical Biblical Commission at the beginning of its mandate. I cordially greet the old and new members of the Commission attending the audience. I greet the "old" members with warm gratitude for the tasks already completed and the "new" members with special joy inspired by hope. I am pleased to have this opportunity to meet you all personally and to say again to each of you how much I appreciate the generosity with which you put your competence as exegetes at the service of the Word of God and the Church's Magisterium.

The theme you have begun to study at this plenary session is of enormous importance; it is, in fact, fundamental for a correct understanding of the mystery of Christ and Christian identity. I would first like to emphasize this usefulness, which we could call *ad intra*, since awareness of one's own identity determines the nature of one's relations with others. In this case it determines the nature of the relations between Christians and Jews.

---

*Editor's Note: This address was delivered to the Pontifical Biblical Commission at the time it was commencing work on a study that would eventually be published in 2001 as *The Jewish People and Their Sacred Scriptures in the Christian Bible.*

2.

Since the second century AD, the Church has been faced with the temptation to separate the New Testament completely from the Old, and to oppose one to the other, attributing to them two different origins. The Old Testament, according to Marcion, came from a god unworthy of the name because he was vindictive and bloodthirsty, while the New Testament revealed a God of reconciliation and generosity. The Church firmly rejected this error, reminding all that God's tenderness was already revealed in the Old Testament. Unfortunately, the Marcionite temptation is making its appearance again in our time. However what occurs most frequently is an ignorance of the deep ties linking the New Testament to the Old, an ignorance that gives some people the impression that Christians have nothing in common with Jews.

Centuries of reciprocal prejudice and opposition have created a deep divide which the Church is now endeavoring to bridge, spurred to do so by the Second Vatican Council's position. The new liturgical Lectionaries have given more space to Old Testament texts, and the *Catechism of the Catholic Church* has been concerned to draw constantly from the treasures of Sacred Scripture.

3.

Actually, it is impossible fully to express the mystery of Christ without reference to the Old Testament. Jesus' human identity is determined on the basis of his bond with the people of Israel, with the dynasty of David and his descent from Abraham. And this does not mean only a physical belonging. By taking part in the synagogue celebrations where the Old Testament texts were read and commented on, Jesus also came humanly to know these texts; he nourished his mind and heart with them, using them in prayer and as an inspiration for his actions.

Thus he became an authentic son of Israel, deeply rooted in his own people's long history. When he began to preach and teach, he drew abundantly from the treasure of Scripture, enriching this treasure with new inspirations and unexpected initiatives. These—let us note—did not aim at abolishing the old revelation but, on the contrary, at bringing it to its complete fulfillment. Jesus understood the increasing opposition he had to face on the way to Calvary in the light of the Old

Testament, which revealed to him the destiny reserved for its prophets. He also knew from the Old Testament that in the end God's love always triumphs.

To deprive Christ of his relationship with the Old Testament is therefore to detach him from his roots and to empty his mystery of all meaning. Indeed, to be meaningful, the Incarnation had to be rooted in centuries of preparation. Christ would otherwise have been like a meteor that falls to the earth and is devoid of any connection with human history.

4.

From her origins, the Church has well understood that the Incarnation is rooted in history and, consequently, she has fully accepted Christ's insertion into the history of the People of Israel. She has regarded the Hebrew Scriptures as the perennially valid Word of God, addressed to her as well as to the children of Israel. It is of primary importance to preserve and renew this ecclesial awareness of the essential relationship to the Old Testament. I am certain that your work will make an excellent contribution in this regard. I am delighted with it and deeply grateful to you.

You are called to help Christians have a good understanding of their identity, an identity that is defined first and foremost by faith in Christ, the Son of God. But this faith is inseparable from its relationship to the Old Testament, since it is faith in Christ who "died for our sins *according to the Scriptures*" and "was raised...*in accordance with the Scriptures*" (1 Cor 15:3–4). The Christian must know that by belonging to Christ he has become "Abraham's offspring" (Gal 3:29) and has been grafted onto a cultivated olive tree (cf. Rom 11:17–24), that is, included among the People of Israel, to "share the richness of the olive tree" (Rom 11:17). If he has this firm conviction, he can no longer allow for Jews as such to be despised, or worse, ill treated.

5.

In saying this I do not mean to disregard the fact that the New Testament preserves traces of obvious tension between the early

Christian communities and some groups of non-Christian Jews. St. Paul himself testifies to this tension in his letters that as a non-Christian Jew he had proudly persecuted the Church of God (cf. Gal 1:13; 1 Cor 15:9; Phil 3:6). These painful memories must be overcome in charity, in accordance with Christ's command. Exegesis must always seek to advance in this direction and thereby help to decrease tensions and clear up misunderstandings.

Precisely in the light of all this, the work that you have begun is highly important and deserves to be carried out with care and commitment. It involves certain difficult aspects and delicate points, but it is very promising and full of great hope. I trust it will be very fruitful for the glory of God. With this wish I assure you of a constant remembrance in prayer and I cordially impart a special Apostolic Blessing to you all.

33

Address to Participants in the Vatican Symposium on "The Roots of Anti-Judaism in the Christian Milieu"

Pope John Paul II, Vatican City, October 31, 1997*

1.

I am happy to receive you during your symposium on the roots of anti-Judaism. I greet in particular Cardinal Roger Etchegaray, president of the committee for the great Jubilee of the Year 2000, who is presiding over your meetings. I thank you for devoting these days to a theological study of great importance.

Your meeting is part of preparations for the great jubilee, for which I have invited the church's members to make an appraisal of the millennium about to end, and especially of our century, in the spirit of a necessary "examination of conscience" on the threshold of what should be a time of conversion and reconciliation (*Tertio Millennio Adveniente*, 27–35).

The goal of your symposium is the correct theological interpretation of the relations of the church of Christ with the Jewish people, for which the conciliar declaration *Nostra Aetate* [*Bridges*, Vol. 1, Document 30] has laid the foundation and about which I have had occasion to speak a number of times in the exercise of my ministry. Indeed, in the Christian world—I am not saying on the part of the church as such— erroneous and unjust interpretations of the New Testament relative to the Jewish people and their presumed guilt circulated for too long, engendering sentiments of hostility toward this people. That con-

---

*Editor's Note: This symposium examining anti-Jewish teachings and attitudes in the Christian world took place while the document *We Remember: A Reflection on the Shoah* (Document 49 below) was in the final stages of composition.

tributed to a lulling of many consciences, so that—when Europe was swept by the wave of persecutions inspired by a pagan antisemitism that in its essence was equally anti-Christian—alongside those Christians who did everything to save those who were persecuted, even to the point of risking their own lives, the spiritual resistance of many was not what humanity expected of Christ's disciples. Your thoughtful attention to the past, in view of achieving a purification of memory, is particularly opportune for showing clearly that antisemitism is without any justification and is absolutely condemnable.

Your efforts complement a reflection conducted notably by the Commission for Religious Relations with the Jews and expressed, among other places, in the *Guidelines* of December 1, 1974 [*Bridges*, Vol. 1, Document 38], and in the *Notes on the Correct Way to Present the Jews and Judaism in Preaching and Catechesis in the Roman Catholic Church* of June 24, 1985 [*Bridges*, Vol. 1, Document 39]. I appreciate the fact that the theological research conducted by your symposium is done with scholarly rigor, in the conviction that to serve the truth is to serve Christ himself and his church.

2.

At the conclusion of some chapters in the Letter to the Romans (9–11) casting critical light on Israel's destiny according to God's plan, St. Paul gives us a resounding hymn of adoration: "Oh, the depth of the riches and wisdom and knowledge of God!" (11:33). In Paul's ardent soul, this hymn echoes a principle he has just expressed, which is in a way the epistle's central theme: "For God delivered all to disobedience, that he might have mercy upon all" (11:32). Salvation history, even when its vicissitudes seem disconcerting to us, is guided by the mercy of him who came to save that which was lost. An attitude of adoration before the unfathomable depths of God's loving providence permits us to just glimpse something of what is a mystery of faith.

3.

At the origin of this little people—situated between great pagan empires whose blaring culture was overpowering—is the act of divine election. This people is assembled and led by Yahweh, creator of heaven and of earth. Its existence is therefore not purely a fact of nature or of culture in the sense that the resourcefulness proper to one's nature is expressed in culture. It is a supernatural fact. This people perseveres despite everything because it is the people of the covenant, and despite human infidelities, Yahweh is faithful to his covenant. To ignore this most basic principle is to adopt a Marcionism against which the church immediately and vigorously reacted, conscious of a vital link with the Old Testament, without which the New Testament itself is emptied of meaning. The Scriptures are inseparable from the people and their history, which leads to Christ, the promised and awaited Messiah, Son of God made man. The church does not cease to confess this, daily taking up in its liturgy the psalms, as well as the canticles of Zechariah, the Virgin Mary and Simeon (cf. Ps 132:17; Luke 1:46–55; 1:68–79; 2:29–32).

This is why those who consider the reality that Jesus was a Jew and that his milieu was the Jewish world to be simple contingent cultural facts—for which it would be possible to substitute another religious tradition from which the person of the Lord could be detached without losing his identity—not only misunderstand the meaning of the history of salvation but, more radically, do damage to the very truth of the incarnation and make an authentic conception of inculturation impossible.

4.

Based on what I have already said, we can draw some conclusions capable of giving direction to the Christian's attitude and the theologian's work. The church firmly condemns all forms of genocide as well as the racist theories that have inspired and claimed to justify them. One recalls the encyclical of Pius XI, *Mit Brennender Sorge* (1937) and that of Pius XII, *Summi Pontificatus* (1939); the latter recalled the law of human solidarity and of charity toward every person, whatever the people to which he belongs. Racism is therefore a negation of the deepest identity of the human being, who is a person created in the image and likeness of God. To the moral malice of all genocide is added, with the Shoah, the malice of a hatred which does violence to

God's salvific plan in history. The church realizes that it also was directly targeted by this hatred.

The teaching of Paul in the Letter to the Romans teaches us what brotherly sentiments, rooted in faith, we ought to have for the children of Israel (cf. Rom 9:4–5). The apostle underlines this: "They are beloved because of the patriarchs. For the gifts and the call of God are irrevocable" (cf. Rom 11:28–29).

5.

Be assured of my gratitude for the work you are doing on a theme of great importance which matters a great deal to me. You thus are contributing to deepening the dialogue between Catholics and Jews; we are pleased at its positive renewal over the course of recent decades.

I offer my best wishes to you and your loved ones, and I willingly give you my apostolic blessing.

34

Homily for the Canonization of Edith Stein / Teresa Benedicta of the Cross (excerpt)

Pope John Paul II, Vatican City, October 11, 1998

Dear brothers and sisters! Because she was Jewish, Edith Stein was taken with her sister Rosa and many other Catholic Jews from the Netherlands to the concentration camp in Auschwitz, where she died with them in the gas chambers. Today we remember them all with deep respect. A few days before her deportation, the woman religious had dismissed the question about a possible rescue: "Do not do it! Why should I be spared? Is it not right that I should gain no advantage from my baptism? If I cannot share the lot of my brothers and sisters, my life, in a certain sense, is destroyed."

From now on, as we celebrate the memory of this new saint from year to year, we must also remember the Shoah, that cruel plan to exterminate a people—a plan to which millions of our Jewish brothers and sisters fell victim. May the Lord let his face shine upon them and grant them peace (cf. Num 6:25ff.).

For the love of God and man, once again I raise an anguished cry: May such criminal deeds never be repeated against any ethnic group, against any race, in any corner of this world! It is a cry to everyone: to all people of goodwill; to all who believe in the Just and Eternal God; to all who know they are joined to Christ, the Word of God made man. We must all stand together; human dignity is at stake. There is only one human family. The new saint also insisted on this: "Our love of neighbor is the measure of our love of God. For Christians—and not only for them—no one is a 'stranger.' The love of Christ knows no borders"...

"God is spirit, and those who worship him must worship in spirit and truth" (John 4:24).

Dear brothers and sisters, the divine Teacher spoke these words to the Samaritan woman at Jacob's well. What he gave his chance but attentive listener we also find in the life of Edith Stein, in her "ascent of Mount Carmel." The depth of the divine mystery became perceptible to her in the silence of contemplation. Gradually, throughout her life, as she grew in the knowledge of God, worshiping him in spirit and truth, she experienced ever more clearly her specific vocation to ascend the Cross with Christ, to embrace it with serenity and trust, to love it by following in the footsteps of her beloved Spouse. St. Teresa Benedicta of the Cross is offered to us today as a model to inspire us and a protectress to call upon.

We give thanks to God for this gift. May the new saint be an example to us in our commitment to serve freedom, in our search for the truth. May her witness constantly strengthen the bridge of mutual understanding between Jews and Christians.

St. Teresa Benedicta of the Cross, pray for us! Amen.

35

Homily at Mount Sinai (excerpt)

Pope John Paul II, Mount Sinai, Egypt, February 26, 2000

1.

In this year of the great jubilee, our faith leads us to become pilgrims in the footsteps of God. We contemplate the path he has taken through time, revealing to the world the magnificent mystery of his faithful love for all humankind. Today, with great joy and deep emotion, the Bishop of Rome is a pilgrim to Mount Sinai, drawn by this holy mountain which rises like a soaring monument to what God revealed here. Here he revealed his name! Here he gave his law, the Ten Commandments of the covenant!

How many have come to this place before us! Here the people of God pitched their tents (cf. Exod 19:2); here the prophet Elijah took refuge in a cave (cf. 1 Kgs 19:9); here the body of the martyr Catherine found a final resting place; here a host of pilgrims through the ages have scaled what St. Gregory of Nyssa called "the mountain of desire" (St. Gregory of Nyssa, *The Life of Moses*, II, 232); here generations of monks have watched and prayed. We humbly follow in their footsteps to "the holy ground" where the God of Abraham, of Isaac and of Jacob commissioned Moses to set his people free (cf. Exod 3:5–8).

2.

God shows himself in mysterious ways—as the fire that does not consume—according to a logic which defies all that we know and expect. He is the God who is at once close at hand and far away; he is in the world but not of it. He is the God who comes to meet us, but who will not be possessed. He is "I AM WHO I AM"—the name which is no name! I AM WHO I AM: the divine abyss in which essence and existence are one! The God who is being itself! Before such a mystery, how can we fail to "take off our shoes" as he commands and adore him on this holy ground?

Here on Mount Sinai, the truth of "who God is" became the foundation and guarantee of the covenant. Moses enters "the luminous darkness" (*The Life of Moses*, II, 164), and there he is given the law "written with the finger of God" (Exod 31:18). But what is this law? It is the law of life and freedom! At the Red Sea the people had experienced a great liberation. They had seen the power and fidelity of God; they had discovered that he is the God who does indeed set his people free as he had promised. But now on the heights of Sinai this same God seals his love by making the covenant that he will never renounce. If the people obey his law, they will know freedom forever. The exodus and the covenant are not just events of the past; they are forever the destiny of all God's people!

3.

The encounter of God and Moses on this mountain enshrines at the heart of our religion the mystery of liberating obedience, which finds its fulfillment in the perfect obedience of Christ in the incarnation and on the cross (cf. Phil 2:8; Heb 5:8–9). We too shall be truly free if we learn to obey as Jesus did (cf. Heb 5:8).

The Ten Commandments are not an arbitrary imposition of a tyrannical Lord. They were written in stone, but before that they were written on the human heart as the universal moral law, valid in every time and place. Today, as always, the Ten Words of the law provide the only true basis for the lives of individuals, societies and nations. Today as always, they are the only future of the human family. They save man from the destructive force of egoism, hatred and falsehood. They point out all the false gods that draw him into slavery: the love of self to the exclusion of God, the greed for power and pleasure that overturns the order of justice and degrades our human dignity and that of our neighbor. If we turn from these false idols and follow the God who sets his people free and remains always with them, then we shall emerge like Moses after forty days on the mountain, "shining with glory" (*The Life of Moses*, II, 230), ablaze with the light of God!

To keep the commandments is to be faithful to God, but it is also to be faithful to ourselves, to our true nature and our deepest aspirations. The wind which still today blows from Sinai reminds us that God wants to be honored in and through the growth of his creatures: *Gloria Dei, homo vivens*. In this sense, that wind carries an insistent invitation to dialogue between the followers of the great monotheistic religions in their service of the human family. It suggests that in God we can find the point of our encounter: in God the all-powerful and all-merciful, Creator of the universe and Lord of history, who at the end of our earthly existence will judge us with perfect justice.

4.

The gospel reading to which we have just listened suggests that Sinai finds its fulfillment on another mountain, the mountain of the transfiguration, where Jesus appears to his apostles shining with the glory of God. Moses and Elijah stand with him to testify that the fullness of God's revelation is found in the glorified Christ.

On the mountain of the transfiguration, God speaks from the cloud, as he did on Sinai. But now he says, "This is my beloved Son; listen to him" (Mark 9:7). He commands us to listen to his Son, because "no one knows the Father except the Son and anyone to whom the Son chooses to reveal him" (Matt 11:27). And so we learn that the true name of God is Father! The name which is beyond all other names: Abba! (cf. Gal 4:6). And in Jesus we learn that our true name is son, daughter! We learn that the God of the exodus and the covenant sets his people free because they are his sons and daughters, created not for slavery but for "the glorious liberty of the children of God" (Rom 8:21).

So when St. Paul writes that we "have died to the law through the body of Christ" (Rom 7:4), he does not mean that the law of Sinai is past. He means that the Ten Commandments now make themselves heard through the voice of the beloved Son. The person delivered by Jesus Christ into true freedom is aware of being bound not externally by a multitude of prescriptions, but internally by the love which has taken hold in the deepest recesses of his heart. The Ten Commandments are the law of freedom: not the freedom to follow our blind passions, but the freedom to love, to choose what is good in every situation, even when to do so is a burden. It is not an impersonal law that we obey; what is required is loving surrender to the Father through Christ Jesus in the Holy Spirit (cf. Rom 6:14; Gal 5:18). In revealing himself on the mountain and giving his law, God revealed man to man himself. Sinai stands at the very heart of the truth about man and his destiny.

36

Address at the Hall of Remembrance, Yad Vashem

Pope John Paul II, Jerusalem, March 23, 2000

The words of the ancient psalm rise from our hearts:

> I have become like a broken vessel.
> I hear the whispering of many—terror on every side!
> as they scheme together against me, as they plot to take my
> life.
> But I trust in you, O Lord; I say, "You are my God."
> (Ps 31:13–15)

1.

In this place of memories, the mind and heart and soul feel an extreme need for silence. Silence in which to remember. Silence in which to try to make some sense of the memories which come flooding back. Silence because there are no words strong enough to deplore the terrible tragedy of the Shoah. My own personal memories are of all that happened when the Nazis occupied Poland during the war. I remember my Jewish friends and neighbors, some of whom perished, while others survived.

I have come to Yad Vashem to pay homage to the millions of Jewish people who, stripped of everything, especially of their human dignity, were murdered in the Holocaust. More than half a century has passed, but the memories remain.

Here, as at Auschwitz and many other places in Europe, we are overcome by the echo of the heartrending laments of so many. Men, women and children cry out to us from the depths of the horror that they knew. How can we fail to heed their cry? No one can forget or ignore what happened. No one can diminish its scale.

2.

We wish to remember. But we wish to remember for a purpose, namely to ensure that never again will evil prevail, as it did for the millions of innocent victims of Nazism.

How could man have such utter contempt for man? Because he had reached the point of contempt for God. Only a godless ideology could plan and carry out the extermination of a whole people.

The honor given to the "righteous gentiles" by the State of Israel at Yad Vashem for having acted heroically to save Jews, sometimes to the point of giving their own lives, is a recognition that not even in the darkest hour is every light extinguished. That is why the psalms, and the entire Bible, though well aware of the human capacity for evil, also proclaim that evil will not have the last word. Evil will not have the last word. Out of the depths of pain and sorrow, the believer's heart cries out: "I trust in you, O Lord; I say, 'You are my God'" (Ps 31:14).

3.

Jews and Christians share an immense spiritual patrimony, flowing from God's self-revelation. Our religious teachings and our spiritual experience demand that we overcome evil with good. We remember, but not with any desire for vengeance or as an incentive to hatred. For us, to remember is to pray for peace and justice, and to commit ourselves to their cause. Only a world at peace, with justice for all, can avoid repeating the mistakes and terrible crimes of the past.

As Bishop of Rome and successor of the Apostle Peter, I assure the Jewish people that the Catholic Church, motivated by the gospel law of truth and love and by no political considerations, is deeply saddened by the hatred, acts of persecution and displays of antisemitism directed against the Jews by Christians at any time and in any place. The Church rejects racism in any form as a denial of the image of the Creator inherent in every human being (cf. Gen 1:26).

4.

In this place of solemn remembrance, I fervently pray that our sorrow for the tragedy which the Jewish people suffered in the twentieth century will lead to a new relationship between Christians and Jews. Let us build a new future in which there will be no more anti-Jewish feeling among Christians or anti-Christian feeling among Jews, but rather the mutual respect required of those who adore the one Creator and Lord, and look to Abraham as our common father in faith (cf. *We Remember* [Document 49 below], V).

The world must heed the warning that comes to us from the victims of the Holocaust and from the testimony of the survivors. Here at Yad Vashem the memory lives on, and burns itself onto our souls. It makes us cry out:

"I hear the whispering of many—terror on every side!
But I trust in you, O Lord; I say, 'You are my God'" (Ps 31:13–15).

Thank you very much.

37

Prayer at the Western Wall

Pope John Paul II, Jerusalem, March 26, 2000*

God of our fathers,
you chose Abraham and his descendants
to bring Your name to the nations:
we are deeply saddened
by the behavior of those
who in the course of history
have caused these children of Yours to suffer,
and asking Your forgiveness
we wish to commit ourselves
to genuine brotherhood
with the people of the Covenant.

Jerusalem, 26 March 2000
Joannnes Paulus II

---

*Editor's Note: During his pilgrimage to Israel, John Paul II prayed at the Western Wall, and according to Jewish custom placed a written prayer, a *kvitle*, in a crack in the wall. The text repeated the prayer for God's forgiveness for Christian sins against the Jewish people that had been offered at St. Peter's Basilica during the Mass of Pardon on March 12, 2000, with the omission, however, of the concluding phrase, "We ask this through Christ our Lord." The prayer, hand signed by the pope, is now housed in Yad Vashem, the Holocaust Memorial in Jerusalem.

38

Address at the Roonstrasse Synagogue of Cologne

Pope Benedict XVI, Cologne, Germany, August 19, 2005

Ladies and Gentlemen,
Dear Brothers and Sisters!

Shalom lechem! It has been my deep desire, during my first visit to Germany since my election as the successor of the Apostle Peter, to meet the Jewish community of Cologne and the representatives of Judaism in Germany. By this visit I would like to return in spirit to the meeting that took place in Mainz on November 17, 1980 between my venerable predecessor Pope John Paul II, then making his first visit to this country, and members of the Central Jewish Committee in Germany and the Rabbinic Conference. Today too I wish to reaffirm that I intend to continue on the path toward improved relations and friendship with the Jewish People, following the decisive lead given by Pope John Paul II (cf. Address to the Delegation of the International Jewish Committee on Interreligious Consultations, June 9, 2005: *L'Osservatore Romano*, June 10, 2005, p. 5).

The Jewish community in Cologne can truly feel "at home" in this city. Cologne is, in fact, the oldest site of a Jewish community on German soil, dating back to the Colonia of Roman times. The history of relations between the Jewish and Christian communities has been complex and often painful. There were times when the two lived together peacefully, but there was also the expulsion of the Jews from Cologne in the year 1424. And in the twentieth century, in the darkest period of German and European history, an insane racist ideology, born of neo-paganism, gave rise to the attempt, planned and systematically carried out by the regime, to exterminate European Jewry. The result has passed into history as the Shoah. The victims of this unspeakable and previously unimaginable crime amounted to seven thousand named individuals in Cologne alone; the real figure was surely much higher. The holiness of God was no longer recognized, and consequently contempt was shown for the sacredness of human life.

This year marks the sixtieth anniversary of the liberation of the Nazi concentration camps, in which millions of Jews—men, women and children—were put to death in the gas chambers and ovens. I make my own the words written by my venerable predecessor on the occasion of the sixtieth anniversary of the liberation of Auschwitz and I too say: "I bow my head before all those who experienced this manifestation of the *mysterium iniquitatis*." The terrible events of that time must "never cease to rouse consciences, to resolve conflicts, to inspire the building of peace" (Message for the Liberation of Auschwitz, January 15, 2005). Together we must remember God and his wise plan for the world which he created. As we read in the Book of Wisdom, he is the "lover of life" (11:26).

This year also marks the fortieth anniversary of the promulgation of the Second Vatican Council's declaration *Nostra Aetate* [*Bridges*, Vol. 1, Document 30], which opened up new prospects for Jewish-Christian relations in terms of dialogue and solidarity. This declaration, in the fourth chapter, recalls the common roots and the immensely rich spiritual heritage that Jews and Christians share. Both Jews and Christians recognize in Abraham their father in faith (cf. Gal 3:7; Rom 4:11ff.) and they look to the teachings of Moses and the prophets. Jewish spirituality, like its Christian counterpart, draws nourishment from the psalms. With Saint Paul, Christians are convinced that "the gifts and the call of God are irrevocable" (Rom 11:29, cf. 9:6,11; 11:1ff.). In considering the Jewish roots of Christianity (cf. Rom 11:16–24), my venerable predecessor, quoting a statement by the German bishops, affirmed that: "whoever meets Jesus Christ meets Judaism" (*Insegnamenti*, vol. III/2, 1980, p. 1272).

The conciliar declaration *Nostra Aetate* therefore "deplores feelings of hatred, persecutions and demonstrations of antisemitism directed against the Jews at whatever time and by whomsoever" (no. 4). God created us all "in his image" (cf. Gen 1:27) and thus honored us with a transcendent dignity. Before God, all men and women have the same dignity, whatever their nation, culture or religion. Hence the declaration *Nostra Aetate* also speaks with great esteem of Muslims (cf. no. 3) and of the followers of other religions (cf. no. 2). On the basis of our shared human dignity the Catholic Church "condemns as foreign to the mind of Christ any kind of discrimination whatsoever between people, or harassment of them, done by reason of race or color, class or religion" (no. 5). The Church is conscious of her duty to transmit this teaching, in her catechesis and in every aspect of her life, to the younger generations which did not witness the terrible events that took place before and during the Second World War. It is a particularly important task, since today, sadly, we are witnessing the rise of new signs of antisemitism and various forms of a general hostility toward foreigners. How can we fail to see in this a reason for concern and vigilance? The Catholic Church is committed—I reaffirm this again today—to tolerance, respect, friendship and peace between all peoples, cultures and religions.

In the forty years that have passed since the conciliar declaration *Nostra Aetate*, much progress has been made, in Germany and throughout the world, toward better and closer relations between Jews and Christians. Alongside official relationships, due above all to cooperation between specialists in the biblical sciences, many friendships have been born. In this regard, I would mention the various declarations by the German Episcopal Conference and the charitable work done by the Society for Jewish-Christian Cooperation in Cologne, which since 1945 have enabled the Jewish community to feel once again "at home" here in Cologne and to establish good relations with the Christian communities. Yet much still remains to be done. We must come to know one another much more and much better. Consequently I would encourage sincere and trustful dialogue between Jews and Christians, for only in this way will it be possible to arrive at a shared interpretation of disputed historical questions, and, above all, to make progress toward a theological evaluation of the relationship between Judaism and Christianity. This dialogue, if it is to be sincere, must not gloss over or underestimate the existing differences; in those areas in which, due to our profound convictions in faith, we diverge, and indeed precisely in those areas, we need to show respect [*orally*: "and love"] for one another.

Finally, our gaze should not only be directed to the past, but should also look forward to the tasks that await us today and tomorrow. Our rich common heritage and our fraternal and more trusting relations call upon us to join in giving an ever more harmonious witness and to work together on the practical level for the defense and promotion of human rights and the sacredness of human life, for family values, for social justice and for peace in the world. The Decalogue (cf. Exod 20; Deut 5) is for us a shared legacy and commitment. The Ten Commandments are not a burden, but a sign-post showing the path leading to a successful life. This is particularly the case for the young people whom I am meeting in these days and who are so dear to me. My wish is that they may be able to recognize in the Decalogue a lamp for their steps, a light for their path (cf. Ps 119:105). Adults have the responsibility of handing down to young people the torch of hope that God has given to Jews and to Christians, so that "never again" will the forces of evil come to power, and that future generations, with God's help, may be able to build a more just and peaceful world, in which all people have equal rights and are equally at home.

I conclude with the words of Psalm 29, which express both a wish and a prayer: "May the Lord give strength to his people, may he bless his people with peace."

May he hear our prayer!

39

Address at Auschwitz

Pope Benedict XVI, Oswiecim (Auschwitz), Poland, May 28, 2006

To speak in this place of horror, in this place where unprecedented mass crimes were committed against God and man, is almost impossible—and it is particularly difficult and troubling for a Christian, for a pope from Germany. In a place like this, words fail; in the end, there can only be a dread silence—a silence which is itself a heartfelt cry to God: Why, Lord, did you remain silent? How could you tolerate all this? In silence, then, we bow our heads before the endless line of those who suffered and were put to death here; yet our silence becomes in turn a plea for forgiveness and reconciliation, a plea to the living God never to let this happen again.

Twenty-seven years ago, on June 7, 1979, Pope John Paul II stood in this place [cf. *Bridges*, Vol. 1, Document 33]. He said: "I come here today as a pilgrim. As you know, I have been here many times. So many times! And many times I have gone down to Maximilian Kolbe's death cell, paused before the execution wall, and walked amid the ruins of the Birkenau ovens. It was impossible for me not to come here as pope." Pope John Paul came here as a son of that people which, along with the Jewish people, suffered most in this place and, in general, throughout the war. "Six million Poles lost their lives during the Second World War: a fifth of the nation," he reminded us. Here too he solemnly called for respect for human rights and the rights of nations, as his predecessors John XXIII and Paul VI had done before him, and added: "The one who speaks these words is...the son of a nation which in its history has suffered greatly from others. He says this, not to accuse, but to remember. He speaks in the name of all those nations whose rights are being violated and disregarded..."

Pope John Paul II came here as a son of the Polish people. I come here today as a son of the German people. For this very reason, I can and must echo his words: I could not fail to come here. I had to come. It is a duty before the truth and the just due of all who suffered here, a duty before God, for me to come here as the successor of Pope John Paul II and as a son of the German people—a son of that people over which a ring of criminals rose to power by false promises of future greatness and the recovery of the nation's honor, prominence and prosperity, but also through terror and intimidation, with the result that our people was used and abused as an instrument of their thirst for destruction and power. Yes, I could not fail to come here. On June 7, 1979, I came as the archbishop of Munich-Freising, along with many other bishops who accompanied the pope, listened to his words and joined in his prayer. In 1980 I came back to this dreadful place with a delegation of German bishops, appalled by its evil, yet grateful for the fact that above its dark clouds the star of reconciliation had emerged. This is the same reason why I have come here today: to implore the grace of reconciliation—first of all from God, who alone can open and purify our hearts, from the men and women who suffered here, and finally the grace of reconciliation for all those who, at this hour of our history, are suffering in new ways from the power of hatred and the violence which hatred spawns.

How many questions arise in this place! Constantly the question comes up: Where was God in those days? Why was he silent? How could he permit this endless slaughter, this triumph of evil? The words of Psalm 44 come to mind, Israel's lament for its woes: "You have broken us in the haunt of jackals, and covered us with deep darkness…because of you we are being killed all day long, and accounted as sheep for the slaughter. Rouse yourself! Why do you sleep, O Lord? Awake, do not cast us off forever! Why do you hide your face? Why do you forget our affliction and oppression? For we sink down to the dust; our bodies cling to the ground. Rise up, come to our help! Redeem us for the sake of your steadfast love!" (Ps 44:19, 22–26). This cry of anguish, which Israel raised to God in its suffering, at moments of deep distress, is also the cry for help raised by all those who in every age—yesterday, today and tomorrow—suffer for the love of God, for the love of truth and goodness. How many they are, even in our own day!

We cannot peer into God's mysterious plan—we see only piecemeal, and we would be wrong to set ourselves up as judges of God and history. Then we would not be defending man, but only contributing to his downfall. No—when all is said and done, we must continue to cry out humbly yet insistently to God: Rouse yourself! Do not forget mankind, your creature! And our cry to God must also be a cry that pierces our very heart, a cry that awakens within us God's hidden presence—so that his power, the power he has planted in our hearts, will not be buried or choked within us by the mire of selfishness, pusillanimity, indifference or opportunism. Let us cry out to God, with all our hearts, at the present hour, when new misfortunes befall us, when all the forces of darkness seem to issue anew from human hearts: whether it is the abuse of God's name as a means of justifying senseless violence against innocent persons, or the cynicism which refuses to acknowledge God and ridicules faith in him. Let us cry out to God, that he may draw men and women to conversion and help them to see that violence does not bring peace, but only generates more violence— a morass of devastation in which everyone is ultimately the loser. The God in whom we believe is a God of reason—a reason, to be sure, which is not a kind of cold mathematics of the universe, but is one with love and with goodness. We make our prayer to God and we appeal to humanity, that this reason, the logic of love and the recognition of the power of reconciliation and peace, may prevail over the threats arising from irrationalism or from a spurious and godless reason.

The place where we are standing is a place of memory, it is the place of the Shoah. The past is never simply the past. It always has something to say to us; it tells us the paths to take and the paths not to take. Like John Paul II, I have walked alongside the inscriptions in various languages erected in memory of those who died here: inscriptions in Belarusian, Czech, German, French, Greek, Hebrew, Croatian, Italian, Yiddish, Hungarian, Dutch, Norwegian, Polish, Russian, Romani, Romanian, Slovak, Serbian, Ukrainian, Judaeo-Spanish and English. All these inscriptions speak of human grief, they give us a glimpse of the cynicism of that regime which treated men and women as material objects and failed to see them as persons embodying the image of God. Some inscriptions are pointed reminders. There is one in Hebrew. The rulers of the Third Reich wanted to crush the entire Jewish people, to cancel it from the register of the peoples of the earth. Thus the words of the Psalm: "We are being killed, accounted as sheep for the slaughter" were fulfilled in a terrifying way. Deep down, those vicious criminals, by wiping out this people, wanted to kill the God who called Abraham, who spoke on Sinai and laid down principles to serve as a guide for mankind, principles that are eternally valid. If this people, by its very existence, was a witness to the God who spoke to humanity and took us to himself, then that God finally had to die and power had to belong to man alone—to those men, who thought that by force they had made themselves masters of the world. By destroying Israel, by the Shoah, they ultimately wanted to tear up the taproot of the Christian faith and to replace it with a faith of their own invention: faith in the rule of man, the rule of the powerful.

Then there is the inscription in Polish. First and foremost they wanted to eliminate the cultural elite, thus erasing the Polish people as an autonomous historical subject and reducing it, to the extent that it continued to exist, to slavery. Another inscription offering a pointed reminder is the one written in the language of the Sinti and Roma people. Here too, the plan was to wipe out a whole people which lives by migrating among other peoples. They were seen as part of the refuse of world history, in an ideology which valued only the empirically useful; everything else, according to this view, was to be written off as *lebensunwertes Leben*—life unworthy of being lived. There is also the inscription in Russian, which commemorates the tremendous loss of life endured by the Russian soldiers who combated the Nazi reign of terror; but this inscription also reminds us that their mission had a tragic twofold effect: they set the peoples free from one dictatorship, but the same peoples were thereby subjected to a new one, that of Stalin and the Communist system.

The other inscriptions, written in Europe's many languages, also speak to us of the sufferings of men and women from the whole continent. They would stir our hearts profoundly if we remembered the victims not merely in general, but rather saw the faces of the individual persons who ended up here in this abyss of terror. I felt a deep urge to pause in a particular way before the inscription in German. It evokes the face of Edith Stein, Theresia Benedicta a Cruce: a woman, Jewish and German, who disappeared along with her sister into the black night of the Nazi-German concentration camp; as a Christian and a Jew, she accepted death with her people and for them. The Germans who had been brought to Auschwitz-Birkenau and met their death here were considered as *Abschaum der Nation*—the refuse of the nation. Today we gratefully hail them as witnesses to the truth and goodness which even among our people were not eclipsed. We are grateful to them, because they did not submit to the power of evil, and now they stand before us like lights shining in a dark night. With profound respect and gratitude, then, let us bow our heads before all those who, like the three young men in Babylon facing death in the fiery furnace, could respond: "Only our God can deliver us. But even if he does not, be it known to you, O King, that we will not serve your gods and we will not worship the golden statue that you have set up" (cf. Dan 3:17ff.).

Yes, behind these inscriptions is hidden the fate of countless human beings. They jar our memory, they touch our hearts. They have no desire to instill hatred in us: instead, they show us the terrifying effect of hatred. Their desire is to help our reason to see evil as evil and to reject it; their desire is to enkindle in us the courage to do good and to resist evil. They want to make us feel the sentiments expressed in the words that Sophocles placed on the lips of Antigone, as she contemplated the horror all around her: my nature is not to join in hate but to join in love.

By God's grace, together with the purification of memory demanded by this place of horror, a number of initiatives have sprung up with the aim of imposing a limit upon evil and confirming goodness. Just now I was able to bless the Center for Dialogue and Prayer. In the immediate neighborhood the Carmelite nuns carry on their life of hiddenness, knowing that they are united in a special way to the mystery of Christ's Cross and reminding us of the faith of Christians, which declares that God himself descended into the hell of suffering and suffers with us. In Oswiecim is the Center of Saint Maximilian Kolbe, and the International Center for Education about Auschwitz and the Holocaust. There is also the International House for Meetings of Young people. Near one of the old prayer houses is the Jewish Center. Finally the Academy for Human Rights is presently being established. So there is hope that this place of horror will gradually become a place for constructive thinking, and that remembrance will foster resistance to evil and the triumph of love.

At Auschwitz-Birkenau humanity walked through a "valley of darkness." And so, here in this place, I would like to end with a prayer of trust—with one of the psalms of Israel which is also a prayer of Christians: "The Lord is my shepherd, I shall not want. He makes me lie down in green pastures; he leads me beside still waters; he restores my soul. He leads me in right paths for his name's sake. Even though I walk through the valley of the shadow of death, I fear no evil; for you are with me; your rod and your staff—they comfort me...I shall dwell in the house of the Lord my whole life long" (Ps 23:1–4, 6).

40

New Tridentine Rite
Good Friday Intercession for Jews

Pope Benedict XVI, Vatican City, February 5, 2008*

Pro conversione Iudaeorum

Let us also pray for the Jews.
    May the Lord our God illuminate their hearts
    so that they may recognize Jesus Christ as savior of all men.

Let us pray.
    Almighty and everlasting God, you who want all men to be
        saved
    and to gain knowledge of the Truth,
    kindly allow that,
    as the fullness of peoples enter into your Church, all of Israel
        may be saved.
    Through Christ our Lord.

---

*Editor's Note: In response to concerns about his recent permission for wider use of the pre–Vatican Council II Tridentine Mass, which on Good Friday included a prayer for Jews that described them as "veiled" and "blind," Pope Benedict composed a new version of the prayer. Its use is required when the Tridentine Rite is employed on Good Friday. A footnote accompanying the new text indicated that the Latin title "For the conversion of the Jews" was retained.

41

Prayer at the Western Wall

Pope Benedict XVI, Jerusalem, May 12, 2009

God of all the ages,
on my visit to Jerusalem, the "City of Peace,"
spiritual home to Jews, Christians and Muslims alike,
I bring before you the joys, the hopes and the aspirations,
the trials, the suffering and the pain of all your people
    throughout the world.
God of Abraham, Isaac and Jacob,
hear the cry of the afflicted, the fearful, the bereft;
send your peace upon this Holy Land, upon the Middle East,
upon the entire human family;
stir the hearts of all who call upon your name,
to walk humbly in the path of justice and compassion.
"The Lord is good to those who wait for him,
to the soul that seeks him!" (Lam 3:25)

42

Address at Yad Vashem: "May the Names of These Victims Never Perish"

Pope Benedict XVI, Jerusalem, May 11, 2009

> *I will give in my house and within my walls a memorial and a name...*
> *I will give them an everlasting name which shall not be cut off.*
> (Isa 56:5)

This passage from the Book of the prophet Isaiah furnishes the two simple words which solemnly express the profound significance of this revered place: *yad*—"memorial"; *shem*—"name." I have come to stand in silence before this monument, erected to honor the memory of the millions of Jews killed in the horrific tragedy of the Shoah. They lost their lives, but they will never lose their names: these are indelibly etched in the hearts of their loved ones, their surviving fellow prisoners, and all those determined never to allow such an atrocity to disgrace mankind again. Most of all, their names are forever fixed in the memory of Almighty God.

One can rob a neighbor of possessions, opportunity or freedom. One can weave an insidious web of lies to convince others that certain groups are undeserving of respect. Yet, try as one might, one can never take away the name of a fellow human being. Sacred Scripture teaches us the importance of names in conferring upon someone a unique mission or a special gift. God called Abram "Abraham" because he was to become the "father of many nations" (Gen 17:5). Jacob was called "Israel" because he had "contended with God and man and prevailed" (Gen 32:29). The names enshrined in this hallowed monument will

219

forever hold a sacred place among the countless descendants of Abraham. Like his, their faith was tested. Like Jacob, they were immersed in the struggle to discern the designs of the Almighty. May the names of these victims never perish! May their suffering never be denied, belittled or forgotten! And may all people of goodwill remain vigilant in rooting out from the heart of man anything that could lead to tragedies such as this!

The Catholic Church, committed to the teachings of Jesus and intent on imitating his love for all people, feels deep compassion for the victims remembered here. Similarly, she draws close to all those who today are subjected to persecution on account of race, color, condition of life or religion—their sufferings are hers, and hers is their hope for justice. As Bishop of Rome and successor of the Apostle Peter, I reaffirm—like my predecessors—that the Church is committed to praying and working tirelessly to ensure that hatred will never reign in the hearts of men again. The God of Abraham, Isaac and Jacob is the God of peace (cf. Ps 85:9).

The Scriptures teach that it is our task to remind the world that this God lives, even though we sometimes find it difficult to grasp his mysterious and inscrutable ways. He has revealed himself and continues to work in human history. He alone governs the world with righteousness and judges all peoples with fairness (cf. Ps 9:9).

Gazing upon the faces reflected in the pool that lies in stillness within this memorial, one cannot help but recall how each of them bears a name. I can only imagine the joyful expectation of their parents as they anxiously awaited the birth of their children. What name shall we give this child? What is to become of him or her? Who could have imagined that they would be condemned to such a deplorable fate!

As we stand here in silence, their cry still echoes in our hearts. It is a cry raised against every act of injustice and violence. It is a perpetual reproach against the spilling of innocent blood. It is the cry of Abel rising from the earth to the Almighty. Professing our steadfast trust in God, we give voice to that cry using words from the Book of Lamentations which are full of significance for both Jews and Christians:

> The favors of the Lord are not exhausted, his mercies are not
> spent;
> They are renewed each morning, so great is his faithfulness.

> My portion is the Lord, says my soul; therefore will I hope in
> him.
> Good is the Lord to the one who waits for him, to the soul
> that seeks him;
> It is good to hope in silence for the saving help of the Lord.
> (Lam 3:22-26)

My dear friends, I am deeply grateful to God and to you for the opportunity to stand here in silence: a silence to remember, a silence to pray, a silence to hope.

43

Address at the Great Synagogue of Rome

Pope Benedict XVI, Rome, January 17, 2010

What marvels the Lord worked for them!
What marvels the Lord worked for us:
Indeed we were glad. (Ps 126)

How good and how pleasant it is
when brothers live in unity. (Ps 133)

Dear Chief Rabbi of the Jewish Community of Rome,
President of the Union of Italian Jewish Communities,
President of the Jewish Community of Rome,
Rabbis,
Distinguished Authorities,
Friends, Brothers and Sisters,

1.

At the beginning of this encounter in the Great Synagogue of the Jews of Rome, the psalms which we have heard suggest to us the right spiritual attitude in which to experience this particular and happy moment of grace: the praise of the Lord, who has worked marvels for us and has gathered us in his *Hèsed*, his merciful love, and thanksgiving to him for granting us this opportunity to come together to strengthen the bonds which unite us and to continue to travel together along the path of reconciliation and fraternity. I wish to express first of all my sincere gratitude to you, Chief Rabbi, Doctor Riccardo Di Segni, for your invitation and for the thoughtful words which you have addressed to me. I wish to thank also the President of the Union of Italian Jewish Communities, Mr. Renzo Gattegna, and the President of the Jewish Community of Rome, Mr. Riccardo Pacifici, for their courteous greetings. My thoughts go to the Authorities and to all present, and they extend in a special way to the entire Jewish Community of Rome and to all who have worked to bring about this moment of encounter and friendship which we now share.

When he came among you for the first time, as a Christian and as pope, my venerable predecessor John Paul II, almost twenty-four years ago, wanted to make a decisive contribution to strengthening the good relations between our two communities, so as to overcome every misconception and prejudice. My visit forms a part of the journey already begun, to confirm and deepen it. With sentiments of heartfelt appreciation, I come among you to express to you the esteem and the affection which the Bishop and the Church of Rome, as well as the entire Catholic Church, have toward this Community and all Jewish communities around the world.

2.

The teaching of the Second Vatican Council has represented for Catholics a clear landmark to which constant reference is made in our attitude and our relations with the Jewish people, marking a new and significant stage. The Council gave a strong impetus to our irrevocable commitment to pursue the path of dialogue, fraternity and friendship, a journey which has been deepened and developed in the last forty years, through important steps and significant gestures. Among them, I should mention once again the historic visit by my venerable predecessor to this Synagogue on April 13, 1986, the numerous meetings he had with Jewish representatives, both here in Rome and during his apostolic visits throughout the world, the Jubilee pilgrimage which he made to the Holy Land in the year 2000, the various documents of the Holy See which, following the Second Vatican Council's declaration *Nostra Aetate* [*Bridges*, Vol. 1, Document 30], have made helpful contributions to the increasingly close relations between Catholics and Jews. I too, in the course of my pontificate, have wanted to demonstrate my closeness to and my affection for the people of the Covenant. I cherish in my heart each moment of the pilgrimage that I had the joy of making to the Holy Land in May of last year, along with the memories of numerous meetings with Jewish communities and organizations, in particular my visits to the synagogues of Cologne and New York.

Furthermore, the Church has not failed to deplore the failings of her sons and daughters, begging forgiveness for all that could in any way have contributed to the scourge of antisemitism and anti-Judaism (cf. Commission for Religious Relations with the Jews, *We Remember: A Reflection on the Shoah*, March 16, 1998 [Document 49 below]). May these wounds be healed forever! The heartfelt prayer which Pope John Paul II offered at the Western Wall on March 26, 2000 [Document 37 above] comes back to my mind, and it calls forth a profound echo in our hearts: "God of our Fathers, you chose Abraham and his descendants to bring your Name to the nations: we are deeply saddened by the behavior of those who in the course of history have caused these children of yours to suffer, and asking your forgiveness we wish to commit ourselves to genuine brotherhood with the people of the Covenant."

3.

The passage of time allows us to recognize in the twentieth century a truly tragic period for humanity: ferocious wars that sowed destruction, death and suffering like never before; frightening ideologies, rooted in the idolatry of man, of race, and of the State, which led to brother killing brother. The singular and deeply disturbing drama of the Shoah represents, as it were, the most extreme point on the path of hatred that begins when man forgets his Creator and places himself at the center of the universe. As I noted during my visit of May 28, 2006 to the Auschwitz concentration camp, which is still profoundly impressed upon my memory, "the rulers of the Third Reich wanted to crush the entire Jewish people," and, essentially, "by wiping out this people, they intended to kill the God who called Abraham, who spoke on Sinai and laid down principles to serve as a guide for mankind, principles that remain eternally valid" [Document 39 above].

Here in this place, how could we not remember the Roman Jews who were snatched from their homes, before these very walls, and who with tremendous brutality were killed at Auschwitz? How could one ever forget their faces, their names, their tears, the desperation faced by these men, women and children? The extermination of the people of the Covenant of Moses, at first announced, then systematically programmed and put into practice in Europe under the Nazi regime, on that day tragically reached as far as Rome. Unfortunately, many remained indifferent, but many, including Italian Catholics, sustained by their faith and by Christian teaching, reacted with courage, often at risk of their lives, opening their arms to assist the Jewish fugitives who were being hunted down, and earning perennial gratitude. The Apostolic See itself provided assistance, often in a hidden and discreet way. The memory of these events compels us to strengthen the bonds that unite us so that our mutual understanding, respect and acceptance may always increase.

4.

Our closeness and spiritual fraternity find in the Holy Bible—in Hebrew *Sifre Qodesh* or "Book of Holiness"—their most stable and lasting foundation, which constantly reminds us of our common roots, our history and the rich spiritual patrimony that we share. It is in pondering her own mystery that the Church, the People of God of the New Covenant, discovers her own profound bond with the Jews, who were chosen by the Lord before all others to receive his word (cf. *Catechism of the Catholic Church*, 839). "The Jewish faith, unlike other non-Christian religions, is already a response to God's revelation in the Old Covenant. To the Jews 'belong the sonship, the glory, the covenants, the giving of the law, the worship, and the promises; to them belong the patriarchs and of their race, according to the flesh is the Christ' (Rom 9:4–5), 'for the gifts and the call of God are irrevocable!' (Rom 11:29)" (ibid).

5.

Many lessons may be learned from our common heritage derived from the Law and the Prophets. I would like to recall some of them:

first of all, the solidarity which binds the Church to the Jewish people "at the level of their spiritual identity," which offers Christians the opportunity to promote "a renewed respect for the Jewish interpretation of the Old Testament" (cf. Pontifical Biblical Commission, *The Jewish People and Their Sacred Scriptures in the Christian Bible* [Document 50 below], 2001, pp. 12 and 55); the centrality of the Decalogue as a common ethical message of permanent value for Israel, for the Church, for non-believers and for all of humanity; the task of preparing or ushering in the Kingdom of the Most High in the "care for creation" entrusted by God to man for him to cultivate and to care for responsibly (cf. Gen 2:15).

6.

In particular, the Decalogue—the "Ten Words" or Ten Commandments (cf. Exod 20:1–17; Deut 5:1–21)—which comes from the Torah of Moses, is a shining light for ethical principles, hope and dialogue, a guiding star of faith and morals for the people of God, and it also enlightens and guides the path of Christians. It constitutes a beacon and a norm of life in justice and love, a "great ethical code" for all humanity. The "Ten Commandments" shed light on good and evil, on truth and falsehood, on justice and injustice, and they match the criteria of every human person's right conscience. Jesus himself recalled this frequently, underlining the need for active commitment in living the way of the Commandments: "If you wish to enter into life, observe the Commandments" (Matt 19:17). From this perspective, there are several possible areas of cooperation and witness. I would like to recall three that are especially important for our time.

The "Ten Commandments" require that we recognize the one Lord, against the temptation to construct other idols, to make golden calves. In our world there are many who do not know God or who consider him superfluous, without relevance for their lives; hence, other new gods have been fabricated to whom man bows down. Reawakening in our society openness to the transcendent dimension, witnessing to the one God, is a precious service which Jews and Christians can offer together.

The "Ten Commandments" call us to respect life and to protect it against every injustice and abuse, recognizing the worth of each human person, created in the image and likeness of God. How often, in every part of the world, near and far, the dignity, the freedom and the rights of human beings are trampled upon! Bearing witness together to the supreme value of life against all selfishness is an important contribution to a new world where justice and peace reign, a world marked by that "shalom" which the lawgivers, the prophets and the sages of Israel longed to see.

The "Ten Commandments" call us to preserve and to promote the sanctity of the family, in which the personal and reciprocal, faithful and definitive "Yes" of man and woman makes room for the future, for the authentic humanity of each, and makes them open, at the same time, to the gift of new life. To witness that the family continues to be the essential cell of society and the basic environment in which human virtues are learned and practiced is a precious service offered in the construction of a world with a more human face.

7.

As Moses taught in the *Shema* (cf. Deut 6:5; Lev 19:34)—and as Jesus reaffirms in the Gospel (cf. Mark 12:19–31)—all of the Commandments are summed up in the love of God and loving-kindness toward one's neighbor. This Rule urges Jews and Christians to exercise, in our time, a special generosity toward the poor, toward women and children, strangers, the sick, the weak and the needy. In the Jewish tradition there is a wonderful saying of the Fathers of Israel: "Simon the Just often said: The world is founded on three things: the Torah, worship, and acts of mercy" (*Avoth* 1:2). In exercising justice and mercy, Jews and Christians are called to announce and to bear witness to the coming Kingdom of the Most High, for which we pray and work in hope each day.

8.

On this path we can walk together, aware of the differences that exist between us, but also aware of the fact that when we succeed in uniting our hearts and our hands in response to the Lord's call, his light comes closer and shines on all the peoples of the world. The progress made in the last forty years by the International Committee for Catholic-Jewish Relations and, in more recent years, by the Mixed Commission of the Chief Rabbinate of Israel and of the Holy See, are a sign of our common will to continue an open and sincere dialogue. Tomorrow here in Rome, in fact, the Mixed Commission will hold its ninth meeting, on "Catholic and Jewish Teaching on Creation and the Environment"; we wish them a profitable dialogue on such a timely and important theme.

9.

Christians and Jews share to a great extent a common spiritual patrimony, they pray to the same Lord, they have the same roots, and yet they often remain unknown to each other. It is our duty, in response to God's call, to strive to keep open the space for dialogue, for reciprocal respect, for growth in friendship, for a common witness in the face of the challenges of our time, which invite us to cooperate for the good of humanity in this world created by God, the Omnipotent and Merciful.

10.

Finally, I offer a particular reflection on this, our city of Rome, where, for nearly two millennia, as Pope John Paul II said, the Catholic Community with its Bishop and the Jewish Community with its Chief Rabbi have lived side by side. May this proximity be animated by a growing fraternal love, expressed also in closer cooperation, so that we may offer a valid contribution to solving the problems and difficulties that we still face.

I beg from the Lord the precious gift of peace in the world, above all in the Holy Land. During my pilgrimage there last May, at the Western Wall in Jerusalem, I prayed to Him who can do all things, asking: "Send your peace upon this Holy Land, upon the Middle East, upon the entire human family; stir the hearts of those who call upon your name, to walk humbly in the path of justice and compassion" (Prayer at the Western Wall of Jerusalem, May 12, 2009 [Document 41 above]).

I give thanks and praise to God once again for this encounter, asking him to strengthen our fraternal bonds and to deepen our mutual understanding.

O praise the Lord, all you nations,
acclaim him, all you peoples.
Strong is his love for us,
He is faithful forever.
Alleluia. (Ps 117)

44

"The Time of the Gentiles"

Excerpt from Jesus of Nazareth, *Part Two,* Holy Week: From the Entrance into Jerusalem to the Resurrection, *by Pope Benedict XVI, published in March, 2011**

A superficial reading or hearing of Jesus' eschatological discourse would give the impression that Jesus linked the end of Jerusalem chronologically to the end of the world, especially when we read in Matthew: "Immediately after the tribulation of those days the sun will be darkened...; then will appear the sign of the Son of man in heaven..." (24:29-30). This direct chronological connection between the end of Jerusalem and the end of the whole world seems to be further confirmed when we come across these words a few verses later: "Truly, I say to you, this generation will not pass away till all these things take place..." (24:34).

On first glance, it seems that Luke was the only one to downplay this connection. In his account we read: "They will fall by the edge of the sword, and be led captive among all nations; and Jerusalem will be trodden down by the Gentiles, until the times of the Gentiles are fulfilled" (21:24). Between the destruction of Jerusalem and the end of the world, "the times of the Gentiles" are here inserted. Luke has been accused of thereby shifting the temporal axis of the Gospels and of Jesus' original message, recasting the end of time as the intermediate time and, thus, inventing the time of the Church as a new phase of salvation history. But if we look closely, we find that these "times of the Gentiles" are also foretold, in different terms and at a different point, in the versions of Jesus' discourse recounted by Matthew and Mark.

---

*Editor's Note: The following is an excerpt from the section in Pope Benedict's book on "Jesus' Eschatological Discourse." In the final paragraphs, he answers in the negative the question of whether there should today be Christian conversionary missions aimed at Jews.

Matthew quotes the following saying of Jesus: "And this gospel of the kingdom will be preached throughout the whole world, as a testimony to all nations; and then the end will come" (24:14). And in Mark we read: "The gospel must first be preached to all nations" (13:10).

We see at once how much care is needed when making connections within this discourse of Jesus; the text is woven together from individual strands of tradition that do not present a straightforward linear argument but that must, as it were, be read in the light of one another. In the third section of this chapter ("Prophecy and Apocalyptic"), we will look in more detail at this redactional question, which is of great significance for a correct understanding of the text.

From the content, it is clear that all three Synoptic Gospels recognize a time of the Gentiles: the end of time can come only when the Gospel has been brought to all peoples. The time of the Gentiles—the time of the Church made up of all the peoples of the world—is not an invention of Saint Luke: it is the common patrimony of all the Gospels.

At this point we encounter once again the connection between the Gospel tradition and the basic elements of Pauline theology. If Jesus says in the eschatological discourse that the Gospel must first be proclaimed to the Gentiles and only then can the end come, we find exactly the same thing in Paul's Letter to the Romans: "A hardening has come upon part of Israel, until the full number of the Gentiles come in, and so all Israel will be saved" (11:25–26). The full number of the Gentiles and all Israel: in this formula we see the universalism of the divine salvific will. For our purposes, though, the important point is that Paul, too, recognizes an age of the Gentiles, which is the present and which must be fulfilled if God's plan is to attain its goal.

The fact that the early Church was unable to assess the chronological duration of these *kairoi* ("times") of the Gentiles and that it was generally assumed they would be fairly short is ultimately a secondary consideration. The essential point is that these times were both asserted and foretold and that, above all else and prior to any calculation of their duration, they had to be understood and were understood by the disciples in terms of a mission: to accomplish now what had been proclaimed and demanded—by bringing the Gospel to all peoples.

The restlessness with which Paul journeyed to the nations, so as to bring the message to all and, if possible, to fulfill the mission within his own lifetime—this restlessness can only be explained if one is aware of the historical and eschatological significance of his exclamation: "Necessity is laid upon me. Woe to me if I do not preach the gospel!" (1 Cor 9:16).

In this sense, the urgency of evangelization in the apostolic era was predicated not so much on the necessity for each individual to acquire knowledge of the Gospel in order to attain salvation, but rather on this grand conception of history: if the world was to arrive at its destiny, the Gospel had to be brought to all nations. At many stages in history, this sense of urgency has been markedly attenuated, but it has always revived, generating new dynamism for evangelization.

In this regard, the question of Israel's mission has always been present in the background. We realize today with horror how many misunderstandings with grave consequences have weighed down our history. Yet a new reflection can acknowledge that the beginnings of a correct understanding have always been there, waiting to be rediscovered, however deep the shadows.

Here I should like to recall the advice given by Bernard of Clairvaux to his pupil Pope Eugene III on this matter. He reminds the Pope that his duty of care extends not only to Christians, but: "You also have obligations toward unbelievers, whether Jew, Greek, or Gentile" (*De Consideratione* III/i, 2). Then he immediately corrects himself and observes more accurately: "Granted, with regard to the Jews, time excuses you; for them a determined point in time has been fixed, which cannot be anticipated. The full number of the Gentiles must come in first. But what do you say about these Gentiles?...Why did it seem good to the Fathers...to suspend the word of faith while unbelief was obdurate? Why do we suppose the word that runs swiftly stopped short?" (*De Consideratione* III/i, 3).

Hildegard Brem comments on this passage as follows: "In the light of Romans 11:25, the Church must not concern herself with the conversion of the Jews, since she must wait for the time fixed for this by God, 'until the full number of the Gentiles come in' (Rom 11:25). On the contrary, the Jews themselves are a living homily to which the Church must draw attention, since they call to mind the Lord's suffering (cf. Ep 363)..." (quoted in *Sämtliche Werke*, ed. Winkler, I, p. 834).

The prophecy of the time of the Gentiles and the corresponding mission is a core element of Jesus' eschatological message. The special mission to evangelize the Gentiles, which Paul received from the risen Lord, is firmly anchored in the message given by Jesus to his disciples before his Passion. The time of the Gentiles—"the time of the Church"—which, as we have seen, is proclaimed in all the Gospels, constitutes an essential element of Jesus' eschatological message.

45

Ecclesia in Medio Oriente (The Church in the Middle East) (excerpt)

An excerpt from the section on "Interreligious Dialogue" in Pope Benedict's post-synodal apostolic exhortation, issued September 14, 2012, in response to the Special Synod on the Middle East, held at the Vatican in October 2010

19. The Church's universal nature and vocation require that she engage in dialogue with the members of other religions. In the Middle East this dialogue is based on the spiritual and historical bonds uniting Christians to Jews and Muslims. It is a dialogue which is not primarily dictated by pragmatic political or social considerations, but by underlying theological concerns which have to do with faith. They are grounded in the sacred Scriptures and are clearly defined in the Dogmatic Constitution on the Church, *Lumen Gentium* [cf. *Bridges*, Vol. 1, Document 29] and in the Declaration on the Church's Relation to Non-Christian Religions, *Nostra Aetate* [*Bridges*, Vol. 1, Document 30].[17] Jews, Christians and Muslims alike believe in one God, the Creator of all men and women. May Jews, Christians and Muslims rediscover one of God's desires, that of the unity and harmony of the human family. May Jews, Christians and Muslims find in other believers brothers and sisters to be respected and loved, and in this way, beginning in their own lands, give the beautiful witness of serenity and concord between the children of Abraham. Rather than being exploited in endless conflicts which are unjustifiable for authentic believers, the acknowledgment of one God—if lived with a pure heart—can make a powerful contribution to peace in the region and to respectful coexistence on the part of its peoples.

20. The bonds uniting Christians and Jews are many and they run deep. They are anchored in a precious common spiritual heritage. There is of course our faith in one God, the Creator, who reveals himself, offers

his unending friendship to mankind and out of love desires to redeem us. There is also the Bible, much of which is common to both Jews and Christians. For both, it is the word of God. Our common recourse to sacred Scripture draws us closer to one another. Moreover, Jesus, a son of the Chosen People, was born, lived and died a Jew (cf. Rom 9:4–5). Mary, his Mother, likewise invites us to rediscover the Jewish roots of Christianity. These close bonds are a unique treasure of which Christians are proud and for which they are indebted to the Chosen People. The Jewishness of the Nazarene allows Christians to taste joyfully the world of the Promise and resolutely introduces them into the faith of the Chosen People, making them a part of that People. Yet the person and the deepest identity of Jesus also divide them, for in him Christians recognize the Messiah, the Son of God.

21. Christians ought to become more conscious of the depth of the mystery of the Incarnation in order to love God with all their heart, with all their soul and with all their might (cf. Deut 6:5). Christ, the Son of God, became flesh in a people, a faith tradition and a culture which, if better known, can only enrich the understanding of the Christian faith. Christians have come to this deeper understanding thanks to the death and resurrection of Christ (cf. Luke 24:26). But they must always be aware of and grateful for their roots. For the shoot grafted onto the ancient tree to take (cf. Rom 11:17–18), it needs the sap rising from the roots.

22. Relationships between the two communities of believers bear the marks of history and human passion. Misunderstandings and reciprocal distrust have abounded. Past persecutions, whether surreptitious or violent, are inexcusable and greatly to be deplored. And yet, despite these tragic situations, the interplay between both communities over the centuries proved so fruitful that it contributed to the birth and expansion of the civilization and culture commonly known as Judeo-Christian. It is as if these two worlds, claiming to be different or opposed for various reasons, had decided to unite in offering humanity a noble alloy. This relationship, which both unites and separates Jews and Christians, ought to open both groups to a new sense of responsibility for and with one another.[18] For both peoples have received the same blessing and the eternal promises which enable them to advance trustingly toward fraternity.

23. The Catholic Church, in fidelity to the teachings of the Second Vatican Council, looks with esteem to Muslims, who worship God

above all by prayer, almsgiving and fasting, revere Jesus as a prophet while not acknowledging his divinity, and honor Mary, his Virgin Mother. We know that the encounter of Islam and Christianity has often taken the form of doctrinal controversy. Sadly, both sides have used doctrinal differences as a pretext for justifying, in the name of religion, acts of intolerance, discrimination, marginalization and even of persecution.[19]

24. Despite this fact, Christians live daily alongside Muslims in the Middle East, where their presence is neither recent nor accidental, but has a long history. As an integral part of the Middle East, Christians have developed over the centuries a type of relationship with their surroundings which can prove instructive. They have let themselves be challenged by Muslim devotion and piety, and have continued, in accordance with their means and to the extent possible, to live by and to promote the values of the Gospel in the surrounding culture. The result has been a particular form of symbiosis. It is proper, then, to acknowledge the contribution made by Jews, Christians and Muslims in the formation of a rich culture proper to the Middle East.[20]

Notes

17. Cf. *Propositio* 40.
18. Cf. Benedict XVI, *Address at Hechal Shlomo Center, Jerusalem* (12 May 2009): AAS 101 (2009), 522–523; Propositio 41.
19. Cf. *Propositio* 5.
20. Cf. *Propositio* 42.

46

Comments on Christian-Jewish Relations

Pope Francis, Vatican City, June–November 2013*

On **Nostra Aetate** *and Interreligious Friendships:*

...I cannot fail to mention what was solemnly stated by the Second Vatican Council in paragraph 4 of the declaration *Nostra Aetate* [*Bridges*, Vol. 1, Document 30], as it remains for the Catholic Church a key point of reference for relations with the Jewish people.

In that Council text, the Church recognizes that "the beginnings of its faith and election are to be found in the patriarchs, Moses and prophets." And, with regard to the Jews, the Council recalls the teaching of Saint Paul, who wrote "the gifts and the call of God are irrevocable" and who also firmly condemned hatred, persecution and all forms of antisemitism. Due to our common roots, a Christian cannot be antisemitic!

The fundamental principles expressed by the Declaration have marked the path of greater awareness and mutual understanding trodden these last decades by Jews and Catholics, a path which my predecessors have strongly encouraged, both by very significant gestures and by the publication of a series of documents to deepen the thinking about theological bases of the relations between Jews and Christians. It is a journey for which we must surely give thanks to God.

Having said that, this is only the most visible element of a whole movement to be found here and there throughout the world, as I know

---

*Editor's Note: In the months after his election as Pope Francis on March 13, 2013, the former archbishop of Buenos Aires, Cardinal Jorge Mario Bergoglio, SJ, spoke repeatedly of the importance of Christian-Jewish relations and the significance for him personally of his friendships with many Argentinean Jews. Presented here are excerpts from some of his writings or addresses on the subject.

from personal experience. During my time as Archbishop of Buenos Aires, I had the joy of maintaining relations of sincere friendship with leaders of the Jewish world. We talked often of our respective religious identities, the image of man found in the Scriptures, and how to keep an awareness of God alive in a world now secularized in many ways. I met with them on various occasions to discuss the challenges which Jews and Christians both face. But above all, as friends, we enjoyed each other's company, we were all enriched through encounter and dialogue, and we welcomed each other, and this helped all of us grow as people and as believers.

[From "Address to the International Jewish Committee on Interreligious Consultations," June 24, 2013]

On the Importance of Dialogue:

...[I]n addition to an integral humanism which respects cultural distinctiveness and fraternal responsibility, I consider essential for facing the present moment: constructive dialogue. Between selfish indifference and violent protest there is always another possible option: that of dialogue. Dialogue between generations, dialogue with the people, because we are all people, the capacity to give and receive, while remaining open to the truth...A basic contribution in this regard is made by the great religious traditions, which play a fruitful role as a leaven of society and a life-giving force for democracy. Peaceful coexistence between different religions is favored by the laicity of the state, which, without appropriating any one confessional stance, respects and esteems the presence of the religious dimension in society, while fostering its more concrete expressions.

When leaders in various fields ask me for advice, my response is always the same: dialogue, dialogue, dialogue. It is the only way for individuals, families and societies to grow, the only way for the life of peoples to progress, along with the culture of encounter, a culture in which all have something good to give and all can receive something good in return. Others always have something to give me, if we know how to approach them in a spirit of openness and without prejudice. I call this attitude of openness and availability without prejudice "social humility," and it is this that favors dialogue. Only in this way can understanding grow between cultures and religions, mutual esteem without needless preconceptions, respectful of the rights of everyone.

Today, either we stand together with the culture of dialogue and encounter, or we all lose, we all lose; from here we can take the right road that makes the journey fruitful and secure.

[From "Address to Brazilian Leaders," July 27, 2013]

On Jewish Fidelity to God:

...[W]hat should be said to the Jewish brethren concerning the promise that God made to them: is that an empty promise? This question, believe me, is a radical one for us Christians because with the help of God, especially in the light of the Second Vatican Council, we have rediscovered that the Jewish people remain for us the holy root from which Jesus was born. I too have cultivated many friendships through the years with my Jewish brothers in Argentina and often while in prayer, as my mind turned to the terrible experience of the Shoah, I looked to God. What I can tell you, with Saint Paul, is that God has never neglected his faithfulness to the covenant with Israel, and that, through the awful trials of these last centuries, the Jews have preserved their faith in God. And for this, we, the Church and the whole human family, can never be sufficiently grateful to them. Moreover, persevering with faith in the God of the Covenant, they remind everyone, including us Christians, that we wait unceasingly as pilgrims for the return of the Lord, and that therefore we should be open to him and not remain entrenched in our achievements.

[From "A Letter to Non-Believers," September 11, 2013]

On Proselytism

Proselytism is downright nonsense; it doesn't make any sense. We need to learn to understand each other, listen to one another, and increase our knowledge about the world around us. It often happens that after one meeting I want to have another one because new ideas emerge and new needs are discovered. This is what is important: to know one another, to listen to one another, broaden the range of thought. The world is full of streets that converge and diverge; the important thing is that they lead to the Good.

[From a conversation with Dr. Eugenio Scalfari, October 21, 2013]

On Educating the Young for Dialogue

To the young, we must be able to convey not only a knowledge of the history of Jewish-Catholic dialogue about past difficulties, but also an awareness of the progress made in recent decades. Above all we must be able to transmit a passion for meeting and coming to know others, promoting an active and responsible involvement of our young people.

[From "Address to Delegation from Simon Wiesenthal Center," October 23, 2013]

On Relations with Judaism

We hold the Jewish people in special regard because their covenant with God has never been revoked, for "the gifts and the call of God are irrevocable" (Rom 11:29). The Church, which shares with Jews an important part of the sacred Scriptures, looks upon the people of the covenant and their faith as one of the sacred roots of her own Christian identity (cf. Rom 11:16–18). As Christians, we cannot consider Judaism as a foreign religion, nor do we include the Jews among those called to turn from idols and to serve the true God (cf. 1 Thess 1:9). With them, we believe in the one God who acts in history, and with them we accept his revealed word.

Dialogue and friendship with the children of Israel are part of the life of Jesus' disciples. The friendship which has grown between us makes us bitterly and sincerely regret the terrible persecutions which they have endured, and continue to endure, especially those that have involved Christians.

God continues to work among the people of the Old Covenant and to bring forth treasures of wisdom which flow from their encounter with his word. For this reason, the Church also is enriched when she receives the values of Judaism. While it is true that certain Christian beliefs are unacceptable to Judaism, and that the Church cannot refrain from proclaiming Jesus as Lord and Messiah, there exists as well a rich complementarity which allows us to read the texts of the Hebrew Scriptures together and to help one another to mine the riches of God's word. We can also share many ethical convictions and a common concern for justice and the development of peoples…

Non-Christians, by God's gracious initiative, when they are faithful to their own consciences, can live "justified by the grace of God,"[199] and thus be "associated to the paschal mystery of Jesus Christ."[200] But due to the sacramental dimension of sanctifying grace, God's working in them tends to produce signs and rites, sacred expressions which in turn bring others to a communitarian experience of journeying toward God.[201] While these lack the meaning and efficacy of the sacraments instituted by Christ, they can be channels which the Holy Spirit raises up in order to liberate non-Christians from atheistic immanentism or from purely individual religious experiences. The same Spirit everywhere brings forth various forms of practical wisdom which help people to bear suffering and to live in greater peace and harmony. As Christians, we can also benefit from these treasures built up over many centuries, which can help us better to live our own beliefs.

[From *Evangelii Gaudium* (The Joy of the Gospel), November 24, 2013]

Notes

199. International Theological Commission, *Christianity and the World Religions* (1996), 72: Enchiridion Vaticanum 15, No. 1061.
200. Ibid.
201. Cf. ibid., 81–87: Enchiridion Vaticanum 15, Nos. 1070–1076.

47

The Interpretation of the Bible in the Church (excerpt)

Pontifical Biblical Commission, Vatican City, April 23, 1993*

3. Limits

So as to remain in agreement with the saving truth expressed in the Bible, the process of actualization should keep within certain limits and be careful not to take wrong directions.

While every reading of the Bible is necessarily selective, care should be taken to avoid tendentious interpretations, that is, readings which, instead of being docile to the text make use of it only for their own narrow purposes (as is the case in the actualization practiced by certain sects, for example Jehovah's Witnesses).

Actualization loses all validity if it is grounded in theoretical principles which are at variance with the fundamental orientations of the biblical text, as, for example, a rationalism which is opposed to faith or an atheistic materialism.

Clearly to be rejected also is every attempt at actualization set in a direction contrary to evangelical justice and charity, such as, for example, the use of the Bible to justify racial segregation, antisemitism or

---

*Editor's Note: In this section of a long document, the Pontifical Biblical Commission discusses the principles, methods, and limits of the interpretive process called "actualization." This can be understood as the rereading of earlier texts in the light of new circumstances, and their application in the world of today. This brief excerpt from Section IV, A of the document specifies that certain types of actualization should be rejected as contrary to the Gospel.

sexism whether on the part of men or of women. Particular attention is necessary, according to the spirit of the Second Vatican Council (*Nostra Aetate* [*Bridges*, Vol. 1, Document 30], 4), to avoid absolutely any actualization of certain texts of the New Testament which could provoke or reinforce unfavorable attitudes to the Jewish people. The tragic events of the past must, on the contrary, impel all to keep unceasingly in mind that, according to the New Testament, the Jews remain "beloved" of God, "since the gifts and calling of God are irrevocable" (Rom 11:28–29).

False paths will be avoided if actualization of the biblical message begins with a correct interpretation of the text and continues within the stream of the living tradition, under the guidance of the church's magisterium.

In any case, the risk of error does not constitute a valid objection against performing what is a necessary task: that of bringing the message of the Bible to the ears and hearts of people of our own time.

48

Fundamental Agreement between the Holy See and the State of Israel

Issued by the Secretariat of State of the Holy See and the State of Israel, December 30, 1993

Preamble

The Holy See and the State of Israel,

Mindful of the singular character and universal significance of the Holy Land;

Aware of the unique nature of the relationship between the Catholic Church and the Jewish people, and of the historic process of reconciliation and growth in mutual understanding and friendship between Catholics and Jews;

Having decided on 29 July 1992 to establish a 'Bilateral Permanent Working Commission,' in order to study and define together issues of common interest, and in view of normalizing their relations;

Recognizing that the work of the aforementioned Commission has produced sufficient material for a first and Fundamental Agreement;

Realizing that such Agreement will provide a sound and lasting basis for the continued development of their present and future relations and for the furtherance of the Commission's task,

Agree upon the following Articles:

Article 1

The State of Israel, recalling its Declaration of Independence, affirms its continuing commitment to uphold and observe the human right to freedom of religion and conscience, as set forth in the

Universal Declaration of Human Rights and in other international instruments to which it is a party.

The Holy See, recalling the Declaration on Religious Freedom of the Second Vatican Ecumenical Council, *Dignitatis Humanae*, affirms the Catholic Church's commitment to uphold the human right to freedom of religion and conscience, as set forth in the Universal Declaration of Human Rights and in other international instruments to which it is a party. The Holy See wishes to affirm as well the Catholic Church's respect for other religions and their followers as solemnly stated by the Second Vatican Ecumenical Council in its Declaration on the Relation of the Church to Non-Christian Religions, *Nostra Aetate*.

Article 2

The Holy See and the State of Israel are committed to appropriate cooperation in combating all forms of antisemitism and all kinds of racism and of religious intolerance, and in promoting mutual understanding among nations, tolerance among communities and respect for human life and dignity.

The Holy See takes this occasion to reiterate its condemnation of hatred, persecution and all other manifestations of antisemitism directed against the Jewish people and individual Jews anywhere, at any time and by anyone. In particular, the Holy See deplores attacks on Jews and desecration of Jewish synagogues and cemeteries, acts which offend the memory of the victims of the Holocaust, especially when they occur in the same places which witnessed it.

Article 3

The Holy See and the State of Israel recognize that both are free in the exercise of their respective rights and powers, and commit themselves to respect this principle in their mutual relations and in their cooperation for the good of the people.

The State of Israel recognizes the right of the Catholic Church to carry out its religious, moral, educational and charitable functions, and to have its own institutions, and to train, appoint and deploy its own personnel in the said institutions or for the said functions to these ends. The Church recognizes the right of the State to carry out its functions, such as promoting and protecting the welfare and the safety of the people. Both the State and the Church recognize the need for dialogue and cooperation in such matters as by their nature call for it.

Concerning Catholic legal personality at canon law the Holy See and the State of Israel will negotiate on giving it full effect in Israeli law, following a report from a joint subcommission of experts.

Article 4

The State of Israel affirms its continuing commitment to maintain and respect the "Status quo" in the Christian Holy Places to which it applies and the respective rights of the Christian communities thereunder. The Holy See affirms the Catholic Church's continuing commitment to respect the aforementioned "Status quo" and the said rights.

The above shall apply notwithstanding an interpretation to the contrary of any Article in this Fundamental Agreement.

The State of Israel agrees with the Holy See on the obligation of continuing respect for and protection of the character proper to Catholic sacred places, such as churches, monasteries, convents, cemeteries and their like.

The State of Israel agrees with the Holy See on the continuing guarantee of the freedom of Catholic worship.

Article 5

The Holy See and the State of Israel recognize that both have an interest in favoring Christian pilgrimages to the Holy Land. Whenever the need for coordination arises, the proper agencies of the Church and of the State will consult and cooperate as required.

The State of Israel and the Holy See express the hope that such pilgrimages will provide an occasion for better understanding between the pilgrims and the people and religions in Israel.

Article 6

The Holy See and the State of Israel jointly reaffirm the right of the Catholic Church to establish, maintain and direct schools and institutes of study at all levels, this right being exercised in harmony with the rights of the State in the field of education.

Article 7

The Holy See and the State of Israel recognize a common interest in promoting and encouraging cultural exchanges between Catholic institutions worldwide, and educational, cultural and research institutions in Israel, and in facilitating access to manuscripts, historical documents and similar source materials, in conformity with applicable laws and regulations.

Article 8

The State of Israel recognizes that the right of the Catholic Church to freedom of expression in the carrying out of its functions is exercised also through the Church's own communications media, this right being exercised in harmony with the rights of the State in the field of communications media.

Article 9

The Holy See and the State of Israel jointly reaffirm the right of the Catholic Church to carry out its charitable functions through its health care and social welfare institutions, this right being exercised in harmony with the rights of the State in this field.

Article 10

The Holy See and the State of Israel jointly reaffirm the right of the Catholic Church to property.

Without prejudice to rights relied upon by the Parties:

The Holy See and the State of Israel will negotiate in good faith a comprehensive agreement, containing solutions acceptable to both Parties, on unclear, unsettled and disputed issues concerning property, economic and fiscal matters relating to the Catholic Church generally, or to specific Catholic Communities or institutions.

For the purpose of the said negotiations, the Permanent Bilateral Working Commission will appoint one or more bilateral subcommissions of experts to study the issues and make proposals.

The Parties intend to commence the aforementioned negotiations within three months of entry into force of the present Agreement, and aim to reach agreement within two years from the beginning of the negotiations.

During the period of these negotiations, actions incompatible with these commitments shall be avoided.

Article 11

The Holy See and the State of Israel declare their respective commitment to the promotion of the peaceful resolution of conflicts among States and nations, excluding violence and terror from international life.

The Holy See, while maintaining in every case the right to exercise its moral and spiritual teaching office, deems it opportune to recall that, owing to its own character, it is solemnly committed to remaining a stranger to all merely temporal conflicts, which principle applies specifically to disputed territories and unsettled borders.

Article 12

The Holy See and the State of Israel will continue to negotiate in good faith in pursuance of the Agenda agreed upon in Jerusalem on 15 July, 1992 and confirmed at the Vatican on 9 July 1992; likewise on issues arising from Articles of the present Agreement, as well as on other issues bilaterally agreed upon as objects of negotiation.

Article 13

In this Agreement the Parties use these terms in the following sense:

The Catholic Church and the Church—including, inter alia, its Communities and institutions,

Communities of the Catholic Church—meaning the Catholic religious entities considered by the Holy See as Churches sui juris and by the State of Israel as Recognized Religious Communities;

The State of Israel and the State—including, inter alia, its authorities established by law.

Notwithstanding the validity of this Agreement as between the Parties, and without detracting from the generality of any applicable rule of law with reference to treaties, the Parties agree that this Agreement does not prejudice rights and obligations arising from existing treaties between either Party and a State or States, which are known and in fact available to both Parties at the time of the signature of this Agreement.

Article 14

Upon signature of the present Fundamental Agreement and in preparation for the establishment of full diplomatic relations, the Holy See and the State of Israel exchange Special Representatives, whose rank and privileges are specified in an Additional Protocol.

Following the entry into force and immediately upon the beginning of the implementation of the present Fundamental Agreement, the Holy See and the State of Israel will establish full diplomatic relations at the level of Apostolic Nunciature, on the part of the Holy See, and Embassy, on the part of the State of Israel.

Article 15

This Agreement shall enter into force on the date of the latter notification of ratification by a Party.

FOR THE GOVERNMENT OF THE STATE OF ISRAEL

FOR THE HOLY SEE

Done in two original copies in the English and Hebrew languages, both texts being equally authentic. In case of divergency, the English text shall prevail.

Signed in Jerusalem, this 30th day of the month of December, in the year 1993, which corresponds to the 16th day of the month of Tevet, in the year 5754.

[signed by:]
Mr. Yossi Beilin, Deputy Foreign Minister for the State of Israel
Msgr. Claudio Celli, Assistant Secretary of State for the Holy See

49

We Remember:
A Reflection on the Shoah

Commission for Religious Relations with the Jews, Vatican City, March 16, 1998

I. The Tragedy of the Shoah and the Duty of Remembrance

The twentieth century is fast coming to a close and a new Millennium of the Christian era is about to dawn. The 2000th anniversary of the Birth of Jesus Christ calls all Christians, and indeed invites all men and women, to seek to discern in the passage of history the signs of divine Providence at work, as well as the ways in which the image of the Creator in man has been offended and disfigured.

This reflection concerns one of the main areas in which Catholics can seriously take to heart the summons which Pope John Paul II has addressed to them in his Apostolic Letter *Tertio Millennio Adveniente*: "It is appropriate that, as the Second Millennium of Christianity draws to a close, the Church should become more fully conscious of the sinfulness of her children, recalling all those times in history when they departed from the spirit of Christ and his Gospel and, instead of offering to the world the witness of a life inspired by the values of faith, indulged in ways of thinking and acting which were truly forms of counter-witness and scandal."[1]

This century has witnessed an unspeakable tragedy, which can never be forgotten: the attempt by the Nazi regime to exterminate the Jewish people, with the consequent killing of millions of Jews. Women and men, old and young, children and infants, for the sole reason of their Jewish origin, were persecuted and deported. Some were killed immediately, while others were degraded, ill-treated, tortured and utterly robbed of their human dignity, and then murdered. Very few of those who entered the Camps survived, and those who did remained scarred for life. This was the Shoah. It is a major fact of the history of this century, a fact which still concerns us today.

Before this horrible genocide, which the leaders of nations and Jewish communities themselves found hard to believe at the very moment when it was mercilessly being put into effect, no one can remain indifferent, least of all the Church, by reason of her very close bonds of spiritual kinship with the Jewish people and her remembrance of the injustices of the past. The Church's relationship to the Jewish people is unlike the one she shares with any other religion.[2] However, it is not only a question of recalling the past. The common future of Jews and Christians demands that we remember, for "there is no future without memory."[3] History itself is *memoria futuri*.

In addressing this reflection to our brothers and sisters of the Catholic Church throughout the world, we ask all Christians to join us in meditating on the catastrophe which befell the Jewish people, and on the moral imperative to ensure that never again will selfishness and hatred grow to the point of sowing such suffering and death.[4] Most especially, we ask our Jewish friends, "whose terrible fate has become a symbol of the aberrations of which man is capable when he turns against God,"[5] to hear us with open hearts.

II. What We Must Remember

While bearing their unique witness to the Holy One of Israel and to the Torah, the Jewish people have suffered much at different times and in many places. But the Shoah was certainly the worst suffering of all. The inhumanity with which the Jews were persecuted and massacred during this century is beyond the capacity of words to convey. All this was done to them for the sole reason that they were Jews.

The very magnitude of the crime raises many questions. Historians, sociologists, political philosophers, psychologists and theologians are all trying to learn more about the reality of the Shoah and its causes. Much scholarly study still remains to be done. But such an event cannot be fully measured by the ordinary criteria of historical research alone. It calls for a "moral and religious memory" and, particularly among Christians, a very serious reflection on what gave rise to it.

The fact that the Shoah took place in Europe, that is, in countries of long-standing Christian civilization, raises the question of the relation

between the Nazi persecution and the attitudes down the centuries of
Christians toward Jews.

III. Relations Between Jews and Christians

The history of relations between Jews and Christians is a tormented one. His Holiness Pope John Paul II has recognized this fact
in his repeated appeals to Catholics to see where we stand with regard
to our relations with the Jewish people.[6] In effect, the balance of these
relations over two thousand years has been quite negative.[7]

At the dawn of Christianity, after the crucifixion of Jesus, there
arose disputes between the early Church and the Jewish leaders and
people who, in their devotion to the Law, on occasion violently
opposed the preachers of the Gospel and the first Christians. In the
pagan Roman Empire, Jews were legally protected by the privileges
granted by the Emperor, and the authorities at first made no distinction between Jewish and Christian communities. Soon however,
Christians incurred the persecution of the State. Later, when the
Emperors themselves converted to Christianity, they at first continued to guarantee Jewish privileges. But Christian mobs who attacked
pagan temples sometimes did the same to synagogues, not without
being influenced by certain interpretations of the New Testament
regarding the Jewish people as a whole. "In the Christian world—I do
not say on the part of the Church as such—erroneous and unjust
interpretations of the New Testament regarding the Jewish people
and their alleged culpability have circulated for too long, engendering
feelings of hostility toward this people."[8] Such interpretations of the
New Testament have been totally and definitively rejected by the
Second Vatican Council.[9]

Despite the Christian preaching of love for all, even for one's enemies, the prevailing mentality down the centuries penalized minorities
and those who were in any way "different." Sentiments of anti-Judaism
in some Christian quarters, and the gap which existed between the
Church and the Jewish people, led to a generalized discrimination,
which ended at times in expulsions or attempts at forced conversions.
In a large part of the "Christian" world, at the end of the eighteenth
century, those who were not Christian did not always enjoy a fully
guaranteed juridical status. Despite that fact, Jews throughout

Christendom held on to their religious traditions and communal customs. They were therefore looked upon with a certain suspicion and mistrust. In times of crisis such as famine, war, pestilence or social tensions, the Jewish minority was sometimes taken as a scapegoat and became the victim of violence, looting, even massacres.

By the end of the eighteenth century and the beginning of the nineteenth century, Jews generally had achieved an equal standing with other citizens in most States and a certain number of them held influential positions in society. But in that same historical context, notably in the nineteenth century, a false and exacerbated nationalism took hold. In a climate of eventful social change, Jews were often accused of exercising an influence disproportionate to their numbers. Thus there began to spread in varying degrees throughout most of Europe an anti-Judaism that was essentially more sociological and political than religious.

At the same time, theories began to appear which denied the unity of the human race, affirming an original diversity of races. In the twentieth century, National Socialism in Germany used these ideas as a pseudo-scientific basis for a distinction between so called Nordic-Aryan races and supposedly inferior races. Furthermore, an extremist form of nationalism was heightened in Germany by the defeat of 1918 and the demanding conditions imposed by the victors, with the consequence that many saw in National Socialism a solution to their country's problems and cooperated politically with this movement.

The Church in Germany replied by condemning racism. The condemnation first appeared in the preaching of some of the clergy, in the public teaching of the Catholic Bishops, and in the writings of lay Catholic journalists. Already in February and March 1931, Cardinal Bertram of Breslau, Cardinal Faulhaber and the Bishops of Bavaria, the Bishops of the Province of Cologne and those of the Province of Freiburg published pastoral letters condemning National Socialism, with its idolatry of race and of the State.[10] The well-known Advent sermons of Cardinal Faulhaber in 1933, the very year in which National Socialism came to power, at which not just Catholics but also Protestants and Jews were present, clearly expressed rejection of the Nazi antisemitic propaganda.[11] In the wake of the Kristallnacht, Bernard Lichtenberg, Provost of Berlin Cathedral, offered public prayers for the Jews. He was later to die at Dachau and has been declared Blessed.

Pope Pius XI too condemned Nazi racism in a solemn way in his Encyclical Letter *Mit brennender Sorge*,[12] which was read in German churches on Passion Sunday 1937, a step which resulted in attacks and sanctions against members of the clergy. Addressing a group of Belgian pilgrims on September 6, 1938, Pius XI asserted: "Antisemitism is unacceptable. Spiritually, we are all Semites."[13] Pius XII, in his very first Encyclical, *Summi Pontificatus*,[14] of October 20, 1939, warned against theories which denied the unity of the human race and against the deification of the State, all of which he saw as leading to a real "hour of darkness."[15]

IV. Nazi Antisemitism and the Shoah

Thus we cannot ignore the difference which exists between antisemitism based on theories contrary to the constant teaching of the Church on the unity of the human race and on the equal dignity of all races and peoples, and the long-standing sentiments of mistrust and hostility that we call anti-Judaism, of which unfortunately, Christians also have been guilty.

The National Socialist ideology went even further, in the sense it refused to acknowledge any transcendent reality as the source of life and the criterion of moral good. Consequently, a human group, and the State with which it was identified, arrogated to itself an absolute status and determined to remove the very existence of the Jewish people, a people called to witness to the one God and the Law of the Covenant. At the level of theological reflection we cannot ignore the fact that not a few in the Nazi party not only showed aversion to the idea of divine Providence at work in human affairs, but gave proof of a definite hatred directed at God himself. Logically, such an attitude also led to a rejection of Christianity, and a desire to see the Church destroyed or at least subjected to the interests of the Nazi state.

It was this extreme ideology which became the basis of the measures taken, first to drive the Jews from their homes and then to exterminate them. The Shoah was the work of a thoroughly modern neo-pagan regime. Its antisemitism had its roots outside of Christianity and, in pursuing its aims, it did not hesitate to oppose the Church and persecute her members also.

But it may be asked whether the Nazi persecution of the Jews was not made easier by the anti-Jewish prejudices imbedded in some

Christian minds and hearts. Did anti-Jewish sentiment among Christians make them less sensitive, or even indifferent, to the persecution launched against the Jews by National Socialism when it reached power?

Any response to this question must take into account that we are dealing with the history of people's attitudes and ways of thinking, subject to multiple influences. Moreover, many people were altogether unaware of the "final solution" that was being put into effect against a whole people; others were afraid for themselves and those near to them; some took advantage of the situation; and still others were moved by envy. A response would need to be given case by case. To do this, however, it is necessary to know what precisely motivated people in a particular situation.

At first the leaders of the Third Reich sought to expel the Jews. Unfortunately, the governments of some Western countries of Christian tradition, including some in North and South America, were more than hesitant to open their borders to the persecuted Jews. Although they could not foresee how far the Nazi hierarchs would go in their criminal intentions, the leaders of those nations were aware of the hardships and dangers to which Jews living in the territories of the Third Reich were exposed. The closing of borders to Jewish emigration in those circumstances, whether due to any anti-Jewish hostility or suspicion, political cowardice or shortsightedness, or national selfishness, lays a heavy burden of conscience on the authorities in question.

In the lands where the Nazis undertook mass deportations, the brutality which surrounded these forced movements of helpless people should have led to suspect the worst. Did Christians give every possible assistance to those being persecuted, and in particular to the persecuted Jews?

Many did, but others did not. Those who did help to save Jewish lives as much as was in their power, even to the point of placing their own lives in danger, must not be forgotten. During and after the war, Jewish communities and Jewish leaders expressed their thanks for all that had been done for them, including what Pope Pius XII did personally or through his representatives to save hundreds of thousands of Jewish lives.[16] Many Catholic bishops, priests, religious and laity have been honored for this reason by the State of Israel.

Nevertheless, as Pope John Paul II has recognized, alongside such courageous men and women, the spiritual resistance and concrete

action of other Christians was not that which might have been
expected from Christ's followers. We cannot know how many
Christians in countries occupied or ruled by the Nazi powers or their
allies were horrified at the disappearance of their Jewish neighbors and
yet were not strong enough to raise their voices in protest. For
Christians, this heavy burden of conscience of their brothers and sisters during the Second World War must be a call to penitence.[17]

We deeply regret the errors and failures of those sons and daughters of the Church. We make our own what is said in the Second
Vatican Council's Declaration *Nostra Aetate* [*Bridges*, Vol. 1, Document
30], which unequivocally affirms: "The Church...mindful of her common patrimony with the Jews, and motivated by the Gospel's spiritual
love and by no political considerations, deplores the hatred, persecutions and displays of antisemitism directed against the Jews at any time
and from any source."[18]

We recall and abide by what Pope John Paul II, addressing the leaders of the Jewish community in Strasbourg in 1988, stated: "I repeat
again with you the strongest condemnation of antisemitism and racism,
which are opposed to the principles of Christianity."[19] The Catholic
Church therefore repudiates every persecution against a people or
human group anywhere, at any time. She absolutely condemns all
forms of genocide, as well as the racist ideologies that give rise to
them. Looking back over this century, we are deeply saddened by the
violence that has enveloped whole groups of peoples and nations. We
recall in particular the massacre of the Armenians, the countless victims in Ukraine in the 1930s, the genocide of the Gypsies, which was
also the result of racist ideas, and similar tragedies which have
occurred in America, Africa and the Balkans. Nor do we forget the
millions of victims of totalitarian ideology in the Soviet Union, in
China, Cambodia and elsewhere. Nor can we forget the drama of the
Middle East, the elements of which are well known. Even as we make
this reflection, "many human beings are still their brothers' victims."[20]

V. Looking Together to a Common Future

Looking to the future of relations between Christians and Jews, in
the first place we appeal to our Catholic brothers and sisters to renew

the awareness of the Hebrew roots of their faith. We ask them to keep in mind that Jesus was a descendant of David; that the Virgin Mary and the Apostles belonged to the Jewish people; that the Church draws sustenance from the root of that good olive tree on to which have been grafted the wild olive branches of the Gentiles (cf. Rom 11:17–24); that the Jews are our dearly beloved brothers, indeed in a certain sense they are "our elder brothers."[21]

At the end of this Millennium the Catholic Church desires to express her deep sorrow for the failures of her sons and daughters in every age. This is an act of repentance (*teshuva*), since, as members of the Church, we are linked to the sins as well as the merits of all her children. The Church approaches with deep respect and great compassion the experience of extermination, the Shoah, suffered by the Jewish people during World War II. It is not a matter of mere words, but indeed of binding commitment. "We would risk causing the victims of the most atrocious deaths to die again if we do not have an ardent desire for justice, if we do not commit ourselves to ensure that evil does not prevail over good as it did for millions of children of the Jewish people...Humanity cannot permit all that to happen again."[22]

We pray that our sorrow for the tragedy which the Jewish people has suffered in our century will lead to a new relationship with the Jewish people. We wish to turn awareness of past sins into a firm resolve to build a new future in which there will be no more anti-Judaism among Christians or anti-Christian sentiment among Jews, but rather a shared mutual respect, as befits those who adore the one Creator and Lord and have a common father in faith, Abraham.

Finally, we invite all men and women of good will to reflect deeply on the significance of the Shoah . The victims from their graves, and the survivors through the vivid testimony of what they have suffered, have become a loud voice calling the attention of all of humanity. To remember this terrible experience is to become fully conscious of the salutary warning it entails: the spoiled seeds of anti-Judaism and anti-semitism must never again be allowed to take root in any human heart.

—Cardinal Edward Idris Cassidy, President
—The Most Reverend Pierre Duprey, Vice-President
—The Reverend Remi Hoeckman, O.P., Secretary

Notes

1. Pope John Paul II, Apostolic Letter *Tertio Millennio Adveniente*, November 10, 1994, 33: *AAS* 87 (1995), 25.

2. Cf. Pope John Paul II, *Address at the Great Synagogue of Rome*, April 13, 1986 [Document 27 above], 4: *AAS* 78 (1986), 1120.

3. Pope John Paul II, *Angelus Prayer*, June 11, 1995: *Insegnamenti* 18/1, 1995, 1712.

4. Pope John Paul II, *Address to Jewish Leaders in Budapest*, August 18, 1991, 4: *Insegnamenti* 14/2, 1991, 349.

5. Pope John Paul II, Encyclical Letter *Centesimus Annus*, May 1, 1991, 17: *AAS* 83 (1991), 814–15.

6. Cf. Pope John Paul II, *Address to Delegates of Episcopal Conferences for Catholic-Jewish Relations*, March 6, 1982 [*Bridges*, Vol. 1, Document 35]: *Insegnamenti* 5/1, 1982, 743–47.

7. Cf. Holy See's Commission for Religious Relations with the Jews, *Notes on the Correct Way to Present the Jews and Judaism in Preaching and Catechesis in the Roman Catholic Church*, June 24, 1985 [*Bridges*, Vol. 1, Document 39], VI, 1: *Ench. Vat.* 9, 1656.

8. Cf. Pope John Paul II, *Address to Symposium on the Roots of Anti-Judaism*, October 31, 1997 [Document 33 above], 1: *L'Osservatore Romano*, November 1, 1997, p. 6.

9. Cf. Second Vatican Ecumenical Council, *Nostra Aetate* [*Bridges*, Vol. 1, Document 30], 4.

10. Cf. B. Statiewski, ed. *Akten Deutscher Bischöfe Über die Lage der Kirche*, 1933–1945, vol. I, 1933-1934 (Mainz 1968), Appendix.

11. Cf. L. Volk, *Der Bayerische Episkopat und der Nationalsoziaismus* 1930–1934 (Mainz 1966), pp. 170–74.

12. The Encyclical is dated March 14, 1937: *AAS* 29 (1937), 145–67.

13. *La Documentation Catholique*, 29 (1938), col. 1460.

14. *AAS* 31 (1939), 413–53.

15. *Ibid.*, 449.

16. The wisdom of Pope Pius XII's diplomacy was publicly acknowledged on a number of occasions by representatives of Jewish Organizations and personalities. For example, on September 7, 1945, Dr. Joseph Nathan, who represented the Italian Hebrew Communities, stated: "Above all, we acknowledge the Supreme Pontiff and the religious men and women who, executing the directives of the Holy Father, recognized the persecuted as their brothers and, with effort and abnegation, hastened to help us, disregarding the terrible dangers to which they were exposed" (*L'Osservatore Romano*, September 8, 1945, p. 2). On September 21 of that same year, Pius XII received in audience Dr. A. Leo Kubowitzki, Secretary General of the World Jewish Congress who came

to present "to the Holy Father, in the name of the Union of Israelitic Communities, warmest thanks for the efforts of the Catholic Church on behalf of Jews throughout Europe during the War" (*L'Osservatore Romano*, September 23, 1945, p. 1). On Thursday, November 29, 1945, the Pope met about eighty representatives of Jewish refugees from various concentration camps in Germany, who expressed "their great honor at being able to thank the Holy Father personally for his generosity toward those persecuted during the Nazi-Fascist period" (*L'Osservatore Romano*, November 30, 1945, p. 1). In 1958, at the death of Pope Pius XII, Golda Meir sent an eloquent message: "We share in the grief of humanity. When fearful martyrdom came to our people, the voice of the Pope was raised for its victims. The life of our times was enriched by a voice speaking out about great moral truths above the tumult of daily conflict. We mourn a great servant of peace."

17. Cf. Pope John Paul II, *Address to the New Ambassador of the Federal Republic of Germany to the Holy See* [Document 30 above], November 8, 1990, 2: *AAS* 83 (1991), 587–88.

18. *Loc. cit.*, no. 4.

19. *Address to Jewish Leaders*, Strasbourg, October 9, 1988, no. 8: *Insegnamenti* 11/3, 1988, 1134.

20. Pope John Paul II, *Address to the Diplomatic Corps*, January 15, 1994, 9: *AAS* 86 (1994), 816.

21. Pope John Paul II, *Address at the Great Synagogue of Rome*, April 13, 1986 [Document 27 above], 4: *AAS* 78 (1986), 1120.

22. Pope John Paul II, *Address on the Occasion of a Commemoration of the Shoah, April 7, 1994,* 3: *Insegnamenti* 17/1, 1994, 897 and 893.

50

The Jewish People
and Their Sacred Scriptures
in the Christian Bible (excerpt)

Pontifical Biblical Commission, Vatican City, May 24, 2001

II. Fundamental Themes in the Jewish Scriptures and
Their Reception into Faith in Christ

19. To the Jewish Scriptures which it received as the authentic Word of God, the Christian Church added other Scriptures expressing its faith in Jesus, the Christ. It follows then that the Christian Bible is not composed of one "Testament," but two "Testaments," the Old and the New, which have complex, dialectical relationships between them. A study of these relationships is indispensable for anyone who wishes to have a proper appreciation of the links between the Christian Church and the Jewish people. The understanding of these relationships has changed over time. The present chapter offers firstly an overview of these changes, followed by a more detailed study of the basic themes common to both Testaments.

A. Christian Understanding of the Relationships between the Old and New Testaments

1. *Affirmation of a reciprocal relationship*

By "Old Testament" the Christian Church has no wish to suggest that the Jewish Scriptures are outdated or surpassed.[37] On the contrary, it has always affirmed that the Old Testament and the New Testament are inseparable. Their first relationship is precisely that. At the beginning of the second century, when Marcion wished to discard the Old Testament, he met with vehement resistance from the post-apostolic Church. Moreover, his rejection of the Old Testament led him to disregard a major portion of the New—he retained only the Gospel of Luke and some Pauline Letters—which clearly showed that his position was indefensible. It is in the light of the Old Testament that the New understands the life, death and glorification of Jesus (cf. 1 Cor 15:3–4).

This relationship is also reciprocal: on the one hand, the New Testament demands to be read in the light of the Old, but it also invites a "re-reading" of the Old in the light of Jesus Christ (cf. Luke 24:45). How is this "re-reading" to be done? It extends to "all the Scriptures" (Luke 24:27) to "everything written in the Law of Moses, the Prophets and the Psalms" (24:44), but the New Testament only offers a limited number of examples, not a methodology.

2. Re-reading the Old Testament in the Light of Christ

The examples given show that different methods were used, taken from their cultural surroundings, as we have seen above.[38] The texts speak of typology[39] and of reading in the light of the Spirit (2 Cor 3:14–17). These suggest a twofold manner of reading, in its original meaning at the time of writing, and a subsequent interpretation in the light of Christ.

In Judaism, re-readings were commonplace. The Old Testament itself points the way. For example, in the episode of the manna, while not denying the original gift, the meaning is deepened to become a symbol of the Word through which God continually nourishes his people (cf. Deut 8:2–3). The Books of Chronicles are a re-reading of the Book of Genesis and the Books of Samuel and Kings. What is specific to the Christian re-reading is that it is done, as we have said, in the light of Christ.

This new interpretation does not negate the original meaning. Paul clearly states that "the very words of God were entrusted" to the Israelites (Rom 3:2) and he takes it for granted that these words of God could be read and understood before the coming of Christ. Although he speaks of a blindness of the Jews with regard to "the reading of the

Old Testament" (2 Cor 3:14), he does not mean a total incapacity to read, only an inability to read it in the light of Christ.

3. Allegorical Re-reading

20. The Hellenistic world had different methods of which Christian exegesis made use as well. The Greeks often interpreted their classical texts by allegorizing them. Commenting on ancient poetry like the works of Homer, where the gods seem to act like capricious and vindictive humans, scholars explained this in a more religious and morally acceptable way by emphasizing that the poet was expressing himself in an allegorical manner when he wished to describe only human psychological conflicts, the passions of the soul, using the fiction of war between the gods. In this case, a new and more spiritual meaning replaced the original one.

Jews in the diaspora sometimes utilized this method, in particular to justify certain prescriptions of the Law which, taken literally, would appear nonsensical to the Hellenistic world. Philo of Alexandria, who had been nurtured in Hellenistic culture, tended in this direction. He developed, often with a touch of genius, the original meaning, but at other times he adopted an allegorical reading that completely overshadowed it. As a result, his exegesis was not accepted in Judaism.

In the New Testament, there is a single mention of "things spoken allegorically" (*allgoroumena*: Gal 4:24), but here it is a question of typology, that is, the persons mentioned in the ancient text, are presented as evoking things to come, without the slightest doubt being cast on their historicity. Another Pauline text uses allegory to interpret a detail of the Law (1 Cor 9:9), but he never adopted this method as a general rule.

The Fathers of the Church and the medieval authors, in contrast, make systematic use of it for the entire Bible, even to the least detail—both for the New Testament as well as for the Old—to give a contemporary interpretation capable of application to the Christian life. For example, Origen sees the wood used by Moses to sweeten the bitter waters (Exod 15:22–25) as an allusion to the wood of the cross; he sees the scarlet thread used by Rahab as a means of recognizing her house (Josh 2:18), as an allusion to the blood of the Savior. Any detail capable of establishing contact between an Old Testament episode and Christian realities was exploited. In every page of the Old Testament, in addition, many direct and specific allusions to Christ and the

Christian life were found, but there was a danger of detaching each detail from its context and severing the relationship between the biblical text and the concrete reality of salvation history. Interpretation then became arbitrary.

Certainly, the proposed teaching had a certain value because it was animated by faith and guided by a comprehensive understanding of Scripture read in the Tradition. But such teaching was not based on the commentated text. It was superimposed on it. It was inevitable, therefore, that at the moment of its greatest success, it went into irreversible decline.

4. Return to the Literal Sense

Thomas Aquinas saw clearly what underpinned allegorical exegesis: the commentator can only discover in a text what he already knows, and in order to know it, he had to find it in the literal sense of another text. From this Thomas Aquinas drew the conclusion: a valid argument cannot be constructed from the allegorical sense, it can only be done from the literal sense.[40]

Starting from the Middle Ages, the literal sense has been restored to a place of honor and has not ceased to prove its value. The critical study of the Old Testament has progressed steadily in that direction culminating in the supremacy of the historical-critical method.

And so an inverse process was set in motion: the relation between the Old Testament and Christian realities was now restricted to a limited number of Old Testament texts. Today, there is the danger of going to the opposite extreme of denying outright, together with the excesses of the allegorical method, all Patristic exegesis and the very idea of a Christian and Christological reading of Old Testament texts. This gave rise in contemporary theology, without as yet any consensus, to different ways of re-establishing a Christian interpretation of the Old Testament that would avoid arbitrariness and respect the original meaning.

5. The Unity of God's Plan and the Idea of Fulfilment

21. The basic theological presupposition is that God's salvific plan which culminates in Christ (cf. Eph 1:3–14) is a unity, but that it is realized progressively over the course of time. Both the unity and the

gradual realization are important; likewise, continuity in certain points and discontinuity in others. From the outset, the action of God regarding human beings has tended toward final fulfillment and, consequently, certain aspects that remain constant began to appear: God reveals himself, calls, confers a mission, promises, liberates, makes a covenant. The first realizations, though provisional and imperfect, already give a glimpse of the final plenitude. This is particularly evident in certain important themes which are developed throughout the entire Bible, from Genesis to Revelation: the way, the banquet, God's dwelling among men. Beginning from a continuous re-reading of events and texts, the Old Testament itself progressively opens up a perspective of fulfillment that is final and definitive. The Exodus, the primordial experience of Israel's faith (cf. Deut 6:20–25; 26:5–9) becomes the symbol of final salvation. Liberation from the Babylonian Exile and the prospect of an eschatological salvation are described as a new Exodus.[41] Christian interpretation is situated along these lines with this difference, that the fulfillment is already substantially realized in the mystery of Christ.

The notion of fulfillment is an extremely complex one,[42] one that could easily be distorted if there is a unilateral insistence either on continuity or discontinuity. Christian faith recognizes the fulfillment, in Christ, of the Scriptures and the hopes of Israel, but it does not understand this fulfillment as a literal one. Such a conception would be reductionist. In reality, in the mystery of Christ crucified and risen, fulfillment is brought about in a manner unforeseen. It includes transcendence.[43] Jesus is not confined to playing an already fixed role—that of Messiah—but he confers, on the notions of Messiah and salvation, a fullness which could not have been imagined in advance; he fills them with a new reality; one can even speak in this connection of a "new creation."[44] It would be wrong to consider the prophecies of the Old Testament as some kind of photographic anticipations of future events. All the texts, including those which later were read as messianic prophecies, already had an immediate import and meaning for their contemporaries before attaining a fuller meaning for future hearers. The messiahship of Jesus has a meaning that is new and original.

The original task of the prophet was to help his contemporaries understand the events and the times they lived in from God's viewpoint. Accordingly, excessive insistence, characteristic of a certain apologetic, on the probative value attributable to the fulfillment of prophecy must be discarded. This insistence has contributed to harsh judgments by Christians of Jews and their reading of the Old Testament: the more reference to Christ is found in Old Testament texts, the more the incredulity of the Jews is considered inexcusable and obstinate.

Insistence on discontinuity between both Testaments and going beyond former perspectives should not, however, lead to a one-sided spiritualization. What has already been accomplished in Christ must yet be accomplished in us and in the world. The definitive fulfillment will be at the end with the resurrection of the dead, a new heaven and a new earth. Jewish messianic expectation is not in vain. It can become for us Christians a powerful stimulant to keep alive the eschatological dimension of our faith. Like them, we too live in expectation. The difference is that for us the One who is to come will have the traits of the Jesus who has already come and is already present and active among us.

6. Current Perspectives

The Old Testament in itself has great value as the Word of God. To read the Old Testament as Christians then does not mean wishing to find everywhere direct reference to Jesus and to Christian realities. True, for Christians, all the Old Testament economy is in movement toward Christ; if then the Old Testament is read in the light of Christ, one can, retrospectively, perceive something of this movement. But since it is a movement, a slow and difficult progression throughout the course of history, each event and each text is situated at a particular point along the way, at a greater or lesser distance from the end. Retrospective re-readings through Christian eyes mean perceiving both the movement toward Christ and the distance from Christ, prefiguration and dissimilarity. Conversely, the New Testament cannot be fully understood except in the light of the Old Testament.

The Christian interpretation of the Old Testament is then a differentiated one, depending on the different genres of texts. It does not blur the difference between Law and Gospel, but distinguishes carefully the successive phases of revelation and salvation history. It is a theological interpretation, but at the same time historically grounded. Far from excluding historical-critical exegesis, it demands it.

Although the Christian reader is aware that the internal dynamism of the Old Testament finds its goal in Jesus, this is a retrospective perception whose point of departure is not in the text as such, but in the events of the New Testament proclaimed by the apostolic preaching. It cannot be said, therefore, that Jews do not see what has been proclaimed in the text, but that the Christian, in the light of Christ and in the Spirit, discovers in the text an additional meaning that was hidden there.

7. Contribution of Jewish Reading of the Bible

22. The horror in the wake of the extermination of the Jews (the Shoah) during the Second World War has led all the Churches to rethink their relationship with Judaism and, as a result, to reconsider their interpretation of the Jewish Bible, the Old Testament. It may be asked whether Christians should be blamed for having monopolized the Jewish Bible and reading there what no Jew has found. Should not Christians henceforth read the Bible as Jews do, in order to show proper respect for its Jewish origins?

In answer to the last question, a negative response must be given for hermeneutical reasons. For to read the Bible as Judaism does necessarily involves an implicit acceptance of all its presuppositions, that is, the full acceptance of what Judaism is, in particular, the authority of its writings and rabbinic traditions, which exclude faith in Jesus as Messiah and Son of God.

As regards the first question, the situation is different, for Christians can and ought to admit that the Jewish reading of the Bible is a possible one, in continuity with the Jewish Sacred Scriptures from the Second Temple period, a reading analogous to the Christian reading which developed in parallel fashion. Both readings are bound up with the vision of their respective faiths, of which the readings are the result and expression. Consequently, both are irreducible.

On the practical level of exegesis, Christians can, nonetheless, learn much from Jewish exegesis practiced for more than two thousand years, and, in fact, they have learned much in the course of history.[45] For their part, it is to be hoped that Jews themselves can derive profit from Christian exegetical research.

Notes

37. ...Today in certain circles there is a tendency to use "First Testament" to avoid any negative connotation attached to "*Old* Testament." But "Old Testament" is a biblical and traditional expression which of itself does not have a negative connotation: the Church fully recognizes the importance of the Old Testament.

38. Cf. I.D: "Jewish Exegetical Methods employed in the New Testament," nos. 12–15.

39. Cf. Rom 5:14; 1 Cor 10:6; Heb 9:24; 1 Pet 3:21.

40. Thomas Aquinas, *Summa Theologica*, 1a, q. 1, a. 10ad 1um; cf. also *Quodl.* VII, 616m.

41. Isa 35:1–10; 40:1–5; 43:1–22; 48:12–21; 62.

42. Cf. below II B.9 and C, nos. 54–65.

43. "Non solum impletur, verum etiam transcenditur," Ambroise Autpert, quoted by H. de Lubac, *Exégèse médiévale*, II.246.

44. 2 Cor 5:17; Gal 6:15.

45. Cf. the document of the Pontifical Biblical Commission, *The Interpretation of the Bible in the Church*, I.C.2: "Approach through Recourse to Jewish Traditions of Interpretation."

51

Dominus Iesus (The Lord Jesus)

Address by Cardinal Walter Kasper at the meeting of the International Catholic-Jewish Liaison Committee, New York, May 1, 2001*

1.

The Declaration *Dominus Iesus*, published in September 2000 by the Congregation for the Doctrine of the Faith, has sparked off various reactions by different people and communities, also by Jews.

Obviously, there have been some misunderstandings. The highly technical language of this document for the instruction of Catholic theologians—a document that is perhaps a little too densely written—raised misunderstandings on the very meaning and intention of the text among people who are not very familiar with Catholic theological "jargon" and with the rules of its correct interpretation. Many of these reactions appear to be based on information which obviously uninformed secular mass-media have thrown into the arena of public opinion.

On the other hand, some substantial difficulty which theologically informed Jews might have had with the document would be more

---

*Editor's Note: On August 6, 2000, the Congregation for the Doctrine of the Faith issued an instruction called "*Dominus Iesus* [The Lord Jesus]: Declaration on the Unicity and Salvific Universality of Christ and the Church." In discussing non-Christian religions, it described them in the category of "belief," the product of human striving toward the transcendent, and not in the category of "faith," the result of divine revelation like Christianity. Since Judaism is by definition a non-Christian religion, some questioned if this delegitimized Judaism as an authentic "faith," thereby contradicting Catholic teaching that the Hebrew Scriptures were divinely revealed. In light of this, Cardinal Kasper, in his first official address as the new president of the Pontifical Commission for Religious Relations with the Jews, considered the special status of Judaism in Catholic thought.

understandable, since it expresses matters—such as the interpretation of Jesus as the Son of God—on which Jews and Christians have parted ways many centuries ago. These differences deserve mutual respect. But, at the same time, they evoke painful memories of the past. This is why the document was often painful for Jews. It was not its intention to hurt or offend. But it did, and for this I can only express my profound regret. My friends' pains are also my pains.

2.

But what was and what is the very problem? The problem raised by this text is linked with the intention of the document. The Declaration mainly deals with Interreligious Dialogue. But it is not itself in a dialogue either with Hindus, nor Moslems nor Jews. It argues against some newer relativistic and to some degree syncretistic theories among Christian theologians, theories spread in India and in the Western so-called postmodern world as well, which advocate a pluralistic vision of religion and classify both Jewish and Christian religion under the category of "world religions." It argues against theories that deny the specific identity of Jewish and Christian religion, and do not take into account the distinction between faith as answer to God's revelation and belief as human search for God and human religious wisdom. Thus, the Declaration defends the specific revelation character of the Hebrew Bible too, which we Christians call the Old Testament, against theories claiming, for example, that the Holy Books of Hinduism are the Old Testament for Hindus.

But this gave rise to misunderstandings. Some Jewish readers tend to think that the Church's attitude toward Jews and Judaism is a subcategory of its attitude toward world religions in general. Yet, such a presumption is a mistake, and so is the presumption that the document represents "a backward step in a concerted attempt to overturn the [in this case Catholic-Jewish] dialogue of recent decades." I am quoting here a comment made by a Jewish scholar.

This misunderstanding can be avoided if the Declaration is read and interpreted—as any magisterial document should—in the larger context of all other official documents and declarations, which are by no means cancelled, revoked or nullified by this document. Read in this wider context, we must say that, with regard to the above-mentioned presumption, Catholic-Jewish relations are not a subset of interreligious relations in general, neither in theory or in practice. In practice: remember that our Commission for Religious Relations with the Jews is not attached to the Pontifical Council for Interreligious Dialogue, but to the Pontifical Council which is responsible for the promotion of the ecumenical dialogue. In theory: remember that Judaism, in the mind of the Church, is unique among the world's religions, because, as *Nostra Aetate* [*Bridges*, Vol. 1, Document 30] states, it is "the root of that good olive tree onto which have been grafted the wild olive branches of the Gentiles" (cf. St. Paul in his letter to the Romans, 11:17–24). Or, as Pope John Paul II has put it on more than one occasion, "our two religious communities are connected and closely related at the very level of their religious identities" (his addresses of March 12, 1979, and March 6, 1982 [*Bridges*, Vol. 1, Documents 32 and 35]); and during his historic visit to the Synagogue of Rome on April 13, 1986 [Document 27 above]: "The Jewish religion is not 'extrinsic' to us, but in a certain way is 'intrinsic' to our own religion. With Judaism, therefore, we have a relationship which we do not have with any other religion. You are our dearly beloved brothers and, in a certain way, it could be said that you are our elder brothers."

On March 6, 1982, the Pope referred to "the faith and religious life of the Jewish people as they are professed and practiced still today." In fact, also the *Notes on the Correct Way to Present the Jews and Judaism in Preaching and Catechesis in the Roman Catholic Church*, published by our Commission on June 24, 1985 [*Bridges*, Vol. 1, Document 39], are concerned that Judaism is not presented in Catholic teaching as being merely a historical and archeological reality. It refers to "the permanent reality of the Jewish people"—"the people of God of the Old Covenant, which has never been revoked" (John Paul II on November 17, 1980, in Mainz [*Bridges*, Vol. 1, Document 34])—as a "living reality closely related to the Church." In fact, the *Notes* remind us, Catholics, that "Abraham is truly the father of our faith (cf. Rom 4:11–12; Roman Canon: *patriarchae nostri Abrahae*). And it is said (1 Cor 10:1): 'Our fathers were all under the cloud, and all passed through the sea.'"

Indeed *Dominus Iesus* also specifically acknowledges the divine revelation in the Hebrew Bible, in contrast to the sacred books of other religions.

Against some relativistic theories that subordinate both Jewish and Christian religion in the category of world religions, this document, referring to the II Vatican Council, states: "The Church's tradition, however, reserves the designation of inspired texts to the canonical books of the Old and New Testament, since these are inspired by the Holy Spirit."

Thus the document *Dominus Iesus* does not affect Catholic-Jewish relations in a negative way. Because of its purpose, it does not deal with the question of the theology of Catholic-Jewish relations, proclaimed by *Nostra Aetate*, and of subsequent Church teaching. What the document tries to "correct" is another category, namely the attempts by some Christian theologians to find a kind of "universal theology" of interreligious relations, which, in some cases, has led to indifferentism, relativism and syncretism. Against such theories we, as Jews and Christians, are on the same side, sitting in the same boat; we have to fight, to argue and to bear witness together. Our common self-understanding is at stake.

I think that Cardinal Joseph Ratzinger, the Prefect of the Congregation for the Doctrine of the Faith, has clarified these questions in his article *"L'eredità di Abramo"* (The Heritage of Abraham, in *L'Osservatore Romano*, December 29, 2000) where he writes: "It is evident that dialogue of us Christians with the Jews stands on a different level with regard to the dialogue with the other religions. The faith witnessed in the Bible of the Jews, the Old Testament of Christians, is for us not a different religion but the foundation of our own faith." I think this is a clear statement, to which I have nothing to add.

3.

Besides the already mentioned main problem raised by *Dominus Iesus*, there are other questions that I cannot deal with in this paper, since they would need a much more thorough discussion. These questions have already been object of our dialogue and should be on the agenda also in the future. In this context, I can only mention them, without claiming to solve them. Neither has *Dominus Iesus* the intention to enter these issues: they are beyond its intra-theological and intra-catholic intention.

One of these questions is how to relate the covenant with the Jewish people, which according to St. Paul is unbroken and not revoked but still in vigor, with what we Christians call the New covenant. As you know, the old theory of substitution is gone since Vatican Council II. For us Christians today the covenant with the Jewish people is a living heritage, a living reality. There cannot be a mere coexistence between the two covenants. Jews and Christians, by their respective specific identities, are intimately related to each other. It is impossible now to enter the complex problem of how this intimate relatedness should or could be defined. Such a question touches the mystery of Jewish and Christian existence as well, and should be discussed in our further dialogue.

The only thing I wish to say is that the document *Dominus Iesus* does not state that everybody needs to become a Catholic in order to be saved by God. On the contrary, it declares that God's grace, which is the grace of Jesus Christ according to our faith, is available to all. Therefore, the Church believes that Judaism, i.e., the faithful response of the Jewish people to God's irrevocable covenant, is salvific for them, because God is faithful to his promises.

This touches the problem of mission toward Jews, a painful question with regard to forced conversion in the past. *Dominus Iesus*, as other official documents, raised this question again, saying that dialogue is a part of *evangelization*. This stirred Jewish suspicion. But this is a language problem, since the term *evangelization*, in official Church documents, cannot be understood in the same way it is commonly interpreted in everyday's speech. In strict theological language, *evangelization* is a very complex and overall term, and reality. It implies presence and witness, prayer and liturgy, proclamation and catechesis, dialogue and social work. Now, presence and witness, prayer and liturgy, dialogue and social work, which are all part of *evangelization*, do not have the goal of increasing the number of Catholics. Thus *evangelization*, if understood in its proper and theological meaning, does not imply any attempt of proselytism whatsoever.

On the other hand, the term *mission*, in its proper sense, is referred to conversion from false gods and idols to the true and one God, who revealed himself in the salvation history with his elected people. Thus mission, in this strict sense, cannot be used with regard to Jews, who believe in the true and one God. Therefore—and this is characteristic— [there] does not exist any Catholic missionary organization for Jews.

There is dialogue with Jews; no mission in this proper sense of the word toward them. But what is *dialogue*? Certainly—as we learned from Jewish philosophers such as Martin Buber—it is more than small talk and mere exchange of opinions. It is also different from academic dispute, however important academic dispute may be within dialogue. Dialogue implies personal commitments and witness of one's own conviction and faith. Dialogue communicates one's faith and, at the same time, requires profound respect for the conviction and faith of the partner. It respects the difference of the other and brings mutual enrichment.

With this kind of dialogue we Catholics will continue in the future; with this kind of dialogue we can continue after *Dominus Iesus*. *Dominus Iesus* is not the end of dialogue but a challenge for a further and even more intensive dialogue. We need this dialogue for our own identity and for the sake of the world. In today's world, we, Jews and Christians, have a common mission: together we should give an orientation. Together we must be ambassadors of peace and bring about *Shalom*.

52

Address on the Thirty-seventh Anniversary of *Nostra Aetate* (excerpt)

Cardinal Walter Kasper, Rome, October 28, 2002

October 28 is a very important date in the hearts of Jews and Christians. [On] that day, thirty-six years ago, the Ecumenical Council Vatican II approved, after years of hard work and much effort, *Nostra Aetate*, the statement by which the Catholic Church intended to mark a new approach to religions and to Judaism [*Bridges*, Vol. 1, Document 30]. In the works of the Council, the link between the brotherly attitude toward Jews and the brotherly attitude toward all believers is dictated by various reasons: if, on one side, the need for purification and penitence for the tragic effects of antisemitism, to which the Church has not been completely estranged, was strong, on the other it wanted to stress that the state of current concrete political affairs was such as to urge not to forget that the disquieting and pacifying mystery inscribed in every man's heart addressed Christians in all parts of the vast worlds, where precious legacies of faith and hope are expressed in the great religions.

Since 1965 many things have occurred. In our memory we want to especially retain the meeting in Assisi fifteen years ago, the pilgrimage of the Pope to Jerusalem, the many encounters that at every level have made possible a respectful and blessed exchange: through these, rediscovering fraternity, we Catholics became aware with greater clarity that the faith of Israel is that of our elder brothers, and, most importantly, that Judaism is as a sacrament of every otherness that as such the Church must learn to discern, recognize and celebrate. It is therefore proper [on] this date for the Pontifical Council to welcome and to encourage any initiative favoring the growth of a bond with Judaism, with its theological and spiritual wealth, and with the culture that is expressed by it. From this starting point—in theological dialogue, in daily diplomatic relationships, in the cultural contact of public opinions—it is possible to embark again on the development of a fruitful encounter.

Today, under the weight of mournful and horrifying events of war, everything appears more arduous: from the city of Jerusalem, dear to the heart and the lips of every man of peace, to many other cities in the United States and the world, it seems that what *Nostra Aetate* and the solemnity of the supreme conciliar teaching wanted to teach the Church has suddenly been overrun by current events. But this is precisely the moment to start again and October 28 marks this effort toward hope, which is more powerful than the fears and the mistakes that have been committed in the past and will be committed in the future.

53

Striving for Mutual Respect
in Modes of Prayer

Cardinal Walter Kasper, L'Osservatore Romano, *April 16, 2008*

I.

The Good Friday prayer for the Jews has a long history. The new formulation of the petition in the extraordinary rite (Roman Missal of 1962) presented by Pope Benedict XVI was timely because on the Jewish side several phrases were felt to be offensive, and were also considered objectionable by many Catholics. The new formulation has made significant improvements over the text of 1962. It has, however, also led to fresh irritations and raised fundamental questions among both Jews and Christians.[1]

The sensitivities aroused on the Jewish side are to a large extent based on emotional rather than rational reasons. But we must nevertheless not hastily dismiss them as hypersensitivity. Even among our Jewish friends who have been taking part in intensive dialogue with Christians for decades, collective memories of compulsory catechesis and forced conversions remain vivid. The traumatic memory of the Shoah is a constituent identifying characteristic of the Jewish community of today. Many Jews consider a mission to the Jews as a threat to their existence; some even speak of it as a Shoah by different means. Therefore, a high degree of sensitivity is still required in relations between Jews and Christians.

II.

Explanations of the reformulated Good Friday prayer have in the meantime been able to clear up the most obvious misunderstandings. The very fact that the Good Friday intercession in the Missal of 1970—the one in the Ordinary Rite used in the overwhelming majority of cases—is to remain fully in force indicates that the reformulated petition, which is used by a very small number of congregations, cannot represent a backward step, reversing the advances made in the Second Vatican Council's declaration *Nostra Aetate* [*Bridges*, Vol. 1, Document 30]. That is all the more so since the substance of *Nostra Aetate* is also present in the formally higher-ranking Constitution on the Church *Lumen Gentium* (n. 16) [cf. *Bridges*, Vol. 1, Document 29]; and consequently, on principle, there is no going back. In addition, since the Council many statements have been made by the popes, including the present Pope, which make reference to *Nostra Aetate* and reaffirm its significance.

As distinct from the text of 1970, the reformulated 1962 text speaks of Jesus as the Christ, the Savior of all mankind and therefore also of the Jews. Many have seen this statement as new and unfriendly toward the Jews. But it is grounded in the whole of the New Testament (cf. 1 Tim 2:4), and it points to the universally acknowledged fundamental difference standing between Christians and Jews. Even if this is not expressly spoken of in *Nostra Aetate* or in the petition of 1970, *Nostra Aetate* cannot be detached from the context of all the other Council documents, any more than the Good Friday prayer of the 1970 Missal can be detached from the whole of the Good Friday liturgy, which is centered precisely on this Christian belief. The reformulation of the Good Friday prayer of 1962 does not therefore say anything really new, but simply expresses what has until now always been taken for granted as self-evident, but which has apparently not been sufficiently raised as an issue in many dialogues.[2]

In the past the belief in Christ which distinguishes Christians from Jews has frequently been made a "language of contempt" (Jules Isaac), with all the evil consequences that have arisen from that. When we strive for mutual respect today, we are striving for mutual recognition of each other in our difference. Therefore, we do not expect of the Jews that they agree with the Christological content of the Good Friday prayer, but we do expect them to respect that we as Christians pray in accordance with our belief, just as we evidently do as regards their mode of prayer. In this regard both sides still have much to learn.

III.

The really controversial question is: Should Christians pray for the conversion of the Jews? Can there be a mission to the Jews? In the reformulated prayer the word conversion does not occur. But it is indirectly incorporated in the petition for the enlightenment of the Jews so that they may recognize Jesus Christ. In addition, the Missal of 1962 contains headings for the individual petitions. The heading for the intercession for the Jews was not altered; it still reads, as it did previously, "*Pro conversione Judaeorum*": "For the conversion of the Jews." Many Jews have read the new formulation through the lens of this heading, and that has called forth the reactions I have already described.

In response to that, one can point to the fact that in contrast to some evangelical circles, the Catholic Church has no organized or institutionalized mission to the Jews. To say this is to clarify the question of a mission to the Jews factually but not theologically. It is the virtue of the reformulation of the Good Friday petition that in the second part it gives a first indication of a fundamental theological response.

The text proceeds once more from the 11th chapter of the Letter to the Romans, which also forms the basis of *Nostra Aetate*.[3] The salvation of the Jews is, for St Paul, a profound mystery of election through divine grace (9:14–29). God's gifts are irrevocable and God's promises to his people have not been revoked by him in spite of their disobedience (9:6; 11:1, 29). The hardening of Israel becomes a boon for the salvation of the Gentiles. The wild branches of the Gentiles have been grafted onto the holy rootstock of Israel (11:16ff.). But God has the power to graft in again the broken-off branches (11:23). When the full number of the Gentiles has entered into salvation, the whole of Israel will be saved (11:25ff.). So Israel remains the bearer of the promise and the blessing.

Paul speaks in apocalyptic language of a mystery (11:25). That means more than the fact that the Jews are sometimes an enigma to other peoples, or that to others their existence bears witness to God. Paul understands mystery as the eternal will of God for salvation which has been revealed in history through the apostle's proclamation. In concrete terms he is referring to Isaiah 59:20 and Jeremiah 31:33ff. In this way he is referring to the eschatological gathering of the peoples on Zion as promised by the prophets and by Jesus, and to the universal peace (*shalom*) that will then arise.[4] Paul sees the whole of his missionary activity among the Gentiles from this eschatological perspective. His mission is to prepare the gathering of the peoples which, when the full number of the Gentiles has entered, will serve the salvation of the Jews and bring forth eschatological peace for the world.

So one can say: God will bring about the salvation of Israel in the end, not on the basis of a mission to the Jews but on the basis of the mission to the Gentiles, when the fullness of the Gentiles has entered. He alone who has caused the hardening of the majority of the Jews can dissolve that hardening again. He will do so when "the Deliverer" comes from Zion (Rom 11:26). On the basis of Paul's use of language (cf. 1 Thess 1:10), that can be none other than Christ at his return. In fact, Jews and Gentiles have the same Lord (Rom 10:12).[5]

IV.

The reformulated Good Friday prayer gives expression to this hope in a prayer of intercession directed to God.[6] Basically, with this prayer the Church is repeating the petition in the Lord's Prayer: "Thy kingdom come" (Matt 6:10; Luke 11:2), and the early Christian liturgical cry "*Maranatha*": "Come Lord Jesus, come soon" (1 Cor 16:22; Rev 22:20: Did 10, 6). Such petitions for the coming of the Kingdom of God and for the realization of the mystery of salvation are not by nature a call to the Church to undertake missionary action to the Jews. Rather, they respect the whole depth of the *Deus absconditus*, of his election through grace, of the hardening and of his infinite mercy. So in this prayer the Church does not take it upon herself to orchestrate the realization of the unfathomable mystery. She cannot do so. Instead, she lays the when and the how entirely in God's hands. God alone can bring about the Kingdom of God in which the whole of Israel is saved and eschatological peace is bestowed on the world.

In order to support this interpretation one can refer to a text of Bernard of Clairvaux, which says that we do not have to concern ourselves with the Jews, for God himself will take care of them.[7] The correctness of this interpretation is demonstrated once more by the concluding doxology of the 11th chapter of the Letter to the Romans: "O the depth of the riches and wisdom and knowledge of God! How unsearchable are his judgments and how inscrutable his ways!" (11:33). This doxology demonstrates once more that the issue here is the glorification in adoration of God and of his unsearchable election through grace, and not a call to some kind of action, not even to mission.

V.

The exclusion of an intentional and institutional mission to the Jews does not mean that Christians should sit about with their hands in their laps. One must distinguish between intentional and organized mission on the one hand and Christian witness on the other. Naturally, wherever appropriate, Christians must offer witness before their elder brothers and sisters in the faith of Abraham (John Paul II) to their faith and the richness and beauty of their belief in Jesus Christ. That is what Paul did. On his missionary journeys each time he went first to the synagogue and only when he found no faith there did he go to the Gentiles (Acts 13:5, 14ff., 42–52; 14:1–6ff.; principally Rom 1:16).

Such witness is demanded of us today too. It should certainly be done tactfully and respectfully; but it would be dishonest if Christians in their encounters with Jewish friends remained silent about their faith or denied it. We expect the same of believing Jews toward us. In the dialogues with which I am familiar this behavior is altogether normal. An honest dialogue between Jews and Christians is only possible on the basis, first, of our shared belief in one God, Creator of heaven and earth, and in the promises given to Abraham and the fathers; and on the other hand in awareness and respect for the fundamental distinction, which consists in our belief in Jesus as the Christ and the Redeemer of all mankind.

The widespread misunderstanding of the reformulated Good Friday prayer is a sign of how great a task still lies before us in Jewish-Christian dialogue. The problems which have arisen should therefore give us occasion to further clarify and deepen the foundations and the goals of the Jewish-Christian dialogue. If a deepening of the dialogue could be initiated in this way, the recent controversy would in the end lead to a good result. We must of course be aware that the dialogue between Jews and Christians will by its very nature always remain difficult and fragile, and will demand a high degree of sensitivity from both sides.

Notes

1. An overview of the first reactions "pro and con" can be found in: *Il Regno*, n. 1029, 2008, 89–91. Apart from such reactions in the media, the Holy See's Commission for Religious Relations with the Jews has in the meantime collected a series of thorough and detailed position statements primarily from the U.S.A., Germany and Italy: see R. di Segni, "La preghiera per gli ebrei," in: *Shalom* 2008, n. 3, 4–7.

2. This does not apply to the international Jewish-Christian dialogue, in which this question arose following the declaration *Dominus Iesus* (2000). The Holy See's Commission for Religious Relations with the Jews has taken this into account and conducted expert discussions in Ariccia, Italy; Louvain, Belgium; and Frankfurt, Germany; the next conversation in Notre Dame (Indiana, U.S.A.) is already being planned.

3. On interpretation I refer above all to the detailed commentary of Thomas of Aquinas, *Super ad Romanos*, ch. 11 lectio 1–5, which is also very fruitful regarding this question. More recent commentaries: E. Peterson, *Der Brief an die Römer* (Ausgew. Schriften, 6), Wurzburg, 1997, 312–30, esp. 323; E. Kasemann, An die Römer (HNT 8a), Tubingen, 1973, 298–308; H. Schlier, Der Römerbrief, (HTHKNT, 6), Freiburg im Breisgau, 1977, 320–50, esp. 337–41; O. Kuss, Der Römerbrief, 3. Lieferung, Regensburg, 1978, 809–25; U. Wilckens, Der Brief an die Römer (EKK, Vl/2), Zürich-Neukirchen, 1980, 234–74, esp. 252–57. Fundamental: the document of the Pontifical Bible Commission *Das jüdische Volk und seine heilige Schrift in der christlichen Bibel* (2001). Also F. Mussner, *Traktat über die Juden*, Munich, 1979, 52–67; J. Ratzinger, *La Chiesa, Israele e le religioni del mondo*, Turin, 2000; J. M. Lustiger, La promessa, Paris, 2002; W. Kasper, "L'antica e la nuova alleanza nel dialogo ebraicocristiano", in: *Nessuno è perduto, Comunione, dialogo ecumenico, evangelizzazione*, Bologna, 2005, 95–119. In addition, a wealth of more recent literature on the question of Jewish-Christian dialogue, mainly in English.

4. Important texts include Is 2:2–5; 49:9–13; 60; Mi 4:1–3 u.a. On this subject: J. Jeremias, Jesu Verheißung für die Völker, Göttingen, 1959.

5. This raises the most fundamental theological issue in current Jewish-Christian dialogue: Is there one single covenant or [are there] two parallel covenants for Jews and Christians? The core issue here is the universality of

salvation in Jesus Christ, which from the Christian perspective is inalienable. See the overview of older literature on this topic in J. T. Pawlikowski, *Judentum und Christentum*, in: TRE 18 (1988) 386–403; on the basis of interventions by myself and others, Pawlikowski has advanced his position significantly and given a thorough report of the current state of this discussion in: "Reflections on Covenant and Mission," in: *Themes in Jewish-Christian Relations*, ed. E. Kessler and M. J. Wright, Cambridge, England, 2005, 273–99.

6. The prayer has altered this text to the extent that it speaks of the entry of the Gentiles "into the Church," which is not found in Paul. That has led some Jewish critics to draw the conclusion that it means the entry of Israel into the Church, which in turn is not stated in the prayer. In the sense of the Apostle Paul one should rather say that the salvation of the greater part of the Jews will indeed be mediated by Jesus Christ, but not by entry into the Church. At the end of days, when the Kingdom of God becomes a final reality, there will no longer be a visible Church. The point here is that at the end of days the one people of God, consisting of Jews and Gentiles who have become faithful, will once more be one and reconciled.

7. Bernard of Clairvaux, *De consideratione*, III, 1, 3. See also: *Sermones super Cantica Canticorum*, Sermo 79, 5.

54

Christians Called to Be Faithful to Abraham's Heritage

An address by Cardinal Kurt Koch at the Jerusalem Studies Institute, Jerusalem, May 24, 2012

The unique but complex history between Christians and Jews[1]

In most countries in Europe today we live in increasingly multi-religious societies in which other religions no longer appear to us Christians as alien phenomena, but instead as realties that we encounter in our daily life, especially since they have taken on a tangible and personal face in everyday contact with believers of other religions. These multi-religious societies represent both an opportunity and a danger for Jewish-Christian encounters. They are an opportunity to the extent that today's society has to have an open ear for the world of the religions and must accordingly display a great readiness for interreligious dialogue. The danger however consists in the fact that even the relationship between Judaism and Christianity may today be located within interreligious dialogue, and thereby be reduced to just another variant of interreligious dialogue, so that its distinctive uniqueness is no longer taken into account.

That for us Christians Judaism is not just one religion among many, but that the relationship between Christianity and Judaism involves an individual and unique connection, finds its expression already in our history, though in a most painful form. For this history proves to be very complex, oscillating between proximity and distance, between familiarity and alienation, between love and hate—and it has been so from the very beginning. On the one hand Jesus cannot be understood without Judaism, the early Christian congregation quite naturally participated in the Jewish liturgy in the temple, and Paul too

283

on his various mission journeys always went to the synagogues first before turning to the Gentiles with his proclamation of the gospel. On the other hand, the schism between synagogue and church formed the first split in the history of the church, which the Catholic theologian Erich Przywara defined as the "primal rift," from which he derived the subsequent progressive loss of wholeness of the Catholica.[2] Even though contemporary research tends to accept that the process of estrangement and dissociation between Judaism and Christianity extended over a longer period than previously assumed and surely only gradually took shape during the second century after the destruction of the Second Temple in 70 AD, there is nevertheless no question that this process was set in place at the very beginning of Jewish-Christian relations, and the relationship between Jews and Christians was marked by conflict already at an early stage. Cardinal Joseph Ratzinger outlined that conflict in these words: "The church was regarded by her mother as an unnatural daughter, while the Christians regarded the mother as blind and obstinate."[3] While this image reminds us that the conflicts between Jews and Christians were still like family quarrels, the relationship between Jews and Christians deteriorated progressively as the awareness of belonging to the same family was gradually lost. It has therefore in the course of history been exposed to great strain and hostility, which has in many cases unfortunately led to anti-Jewish attitudes involving outbreaks of violence and pogroms against the Jews.

Pagan antisemitism and Christian anti–Judaism

The distinctive uniqueness of Jewish-Christian relations in its negative aspect is permanently connected with its history in the past century. The mass murder of European Jews, planned and executed with industrial perfection by the National Socialists, has more than ever before made the Jewish-Christian relationship historically unique. The Shoah must be judged as the lowest possible nadir of that primitive racist antisemitism of Nazi ideology which had developed already in the nineteenth century. This thoroughly racist antisemitism is of course fundamentally alien to Christianity, and was repeatedly sharply condemned by Popes Pius XI and Pius XII above all. The Shoah can and should not however be attributed to Christianity as such: it was in fact led by a godless, anti-Christian and neo-pagan ideology. The Goebbels diaries at the latest have brought to light the fact that Hitler hated Christianity just as much as Judaism, and that he saw in Catholicism above all the virtual Trojan Horse of Judaism within Christianity. Thus we read in these diaries for example Goebbels' statement about Hitler: "The Führer is deeply religious but deeply anti-Christian. He sees in Christianity a symptom of decay, a branch of the Jewish race, an absurdity which he intends to gradually undermine on all fronts. He hates Christianity, which transformed the light and airy temple of antiquity into a gloomy cathedral with a pain-wracked crucified Christ."[4]

If the Shoah must therefore be judged as the horrific nadir of a neo-pagan world view which intended to annihilate not only Judaism but also the Jewish heritage in Christianity, one can also understand that Pope Benedict XVI during his visit to the extermination camp Auschwitz-Birkenau wished to give expression to this fatal connection: "By destroying Israel they ultimately wanted to tear up the taproot of the Christian faith and to replace it with a faith of their own invention: faith in the rule of man, the rule of the powerful."[5] In these words by the Pope one should not see, as has so often been done, an evasion of the guilty complicity of Christians, but rather recognize his conviction that Christianity is most profoundly rooted in Judaism, and that Christianity could not exist without these vital Jewish roots.[6] With deep shame we Christians must also acknowledge that Hitler, with his joint rejection of both Judaism and Christianity, had grasped the true essence of Christianity and its intrinsic relationship with Judaism better that not a few Christians themselves. This shared National Socialist hostility should have aroused among us Christians much more empathetic compassion than in fact did come into effect.

We Christians therefore have every cause to remember our complicity in the horrific developments, and above all to confess that Christian resistance to the boundless inhuman brutality of the ideologically and racially based National Socialism did not display that vigor and clarity which one should by rights have expected. Resistance by Christians may well have also been so inadequate because a theological Christian anti-Judaism had been in effect for centuries, fostering a widespread antisemitic apathy against the Jews. Thus an ancient anti-Jewish legacy was embedded in the furrows of the souls of not a few Christians. We Christians must therefore sincerely regret that only the unparalleled crime of the Shoah was able to bring about a genuine re-thinking.

The new beginning at the Second Vatican Council, and remaining dangers

In this regard the fourth chapter of the Second Vatican Council declaration *Nostra Aetate* [*Bridges*, Vol. 1, Document 30], which the German Cardinal Augustin Bea was commissioned to prepare and which was promulgated by Pope Paul VI in 1965 after controversial discussions during the last session of the Council, enabled a fundamental new beginning in the relationship between Jews and Christians.[7] With this declaration the Second Vatican Council not only repudiated and condemned all outbreaks of hatred, persecutions, slanders and manifestations of force directed against the Jews on the part of so-called Christians. In a positive sense the Council also affirmed the shared patrimony of Jews and Christians, and pointed to the Jewish roots of Christianity. Finally the Council expressed the ardent desire that the reciprocal understanding and the resulting mutual respect of Jews and Christians be fostered. This demands above all that the unique and distinctive individual relationship between Christianity and Judaism must be recalled into Christian consciousness and remain present there, as it was expressed by Pope John Paul II in the vivid and impressive words: "The Jewish religion is not something 'extrinsic' to us but in a certain way is 'intrinsic' to our own religion. With Judaism we therefore have a relationship we do not have with any other religion. You are our dearly beloved brothers and in a certain way it could be said, our elder brothers."[8]

These instructions contained in *Nostra Aetate* have been reaffirmed and reinforced on a number of occasions by the popes in the period since the Council, not least through the visits to the Great Synagogue in Rome by Pope John Paul II on April 13, 1986 and by Pope Benedict XVI on January 17, 2010 [cf. Documents 27 and 43 above]. The epoch-making new course set by the Council regarding the relationship between Jews and Christians is of course repeatedly put to the test. On the one hand the scourge of antisemitism seems to be ineradicable in today's world; and even in Christian theology the age-old Marcionism and anti-Judaism re-emerge with a vengeance again and again, and in fact not only on the part of the traditionalists but also on the liberal side, for example when Jesus' conflict with the Judaism of his day is seen as grounded in the Torah, which is misinterpreted as slavish adherence to external observances from which Jesus brought liberation. I also observe again and again with regret how the roots in the Jewish liturgy are often cut off[9] if in the Sunday worship the prescribed Old Testament reading is omitted, or if the Eucharist is not performed according to the ecclesial norms.

In view of such phenomena and developments the church must be reminded that by excluding Marcion from the Christian congregation in 144, the church rejected his concept of a purely "Christian" bible purged of all Old Testament elements; today too the church is obliged to denounce anti-Judaism and Marcionism as a betrayal of its own Christian faith, and to call to mind that the spiritual kinship between Jews and Christians has its firm and eternal foundation in Holy Scripture. On the other hand, the demand by the Second Vatican Council to foster mutual understanding and respect between Jews and Christians must continue to be accorded due attention. That is the indispensable prerequisite for guaranteeing not only that there will be no recurrence of the dangerous estrangement between Christians and Jews, but also that the regained understanding of the Jewish roots of Christianity does not lapse once more into oblivion.

Jewish roots and Christian graft

The discourse of Jewish roots is indeed to be understood in a strictly theological sense, as already demonstrated by the expressive image of Saint Paul, who spoke of the root of Israel into which the wild branches of the Gentiles have been grafted (cf. Rom 11:16–20). This image represents for Paul the key to thinking of the relationship between Israel and the church in the light of faith: "Nothing but a single olive tree. God's whole history with humanity is like an olive tree with sacred roots and branches cut out and grafted in and artificially ennobled in this way. All God's dealings are like his way of dealing with this tree."[10] With this image Paul gives expression to a duality with regard to the unity and divergence of Israel and the church: on the one hand the image is to be taken seriously in the sense that the grafted wild branches have not grown out of the root itself and or sprung from it but represent a new reality and a new work of salvation by God, so that the Christian church cannot merely be understood as a branch or a fruit of Israel. On the other hand, the image is also to be taken seriously in the sense that the church is only able to survive when it draws nourishment and strength from the root of Israel, and that the grafted branches would wither or even die if they were cut off from the root of Israel. Speaking literally rather than metaphorically, this means that Israel and the church are related to and interdependent on one another, precisely because they exist in a state not only of unity but also of difference. Israel and the church thus remain to that extent bound up with one another, and indeed both unmixed yet undivided.

Unity and difference between Judaism and Christianity come to the fore in the first instance with the testimonies of divine revelation. Because Israel is the beloved people of God's covenant which has never been revoked or repudiated, Israel's book of the covenant, the Old Testament, is part of the lasting heritage of the Christian church. With the existence of the Old Testament as an integral part of the one Christian bible, there is a deeply rooted sense of the intrinsic inseparability and kinship between Judaism and Christianity. The roots of Christianity lie in the Old Testament, and Christianity constantly draws nourishment from this Old Testament root. On the other hand the existence of the New Testament also brings with it a fundamental tension into the relationship of the two faith communities insofar as Christians read the Old Testament in the light of the New, in the conviction expressed by Augustine in the indelible formula: "In the Old Testament the New is concealed and in the New the Old is revealed."[11]

The New Testament sees itself as the fulfillment of what is promised in the Old, but fulfillment cannot mean substitution. This crucial distinction is evident already from the historical fact that Judaism too found itself compelled to adopt a new reading of the Old Testament after the catastrophe of the destruction of the Second Temple in the year 70. Since only the Pharisees survived the catastrophe of the destruction of the temple, they developed their particular mode of reading and interpreting the Old Testament in a period during which there was no temple, taking the Torah as its center. On the basis of this historical situation, Pope Benedict XVI rightly concluded from this in the second part of his book on Jesus of Nazareth, that there were as a consequence "two responses to this situation," or more precisely, "two ways of reading the Old Testament anew after the year 70,"[12] namely the Christian exegesis of the Christians and the rabbinical exegesis of that form of Judaism which arose from the destruction of the temple. Since the Christian church and post-biblical rabbinical and Talmudic Judaism developed in parallel and since both modes each involved a new interpretation of the Old Testament, the crucial new question must be precisely how these two modes are related to one another. Pope Benedict XVI gave a helpful answer to this question with his instruction: "After centuries of antagonism, we now see it as our task to bring these two ways of rereading the biblical texts—the Christian way and the Jewish way—into dialogue with one another, if we are to understand God's will and his word aright."[13] Here Pope Benedict takes up once more a finding that the Pontifical Biblical Commission formulated in its 2001 document "The Jewish People and Their Sacred Scriptures in the Christian Bible" [cf. Document 50 above], that Christians can and must admit "that the Jewish reading of the Bible is a possible one, in continuity with the Jewish scriptures of the Second Temple period, analogous to the Christian reading which developed in parallel fashion"; it then draws the conclusion: "Both readings are bound up with the vision of their respective faiths, of which the readings are the result and expression. Consequently, both are irreducible."[14]

Neither two different paths to salvation nor Jewish Mission

Since in the view of Pope Benedict the two readings each serve the purpose of "rightly understanding God's will and word," it is clear how much importance he attaches to the issue of the Christian faith being rooted in Judaism before and in the turn of the eras, without of course obscuring the irreducible newness of the Christian faith.[15] At that point the question must arise of the precise relationship between Christianity and Judaism, above all in regard to the question of salvation. In this regard the assumption has gained increasing plausibility in recent years that there may be two different paths to salvation, the Jewish path without Christ and the path for all other people which leads through Jesus Christ. Such a view however threatens to call into question the groundbreaking discovery of the Second Vatican Council, that Jews and Christians do not belong to two different peoples of God but in their difference form one people of God, which however lives in two parts in a state of division. The Vatican Commission for Religious Relations with the Jews gave expression to this interpretation already in 1985 in its *Notes on the Correct Way to Present the Jews and Judaism in Preaching and Catechesis in the Roman Catholic Church* when it maintained that the church and Judaism cannot be represented as "two parallel ways to salvation," but that the church must "witness to Christ as the Redeemer for all." The Christian faith stands or falls by the confession that God wants to lead all people to salvation, that he follows this path in Jesus Christ as the universal mediator of salvation, and that there is no "other name under heaven given to the human race by which we are to be saved" (Acts 4:12).

The Christian confession that there can be only one path to salvation, however, does not in any way lead to a demand for organized mission to the Jews. Christians need to be aware that this represents a very delicate and sensitive matter for the Jews because in their eyes it involves the very existence of Israel itself. In this regard however Cardinal Karl Lehmann rightly discerned in his detailed examination of this question that—in contrast to evangelically oriented Protestantism—one finds "as good as no institutional Jewish mission in Catholic mission history": "We have an abundant share in other forms of inappropriate attitudes toward the Jews and therefore have no right to elevate ourselves above others. But in respect to a specific and exclusive mission to the Jews there should be no false consternation or unjustified self-accusation in this regard."[16] The principal rejection of an institutional Jewish mission does not on the other hand exclude Christians from bearing witness to their faith in Jesus Christ also to Jews, but they should do so in a humble and unassuming manner, particularly in view of the great tragedy of the Shoah.

The most profound reason why there cannot be any organized mission to the Jews has in turn been expressed by St. Paul when he proceeds from the conviction that not only salvation comes from the Jews, but also that in the "time of the Gentiles" God entrusted Israel with a specific individual mission. Paul therefore definitively negates the question he himself has posed in the Letter to the Romans, whether God has repudiated his own people, and lets his soteriological reflections on the irrevocable redemption of Israel against the background of the Christ-mystery culminate in a mysterious doxology: "Oh, the depth of the riches and wisdom and knowledge of God! How inscrutable are his judgments and how unsearchable his ways" (Rom

11:33). In the same sense Pope Benedict XVI in the second part of his book on Jesus of Nazareth allows Bernard of Clairvaux to say in reference to this confronting problem, that for the Jews "a determined point in time has been fixed which cannot be anticipated."[17]

Reconciliation in the covenant community of Abraham

This sensitive tightrope walk which does justice to both the Jewish and the Christian faith convictions,[18] enables a promising future for Jewish-Christian dialogue, on the foundation of the covenant which God concluded with Abraham and which is of fundamental significance for Jewish-Christian dialogue. For Abraham is not only the father of Israel but also the father of the faith of Christians. In this covenant community it must be evident for Christians that the covenant that God concluded with Israel has never been revoked but remains valid on the basis of God's unfailing faithfulness to his people, and consequently the New Covenant which Christians believe in can only be understood as the surpassing affirmation and fulfillment of the Old, and never as a replacement. We Christians are therefore also convinced that through the new covenant the Abrahamic covenant has obtained that universality for all peoples which was of course originally intended. This recourse to the Abrahamic covenant is so essentially constitutive of the Christian faith that the Christian church without Israel would be in danger of losing its locus in the history of salvation and degenerating into an ultimately unhistorical gnosis. By the same token, Jews could with regard to the Abrahamic covenant arrive at the insight that Israel without the church would be in danger of remaining too particularist and failing to grasp the universality of its experience of God, opened up for all peoples through Christianity.

In this fundamental sense Israel and the church remain bound up with one another according to the covenant and interdependent on one another, by accepting one another in a profound internal reconciliation drawn from the depths of their respective faiths, thus becoming a sign and instrument of reconciliation to the world. That reconciliation can be possible even after a very complex and often enough difficult and sadly all too often painful history is vouched for by the Jewish-Christian dialogue in the past decades, and this is a sign of hope for continuing the tried and true shared pilgrim path of reconciliation.

Notes

1. Lecture held at the Jerusalem Studies Institute (JIIS), Jerusalem, on May 24, 2012.

2. "The rift between the Eastern and the Western church, the rift between the Roman church and the pluriversum of the Reformation (the countless churches and sects) form part of the primal rift between Judaism (the non-Christian Jews) and Christianity (the 'Gentiles' in the language of the Pauline letters)." Cf. E. Przywara, "Römische Katholizität—All-christliche Ökumenizität," in: J. B. Metz et al. (eds.), *Gott in Welt. Festgabe für K. Rahner* (Freiburg i. Br. 1964), 524-528, citation p. 526.

3. J. Cardinal Ratzinger, "Das Erbe Abrahams," in *Weggemeinschaft des Glaubens. Kirche als Communio* (Augsburg 2002), 235–38, citation p. 237.

4. Cf. H. G. Hockerts, *Die Goebbels–Tagebücher 1932–1941.* Cf. also V. Conzemius, "Zwischen Anpassung und Widerstand. Die Christen und der Nationalsozialismus," in: *Communio. Internationale katholische Zeitschrift* 23 (1994), 483–502.

5. Benedict XVI, "Dovevo venire. Auschwitz-Birkenau: La visita al campo di concentramento il 28 maggio 2006," in: *Insegnamenti di Benedetto XVI* II, 1 2006 (Città del Vaticano 2007), 724–29 [cf. Document 39 above].

6. Cf. C. Sedmak, "Europa und eine Ethik des Gedächtnisses: Papst Benedikt und der Holocaust," in: C. Sedmak /St. O. Horn (eds.), *Die Seele Europas. Papst Benedikt XVI. und die europäische Identität* (Regensburg 2011), 155–83.

7. Cf. A. Cardinal Bea, *Die Kirche und das jüdische Volk* (Freiburg i. Br. 1966), esp. 21-25: "Hinweise zur Geschichte und Entwicklung des Konzils-dokuments."

8. John Paul II, "Ringraziamo il Signore per la ritrovata fratellanza e per la profonda intesa tra la Chiesa e l Ebraismo. Allocuzione nella Sinagoga durante l incontro con la Comunità Ebraica della Città di Roma il 13 aprile 1986" [cf. Document 27 above], in: *Insegnamenti di Giovanni Paolo II* IX, 1 1986 (Città del Vaticano 1986), 1024–1031, citation p. 1027.

9. Cf. B. Pitre, *Jesus and the Jewish Roots of the Eucharist. Unlocking the Secrets of the Last Supper* (New York 2011).

10. Cf. K. Berger, *Gottes einziger Ölbaum. Betrachtungen zum Römerbrief* (Stuttgart 1990), 229.

11. Augustinus, *Quaestiones in Heptateuchum* 2, 73.

12. J. Ratzinger /Benedict XVI, *Jesus of Nazareth. Holy Week: From the Entrance into Jerusalem to the Resurrection* [cf. Document 44 above] (San Francisco, 2011), 33.

13. Ibid., 33–34.

14. II. A. 7.22.

15. Cf. J. Wohlmuth, "Die Sicht auf das Judentum im zweiten Band des Jesusbuches" in: H. Häring (Hrsg.), *Der Jesus des Papstes. Passion, Tod und Auferstehung im Disput* (Münster 2011), 179–93.

16. K. Cardinal Lehmann, "Judenmission. Hermeneutische und theologische Überlegungen zu einer Problemanzeige im jüdisch-christlichen Gespräch," in: H. Frankemölle / J. Wohlmuth (eds.), *Das Heil der Anderen. Problemfeld "Judenmission"* (Freiburg i. Br. 2010), 142–67, citation p. 165.

17. J. Ratzinger / Benedict XVI. *Jesus of Nazareth. Holy Week: From the Entrance into Jerusalem to the Resurrection* [cf. Document 44 above] (San Francisco 2011), 44.

18. This tightrope walk is expressed particularly in the re-formulation of the Good Friday Prayer for the Jews in the extraordinary form of the Roman rite undertaken by Pope Benedict XVI, who explained that he altered the Good Friday prayer in such a way "to express our faith that Christ is the Savior for all, that there are not two channels of salvation, so that Christ is also the redeemer of the Jews, and not just of the Gentiles. But the new formulation also shifts the focus from a direct petition for the conversion of the Jews in a missionary sense to a plea that the Lord might bring about the hour of history when we may all be united." Cf. *Benedict XVI, Light of the World. The Pope, the Church, and the Signs of the Times. A Conversation with Peter Seewald* (San Francisco 2010), 107.

55

God's Mercy Endures Forever: Guidelines on the Presentation of Jews and Judaism in Catholic Preaching

United States Conference of Catholic Bishops' Committee on the Liturgy, Washington, DC, September 18, 1988

Introduction

On June 24, 1985, the solemnity of the Birth of John the Baptist, the Holy See's Commission for Religious Relations with the Jews issued its *Notes on the Correct Way to Present the Jews and Judaism in Preaching and Catechesis in the Roman Catholic Church* [*Bridges*, Vol. 1, Document 39] (hereafter, 1985 *Notes*; USCC Publication No. 970). The 1985 *Notes* rested on a foundation of previous church statements, addressing the tasks given Catholic homilists by the Second Vatican Council's *Declaration on the Relationship of the Church to Non-Christian Religions* (*Nostra Aetate*) [*Bridges*, Vol. 1, Document 30], no. 4.

On December 1, 1974, for example, the Holy See had issued *Guidelines and Suggestions for Implementing the Conciliar Declaration "Nostra Aetate," no. 4* [*Bridges*, Vol. 1, Document 38] (hereafter, 1974 *Guidelines*). The second and third sections of this document placed central emphasis on the important and indispensable role of the homilist in ensuring that God's Word be received without prejudice toward the Jewish people or their religious traditions, asking "with respect to liturgical readings," that "care be taken to see that homilies based on them will not distort their meaning, especially when it is a question of passages which seem to show the Jewish people as such in unfavorable light" (1974 *Guidelines*, no. 2).

In this country, the National Conference of Catholic Bishops, in 1975, similarly urged catechists and homilists to work together to develop among Catholics increasing "appreciation of the Jewishness of that heritage and rich spirituality which we derive from Abraham, Moses, the prophets, the psalmists, and other spiritual giants of the Hebrew Scriptures" (*Statement on Catholic-Jewish Relations*, November 20, 1975 [*Bridges*, Vol. 1, Document 40], no. 12).

Much progress has been made since then. As it continues, sensitivities will need even further sharpening, founded on the Church's growing understanding of biblical and rabbinic Judaism.

It is the purpose of these present *Guidelines* to assist the homilist in these continuing efforts by indicating some of the major areas where challenges and opportunities occur and by offering perspectives and suggestions for dealing with them.

Jewish Roots of the Liturgy

1. "Our common spiritual heritage [with Judaism] is considerable. To assess it carefully in itself and with due awareness of the faith and religious life of the Jewish people as they are professed and practiced still today, can greatly help us to understand better certain aspects of the life of the Church. Such is the case with the liturgy, whose Jewish roots remain still to be examined more deeply, and in any case should be better known and appreciated by the faithful" (Pope John Paul II, March 6, 1982) [*Bridges*, Vol. 1, Document 35].

2. Nowhere is the deep spiritual bond between Judaism and Christianity more apparent than in the liturgy. The very concepts of a liturgical cycle of feasts and the *lectio continua* principle of the lectionary that so mark Catholic tradition are adopted from Jewish liturgical practice. Easter and Pentecost have historical roots in the Jewish feasts of Passover and Shavuot. Though their Christian meaning is quite distinct, an awareness of their original context in the story of Israel is vital to their understanding, as the lectionary readings themselves suggest. Where appropriate, such relationships should be pointed out. The homilist, as a "mediator of meaning" (NCCB Committee on Priestly Life and Ministry, *Fulfilled in Your Hearing*, 1982) interprets for the liturgical assembly not only the Scriptures but their liturgical context as well.

3. The central action of Christian worship, the Eucharistic celebration, is likewise linked historically with Jewish ritual. The term for
Church, *ecclesia*, like the original sense of the word *synagogue*, is an
equivalent for the Hebrew *keneset* or *kenessiyah* (assembly). The
Christian understanding of *ecclesia* is based on the biblical understanding of *qahal* as the formal "gathering" of the people of God. The
Christian *ordo* (order of worship) is an exact rendering of the earliest
rabbinic idea of prayer, called a *seder*, that is, an "order" of service.
Moreover, the Christian *ordo* takes its form and structure from the
Jewish *seder*: the Liturgy of the Word, with its alternating biblical read-
ings, doxologies, and blessings; and the liturgical form of the Eucharist,
rooted in Jewish meal liturgy, with its blessings over bread and wine.
Theologically, the Christian concept of *anamnesis* coincides with the
Jewish understanding of *zikkaron* (memorial reenactment). Applied to
the Passover celebration, *zikkaron* refers to the fact that God's saving
deed is not only recalled but actually relived through the ritual meal.
The synoptic gospels present Jesus as instituting the Eucharist during
a Passover *seder* celebrated with his followers, giving to it a new and
distinctly Christian "memory."

4. In addition to the liturgical seasons and the Eucharist, numerous details of prayer forms and ritual exemplify the Church's continuing relationship with the Jewish people through the ages. The liturgy
of the hours and the formulas of many of the Church's most memo-
rable prayers, such as the "Our Father," continue to resonate with rabbinic Judaism and contemporary synagogue prayers.

Historical Perspectives and Contemporary Proclamation

5. The strongly Jewish character of Jesus' teaching and that of the
primitive Church was culturally adapted by the growing Gentile majority
and later blurred by controversies alienating Christianity from emerging
rabbinic Judaism at the end of the first century. "By the third century,
however, a de-Judaizing process had set in which tended to undervalue
the Jewish origins of the Church, a tendency that has surfaced from time
to time in devious ways throughout Christian history" (*Statement on
Catholic-Jewish Relations* [*Bridges*, Vol. 1, Document 40], no. 12).

6. This process has manifested itself in various ways in Christian
history. In the second century, Marcion carried it to its absurd extreme,

teaching a complete opposition between the Hebrew and Christian Scriptures and declaring that different Gods had inspired the two Testaments. Despite the Church's condemnation of Marcion's teachings, some Christians over the centuries continued to dichotomize the Bible into two mutually contradictory parts. They argued, for example, that the New Covenant "abrogated" or "superseded" the Old, and that the Sinai Covenant was discarded by God and replaced with another. The Second Vatican Council, in *Dei Verbum* and *Nostra Aetate*, rejected these theories of the relationship between the Scriptures. In a major address in 1980, Pope John Paul II linked the renewed understanding of Scripture with the Church's understanding of its relationship with the Jewish people, stating that the dialogue, as "the meeting between the people of God of the Old Covenant, never revoked by God, is at the same time a dialogue within our Church, that is to say, a dialogue between the first and second part of its Bible" (Pope John Paul II, Mainz, November 17, 1980 [*Bridges*, Vol. 1, Document 34]).

7. Another misunderstanding rejected by the Second Vatican Council was the notion of collective guilt, which charged the Jewish people *as a whole* with responsibility for Jesus' death (cf. nos. 21–25 below, on Holy Week). From the theory of collective guilt, it followed for some that Jewish suffering over the ages reflected divine retribution on the Jews for an alleged "deicide." While both rabbinic Judaism and early Christianity saw in the destruction of the Jerusalem Temple in AD 70 a sense of divine punishment (see Luke 19:42–44), the theory of collective guilt went well beyond Jesus' poignant expression of his love as a Jew for Jerusalem and the destruction it would face at the hands of Imperial Rome. Collective guilt implied that because "the Jews" had rejected Jesus, God had rejected them. With direct reference to Luke 19:44, the Second Vatican Council reminded Catholics that "nevertheless, now as before, God holds the Jews most dear for the sake of their fathers; he does not repent of the gifts he makes or of the calls he issues," and established as an overriding hermeneutical principle for homilists dealing with such passages that "the Jews should not be represented as rejected by God or accursed, as if this followed from Holy Scripture" (*Nostra Aetate*, no. 4; cf. 1985 *Notes*, VI:33).

8. Reasons for increased sensitivity to the ways in which Jews and Judaism are presented in homilies are multiple. First, understanding of the biblical readings and of the structure of Catholic liturgy will be enhanced by an appreciation of their ancient sources

and their continuing spiritual links with Judaism. The Christian proclamation of the saving deeds of the One God through Jesus was formed in the context of Second Temple Judaism and cannot be understood thoroughly without that context. It is a proclamation that, at its heart, stands in solidarity with the continuing Jewish witness in affirming the One God as Lord of history. Further, false or demeaning portraits of a repudiated Israel may undermine Christianity as well. How can one confidently affirm the truth of God's covenant with all humanity and creation in Christ (see Rom 8:21) without at the same time affirming God's faithfulness to the Covenant with Israel that also lies at the heart of the biblical testimony?

Advent: The Relationship between the Scriptures

9. As Catholic homilists know, the liturgical year presents both opportunities and challenges. One can show the parallels between the Jewish and Catholic liturgical cycles. And one can, with clarity, confront misinterpretations of the meaning of the lectionary readings, which have been too familiar in the past. Specifically, homilists can guide people away from a triumphalism that would equate the pilgrim Church with the Reign of God, which is the Church's mission to herald and proclaim. Likewise, homilists can confront the unconscious transmission of anti-Judaism through clichés that derive from an unhistorical overgeneralization of the self-critical aspects of the story of Israel as told in the Scriptures (e.g., "hardheartedness" of the Jews, 'blindness," "legalism," "materialism," "rejection of Jesus," etc.). From Advent through Passover/Easter, to Yom Kippur and Rosh Hashana, the Catholic and Jewish liturgical cycles spiral around one another in a stately progression of challenges to God's people to repent, to remain faithful to God's call, and to prepare the world for the coming of God's Reign. While each is distinct and unique, they are related to one another. Christianity is engrafted on and continues to draw sustenance from the common root, biblical Israel (Rom 11:13–24).

10. In this respect, the 1985 *Notes*, stressing "the unity of the divine plan" (no. 11), caution against a simplistic framing of the relationship of Christianity and Judaism as "two parallel ways of salvation" (no. 7). The Church proclaims the universal salvific significance of the Christ-event and looks forward to the day when "there shall be one flock and

one shepherd" (John 10:16; cf. Isa 66:2; Zeph 3:9; Jer 23:3; Ezek 11:17; see also no. 31e below). So intimate is this relationship that the Church "encounters the mystery of Israel" when "pondering her own mystery" (1974 *Guidelines*, no. 5).

11. The lectionary readings from the prophets are selected to bring out the ancient Christian theme that Jesus is the "fulfillment" of the biblical message of hope and promise, the inauguration of the "days to come" described, for example, by the daily Advent Masses, and on Sundays by Isaiah in cycle A and Jeremiah in cycle C for the First Sunday of Advent. This truth needs to be framed very carefully. Christians believe that Jesus is the promised Messiah who has come (see Luke 4:22), but also know that his messianic kingdom is not yet fully realized. The ancient messianic prophecies are not merely temporal predictions but profound expressions of eschatological hope. Since this dimension can be misunderstood or even missed altogether, the homilist needs to raise clearly the hope found in the prophets and heightened in the proclamation of Christ. This hope includes trust in what is promised but not yet seen. While the biblical prophecies of an age of universal *shalom* are "fulfilled" (i.e., irreversibly inaugurated) in Christ's coming, that fulfillment is not yet completely worked out in each person's life or perfected in the world at large (1974 *Guidelines*, no. 2). It is the mission of the Church, as also that of the Jewish people, to proclaim and to work to prepare the world for the full flowering of God's Reign, which is, but is "not yet" (cf. 1974 *Guidelines*, II). Both the Christian "Our Father" and the Jewish *Kaddish* exemplify this message. Thus, both Christianity and Judaism seal their worship with a common hope: "Thy kingdom come!"

12. Christians proclaim that the Messiah has indeed come and that God's Reign is "at hand." With the Jewish people, we await the complete realization of the messianic age.

In underlining the eschatological dimension of Christianity, we shall reach a greater awareness that the people of God of the Old and the New Testament are tending toward a like end in the future: the coming or return of the Messiah—even if they start from two different points of view (1985 *Notes*, nos. 18–19).

13. Other difficulties may be less theologically momentous but can still be troublesome. For example, the reading from Baruch in cycle C or from Isaiah in cycle A for the Second Sunday of Advent can leave the impression that pre-Jesus Israel was wholly guilt-ridden and in

mourning, and Judaism virtually moribund. In fact, in their original historical settings, such passages reveal Judaism's remarkable capacity for self-criticism. While Israel had periods of deep mourning (see Lamentations) and was justly accused of sinfulness (e.g., see Jeremiah), it also experienced periods of joy, return from Exile, and continuing *teshuvah*, turning back to God in faithful repentance. Judaism was and is incredibly complex and vital, with a wide variety of creative spiritual movements vying for the people's adherence.

14. The reform of the liturgy initiated by the Second Vatican Council reintroduced regular readings from the Old Testament into the lectionary. For Catholics, the Old Testament is that collection that contains the Hebrew Scriptures and the seven deuterocanonical books. Using postbiblical Jewish sources, with respect for the essential differences between Christian and Jewish traditions of biblical interpretation, can enliven the approach to the biblical text (cf. nos. 31a and 31i below). The opportunity also presents a challenge for the homilist. Principles of selection of passages vary. Sometimes the readings are cyclic, providing a continuity of narrative over a period of time. At other times, especially during Advent and Lent, a reading from the prophets or one of the historical books of the Old Testament and a gospel pericope are "paired," based on such liturgical traditions as the *sensus plenior* (fuller meaning) or, as is especially the case in Ordinary Time, according to the principle of *typology*, in which biblical figures and events are seen as "types" prefiguring Jesus (see no. 31e below).

15. Many of these pairings represent natural associations of similar events and teachings. Others rely on New Testament precedent and interpretation of the messianic psalms and prophetic passages. Matthew 1:23, for example, quotes the Septuagint, which translates the Hebrew *almah* (young woman) as the Greek for *virgin* in its rendering of Isaiah 7:14. The same biblical text, therefore, can have more than one valid hermeneutical interpretation, ranging from its original historical context and intent to traditional Christological applications. The 1985 *Notes* describe this phenomenon as flowing from the "unfathomable riches" and "inexhaustible content" of the Hebrew Bible. For Christians, the unity of the Bible depends on understanding all Scripture in the light of Christ. Typology is one form, rooted in the New Testament itself, of expressing this unity of Scripture and of the divine plan (see no. 31e below). As such, it "should not lead us to forget that it [the Hebrew Bible] retains its own value as Revelation that

the New Testament often does no more than resume" (1985 *Notes*, no. 15; cf. *Dei Verbum*, 14–18).

Lent: Controversies and Conflicts

16. The Lenten lectionary presents just as many challenges. Prophetic texts such as Joel (Ash Wednesday), Jeremiah's "new covenant" (cycle B, Fifth Sunday), and Isaiah (cycle C, Fifth Sunday) call the assembly to proclaim Jesus as the Christ while avoiding negativism toward Judaism.

17. In addition, many of the New Testament texts, such as Matthew's references to "hypocrites in the synagogue" (Ash Wednesday), John's depiction of Jesus in the Temple (cycle B, Third Sunday), and Jesus' conflicts with the Pharisees (e.g., Luke, cycle C, Fourth Sunday) can give the impression that the Judaism of Jesus' day was devoid of spiritual depth and essentially at odds with Jesus' teaching. References to earlier divine punishments of the Jews (e.g., 1 Cor, cycle C, Third Sunday) can further intensify a false image of Jews and Judaism as a people rejected by God.

18. In fact, however, as the 1985 *Notes* are at pains to clarify (sec. III and IV), Jesus was observant of the Torah (e.g., in the details of his circumcision and purification given in Luke 2:21–24), he extolled respect for it (see Matt 5:17–20), and he invited obedience to it (see Matt 8:4). Jesus taught in the synagogues (see Matt 4:23 and 9:35; Luke 4:15–18; John 18:20) and in the Temple, which he frequented, as did the disciples even after the Resurrection (see Acts 2:46; 3:1ff). While Jesus showed uniqueness and authority in his interpretation of God's word in the Torah—in a manner that scandalized some Jews and impressed others—he did not oppose it, nor did he wish to abrogate it.

19. Jesus was perhaps closer to the Pharisees in his religious vision than to any other group of his time. The 1985 *Notes* suggest that this affinity with Pharisaism may be a reason for many of his apparent controversies with them (see no. 27). Jesus shared with the Pharisees a number of distinctive doctrines: the resurrection of the body; forms of piety such as almsgiving, daily prayer, and fasting; the liturgical practice of addressing God as Father; and the priority of the love commandment (see no. 25). Many scholars are of the view that Jesus was not so much arguing against "the Pharisees" as a group, as

he was condemning excesses of some Pharisees, excesses of a sort that can be found among some Christians as well. In some cases, Jesus appears to have been participating in internal Pharisaic debates on various points of interpretation of God's law. In the case of divorce (see Mark 10:2–12), an issue that was debated hotly between the Pharisaic schools of Hillel and Shammai, Jesus goes beyond even the more stringent position of the House of Shammai. In other cases, such as the rejection of a literal interpretation of the *lex talionis* ("An eye for an eye... "), Jesus' interpretation of biblical law is similar to that found in some of the prophets and ultimately adopted by rabbinic tradition as can be seen in the *Talmud*.

20. After the Church had distanced itself from Judaism (cf. no. 5 above), it tended to telescope the long historical process whereby the gospels were set down some generations after Jesus' death. Thus, certain controversies that may actually have taken place between church leaders and rabbis toward the end of the first century were "read back" into the life of Jesus.

Some [New Testament] references hostile or less than favorable to Jews have their historical context in conflicts between the nascent Church and the Jewish community. Certain controversies reflect Christian-Jewish relations long after the time of Jesus. To establish this is of capital importance if we wish to bring out the meaning of certain gospel texts for the Christians of today. All this should be taken into account when preparing catechesis and homilies for the weeks of Lent and Holy Week (1985 *Notes*, no. 29; see no. 26 below).

Holy Week: The Passion Narratives

21. Because of the tragic history of the "Christ-killer" charge as providing a rallying cry for antisemites over the centuries, a strong and careful homiletic stance is necessary to combat its lingering effects today. Homilists and catechists should seek to provide a proper context for the proclamation of the passion narratives. A particularly useful and detailed discussion of the theological and historical principles involved in presentations of the passions can be found in *Criteria for the Evaluation of Dramatizations of the Passion* issued by the Bishops' Committee for Ecumenical and Interreligious Affairs (March 1988) [Document 56 below].

22. The message of the liturgy in proclaiming the passion narratives in full is to enable the assembly to see vividly the love of Christ for each person, despite their sins, a love that even death could not vanquish. "Christ in his boundless love freely underwent his passion and death because of the sins of all so that all might attain salvation" (*Nostra Aetate*, no. 4). To the extent that Christians over the centuries made Jews the scapegoat for Christ's death, they drew themselves away from the paschal mystery. For it is only by dying to one's sins that we can hope to rise with Christ to new life. This is a central truth of the Catholic faith stated by the *Catechism* of the Council of Trent in the sixteenth century and reaffirmed by the 1985 *Notes* (no. 30).

23. It is necessary to remember that the passion narratives do not offer eyewitness accounts or a modern transcript of historical events. Rather, the events have had their meaning focused, as it were, through the four theological "lenses" of the gospels. By comparing what is shared and what distinguishes the various gospel accounts from each other, the homilist can discern the core from the particular optics of each. One can then better see the significant theological differences between the passion narratives. These differences also are part of the inspired Word of God.

24. Certain historical essentials are shared by all four accounts: a growing hostility against Jesus on the part of some Jewish religious leaders (note that the Synoptic gospels do not mention the Pharisees as being involved in the events leading to Jesus' death, but only the "chief priests, scribes, and elders"); the Last Supper with the disciples; betrayal by Judas; arrest outside the city (an action conducted covertly by the Roman and Temple authorities because of Jesus' popularity among his fellow Jews); interrogation before a high priest (not necessarily a Sanhedrin trial); formal condemnation by Pontius Pilate (cf. the Apostles' and Nicene Creeds, which mention *only* Pilate, even though some Jews were involved); crucifixion by Roman soldiers; affixing the title "King of the Jews" on the cross; death; burial; and resurrection. Many other elements, such as the crowds shouting "His blood be on us and on our children" in Matthew, or the generic use of the term "the Jews" in John, are unique to a given author and must be understood within the context of that author's overall theological scheme. Often, these unique elements reflect the perceived needs and emphases of the author's particular community at the end of the first century, *after* the split between Jews and Christians was well under way.

The bitterness toward synagogue Judaism seen in John's gospel (e.g., John 9:22; 16:2) most likely reflects the bitterness felt by John's own community after its "parting of the ways" with the Jewish community, and the martyrdom of St. Stephen illustrates that verbal disputes could, at times, lead to violence by Jews against fellow Jews who believed in Jesus.

25. Christian reflection on the passion should lead to a deep sense of the need for reconciliation with the Jewish community today. Pope John Paul II has said:

> Considering history in the light of the principles of faith in God, we must also reflect on the catastrophic event of the Shoah...
>
> Considering this mystery of the suffering of Israel's children, their witness of hope, of faith, and of humanity under dehumanizing outrages, the Church experiences ever more deeply her common bond with the Jewish people and with their treasure of spiritual riches in the past and in the present."
> (*Address to Jewish Leadership*, Miami, September 11, 1987)

The Easter Season

26. The readings of the Easter season, especially those from the book of Acts, which is used extensively throughout this liturgical period, require particular attention from the homilist in light of the enduring bond between Jews and Christians. Some of these readings from Acts (e.g., cycles A and B for the Third and Fourth Sundays of Easter) can leave an impression of collective Jewish responsibility for the crucifixion ("You put to death the author of life..." Acts 3:15). In such cases, the homilist should put before the assembly the teachings of *Nostra Aetate* in this regard (see no. 22 above), as well as the fact noted in Acts 3:17 that what was done by some individual Jews was done "out of ignorance" so that no unwarranted conclusion about collective guilt is drawn by the hearers. The Acts may be dealing with a reflection of the Jewish-Christian relationship as it existed toward the end of the first century (when Acts was composed) rather than with the actual attitudes of the post-Easter Jerusalem Church. Homilists should desire to convey the spirit and enthusiasm of the early Church that marks these Easter season readings. But in doing so, statements about

Jewish responsibility have to be kept in context. This is part of the reconciliation between Jews and Christians to which we are all called.

Pastoral Activity during Holy Week and the Easter Season

27. Pope John Paul II's visit to the Chief Rabbi of Rome on Good Friday, 1987, gives a lead for pastoral activities during Holy Week in local churches. Some dioceses and parishes, for example, have begun traditions such as holding a "Service of Reconciliation" with Jews on Palm Sunday, or inviting Holocaust survivors to address their congregations during Lent.

28. It is becoming familiar in many parishes and Catholic homes to participate in a Passover Seder during Holy Week. This practice can have educational and spiritual value. It is wrong, however, to "baptize" the Seder by ending it with New Testament readings about the Last Supper or, worse, turn it into a prologue to the Eucharist. Such mergings distort both traditions.

The following advice should prove useful:

> When Christians celebrate this sacred feast among themselves, the rites of the *haggadah* for the seder should be respected in all their integrity. The seder…should be celebrated in a dignified manner and with sensitivity to those to whom the seder truly belongs. The primary reason why Christians may celebrate the festival of Passover should be to acknowledge common roots in the history of salvation. Any sense of "restaging" the Last Supper of the Lord Jesus should be avoided…The rites of the Triduum are the [Church's] annual memorial of the events of Jesus' dying and rising (Bishops' Committee on the Liturgy *Newsletter*, March 1980, p. 12).

Seders arranged at or in cooperation with local synagogues are encouraged.

29. Also encouraged are joint memorial services commemorating the victims of the Shoah (Holocaust). These should be prepared for with catechetical and adult education programming to ensure a proper spirit of shared reverence. Addressing the Jewish community of Warsaw, Pope John Paul II stressed the uniqueness and significance of

Jewish memory of the Shoah: "More than anyone else, it is precisely you who have become this saving warning. I think that in this sense you continue your particular vocation, showing yourselves to be still the heirs of that election to which God is faithful. This is your mission in the contemporary world ...all of humanity" (Warsaw, June 14, 1987 [Document 29 above]). On the Sunday closest to *Yom Hashoah*, Catholics should pray for the victims of the Holocaust and their survivors. The following serve as examples of petitions for the general intercessions at Mass:

- For the victims of the Holocaust, their families, and all our Jewish brothers and sisters, that the violence and hatred they experienced may never again be repeated, we pray to the Lord.
- For the Church, that the Holocaust may be a reminder to us that we can never be indifferent to the sufferings of others, we pray to the Lord.
- For our Jewish brothers and sisters, that their confidence in the face of long-suffering may spur us on to a greater faith and trust in God, we pray to the Lord.

Preaching throughout the Year

30. The challenges that peak in the seasons of Advent, Lent, and Easter are present throughout the year in the juxtaposition of the lectionary readings. There are many occasions when it is difficult to avoid a reference either to Jews or Judaism in a homily based upon a text from the Scriptures. For all Scripture, including the New Testament, deals with Jews and Jewish themes.

31. Throughout the year, the following general principles will be helpful:

    a. Consistently affirm the value of the whole Bible. While "among all the Scriptures, even those of the New Testament, the Gospels have a special preeminence" *(Dei Verbum*, 18), the Hebrew Scriptures are the word of God and have validity and dignity in and of themselves (ibid., 15). Keep in view the intentions of the biblical authors (ibid., 19).

    b. Place the typology inherent in the lectionary in a proper context, neither overemphasizing nor avoiding it. Show that the meaning of the Hebrew Scriptures for their original audience is not limited to nor diminished by New Testament applications (1985 *Notes*, II).

c. Communicate a reverence for the Hebrew Scriptures and avoid approaches that reduce them to a propaedeutic or background for the New Testament. It is God who speaks, communicating himself through divine revelation (*Dei Verbum*, 6).

d. Show the connectedness between the Scriptures. The Hebrew Bible and the Jewish tradition founded on it must not be set against the New Testament in such a way that the former seems to constitute a religion of only retributive justice, fear, and legalism, with no appeal to love of God and neighbor (cf. Deut 6:5; Lev 19:18,32; Hos 11:1–9; Matt 22:34–40).

e. Enliven the eschatological hope, the "not yet" aspect of the *kerygma*. The biblical promises are realized in Christ. But the Church awaits their perfect fulfillment in Christ's glorious return when all creation is made free (1974 *Guidelines*, II).

f. Emphasize the Jewishness of Jesus and his teachings and highlight the similarities of the teachings of the Pharisees with those of Christ (1985 *Notes*, III and IV).

g. Respect the continuing validity of God's covenant with the Jewish people and their responsive faithfulness, despite centuries of suffering, to the divine call that is theirs (1985 *Notes*, VI).

h. Frame homilies to show that Christians and Jews together are "trustees and witnesses of an ethic marked by the Ten Commandments, in the observance of which humanity finds its truth and freedom" (John Paul II, Rome Synagogue, April 13, 1986 [Document 27 above]).

i. Be free to draw on Jewish sources (rabbinic, medieval, and modern) in expounding the meaning of the Hebrew Scriptures and the apostolic writings. The 1974 *Guidelines* observe that "the history of Judaism did not end with the destruction of Jerusalem, but went on to develop a religious tradition…, rich in religious values." The 1985 *Notes* (no. 14) thus speak of Christians "profiting discerningly from the traditions of Jewish readings" of the sacred texts.

32. The 1985 *Notes* describe what is central to the role of the homilist: "Attentive to the same God who has spoken, hanging on the same word, we have to witness to one same memory and one common hope in him who is master of history. We must also accept our responsibility to prepare the world for the coming of the Messiah by working together for social justice, respect for the rights of persons and nations, and for social and international reconciliation. To this we are driven, Jews and Christians, by the command to love our neighbor, by a common hope for the kingdom of God, and by the great heritage of the prophets" (1985 *Notes*, no. 19; see also Lev 19:18, 32).

56

Criteria for the Evaluation of Dramatizations of the Passion

United States Conference of Catholic Bishops' Committee for Ecumenical and Interreligious Affairs, Washington, DC, March, 1988

Preliminary Considerations

On June 24, 1985, the Vatican Commission for Religious Relations with the Jews issued *Notes on the Correct Way to Present the Jews and Judaism in Preaching and Catechesis of the Roman Catholic Church* [*Bridges*, Vol. 1, Document 39]. That document, like its predecessor, *Guidelines and Suggestions for Implementing the Conciliar Declaration* "Nostra Aetate" *(n. 4)* (December 1, 1974) [*Bridges*, Vol. 1, Document 38], drew its inspiration from the Second Vatican Council and was intended to be an offering on the part of the Holy See to Catholics on how the Conciliar mandate can properly be fulfilled "in our time."

The present document, in its turn, seeks to specify the catechetical principles established in the *Notes* with reference to depictions and presentations of the events surrounding the passion and death of Jesus, including but not limited to dramatic, staged presentations of Jesus' death most popularly known as "passion plays." The principles here invoked are applicable as the *Guidelines* suggest (ch. III) to "all levels of Christian instruction and education," whether written (textbooks, teachers manuals, etc.) or oral (preaching, the mass media).

Specifically, the present document aims to provide practical applications regarding such presentations as they flow from the more general principles of the *Guidelines* and of sections III and IV of the *Notes* concerning the "Jewish Roots of Christianity" and the portrayal of

"Jews in the New Testament." These principles (sec. A, below) lead to both negative and positive criteria (sec. B) for the evaluation of the many ways in which the Christian community throughout the world seeks, with commendable and pious intent, to remind itself of the universal significance and eternal spiritual challenge of the Savior's death and resurrection. A final section (C) acknowledges the many difficulties facing those attempting to dramatize the gospel narratives. It is hoped that this section will be helpful in providing perspectives on the many complex questions that can arise.

It has been noted by scholars that dramatizations of the passion were among the very last of the forms of "miracle" or "morality" plays to be developed in the Middle Ages. This hesitancy on the part of our ancestors in the faith can today only be regarded as most seemly, for the Church's primary reflection on the meaning of Jesus' death and resurrection takes place during Holy Week, as the high point of the liturgical cycle, and touches upon the most sacred and central mysteries of the faith.

It is all the more important, then, that extraliturgical depictions of the sacred mysteries conform to the highest possible standards of biblical interpretation and theological sensitivity. What is true of Catholic teaching in general is even more crucial with regard to depictions of Jesus' passion. In the words of Pope John Paul II as cited at the beginning of the *Notes*: "We should aim, in this field, that Catholic teaching at its different levels...presents Jews and Judaism, not only in an honest and objective manner, free from prejudices and without any offenses, but also with full awareness of the heritage common [to Jews and Christians]."

A. The Mystery of the Passion

1. The overall aim of any depiction of the passion should be the unambiguous presentation of the doctrinal understanding of the event in the light of faith, that is, of the Church's traditional interpretation of the meaning of Christ's death for all humanity. *Nostra Aetate* states this central gospel truth quite clearly: "Christ in his boundless love freely underwent his passion and death because of the sins of all, so that all might attain salvation" (cf. *Notes* IV, 30).

Therefore, any presentations that explicitly or implicitly seek to shift responsibility from human sin onto this or that historical group, such as the Jews, can only be said to obscure a core gospel truth. It has rightly been said that "correctly viewed, the disappearance of the charge of collective guilt of Jews pertains as much to the purity of the Catholic faith as it does to the defense of Judaism" (*Statement* of the National Conference of Catholic Bishops, November 20, 1975 [*Bridges*, Vol. 1, Document 40]).

2. The question of *theological* responsibility for Jesus' death is a long settled one. From the theological perspective, the *Catechism* of the Council of Trent (cited in the *Notes* IV, 30) articulated without hesitancy what should be the major dramatic or moral focus of any dramatization of the event for Christians—a profound self-examination of our own guilt, through sin, for Jesus' death:

> In this guilt are involved all those who fall frequently into sin; for, as our sins consigned Christ the Lord to the death of the cross, most certainly those who wallow in sin and iniquity crucify to themselves again the Son of God...This guilt seems more enormous in us than in the Jews since, if they had known it, they would never have crucified the Lord of glory; while we, on the contrary, professing to know him, yet denying him by our actions, seem in some sort to lay violent hands on him (*Catechism* of the Council of Trent).

3. The central creeds of the Church focus precisely on this theological message, without reference to the extremely complex historical question of reconstructing what various individuals might have done or not done. Only Pilate is mentioned, as the person with sole legal responsibility for the case: "He was also crucified for us, suffered under Pontius Pilate and was buried" (Nicene Creed). This fact gives a certain hermeneutic guidance for the use of various materials from the gospel passion narratives in a dramatic context (cf. sec. C, below).

4. In the development and evaluation of passion performances, then, the central criterion for judgment must be what the *Guidelines* called "an overriding preoccupation to bring out explicitly the *meaning* of the [gospel] text while taking scriptural studies into account" (II, emphasis added). Anything less than this "overriding preoccupation" to

avoid caricaturing the Jewish people, which history has all too frequently shown us, will result almost inevitably in a violation of the basic
hermeneutic principle of the Council in this regard: "the Jews should
not be presented as rejected or accursed by God as if this followed from
Sacred Scripture" (*Nostra Aetate* [*Bridges*, Vol. 1, Document 30]).

5. The 1985 *Notes* also provide a model for the positive understanding of the relationship between the Church and the Jewish people that
should form a key element of the vision underlying presentations of the
passion. As the *Notes* state: "The question is not merely to uproot from
among the faithful the remains of antisemitism still to be found here
and there, but much rather to arouse in them, through educational
work, an exact knowledge of the wholly unique 'bond' (*Nostra Aetate*,
4) which joins us as a Church to the Jews and to Judaism" (I, 8; cf. II,
10–11).

B. Avoiding Caricatures and False Oppositions

1. Any depiction of the death of Jesus will, to a greater or lesser
extent, mix theological perspectives with historical reconstructions of
the event based with greater or lesser fidelity on the four gospel
accounts and what is known from extra-biblical records.

The nature of such mixtures leaves the widest possible latitude for
artistic creativity and insight, but also for abuses and prejudices. What
the *Notes* state in their conclusion regarding Christian-Jewish relations
generally is equally, and perhaps especially, true of the history of the
development of passion plays in their various forms: "There is evident,
in particular, a painful ignorance of the history and traditions of
Judaism, of which only negative aspects and often caricature seem to
form part of the stock ideas of many Christians."

2. Judaism in the first century, especially, incorporated an extraor-
dinarily rich and diverse set of groups and movements. Some sought a
certain accommodation with Hellenic/Roman culture in the Diaspora
and in the Land of Israel. Others vigorously opposed any cultural compromise, fearing ultimate religious assimilation. Some argued for
armed rebellion against Rome (Zealots), others for peaceful but firm
resistance to cultural oppression (some Pharisees) and a few, such as
the Temple priesthood and its party (Sadducees) acted in the eyes of
the people as collaborators with Rome.

Emotions and hopes (both practical and spiritual) ran high, and rhetoric often higher. Thus, along the lines of great issues of the day, and reacting to the pressure of Roman occupation, there moved a variety of groups, each with its own wide range of internal diversity: Sadducees, Zealots, apocalypticists, Pharisees (of varying dispositions, especially the two major schools of Hillel and Shammai), Herodians, Hellenists, scribes, sages, and miracle workers of all sorts. Scripture was understood variously: literally, mystically, allegorically, and through mediating principles of interpretation.

Jesus and his teachings can only be understood within this fluctuating mixture of Jewish trends and movements. In point of fact, various groups and leaders of Jesus' time (perhaps especially certain Pharisees) would have espoused many of Jesus' ideas, such as the nearness of the kingdom of God, resurrection of the body, opposition to the policies of the Temple, and so forth. The gospels reflect only some of this diversity. Succeeding generations of Christians, perhaps misconstruing the theological thrust of St. John's use of the term *Ioudaioi* ("the Jews" or "Judeans"), tended to flatten it into a monolithic, usually negative stereotype. Thus, caricature came to form the basis of the pejorative "stock ideas" rejected so forcefully by the *Notes.* Presentations of the passion, on the contrary, should strive to present the diversity of Jewish communities in Jesus' time, enabling viewers to understand that many of Jesus' major concerns (e.g., critique of Temple policies) would have been shared by other Jews of his time.

3. Many of these negative "stock ideas," unfortunately, can become vividly alive in passion dramatizations. It is all too easy in dramatic presentations to resort to artificial oppositions in order to heighten interest or provide sharp contrasts between the characters. Some of these erroneous oppositions, which are to be carefully avoided, are the following:

> a) Jesus must not be depicted as opposed to the Law (Torah). In fact, as the *Notes* describe in greater detail, "there is no doubt that he wished to submit himself to the law (Gal 4:4)...extolled respect for it (Matt 5:17–20), and invited obedience to it (Matt 8:4) (cf. *Notes* III, 21, 22). Jesus should be portrayed clearly as a pious, observant Jew of his time (*Notes* III, 20 and 28).
>
> b) The Old Testament and the Jewish tradition founded on it must not be set against the New Testament in such a way that the former seems to constitute a religion of only justice, fear,

and legalism with no appeal to the love of God and neighbor (Deut 6:5; Lev 19:18; Matt 22:34–40; cf. *Guidelines* III).

c) Jesus and the disciples must not be set dramatically in opposition to his people, the Jews. This is to misread, for example, the technical terminology employed by John's gospel (*Guidelines* II). It also ignores those parts of the gospel that show the Jewish populace well disposed toward Jesus. In his life and teaching, "Jesus was and always remained a Jew" (*Notes* III, 20), as, indeed, did the apostles (*Notes* III, 22).

d) Jews should not be portrayed as avaricious (e.g., in Temple money-changer scenes); blood thirsty (e.g., in certain depiction's of Jesus' appearances before the Temple priesthood or before Pilate); or implacable enemies of Christ (e.g., by changing the small "crowd" at the governor's palace into a teeming mob). Such depictions, with their obvious "collective guilt" implications, eliminate those parts of the gospels that show that the secrecy surrounding Jesus' "trial" was motivated by the large following he had in Jerusalem and that the Jewish populace, far from wishing his death, would have opposed it had they known and, in fact, mourned his death by Roman execution (cf. Luke 23:27).

e) Any crowd or questioning scene, therefore, should reflect the fact that some in the crowd and among the Jewish leaders (e.g., Nicodemus, Joseph) supported Jesus and that the rest were manipulated by his opponents, as is made clear in the gospels (cf. *Nostra Aetate*, n. 4, "Jewish authorities"; *Notes* IV, 30).

f) Jesus and his teachings should not be portrayed as opposed to or by "the Pharisees" as a group (*Notes* III, 24). Jesus shared important Pharisaic doctrines (*Notes* III, 25) that set them apart from other Jewish groups of the time, such as the Sadducees. The Pharisees, in fact, are not mentioned in accounts of the passion except once in Luke, where Pharisees attempt to warn him of a plot against him by the followers of Herod (Luke 13:31). So, too, did a respected Pharisee, Gamaliel, speak out in a later time before the Sanhedrin to save the lives of the apostles (Acts 5). The Pharisees, therefore, should not be depicted as party to the proceedings against Jesus (*Notes* III, 24–27).

g) In sum, Judaism and Jewish society in the time of Christ and the apostles were complex realities, embracing many different trends, many spiritual, religious, social, and cultural values (*Guidelines* III). Presentations of the passion should strive to reflect this spiritual vitality, avoiding any implication that Jesus' death was a result of religious antagonism between a stereotyped "Judaism" and Christian doctrine. Many of the controversies (or "antitheses") between Jesus and his fellow Jews, as recorded in the gospels, we know today in fact reflect conflicts that took place long after the time of Christ between the early Christian communities and various Jewish communities (*Notes* IV, 29 A). To generalize from such specific and often later conflicts to an either/or opposition between Jesus and Judaism is to anachronize and, more basically, to vitiate the spirit and intent of the gospel texts (*Notes* III, 28; IV, 29 F).

h) In the light of the above criteria, it will also be useful to undertake a careful examination of the staging and costuming aspects of particular productions where this may apply. To give just one example, it is possible to project subtly yet powerfully any or all of the above "oppositions" by costuming: arraying Jesus' enemies in dark, sinister costuming and makeup, with Jesus and his friends in lighter tones. This can be effective on the stage. But it can also be disastrous if the effect is to isolate Jesus and the apostles from "the Jews," as if all were not part of the same people. It is important to portray Jesus and his followers clearly as Jews among Jews, both in dress and in actions such as prayer.

i) Similarly, the use of religious symbols requires careful evaluation. Displays of the menorah, tablets of the law, and other Jewish symbols should appear throughout the play and be connected with Jesus and his friends no less than with the Temple or with those opposed to Jesus. The presence of Roman soldiers should likewise be shown on the stage throughout the play, to represent the oppressive and pervasive nature of the Roman occupation.

C. Difficulties and Sensitivities in Historical Reconstruction Based on the Four Gospel Accounts

The mixture of theological, historical, and artistic aspects mentioned above (B 1) gives rise to many difficulties in constructing an adequate presentation of the passion narratives (Matt 26–28; Mark 14–15; Luke 22–23; John 18–19). Below are some examples of the difficult choices facing those who would seek to do so with faithfulness to the gospels. In each, an attempt will be made to apply to the question principles adduced in sections A and B, above, in the hope that such discussion will be of help to those charged with evaluations of the wide range of possible depictions existing today.

1. The Question of Selectivity

a) Those constructing a single narrative from the versions of the events in the four gospels are immediately aware that the texts differ in many details. To take just two examples, the famous phrase, "His Blood be upon us and on our children," exists only in the Matthean text (Matt 27:24–25), while the question of whether or not there was a full Sanhedrin trial is given widely differing interpretations in each of the gospel narratives. John, for example, has no Sanhedrin trial scene as such, but only a questioning before the two chief priests at dawn (18:19). Also in John, it is a Roman cohort, merely accompanied by Temple guards, that arrests Jesus (John 18:3, 12). How is one to choose between the differing versions?

b) First, it must be understood that the gospel authors did not intend to write "history" in our modern sense, but rather "sacred history" (i.e., offering "the honest truth about Jesus") (*Notes* IV, 29 A) in light of revelation. To attempt to utilize the four passion narratives literally by picking one passage from one gospel and the next from another gospel, and so forth, is to risk violating the integrity of the texts themselves, just as, for example, it violates the sense of Genesis 1 to reduce the magnificence of its vision of the Creation to a scientific theorem.

c) A clear and precise hermeneutic and a guiding artistic vision sensitive to historical fact and to the best biblical scholarship are obviously necessary. Just as obviously, it is not sufficient for the producers of passion dramatizations to respond to responsible criticism simply by appealing to the notion that "it's in the Bible." One must account for one's selections.

In the above instances, for example, one could take from John's gospel the phrase "the Jews" and mix it with Matthew 27:24–25, clearly implying a "blood guilt" on all Jews of all times in violation of *Nostra*

Aetate's dictum that "what happened in his passion cannot be blamed on all the Jews then living without distinction nor upon the Jews of today." Hence, if the Matthean phrase is to be used (not here recommended), great care would have to be taken throughout the presentation to ensure that such an interpretation does not prevail. Likewise, the historical and biblical questions surrounding the notion that there was a formal Sanhedrin trial argue for extreme caution and, perhaps, even abandoning the device. As a dramatic tool, it can too often lead to misunderstanding.

d) The greatest caution is advised in all cases where "it is a question of passages that seem to show the Jewish people as such in an unfavorable light" (*Guidelines* II). A general principle might, therefore, be suggested that if one cannot show beyond reasonable doubt that the particular gospel element selected or paraphrased will not be offensive or have the potential for negative influence on the audience for whom the presentation is intended, that element cannot, in good conscience, be used. This admittedly, will be a difficult principle to apply. Yet, given what has been said above, it would seem to be a necessary one.

2. Historical Knowledge and Biblical Scholarship

a) Often, what we have come to know from biblical scholarship or historical studies will place in doubt a more literalist reading of the biblical text. Here again, the hermeneutical principles of *Nostra Aetate*, the *Guidelines*, and the *Notes* should be of "overriding" concern. One such question suggests itself by way of example. This is the portrait of Pontius Pilate (cf. sec. A 3, above). It raises a very real problem of methodology in historical reconstruction of the events of Jesus' last days.

b) *The Role of Pilate*. Certain of the gospels, especially the two latest ones, Matthew and John, seem on the surface to portray Pilate as a vacillating administrator who himself found "no fault" with Jesus and sought, though in a weak way, to free him. Other data from the gospels and secular sources contemporary with the events portray Pilate as a ruthless tyrant. We know from these latter sources that Pilate ordered crucified hundreds of Jews without proper trial under Roman law, and that in the year 36 Pilate was recalled to Rome to give an account. Luke, similarly, mentions "the Galileans whose blood Pilate mingled with their sacrifices" in the Temple (Luke 13:1–4), thus corroborating the contemporary secular accounts of the unusual cruelty of Pilate's administration. John, as mentioned above, is at pains to show that Jesus' arrest and trial were essentially at Roman hands. Finally, the gospels agree that Jesus' "crime," in Roman eyes, was that of political sedition—crucifixion being the Roman form of punishment for such charges. The threat to Roman rule is implicit in the charge: "King of the Jews," nailed to the cross at Pilate's order (Matt 27:37; Mark 15:26; Luke 23:38; John 19:19). Matthew 27:38 and Mark 15:27 identify the "criminals" crucified with Jesus on that day as "insurgents." There is, then, room for more than one dramatic style of portraying the character of Pilate while still being faithful to the biblical record. Again, it is suggested here that the hermeneutical insight of *Nostra Aetate* and the use of the best available biblical scholarship cannot be ignored in the creative process and provide the most prudent and secure criterion for contemporary dramatic reconstructions.

Conclusion

The *Notes* emphasize that because the Church and the Jewish people are "linked together at the very level of their identity," an accurate, sensitive, and positive appreciation of Jews and Judaism "should not occupy an occasional or marginal place in Christian teaching," but be considered "essential" to Christian proclamation (I, 2; cf. I, 8).

This principle is nowhere more true than in depiction of the central events of the Paschal mystery. It is a principle that gives renewed urgency to the evaluation of all contemporary dramatizations of the passion and a renewed norm for undertaking that delicate and vital task.

Bishops' Committee for Ecumenical and Interreligious Affairs
The Most Rev. J. Francis Stafford, Archbishop of Denver, Chairman

Secretariat for Catholic-Jewish Relations
The Most Rev. William H. Keeler, Bishop of Harrisburg, Episcopal Moderator
Dr. Eugene J. Fisher, Executive Secretary
Rt. Rev. Msgr. George C. Higgins, Chair, Advisory Committee to the Secretariat

57

Catholic Teaching on the Shoah: Implementing the Holy See's "We Remember"

United States Conference of Catholic Bishops' Committee for Ecumenical and Interreligious Affairs, Washington, DC, March, 2001. The text has been slightly abridged below.

A Word on the Present Document

The following reflections are intended to help Catholic schools on all levels, including seminaries and universities, to implement the mandate of the Holy See's 1998 statement, *We Remember: A Reflection on the Shoah* [Document 49 above].[1] These reflections do not in themselves form a curriculum, but rather are designed to help Catholic educators begin developing curricula and other educational programs on the Holocaust…

Why Do Catholics Study the Shoah?

The Shoah can briefly be described as Nazi Germany's systematic and nearly successful attempt, from its foreshadowing on *Kristallnacht* in 1938 to its actual implementation from 1942 to 1945, to murder every Jewish woman, man and child in Europe. By the end two out of every three members of the ancient European Jewish community had been killed—some six million people—along with millions of Gypsies (Romani), homosexuals, Poles, and other "subhumans" (*untermenschen*). So horrendous was this mass killing that the Church at the end of the twentieth century (which Pope John Paul II has not hesitated to call "the Century of the Shoah"),[2] has in *We Remember* called on its members

319

collectively to repent not only for the sins of omission and commission of its members during the Shoah, but also for many centuries of negative teachings about Jews and Judaism that, in the pope's words, "lulled the consciences" of so many European Christians that they were not able to organize an effective resistance to Nazi genocide:[3]

> At the end of this millennium the Catholic Church desires to express her deep sorrow for the failure of her sons and daughters in every age. This is an act of repentance (*teshuvah*), since as members of the Church we are linked to the sins as well as the merits of all her children. The Church approaches with deep respect and great compassion the experience of extermination, the Shoah suffered by the Jewish people during World War II. It is not a matter of mere words, but indeed of binding commitment...We pray that our sorrow for the tragedy which the Jewish people has suffered in our century will lead to a new relationship with the Jewish people. We wish to turn awareness of past sins into a firm resolve to build a new future in which there is no more anti-Judaism among Christians..., but rather a shared mutual respect as befits those who adore the one Creator and Lord and have a common father in faith, Abraham.[4]

The pope and the Holy See here distill the essential and overriding reasons for Catholic education to grapple with the Shoah as part of its central curriculum. First, the Shoah was not a random act of mass murder nor simply the result of a war or ancient enmity between two peoples (as most other genocides are and have been). It was a war against the Jews as the People of God, the First Witnesses to God's Revelation and the eternal bearers of that witness through all the centuries since. It is not accidental that the first direct physical attack on the Jews, *Kristallnacht*, came in 1938 in the form of the burning of synagogues throughout the Nazi-dominated parts of Europe. To create its Third Reich, conceived as a millennium of Aryan domination over the entire earth, the Nazi regime, in its ideology, quite rightly saw that it would have to destroy all memory of divine revelation by destroying first the Jews and then the Church. Only by eliminating the moral inhibitions of Judaism and Christianity from the European conscience would Nazism be able to recreate humanity in its own warped, racialist image and likeness.

The second reason to include the Shoah in Catholic education is that the Church today, speaking for and to all Catholics, needs to remind future generations to be ever-vigilant so that "the spoiled seeds of anti-Judaism and antisemitism [will] never again be allowed to take root in any human heart."[5] These underlying mandates of *We Remember* can be set down as educational goals as follows, noting of course that in specific circumstances other articulations and emphases may be appropriate.

Goals for Shoah Education in a Catholic Context

1. To provide Catholics with accurate knowledge of and respect for Judaism, the eternal covenant between God and the Jewish People, and the spiritual bond of kinship between Jews and Christians.[6] Accomplishing this goal educationally will involve students in "learn[ing] by what essential traits the Jews define themselves in the light of their own religious experience."[7]

2. To encourage a positive appreciation of Jews and Judaism and the ongoing role of the Jewish People in God's plan of salvation. This role, the Church teaches, was not exhausted in preparing the way for and giving birth to Jesus. It will continue until the End of Time. Thus, Pope John Paul II has spoken of the Church and the Jewish People being "joint trustees and witnesses of an ethic," and of "our common heritage in the Law and the Prophets." Our joint witness with Jews to the world, the pope concludes, should be "marked by the Ten Commandments, in the observance of which [humanity] finds [its] truth and freedom."[8] Likewise, the Pope has spoken of the need for joint Catholic-Jewish witness to the memory of the Shoah.[9]

3. To promote the spirit of repentance and conversion called for by *We Remember* and integral to the observance of Jubilee 2000 and beyond.[10] In particular, Catholic institutions of higher learning are called to study "the fact that the Shoah took place in Europe, that is, in countries of long-standing Christian civilization, [which] raises the question of the relationship between the Nazi persecution and the attitudes down the centuries of Christians toward Jews."[11]

4. To arm Catholics for the ongoing fight against traditional Christian anti-Judaism and modern racial antisemitism, by studying the causes and conditions for genocide in order to prevent such atrocities

from happening to Jews or any other group in the future.[12] Study of the Shoah demonstrates vividly to what lengths of destruction prejudice, whether religious or secular in origin, can lead....

Framing Issues Properly and Sensitively

The Shoah was a complex event that took place within the context of the most widespread and destructive war humanity has ever known...

The issues need to be framed for Catholic students with care and concern. On the one hand, as we have seen, this catastrophe was so unprecedented that many people, whether Jews or Christians, found the very fact of it hard to comprehend until it was too late to oppose. On the other hand, many people, Jews and Christians, did sense what was at stake and fought against it. The role of these "righteous," the rescuers, when placed in a proper, subordinated perspective, will provide a necessary model for future generations.

Similarly, because of the Shoah's unprecedented nature, a new word, "genocide," had to be invented to describe it. But once invented "genocide" can justly be applied to other victims of the Nazis, such as Gypsies and Poles, and to other events in this century, such as mass murders in Asia, Africa and Europe. The similarities and differences between these phenomena can fruitfully be explored and analyzed in the classroom.

In confronting the Shoah, honesty and objectivity are vital tools for educators, even dealing with matters that may appear unfavorable to Christians or to the Church. Pope John Paul II reminded Catholic scholars who were gathered at the Vatican to study "The Roots of Anti-Judaism in the Christian Milieu," on October 31, 1997 [Document 33 above]: "I appreciate the fact that the theological research conducted by your symposium is done with scholarly rigor, in the conviction that to serve the truth is to serve Christ himself and his church."

At the same time, the chaotic and intimidating situation faced by ordinary people caught up in a conflagration of unprecedented scope will need to be taken into account. Situations varied tremendously from one area of Europe to another. The Nazis treated local populations differently according to their place on the racial ladder. Slavs, being in Nazi eyes less than fully human, were considered fit only to be slaves, while Danes were seen as fellow Aryans who might have a place in the Nazi Millennium. In Poland alone it was a capital offense to aid a Jew in any way. Whole families and entire Polish villages were murdered by the Nazis for harboring Jews, and a Pole could be killed even for offering a Jew a crust of bread.

In some countries, such as Italy, Denmark and Bulgaria, virtually the entire population rose to the occasion to save the lives of their fellow citizens of Jewish birth. In others, such as France and Austria, heroic resistance and craven collaboration co-existed. In such a complex situation, few generalities can be made about historical precedents, perpetrators, bystanders, rescuers and ordinary people. The following sections raise two issues where particular care is needed: presenting the stories of the Rescuers and the importance of making proper distinctions.

The Rescuers

Israel's major Holocaust museum, Yad Vashem in Jerusalem, remembers and honors the "righteous gentiles" who risked their own lives to save Jews. The U.S. Holocaust Memorial Museum in Washington, DC, similarly honors them, not only listing the names of individuals but offering special exhibits on countries such as Denmark and Italy, each of which saved over 80 percent of the Jews of their countries, and groups such as Zegota, a Polish Catholic organization dedicated to saving Jewish lives.

Again, a sense of balance is needed. Cardinal William H. Keeler of Baltimore, in an address honoring Catholic rescuers at the U.S. Holocaust Memorial Museum in April 1997, placed the occasion firmly within the context of the overall need for repentance on the part of Catholics worldwide, as called for by the pope and the Holy See. The rescuers were, after all, relatively few islands of light in a continent overwhelmed by the darkness of evil. Still, the rescuers remain crucial models for future generations of Catholics. Studies have revealed some widespread characteristics of rescuers that can be inculcated educationally.

First, a sense of morality was deeply implanted in the fiber of their being, whether they were sophisticated and well educated or ordinary people. Rescuers frequently had to make life-or-death decisions (not only for themselves but for their families) on short notice. Most in postwar interviews have said that they felt they had little choice. They could only do "what was right," thus exhibiting a reflex toward the good, often enough despite full awareness of the risks involved.

Second, the righteous had a sense that life has ultimate meaning beyond the present. While their understanding of that meaning may have varied, their experience reminds us to place our lives in a wider context of human meaning and interrelatedness. For Catholics this sense of openness to the transcendent dimension underscores the critical importance of faith in God.

Third, many of the righteous had prior acquaintance with Jews, though not necessarily with the people they actually rescued. From this we learn the importance of building human bonds across religious, racial, and ethnic lines.

Distinctions and Connections

The essence of a good education may lie in developing the skills necessary to make proper distinctions and connections among related phenomena. In this way biology distinguishes and relates the wealth of the world's flora and fauna by classifying them into genus and species in order to understand how life on earth "works." The same is true of theology and the social sciences.

Some responses, Catholic as well as Jewish, to *We Remember* questioned certain distinctions made by the Holy See's commission. These, however, flow from the Church's traditional understanding of itself as a divinely founded institution, and from a careful consideration of history. The chief signer of the document, Cardinal Edward I. Cassidy, clarified what was meant at a meeting with the American Jewish Committee in May 1998.[14] The Pope's liturgy of repentance at St. Peter's in Rome in March 2000, his statement the next week at Yad Vashem [Document 36 above], and the petition for forgiveness that he placed, in the name of the whole Church, in the Western Wall (*Kotel*) in Jerusalem [Document 37 above] all presume these distinctions. Properly interpreted, the distinctions made by the Holy See are crucial to Catholic Shoah education. They are elaborated upon at some length in the statement of the Vatican's International Theological Commission,

Memory and Reconciliation: The Church and the Faults of the Past, issued on Ash Wednesday of the Jubilee Year 2000 in order to explain the precise meaning of the pope's Liturgy of Repentance on the First Sunday of Lent that year.[15]

The Church, Its Members, and Responsibility for the Shoah

The distinction made by the documents between "the Church as such" and her "sons and daughters" is a traditional one familiar to most Catholics. No one—not popes or bishops or priest or laity—is exempt from sin, as Cardinal Cassidy explained. Thus the petition for forgiveness that Pope John Paul II placed in the Western Wall prayed to the "God of our fathers" in the name of the whole Church. The pope did not mean to exclude anyone by reason of rank or clerical status from responsibility for their acts toward Jews over the centuries: "We are deeply saddened / by the behavior of those / who in the course of history / have caused these people of yours to suffer." This statement of repentance at the Wall, coming just after the Pope's prayerful visit to Yad Vashem, includes the sins of omission and commission by Catholics toward Jews both in the centuries leading up to the Shoah and during it.

At the same time, the Church is more than a human institution. It is the Body of Christ incarnate in the world after his Ascension into heaven, the sacrament of the encounter between the divine and the human, the sure instrument of salvation offered to all humanity. *Memory and Reconciliation*, referring to Augustine and Thomas Aquinas, notes the seeming paradox that the Church is at once indefectibly holy and in need of "continual renewal" through repentance,[16] and the statement makes clear that "the fullness of holiness belongs to eschatological time; in the meantime, the church still on pilgrimage should not deceive herself by saying that she is without sin."[17]

These paired theological affirmations, we believe, take on particular urgency when applied to Christian-Jewish relations over the centuries and especially during the Holocaust. The polemical teachings of the Church Fathers against Judaism beginning in the second century (as the pope noted in 1997) and the severe persecutions of Jews that so marred the second millennium, were so pervasive over time that the consciences of twentieth-century Christians were "lulled." The result was that a continent, "Christian" for centuries, found all too few

Christians capable of resisting the virus of racial antisemitism propagated by Nazism. A few did, and their heroism in saving Jewish lives is a model for students today. But many more did not, and for this the Church as a whole, in the moving phrases of Pope John Paul II and of *We Remember*, must repent and take responsibility. As *We Remember* puts it so well: "At the end of this millennium, the Catholic Church desires to express her deep sorrow for the failures of her sons and daughters in every age. This is an act of repentance (*teshuvah*), since as members of the Church we are linked to the sins as well as the merits of all her children."[18]

Anti-Judaism and Antisemitism

We Remember distinguishes broadly between the theological polemics against Judaism developed by Christian teachers as early as the second century and the more modern racial and neo-pagan ideology of antisemitism that was developed in the eighteenth and nineteenth centuries to euphemize racial hatred directed against Jews. Again, the distinction is crucial to understanding. The classic Christian approach to Judaism, as formulated by St. Augustine and set into lasting canonical precedent by Pope St. Gregory the Great, was fundamentally ambiguous in theory and practice. On the one hand, Jews were considered "blind" to the true meaning of their own Scriptures, not seeing their fulfillment in Christ. But their witness to the validity of the Hebrew Bible as divine revelation was seen as essential to the witness of the Church to Christ. Hence, Jews were to be allowed to worship (relatively) freely and were not to be forced to convert to Christianity. Judaism was thus the only licit religion besides Christianity in Christendom throughout the Middle Ages. The popes could be and often were successfully appealed to by Jewish communities when local civil authorities attempted to abuse them.

What specifically Christian anti-Judaism led to when it was abused was forced conversion; occasional, mindless massacres like those of the Crusaders in 1096; expulsion by secular rulers (beginning with England in the twelfth century and culminating in the expulsion from Spain in 1492); and the ghettoization of the remaining Jews of Western Europe.[19] These Christian sins are indefensible. But when the Church was able to exercise authority in the civil societies of Europe (i.e., from the fourth century to the Enlightenment) the moral teaching of Church law acted at times as a restraint. At no time did the plight of Jews degenerate into anything near the systematic attempt at genocide that was the direct result of the adoption of a neo-pagan set of racial ideologies by the Nazi Reich in Germany. This total dehumanization of Jews allowed those who adopted it to conceive and implement the "final solution" for ridding Europe of the "infestation" of its Jewish population.

But Christian anti-Judaism did lay the groundwork for racial, genocidal antisemitism by stigmatizing not only Judaism but Jews themselves for opprobrium and contempt. So the Nazi theories tragically found fertile soil in which to plant the horror of an unprecedented attempt at genocide. One way to put the "connectedness" between the Christian teaching of anti-Judaism (leading to anti-Jewishness) and Nazi antisemitism is that the former is a "necessary cause" to consider in explaining the development and success of the latter in the twentieth century, but not a "sufficient cause." To account for the Holocaust, one must acknowledge the historical role of Christian anti-Judaism. But Christian anti-Judaism alone cannot account for the Holocaust. Semi-scientific racial theories and specific historical, ideological, economic, and social realities within Germany must also be taken into account to begin grappling with why Nazism succeeded in mobilizing virtually the entire intellectual and technological apparatus of a modern industrial state to its warped purpose of eliminating from human history God's People, the Jews.

Guilt and Responsibility

It may be necessary to explain to students that the universal call to repentance before God for Christian sins against Jews that the Holy Father mandated during the Jubilee Year 2000, as well as *We Remember*'s call for the Church's ongoing repentance for these sins, will involve for most Christians an assumption of responsibility for our collective Christian past, not personal guilt. Moral guilt—and it must be remembered that antisemitism is and was a most serious sin—inheres only in the sinner. It cannot be passed on to others. Americans in the generation of Nazi tyranny in Europe fought to defeat it, although our refusal to let in more than a handful of the Jewish refugees should give us reason to examine our national conscience as well.[20] In any event, those born after the war have no reason to feel personal guilt; but members of the one Body of Christ, the Church, have every reason to assume responsibility to ensure that nothing like it can ever happen again.

The Holy See's *Memory and Reconciliation* takes up this issue in some depth, pointing to the biblical writers' strong sense of solidarity in good and evil among the generations ("corporate personality") as the model for us today: "This is how the Jews prayed after the exile (Dan 3:26–30; Bar 2:11–13), accepting the responsibility for the sins committed by their fathers. The church imitates their example and also asks forgiveness for the historical sins of her children."[21]

Again, *We Remember* says well what needs to be said: "It is not a matter of mere words, but indeed of binding commitment...We wish to turn awareness of past sins into a firm resolve to build a new future in which there will be no more anti-Judaism among Christians."[22]

Suggestions for Teaching Courses on the Shoah

The course should fit into the mission of the particular Catholic school or program developing it. Courses offered in Catholic universities, theological schools, and seminaries, for example, will engage the students and faculty in complex theological issues regarding the Church as a whole and its understanding of Scripture, ecclesiology, and especially the liturgy, while courses on the elementary level might focus more helpfully on individual narratives of victims and rescuers, bringing out the moral implications in order to prepare students to be morally grounded leaders for tomorrow. The Shoah destroyed a vibrant culture along with innumerable institutions of higher learning, especially religious learning. Courses, as the outline below suggests, should include some history of Jewish thought, devotion and culture.

Many fields of study are relevant to Shoah education, ranging from history, psychology and sociology to philosophy, theology and the arts. Team-taught, interdisciplinary, and interreligious (led by a Catholic and a Jewish teacher) approaches have much to recommend them in a given academic context...

Since it is impossible to teach all aspects of the Shoah in a single semester, goals will need to be prioritized depending on resources available to the school and in the community.

Prior History of Jewish-Christian Relations
1. Pre-Christian antipathy to Jews
2. Origins and development of the Christian teaching of contempt for Jews and Judaism, and the papal and canonical legislation that nevertheless offered Jews a legal place in Christian society and often sought to protect them from exploitation by civil leaders
3. Spiritual and intellectual creativity of post–New Testament Jewish history (Talmud, Maimonides, Rashi, mysticism, etc.) and its contributions to Western civilization
4. Marginalization and demonization of Jews in Christendom
5. Racial antisemitism—distinct in theory and ideology, but historically and socially connected to Christian theological anti-Judaism

General Preconditions
1. Technological change
2. Economic and political instability
3. Secularized society (and the diminution of Christian moral restraints on certain actions)

Events of the Shoah Itself
1. Basic history, including the destruction of a vital culture
2. Jewish and non-Jewish victims of Nazism
3. Perpetrators, bystanders, beneficiaries, and average citizens —some whom were led by their own apathy to turn their heads away, while others may have harbored fears for their own families which lead them to be silent bystanders.
4. Resistors and rescuers
5. Roles and responses of Catholic, Protestant and Orthodox Churches and how they varied from country to country, region to region
6. Roles and responses of various Christian international bodies, especially the Holy See and the World Council of Churches, and of other international agencies, such as the Red Cross.

Aftermath of the Shoah
1. Jewish responses: theological challenges, State of Israel, creation of memory

2. Christian responses: e.g., the Second Vatican Council twenty years after the event, though issues had been raised by individual Protestants and Catholics sooner, such as facing the history of the "teaching of contempt," replacement theology (supersessionism), challenges to internal theological issues (e.g., teachings about Christian love, value of life), theological methodologies and Christian worship (e.g., *God's Mercy Endures Forever* [Document 55 above]).

3. Moral implications for our world: responses to genocide, prejudice, and antisemitism in its various forms, including in international relations

4. General challenge to our conceptions of Western civilization, including liberal learning, academia, and the professions

5. Challenges raised in remembering and canonizing individuals from the time of the Shoah, questions of biography and hagiography (i.e., Lichtenberg, Kolbe, Stein, Titus Brandsma)[23]

Pedagogical Issues

Experiential Aspects

It is beneficial to use film, testimonies (of survivors, rescuers, liberators, and children of survivors), literature, Internet resources, and/or museum visits to engage students affectively in their studies. Care must be taken not to horrify younger students to the point that they are desensitized or refuse to relate to the issues. Sensitivity to the feelings of guilt or victimization that can arise is imperative.

Contextual Issues

1. The Shoah should not be the only context in which Jews and Judaism are encountered in a curriculum. Even within a Shoah course, Jews and Judaism should not be encountered only as the Shoah's victims or as perennial scapegoats of Christian persecutions.

2. The Shoah must also be confronted within various contexts of general European history, especially of Germany and Austria, but also of all the other countries in which the Nazis were able to operate. The differences between these contexts need to be brought out.

Construction of Memory

1. The instructor should be conscious of the moral imperative to construct a memory of the Shoah that will positively influence the moral formation of students. In a Catholic setting, students should come to accept and regret that the perpetrators, bystanders, and cowed majority in Europe came from within the Christian community. Similarly, Jewish students should come to identify with the victims. Both Catholic and Jewish students should also learn something about the more positive relations between Jews and Catholics as fellow immigrants in America. The need to create this memory and identification should shape the structure of the course. The formation of an empathetic imagination for the memories and sensibilities of others should also be pursued.

2. Students must be conscious that this construction of memory is different depending on the person's entry into identification (positive or negative) with the people involved in the Shoah. They should be aware that memory of the Shoah for Jews is necessarily a radically different memory from that of most Christians. The distinctive victimization of such groups as Poles and other Slavs, gypsies, homosexuals, and the physically or mentally impaired also has an impact on the construction of memory of individual students.

3. While the Shoah was in many respects a unique event, victims of the all-too-numerous other incidents of mass murder will find analytical distinctions trivial to their experience of suffering.

Beyond Courses on the Shoah

The issues of the Shoah and of Jewish-Christian relations are vast topics that most students will encounter only as elective offerings in their total programs of study. Yet their enormous importance requires their integration wherever possible throughout the Catholic curricula. This is especially, though not solely, important for seminaries and theological schools. In biblical studies, for example, courses on books of the Shared Testament (Hebrew Scriptures) should convey esteem for the profundity and permanence of Israel's experience of God and its inspired sacred texts. Courses on the New Testament will benefit from taking seriously the Jewishness of Jesus and the Apostles, and of the

Evangelists, Paul and other authors of the New Testament. They can help improve future sermons and Catholic texts by confronting honestly the anti-Jewish potential of certain passages, especially those concerning the crucifixion, the Pharisees, the Torah [Law], and the permanence of Israel's covenant.[24] Christological courses will be enriched by accurately reflecting the complexities of Judaism in late antiquity as the context of Jesus' teaching and of the early Church's understanding of the significance of the Christ event.

In courses in patristic studies the pervasive—and now repudiated—idea that Christianity replaced or "superseded" Judaism in God's plan of salvation needs to be challenged. Here, it is worthy of note: "It has rightly been stressed that of all the documents promulgated by the Second Vatican Council, that on the Jews [*Nostra Aetate*] is the only one which contains no reference whatsoever to any of the Church's teachings—patristic, conciliar, or pontifical. This alone shows the revolutionary character of the act."[25] Courses on church history and European history will benefit greatly when seen from the vantage point of the perennially marginalized Jewish community, the only religious tradition in Europe that pre-dated Christianity and still exists intact and in continuity with its past.

Homiletics courses and courses devoted to the Rite of Christian Initiation of Adults can explore the relationship between the two testaments of the Christian Bible so as to avoid presentations that explicitly or subtly promote supersessionism. Ethics courses can examine the situations and behaviors of the churches during the Shoah, and benefit from the "double lens" of how Christians and Jews over the centuries have variously interpreted the moral commandments of the Scriptures we share.

To understand the liturgical renewal of the twentieth century and the origins of much that is central to Christian practice, the Jewish roots of our forms of worship need to be understood. Spirituality courses can treat the writings of Jewish commentators and mystics.

These issues need to be integrated into other parts of the daily life of Catholic educational institutions through special events such as commemorations of *Yom Hashoah* (the Jewish day of remembering the victims of the Holocaust), film showings, drama, art exhibits, colloquia and public lectures, joint pilgrimages and retreats with Jewish clergy and laity, and faculty and student exchanges like the American Jewish Committee's CJEEP (Catholic-Jewish Educational Exchange Program).

Notes

1. Similarly, the Bishops' Committee for Ecumenical and Interreligious Relations (BCEIA) sought to implement locally the Holy See's statements of 1974 and 1985 with the 1975 NCCB *Statement on Catholic-Jewish Relations* [*Bridges*, Vol. 1, Document 40] and our own 1988 *Criteria for the Evaluation of Dramatizations of the Passion* [Document 56 above] (Washington, DC: United States Catholic Conference). The Bishops' Committee on the Liturgy further drew out the liturgical implications of the Holy See's 1985 statement in its own statement, *God's Mercy Endures Forever: Guidelines on the Presentation of Jews and Judaism in Catholic Preaching* [Document 55 above] (Washington, DC: United States Catholic Conference, 1989). The Holy See's 1998 statement *We Remember* [Document 49 above], along with related statements of European and U.S. bishops' conferences, is contained in *Catholics Remember the Holocaust* (Washington, DC: United States Catholic Conference, 1998). In *We Remember*, the Holy See wisely uses the Hebrew word Shoah to describe the Holocaust. While not diminishing the suffering of Nazism's many other victims, such as the Romani (Gypsies) and Poles, this term preserves a central focus on Nazism's central victim-group, God's People, the Jews. The present reflection follows this precedent.

2. John Paul II's Address to the Jewish Community of Australia, November 26, 1986 [Document 28 above]. This and other papal texts on Jews and Judaism between 1979 and 1995 can be found, with introduction and commentary, in John Paul II, *Spiritual Pilgrimage: Texts on Jews and Judaism*, ed. Eugene Fisher and Leon Klenicki (New York: Crossroad, 1995).

3. John Paul II, Speech to Symposium on the Roots of Anti-Judaism, October 31, 1997 [Document 33 above]. *L'Osservatore Romano* 6:1 (November 6, 1997).

4. *We Remember*, Part 5. In *Catholics Remember the Holocaust*, p. 54. On the distinction between anti-Judaism and antisemitism, see Part 4.

5. Ibid., p. 55.

6. In a 1985 statement, the Vatican's Commission for Religious Relations with the Jews had this to say regarding Catholic teachings on Judaism: "The urgency and importance of precise, objective and rigorously accurate teaching on Judaism for our faithful follows too from the danger of antisemitism which is always ready to reappear under different guises. The question is not merely to uproot from among the faithful the remains of antisemitism still to be found here and there, but much rather to arouse in them, through educational work, an exact knowledge of the wholly unique 'bond' (*Nostra Aetate*, 4) which joins us as a Church to the Jews and to Judaism" *Notes on the Correct Way to Present the Jews and Judaism in Preaching and Catechesis in the Roman Catholic Church* (June 24, 1985) [*Bridges*, Vol. 1, Document 39], section 1, no. 8. In *Catholic*

Jewish Relations: Documents from the Holy See (London: Catholic Truth Society, 1999).

7. Vatican Commission for Religious Relations with the Jews, *Guidelines and Suggestions for Implementing of the Conciliar Declaration* Nostra Aetate, *no. 4* (December 1, 1974) [*Bridges*, Vol. 1, Document 38], preamble. In *Catholic Jewish Relations.*

8. John Paul II, Address in the Great Synagogue of Rome (April 13, 1986) [Document 27 above], no. 6. In *Spiritual Pilgrimage*, p. 65.

9. Addressing the Jewish leaders of Warsaw on June 14, 1987 [cf. Document 29 above], the Holy Father expanded his vision of ongoing Jewish witness to include the Shoah itself: "I think that today…, you have become a loud warning voice for all humanity…More than anyone else, it is precisely you who have become this saving warning…in this sense you continue your particular vocation, showing yourselves to be still the heirs of that election to which God is faithful. This is your mission in the contemporary world before the peoples, the nations, all of humanity, the Church. And in this Church all peoples and nations feel united to you in this mission." In *Spiritual Pilgrimage*, p. 99.

10. John Paul II, *On the Coming of the Third Millennium (Tertio Millennio Adveniente)*, no. 33 (Washington, D.C.: United States Catholic Conference, 1994).

11. *We Remember*, part 2. In *Catholics Remember the Holocaust*, p. 49.

12. "We would risk causing the victims of the most atrocious deaths to die again if we do not have an ardent desire for justice, if we do not commit ourselves to ensure that evil does not prevail over good as it did for millions of the children of the Jewish people…Humanity cannot permit all that to happen again." *We Remember*, part 5, citing John Paul II. In *Catholics Remember the Holocaust*, p. 55….

14. The text of Cardinal Cassidy's "Reflections Regarding the Vatican's Statement on the Shoah,' originally published in *Origins*, is included in *Catholics Remember the Holocaust*, pp. 61–76.

15. International Theological Commission, *Memory and Reconciliation: The Church and the Faults of the Past*, in *Origins* 29:39 (March 16, 2000): 625–44.

16. Ibid., no. 3.3.

17. Ibid.

18. *We Remember*, part 5. In *Catholics Remember the Holocaust*, p. 54. See also *Memory and Reconciliation*, nos. 3.4 and 5.4.

19. It should be noted that Jews were never expelled from Italy, where papal authority continued the tradition of protection of Jews. Likewise, many Jews found refuge in Eastern Europe, especially Poland, which by the twentieth century enjoyed the largest Jewish population in the world.

20. See Archbishop Oscar Lipscomb (BCEIA chairman) "Commemorating the [50th Anniversary of the] Liberation of Auschwitz." In *Catholics Remember the Holocaust*, pp. 16–20.

21. *Memory and Reconciliation*, no. 2.1.

22. *We Remember*, part 5. In *Catholics Remember the Holocaust*, p. 54.

23. Cf. Cardinal William H. Keeler, "Lessons to Learn from Catholic Rescuers." In *Catholics Remember the Holocaust*, pp. 29–30.

24. See *God's Mercy Endures Forever*.

25. Gerhart M. Riegner, *Nostra Aetate: Twenty Years After*. In: International Catholic-Jewish Liaison Committee, *Fifteen Years of Catholic-Jewish Dialogue, 1970–1985: Selected Papers*, p. 276 (Vatican City: Libreria Editrice Vaticana, 1988).

58

Accepting the Burden of History

Common Declaration of the Bishops' Conferences of the German Federal Republic, of Austria, and of Berlin on the Fiftieth Anniversary of the Pogroms against the Jewish Community on the Night of November 9/10, 1938, November 9, 1988

1. Historical Review

"Those inconceivable sufferings, sorrows and tears are before my eyes and they have impressed themselves deeply on my soul. Indeed, only the one you know, you can love."

It was with these words that Pope John Paul II remembered the events of fifty years ago, during a meeting on June 24, 1988 with the representatives of the Jewish communities.[1] At that time, during the night of the November 9–10, 1938, and the following day, everywhere in the Grossdeutschen Reich, of which Austria had become a part since the Anschluss, synagogues were set on fire or destroyed, Jewish cemeteries were desecrated and countless Jewish shops and homes were demolished and looted. Many Jews were murdered in these pogroms, instigated by the N.S. (National Socialist) leadership, and countless Jews were maltreated. Tens of thousands were deported for days or weeks to the concentration camps at Dachau, Buchenwald and Sachsenhausen. Most of them left this place of their humiliation and affliction seriously hurt in body and soul. There was the added insult and mockery that those who were wronged had to pay a "compensation" of one thousand million Reichsmark.

The N.S. press presented these riots as "spontaneous" actions of revenge of an infuriated populace; soon the word Kristallnacht, made to sound inoffensive, was passed round. But everybody knew that in reality the November pogroms had been street terror of the vilest dimensions, ordered from above, but organized on the spot. That is why there could be found in the population, besides active participation, demonstrative staying away; besides malicious joy, also shame; besides indifference, also inner horror, and besides a timid looking away, also a readiness to help. But nowhere could be found rallies of protest.

Today many complain that at that time even the Christian churches did not speak a public word of condemnation. Sure enough, many priests and lay people were disciplined by the N.S. authorities because of their public criticism of the anti-Jewish outrages. We know of the witness of the Berlin Canon Bernhard Lichtenberg, who later went to his death for his brave actions. However, our predecessors in the episcopate did not raise a common protest from the pulpit.

Their silence also raises questions, because there could be no doubt as to an uncompromising "no" of the Church toward Hitler's race politics. In his encyclical letter *Mitbrennender Sorge*, on March 14, 1937, Pope Pius XI declared that whoever exalted race, people or nation to the highest norm, falsified "the divinely created and divinely ordained order of things."[2] A year later, on April 13, 1938, the same Pope appealed to all Catholic universities and Catholic theological faculties to fight antisemitism in word and writing. In September 1938, he said, "Antisemitism is a revolting movement, of which we Christians cannot be part. Antisemitism cannot be justified. Spiritually we are all Semites."[3]

The German bishops decided—before November 9, 1938—on Guidelines for the clergy concerning N.S. ethnology. In these they declared: "…In the Church there is fundamentally no difference between people and people, race and race." This, certainly, was no direct intervention on behalf of the Jews, but from the point of view of the dictators, it was absolutely clear and therefore provocative. For, through permanently questioning the racist ideology, the Church was shaking the ideological foundations of the regime. In a basic statement of Cologne's Cardinal Schulte, it was pointed out that the main aim of all pastoral care ought to be "to deepen and strengthen the life of faith in as many Catholics as possible to such a degree that they were able to withstand the trials of the time, even if the ultimate witness to their faith was demanded of them." This statement caused the Church to become, in the eyes of the National Socialists, the main opponent to their ideology. Shortly after the November pogroms, an official government opinion poll stated, "It is only those circles influenced by the Church that still stand aloof from the 'Jewish question.'"[4]

But was this enough: the education of conscience and ideological immunization, in the face of burning synagogues and thousands of

abused Jewish fellow-citizens? These questions we ask ourselves, looking back after fifty years. Would not public protest, a clearly recognizable gesture of humaneness and sympathy, have been the duty
demanded from the Church's office as guardian?

These questions depress us all the more, as we—in contrast to
those of that era—ask them, with our knowledge of "Auschwitz." But
it is difficult to find a clear, unambiguous answer to these questions.
We do not know the reasons of the episcopate; moreover, we lack the
sources as to the attitudes and expectations of the laity. But one thing
is certain: the bishops' caution can only be understood against the
background of the National Socialist fight against the Church, which
was a question of life or death for the Church.

At the beginning of October 1938, this battle against the Church in
Austria had reached its first climax with the destruction of the
Archbishop's Palace in Vienna. In Munich, simultaneously with the
November pogroms, under the slogan, "Against world Jewry and its black
and red cronies," the residence of Cardinal Faulhaber was stormed.[5] A
few weeks prior to this, Bishop Sproll of Rottenburg had been expelled
from his diocese after staged riots. Therefore, a great part of the population saw the anti-Jewish outrages as a rehearsal for future attacks on the
Catholic (and Protestant) Church. This, too, was the bishops' fear. In
their common pastoral letter, of August 19, 1938, they described as the
aim of the N.S. Church Politics, "The destruction of the Catholic
Church among our people, yes, even the annihilation of Christianity." So,
to all appearances, the bishops tried everything not to provoke a further
escalation of this fight against the Church. But in the following years they
intensified their practical, but non-spectacular charitable efforts in favor
of the persecuted. The Raphael's Society, the Caritas and the aid organizations of Bishop Preysing (Berlin), Archbishop Groeber (Freiburg) and
Cardinal Innitzer (Vienna) were, for many, the last chance of rescue
before deportations to the death camps of the East started in 1942.

But apart from all these considerations of expediency, we ask if in
November 1938 yet other expressions of brotherly solidarity would not
have been possible and expected; for example, a common prayer for the
innocently persecuted, or a demonstrative, renewed intensification of
the Christian law of love. That this was neglected, saddens us today
when we perceive the defense of basic human rights as a duty that goes
beyond denominations, classes and races.

One has to consider, though, that many an attitude [that] we consider self-evident today grew only as a result of a tough confrontation

with the N.S. regime. The readiness to champion other people's human rights, beyond the interests of one's own church, is just as much part of it as the rejection of any special law against individual groups of society. It has long been Catholic tradition to examine state laws and state activities in the light of norms of natural rights, which are not at the disposal of dictators. The bishops and the faithful had to learn—just like others—painful lessons in the face of N.S. injustice that mocked human dignity and human rights. This was accompanied by enormous tensions, which brought the Fulder Bishops' Conference to the brink of breaking apart.

We know that with this historical review and with a presentation of the circumstances of the time not everything can be explained and certainly not excused. Among us Catholics, too, there has been failure and guilt. In August 1945, the Fulder Bishops' Conference declared: "Many Germans, also from our ranks, allowed themselves to be deluded by the false teachings of National Socialism. They remained indifferent in the face of crimes against human freedom and human dignity; many supported these crimes through their attitude; many became criminals themselves. A heavy responsibility weighs on those who, because of their rank, were in a position to know what was happening among us; who could have prevented such crimes by their influence and did not do it; who even made these crimes possible and so placed themselves in solidarity with the criminals."

The bishops in the Federal Republic of Germany took this up, when they said in a statement in 1980 [*Bridges*, Vol. 1, Document 43], "Integral to the duty of Christian charity toward the Jews is also the continuous prayer for the millions of Jews murdered in the course of history, and the continuous plea to God for forgiveness of the many failures and omissions of which Christians have been guilty in their attitude toward the Jews. In Germany we have a special reason to ask for forgiveness of God and our Jewish brothers." Thus we repeat the psalmist's cry, "If you, O Lord, should mark our guilt, Lord, who would survive? but with you is found forgiveness; for this we revere you." (Ps 130:3ff.)

2. Reflection and Conversion

The memory of November 1938 and the twelve years of N.S. rule is depressing. Therefore, some of us ask whether the remembering of the past ought not, at some time, to come to an end. However, one cannot accept one's own history in a selective fashion and block out those things that incriminate. We have to accept the burden of history. We owe this to the victims, whose sufferings and death may not be forgotten. We owe this to the survivors and relatives because, otherwise, every dialogue with them and each new "being-with-one-another" would be impossible. But we also owe this to the Church and to yes ourselves. For history is not something exterior, it is part of the particular identity of the Church and is able to remind us that the Church, which we proclaim as holy, and which we honor as a mystery, is also a sinful Church and in need of conversion. Therefore our interest must ever slacken to represent this history to ourselves in as comprehensive and as exact a way as possible. For this reason we shall also, in future, advance the research and presentation of our history with all our strength, and do all that is in our power to ensure that the historical truth will be fully told in the teaching of religion, in catechesis and in other fields. For the sake of this truth we shall also oppose all attempts of manipulating history for the sake of present-day differences of opinion in the Church, the state or in society and to misuse it for personal attacks against individuals or whole groups. Respect for the victims demands this as well.

To accept history means to allow oneself to be challenged by its bright and dark sides. Under the National Socialist rule of terror there has been not only failure and guilt, but refusal to give-in and sympathy with the victims as well. Occasionally both were closed to each other and concerned one and the same person. Guilt or refusal to give-in are always the consequences of the individual's free, personal decision. Therefore it is difficult to prove them through subsequent analyses and to attribute them to the individual or even to whole groups of society. But even if one cannot and may not condemn a whole people, there still remains the co-responsibility of all for the things that happened in the name of all and for its consequences. This is also true for the Church. The German Bishops' Conference of September 1st, 1979 stated: "We know that there has been guilt in the Church as well. We know ourselves bound in conscience to an ongoing effort to draw the consequences from the mistakes and confusion of that terrible time."[6]

Days of remembrance repeatedly remind us of these commitments. The remembrance, too, during these days, of the November pogroms of 1938 should be a warning sign for us. But days of remembrance must not remain isolated events. They have to be embedded in a constant effort to contribute to a positive change of attitudes and actions, through remembering the past. The main challenge lies in this duty that constantly recurs. We have to confront it. Occasional setbacks and misunderstandings may also occur in the process. These we have to face with the inner calmness which one can obviously only achieve, if the focus remains firmly in sight. We have to be ready occasionally to allow ourselves to be overtaxed without—as was said on the first German post-war Catholics' Day (*Katholiken Tag*), 1948—"forfeiting one's composure or even one's love."[7] But there are also signs and openings that encourage us. We gratefully call to mind that this process of re-thinking has been co-initiated and sustained by the Jewish side, as well, when prominent representatives of Jewry took the dialogue on their own initiative. We have to continue on this path. A special emphasis will have to be given to the efforts of a genuine understanding and presentation of Judaism and Jewish religion in theology and catechesis. Furthermore, nothing ought to be left untried to promote the understanding between Jews and Christians through direct encounter and to draw from the past the necessary consequences for their joint service of God's word.

With these key words those areas are dealt with which were and still are of special importance in the efforts of the past years to create a new togetherness between Jews and Christians. They have been taken up in a great number of basic statements and declarations, which were presented by the Holy See, numerous local churches, lay people and also joint discussion groups of Jews and Christians. Of special importance among these documents is the Declaration *Nostra Aetate* [*Bridges*, Vol. 1, Document 30] (article 4), promulgated by Vatican II in 1965, which introduced a new beginning in Christian Jewish relations. Related to this document are the *Guidelines* for its implementation, as well as recommendations for preaching and teaching, which were issued in 1974 and 1985 by the Pontifical Commission for Religious Relations with the Jews [*Bridges*, Vol. 1, Documents 38 and 39]. In various countries these recommendations have been taken up and have been concretized in particular texts for specific occasions. In this way the German Bishops' Conference (1980) [*Bridges*, Vol. 1, Document 43], the Austrian Bishops' Conference (1982) and the Berlin Bishops' conference (1988) [Document 58 above] have clearly stated their position.[8] Apart from these, the working paper published in 1979 and the declaration of the discussion panel, "Jews and Christians," at the Central Committee of the German Catholics of 1988 deserve special attention, because they had been worked out jointly by Jews and Christians.[9] These and other documents, as well as the repeated meetings of Church representatives with representatives of Jewish organizations—the last during the pastoral visit of Pope John Paul II in Austria—are indications of the serious desire of many "that the old prejudices may be overcome and that space may be given for an ever fuller recognition of that 'bond' and of the 'spiritual common heritage' which exist between Jews and Christians" (John Paul II, April 13, 1986 [cf. Document 27 above]). The remembrance of the November pogroms ought to be a renewed incentive to interiorize these documents in their intentions and contents and to continue on this road that has been prepared.

3. "You Are Our Dearly Beloved"

The need to encounter one another is especially evident in theology. Over centuries, errors, misunderstandings and prejudices concerning faith and religion have heavily burdened the relationship between Jews and Christians on both sides. Here are to be found—besides political, social and economic resentments—the sources of anti-Judaism, which was also propagated among Catholics. These traditional prejudices have weakened the forces of resistance against the new phenomenon of modern antisemitism, which elevated race to the highest principle and which became the central feature of the National Socialist ideology. The extermination of Jews in the "Third Reich" has painfully brought home to us our own deficiencies and failures. "The terrible persecutions which the Jews have suffered in the various epochs of history have finally opened the eyes and roused the hearts" (Pope John Paul II, March 6, 1982 [cf. *Bridges*, Vol. 1, Document 35]). In the process we were able to rediscover—both in shame and gratitude—the Jewish people as the people of God's first and never-revoked covenant with man. Following the teaching of the Council (Vatican II), Pope John Paul II said during his visit to the Synagogue of Rome on April 13, 1986, "For us, the Jewish religion is not something 'exterior,' but in a certain sense belongs to the innermost part of our religion. Our relationships to it are unlike any of those we have to other religions. You are our dearly beloved brothers and, one could even say, our elder brothers."

This special bond between Christians and Jews is clearly evident if one traces the roots of Christianity and if one considers the spiritual heritage of Israel for the Church. The faith in one creator God is just as common to both as the commandments of the Decalogue or the hope for the messiah. We Christians are called upon to reexamine our understanding of Jews and Judaism from this point of view of mutuality and to change where necessary. But there can be no question of denying what truly separates us or to make false compromises. The person of Jesus both unites and separates us; Jesus, who was a Jew and who for us Christians is Son of God and redeemer of the world. But illuminating the common roots gives us a better understanding of Judaism in its true identity and at the same time helps us to uncover dimensions of our faith that have perhaps been buried. This clarification should, wherever possible, be sought by Christians and Jews together. A dialogue can unfold—fruitful for both sides—about the Old Testament or the importance of Jesus. This joint engagement, however, of Jews and Christians is urgently demanded and is of greatest importance if it concerns faith in the one God. In the face of the temptations coming from new, esoteric myths and promises of salvation, the witness is indispensable of all those who believe in God the creator and redeemer of the whole world.

4. Preaching and Teaching—
To Speak Correctly about Jews and Judaism

With the Declaration *Nostra Aetate*, Vatican II has expressly brought to mind the bond "by which the people of the New Covenant [are] spiritually united with the seed of Abraham." In order to bring about a genuine dialogue between Christians and Jews, the Council has emphasized the importance of "mutual knowledge and esteem." The *Guidelines* of the Vatican Commission for Religious Relations with the Jews [*Bridges*, Vol. 1, Document 38] concretize this concern and urge Christians to learn "by what essential traits the Jews define themselves in the light of their own religious experience." In this way not only individual areas of information and instruction are addressed, but "all levels of Christian doctrine and education." The range of information-media thus envisaged extends from catechetical writings and historical representations to the "media of mass-communication (press, radio, film, television)." A few years ago the same Commission took up again the ideas of the *Guidelines* and presented—with regard to the contents—"Instructions for a Correct Presentation of Jews and Judaism in the Preaching and Teaching of the Catholic Church" [*Bridges*, Vol. 1, Document 39].

Corresponding to these documents and efforts on a world-wide level there are numerous initiatives and activities in various local churches which aim at a proper presentation and appreciation of Jews and Judaism within preaching. The above-mentioned statements of the three Bishops' Conferences fit within this framework just as much as the proclamations of the discussion group "Jews and Christians" at the Central Committee of the German Catholics. These incentives and aids are already producing their first fruits. This issue assumes a new value in the formation of priests, in religious education and in catechesis, during conferences of Catholic academies and educational institutions, or in Church publications. We should not forget to mention the impressive German Catholics' Day (*Katholiken Tag*), during which, with a great participation of young people, the Christian Jewish dialogue and the joint prayer have formed a special focal point for quite some time. Moreover, there are the two Vienna conferences entitled "Shalom," because in Austria these have greatly contributed in helping the representatives of the "Israelite Cult Community" (Kultusgemeinde) to prepare their on-going dialogue. During the Dresden Catholics' Meeting, 1987, as well, the question of the Christian-Jewish dialogue played an essential role. This is no reason for complacency. It gives courage, however, to continue and not to slacken in our efforts. Particularly encouraging is the fact that a part of these initiatives is also carried by the Jews. We owe them grateful recognition.

5. Efforts For Reconciliation

During the Third Reich great wrong has been inflicted on numerous peoples and groups in the name of Germany. In 1945 it was rather doubtful whether it would be possible once more to succeed in establishing a relationship with our neighbors, which was born out of trust and mutual esteem. And yet, the unbelievable has happened. The victims themselves have decisively contributed to this—as the late Cardinal Hoffner commented.[10]

To attain a reconciliation with the Jews all over the world is a still greater task which is far from being accomplished. The hurts are deep. The Jews have been threatened with the "Final Solution," total annihilation. The sacrifices of the Jews in the "Shoah" are immeasurable. And yet we have constantly to make every effort to obtain a reconciliation. In this effort the common religious and cultural roots of Jews and Christians can form a particular point of contact and can contribute to a mutual openness. Central, however, is personal encounter. In this sense, all initiatives which allow immediate contacts, everything that makes dialogue possible and all that widens our horizon across the frontiers of peoples, faiths, and social groupings, deserve ongoing support. Much has been done. Much is still to be done. We place great hopes in the openness and readiness for mutual understanding of the youth, which, in future, will have to build up the relationship between Jews and Christians. It may succeed, in causing the common memory to bring forth a new togetherness and a mutual responsibility for the shaping of the future. The will to openness and readiness for dialogue is necessary on both sides. But just as we MAY not forget, we must accept that many Jews CANNOT forget. Many of those, who themselves had to suffer under the persecutions, but also many of the succeeding generation cannot yet show this openness. Their hurt is too deep. We have to meet them with respect. Reconciliation can neither be forced nor bought, but only be achieved through a long process of walking toward one another.

6. Common Tasks in the World

During the visit of Pope John Paul II to the Synagogue of Rome, Chief Rabbi Toaff said [Document 88 below], "We cannot…forget the past. However, full of confidence and hope, we want to mark today the beginning of a new era of history which promises to be fruitful through joint action, which eventually, in the spirit of partnership, of equality and of mutual respect, may profit the whole of humanity." This consciousness of mutuality among Christians and Jews, but also among all human beings of good-will, grew under National Socialist affliction. It broke away from a pattern of thinking and acting which envisaged, above all, the interests of one's own group—whether political party, trade union or church—and which left little space for a mutual sense of responsibility. Yet, at the same time, the conditions for a mutual engagement of Jews and Christians for and with one another are given in a special manner: both respect the dignity of human beings and acknowledge a task in the human fashioning of the world, because they believe in the creative act of God guaranteed in the Book of Genesis. Therefore both ought determinedly to take their part in ensuring that this consciousness of mutuality is not buried again and that a new "thinking in categories" cannot once more gain a footing in the state and in society.

The areas for mutual engagement of Jews and Christians in the shaping of the world are manifold and also different from one country to another: in the forefront are the efforts in promoting human dignity, the ethical consolidation of the ordering of State and society and the guaranteeing of human rights. In spite of all public protestations and international agreements, human rights are still endangered world-wide—be it for racial, religious, social or political reasons. Especially endangered is the first right of man, the right of life. This is not only true of regions of special oppression and crisis, but also for ourselves, where every year hundreds of thousands of children are killed in their mothers' wombs. The experiences of history teach us that all barriers are breaking where the life of the individual is no longer respected. "Nobody's life is safe unless it is stated incontestably: 'You shall not kill'" (Fulder Bishops' Conference, 1942).

However, Christians and Jews should also work together if it is a question of fighting against any unjustified disadvantage and discrimination of individuals or of whole groups for ideological, religious or other reasons. Religious freedom and freedom of conscience are precious gifts. Therefore Christians and Jews ought to support a just social order, which is marked by mutual respect and tolerance, which safeguards everybody's inalienable rights and which does not give room to antisemitism or any other ideology that holds human beings in contempt. In this way Christians and Jews are called in a special manner to a service of justice and peace.

Furthermore, they are called to a service of peace in the world, the dangers of which are well known to us. The first step toward this is also here to recognize the human being in the other and neither to question his right to life nor his opportunities for development. Just as within a state, so also among nations, the word holds true: "justice creates peace" (Isa 32:17)—the word which—referring to the motto of Pope Pius XII—stands above the present efforts of the Christian churches to work for peace, justice and the preservation of creation.

And finally, our engagement for the preservation of creation is demanded. The way our natural surroundings are threatened by technical civilization is a reminder for us of the task to deal responsibly and competently with creation, not to pillage the treasure of the earth irresponsibly and to consider the consequences of our actions for ourselves and the successive generations. We ought to impress upon our minds and that of others that we are all "creatures," not masters of this world.

For each one of us and for all of us together a vast scope of tasks presents itself here, where what is uniting carries more weight than what divides. History shows us the necessity of acting creatively in good time. In proportion to this manner of acting will grow—thus, we hope—not only the insight into the mutuality of Jews and Christians, but also into the mutuality of all people of good will.

"Reconciliation comes about through remembering" (Martin Buber). One cannot create this reconciliation with one's own hands; it is basically God's work. As a conclusion to this statement we would like to bring in prayer before the Lord of history those events, which are the cause of our remembrance. Only from there can strength and courage flow toward us on the difficult path to reconciliation.

To mark the fiftieth anniversary of the Kristallnacht, the bishops of East Germany made a collection among that country's Catholics on November 13, toward the rebuilding of the new synagogue on the Oranienburgerstrasse in East Berlin. Donations, said the bishop, would be a "sign of solidarity with the people of God of the Old Testament" (*The Tablet*, 19/11/88).

Notes

1. *L'Osservatore Romano*, German edition of July 1, 1988. The texts related to the Christian-Jewish dialogue are collected in the volume, *Die Kirchen und das Judentum. Dokumente von 1945–85* (The Churches and Judaism: Documents from 1945 to 1985): Paderborn, Munich 1988, edited by Rolf Rendtorff and Hans Hermann Henrix. Individual references are therefore given only for those texts that are not included in this volume. [See also for later documents *Die Kirche und das Judentum*, Band II. *Dokumente von 1986–2000* (The Churches and Judaism: Documents from 1986 to 2000): Paderborn, Munich, 2001, edited by Hans Hermann Henrix and Wolfgang Kraus.] As to the historic sources, reference is made to the *Documents of the German Bishops on the Situation of the Church 1933–1945*, Volumes 1–6, Mainz 1968–1985, published by Bernhard Stasiewski and then by Ludwig Volk. Individual references are given here as well only for those sources which are not printed in this series.

2. Printed in Dieter Albrecht (revised), *Exchange of Diplomatic Notes Between the Holy See and the Government of the German Reich*, Volume 1, Mainz 1965, pp. 402–43.

3. Annotation from Rudolf Lill, "Catholicism After 1848," in Karl Heinrich Rengstorf, Siegfried von Kortzfleisch (Publ.), *Church and Synagogue. A Handbook on the History of Christians and Jews. Presentation and Sources*, Volume 2, Stuttgart 1970, p. 366.

4. Helmut Witetschek, *The Church's Position in Bavaria According to the President's Reports, 1933-1943*, Volume 1; *Administrative District of Upper Bavaria*, Mainz 1966, p. 300.

5. Ludwig Volk (Revised): *Documents of Cardinal Michael von Faulhaber 1917–1945*, Volume 2, Mainz 1978, p. 604.

6. Statement of the German Bishops of August 27, 1979, on the occasion of the Fortieth Anniversary of the outbreak of World War II, in Secretariat of the German Bishops' Conference (ed.), *Remembrance and Responsibility*, Working Aids 30, (Bonn 1983).

7. *The Christian in the Peril of the Era*, Paderborn 1949, p. 216.

8. The German Bishops' Statement on the Church's Attitude to Judaism, of April 28, 1980 [*Bridges*, Vol. 1, Document 43], in Rendtorff/Henrix, pp. 260–80. Bishops' Conference of Austria/Pastoral Commission of Austria, "Christians and Judaism," April 1982, in Rendtorff/Henrix, pp. 205–15. Pastoral Letter of the Berlin Bishops' Conference on the Fiftieth Anniversary of the Reich's Night of Pogrom (Kristallnacht), November 1988.

9. Dialogue Group Jews and Christians, at the Central Committee of German Catholics; working paper: "Theological Emphases of the Jewish-Christian Dialogue" of May 8, 1979, in Rendtorff/Henrix, pp. 252–60; "After Fifty Years: How to Talk of Guilt, Sorrow and Reconciliation?"—Statement of the Dialogue Group Jews and Christians of the Central Committee of German Catholics, Fifty years after the Reich's Night of Pogroms (Kristallnacht)" in *Reports and Documents* 68, pp. 30–46 (see SIDIC XXI:3 1988 p. 26).

The Central Committee of German Catholics is the agency recognized by the German Bishops' Conference for the coordinating of the efforts of the lay-apostolate and for the promotion of apostolic activity of the Church in the Federal Republic of Germany and in West Berlin. Membership consists mainly of representatives of the diocesan councils and of the central associations and organizations.

10. Joseph Cardinal Heffner, Sermon in the Ecumenical Service in Cologne Cathedral, May 8, 1985, in Press and Information Office of the Government of the Federal Republic (ed.), *Remembrance, Grief and Reconciliation. Addresses and Statements on the Occasion of the 40th Anniversary of the End of the War*.

59

Pastoral on Jewish-Catholic Relations

Polish Conference of Catholic Bishops, November 30, 1990

We address you today about the very important issue of our relationship to the Jewish people and to the Mosaic religion, with which we Christians are uniquely linked. We do this on the occasion of the twenty-fifth anniversary of the proclamation of the conciliar declaration *Nostra Aetate* [*Bridges*, Vol. 1, Document 30], in which the church defined more precisely its relations to non-Christian religions, among them the Jewish religion.

This declaration, adopted on October 27, 1965, has lost none of its importance or contemporary value today. Our Holy Father John Paul II has repeated this on numerous occasions, saying "I would like to confirm with the deepest conviction that the teaching of the church, given during the Second Vatican Council in the declaration *Nostra Aetate*...always remains for us, for the Catholic Church, for the episcopate...and for the pope, a teaching to which one must adhere, a teaching which one must accept not only as something relevant but even more, as an expression of faith, as an inspiration of the Holy Spirit, as a word of divine wisdom" (Speech to the Jewish community in Venezuela, January 15, 1985).

The conciliar declaration points out first and foremost the multiplicity and diversity of ties that exist between the church, the Jewish religion and the Jewish people. There is no other religion with which the church has such close relations nor is there any other people with which it is so closely linked. "The church of Christ," write the fathers of the council, "acknowledges that in God's plan of salvation the beginning of her faith and election is to be found in the patriarchs, Moses and the prophets" (*Nostra Aetate*, 4). Therefore, John Paul II, who after St. Peter, was the first of his successors to visit a synagogue, having visited the synagogue in Rome on April 13, 1986, could address the Jews as "our elder brothers" in the faith [cf. Document 27 above].

"Many Poles saved Jews during the last war. Hundreds, if not thousands, paid for this with their own lives...In spite of so many heroic examples of help on the part of Polish Christians, there were also people who remained indifferent to this incomprehensible tragedy."

The church is rooted in the Jewish people and in the faith of the Jews most of all because of the fact that Jesus Christ, according to the flesh, came from that people. This central event in the history of salvation was from its very inception intended by God in his original plan of salvation. To that people God disclosed his name and made a covenant with them. This election was not only an exclusive privilege, but also a great commitment to the faith and fidelity to the one God, including the testimony of suffering and, quite often, of death as well. To this people God entrusted the special mission of uniting everyone in the true faith in one God and awaiting the Messiah, the Savior. When the time was fulfilled, the eternally true word of God, the only begotten Son of the Father, took flesh from the Virgin Mary, a daughter of the Jewish people. Announced by the prophets and awaited by his own people, Jesus Christ was born in Bethlehem as "a son of David, a son of Abraham" (Matt 1:1). From the Jewish people came also "the apostles, the pillars on which the church stands," as well as "many of those early disciples who proclaimed the Gospel of Christ to the world" (*Nostra Aetate*, 4).

The church, as God's people of the new election and covenant, did not disinherit God's people of the first election and covenant of the gifts received from God. As St. Paul teaches, the Israelites, because of their forefathers, are the subject of love (Rom 11:28), and therefore the gift of grace and the calling of God are irrevocable (Rom 11:29). To them belong also "the sonship, the glory, the covenants, the giving of the law, the worship and the promises" (Rom 9:4). God thus has not revoked his selection of the Jewish people as the chosen people, but continues to bestow his love. He and only he, the almighty and merciful God, knows the day "when all people will call on God with one voice and serve him shoulder to shoulder" (*Nostra Aetate*, 4).

The fathers of the council, in the declaration, deny in a clear and decisive manner the main accusation that all Jews bear responsibility for the death of Christ. The declaration states, "Even though the Jewish authorities and those who followed their lead pressed for the death of Christ, neither all Jews indiscriminately at that time nor Jews today can be charged with the crimes committed during his passion" (ibid.). Some people, however, quoting the words of St. Matthew's

Gospel, "Let his blood be upon us and upon our children" (Matt 27:25), accuse the Jews of the death of Christ. In reality, these words mean: We accept the full responsibility for that death. But it was not the entire Jewish people who said this, only the unruly crowd gathered in front of Pilate's palace. One should not forget that for these people, as for all of us, Jesus prayed on the cross: "Father, forgive them, for they know not what they do" (Luke 23:34).

The catechism of the Council of Trent treats the question of the responsibility for the death of Christ as follows: "Christian sinners are more responsible for the death of Christ in comparison with certain Jews who participated in it. The latter really did not know what they did, whereas we know only too well... (Part 1, Chap. 5, Quest. 9). The declaration *Nostra Aetate* reminds us of the traditional teaching of the church that "Christ...freely underwent suffering and death because of the sins of all" (No. 4).

The teaching of the church in that declaration was developed in later documents of the Apostolic See. Especially important is a document of 1985 titled *Notes on the Correct Way to Present the Jews and Judaism in Preaching and Catechesis in the Roman Catholic Church* [*Bridges*, Vol. 1, Document 39]. This deserves the widest possible dissemination, especially among pastors and catechists.

We Poles have particular ties with the Jewish people from as early as the first centuries of our history. Poland became for many Jews a second fatherland. The majority of Jews living in the world today are by origin from the territories of the previous and current Polish commonwealth. Unfortunately, in our century this particular land became the grave for several million Jews. Not by our wish, and not by our hands. Here is what our Holy Father said recently, on September 26 of this year, about our common history: "There is still one other nation, one particular people: the people of the patriarchs, of Moses and the prophets, the inheritors of the faith of Abraham...This people lived side by side with us for generations on the same land, which became, as it were, a new fatherland of their diaspora. This people underwent the terrible death of millions of their sons and daughters. At first they were stigmatized in a particular way. Later, they were pushed into the ghetto in separate neighborhoods. Then they were taken to the gas chambers, they underwent death—only because they were children of this people. Murderers did this on our land—perhaps in order to dishonor it. One cannot dishonor a land by the death of innocent victims.

Through such death a land becomes a sacred relic" (Speech to Poles during a Wednesday audience, September 26, 1990).

"The most important way to overcome the difficulties that still exist today is the establishment of a dialogue which would lead to the elimination of distrust, prejudices and stereotypes."

During his historic meeting in 1987 with the few Jews living in Poland, in Warsaw, the Holy Father said [cf. Document 29 above], "Be assured, dear brothers, that the Poles, this Polish church is in a spirit of profound solidarity with you when she looks closely at the terrible reality of the extermination—the unconditional extermination—of your nation, an extermination carried out with premeditation. The threat against you was also a threat against us; this latter was not realized to the same extent because it did not have time to be realized to the same extent. It was you who suffered this terrible sacrifice of extermination: One might say that you suffered it also on behalf of those who were likewise to have been exterminated" (*L'Osservatore Romano*, June 1987).

Many Poles saved Jews during the last war. Hundreds, if not thousands, paid for this with their own lives and the lives of their loved ones. For each of the Jews saved there was a whole chain of hearts of people of good will and helping hands. The express testimony of that help to Jews in the years of the Hitler occupation are the many trees dedicated to Poles in Yad Vashem, the place of national memory in Jerusalem, with the honored title, "The Just among the Nations" given to many Poles. In spite of so many heroic examples of help on the part of Polish Christians, there were also people who remained indifferent to this incomprehensible tragedy. We are especially disheartened by those among Catholics who in some way were the cause of the death of Jews. They will forever gnaw at our conscience on the social plane. If only one Christian could have helped and did not stretch out a helping hand to a Jew during the time of danger or caused his death, we must ask for forgiveness of our Jewish brothers and sisters. We are aware that many of our compatriots still remember the injustices and injuries committed by the postwar communist authorities, in which people of Jewish origin also took part. We must acknowledge, however, that the source of inspiration of their activity was clearly neither their origin nor religion, but the communist ideology, from which the Jews themselves, in fact, suffered many injustices.

We express our sincere regret for all the incidents of antisemitism which were committed at any time or by anyone on Polish soil. We do this with the deep conviction that all incidents of antisemitism are contrary to the spirit of the Gospel and—as Pope John Paul II recently emphasized—"remain opposed to the Christian vision of human dignity" (John Paul II on the fiftieth anniversary of the outbreak of World War II).

In expressing our sorrow for all the injustices and harm done to Jews, we cannot forget that we consider untrue and deeply harmful the use by many of the concept of what is called "Polish antisemitism" as an especially threatening form of that antisemitism; and in addition, frequently connecting the concentration camps not with those who were actually involved with them, but with Poles in a Poland occupied by the Germans. Speaking of the unprecedented extermination of Jews, one cannot forget and even less pass over in silence the fact that the Poles as a nation were one of the first victims of the same criminal racist ideology of Hitler's Nazism.

The same land, which for centuries was the common fatherland of Poles and Jews, of blood spilled together, the sea of horrific suffering and of injuries shared—should not divide us but unite us. For this commonality cries out to us—especially the places of execution and, in many cases, common graves. We Christians and Jews are also united in our belief in one God, the Creator and Lord of the entire universe, who created man in his image and likeness. We are united by the commonly accepted ethical principles included in the Ten Commandments, crowned by the love of God and neighbor. We are united in our respect for the biblical books of the Old Testament as the word of God and by common traditions of prayer. Last, we are united in the common hope of the final coming of the kingdom of God. Together we await the Messiah, the Savior, although we, believing that he is Jesus Christ of Nazareth—await not his first, but his final coming, no more in the poverty of the manger in Bethlehem, but in power and glory.

The most important way to overcome the difficulties that still exist today is the establishment of a dialogue, which would lead to the elimination of distrust, prejudices and stereotypes, and to mutual acquaintance and understanding based on respect for our separate religious traditions as well as opening the way to cooperation in many fields. It is important, moreover, that while doing this, we learn to experience and appreciate the proper religious contexts of Jews and Christians as they are lived by Jews and Christians themselves.

We conclude our pastoral homily, dear brothers and sisters, recalling the recent statement of the Holy Father about our common temporal and final destinies: "The (Jewish) people who lived with us for many generations remained with us after the terrible death of many millions of their sons and daughters. Together we wait for the day of judgment and resurrection" (Speech to Poles during the Wednesday audience, Sept. 26, 1990).

Commending to the merciful God all the victims of force and hatred, we bless you from our hearts, praying that "the God of peace may be always with you" (Phil 4:9).

60

Declaration of Repentance

Catholic Bishops of France, Drancy, September 30, 1997

As one of the major events of the twentieth century, the planned extermination of the Jewish people by the Nazis raises particularly challenging questions of conscience which no human being can ignore. The Catholic Church, far from wanting it to be forgotten, knows full well that conscience is formed in remembering, and that, just as no individual person can live in peace with himself, neither can society live in peace with a repressed or untruthful memory.

The Church of France questions itself. It, like the other churches, has been called to do so by Pope John Paul II as the third millennium draws near: "It is good that the church should cross this threshold fully conscious of what she has lived through...Recognizing the failings of yesteryear is an act of loyalty and courage which helps us strengthen our faith, which makes us face up to the temptations and difficulties of today and prepares us to confront them."[1]

Following this year's celebration of the fiftieth anniversary of the Declaration of Seelisburg [*Bridges*, Vol. 1, Document 56] (that tiny village in Switzerland where, immediately after the war, on August 5, 1947, Jews and Christians drew up guidelines proposing a new understanding of Judaism), the undersigned bishops of France, because of the presence of internment camps in their dioceses, on the occasion of the forthcoming anniversary of the first statutes concerning the Jews drawn up by the Marshall Petain government (October 3, 1940), wish to take a further step. They do so in response to what their conscience, illuminated by Christ, demands.

The time has come for the church to submit her own history, especially that of this period, to critical examination and to recognize without hesitation the sins committed by members of the church, and to beg forgiveness of God and humankind.

In France, the violent persecution did not begin immediately. But very soon, in the months that followed the 1940 defeat, antisemitism was sown at the state level, depriving French Jews of their rights and foreign Jews of their freedom; all of our national institutions were drawn into the applications of these legal measures. By February 1941, some 40,000 Jews were in French internment camps. At this point, in a country which had been beaten, lay prostrate and was partially occupied, the hierarchy saw the protection of its own faithful as its first priority, assuring as much as possible its own institutions. The absolute priority which was given to these objectives, in themselves legitimate, had the unhappy effect of casting a shadow over the biblical demand of respect for every human being created in the image of God.

This retreat into a narrow vision of the church's mission was compounded by a lack of appreciation on the part of the hierarchy of the immense global tragedy which was being played out and which was a threat to Christianity's future. Yet many members of the church and many non-Catholics yearned for the church to speak out at a time of such spiritual confusion and to recall the message of Jesus Christ.

For the most part, those in authority in the church, caught up in a loyalism and docility which went far beyond the obedience traditionally accorded to civil authorities, remained stuck in conformity, prudence and abstention. This was dictated in part by their fear of reprisals against the church's activities and youth movements. They failed to realize that the church, called at that moment to play the role of defender within a social body that was falling apart, did in fact have considerable power and influence, and that in the face of the silence of other institutions, its voice could have echoed loudly by taking a definitive stand against the irreparable.

It must be borne in mind: During the occupation no one knew the full extent of the Hitlerian genocide. While it is true that mention could be made of a great number of gestures of solidarity, we have to ask ourselves whether acts of charity and help are enough to fulfill the demands of justice and respect for the rights of human persons.

So it is that, given the antisemitic legislation enacted by the French government—beginning with the October 1940 law on Jews and that of June 1941, which deprived a whole section of the French people of their rights as citizens, which hounded them out and treated them as inferior beings within the nation—and given the decision to put into internment camps foreign Jews who had thought they could rely on the right of asylum and hospitality in France, we are obliged to admit that the bishops of France made no public statements, thereby acquiescing by their silence in the flagrant violation of human rights and leaving the way open to a death-bearing chain of events.

We can pass no judgment either on the consciences of the people of that era; we are not ourselves guilty of what took place in the past; but we must be fully aware of the cost of such behavior and actions. It is our church, and we are obliged to acknowledge objectively today that ecclesiastical interests, understood in an overly restrictive sense, took priority over the demands of conscience—and we must ask ourselves why.

Over and above the historical circumstances which we have already recalled, we need to pay special attention to the religious reasons for this blindness. To what extent did secular antisemitism have an influence? Why is it, in the debates which we know took place, that the church did not listen to the better claims of its members' voices? Before the war, Jacques Maritain, both in articles and in lectures, tried to open Christians up to a different perspective on the Jewish people. He also forcefully warned against the perversity of the antisemitism that was developing. Just before the war broke out, Cardinal Saliege advised Catholics of the twentieth century to seek light in the teaching of Pius XI rather than in that of the thirteenth-century edicts of Innocent III. During the war, theologians and exegetes in Paris and in Lyons spoke out prophetically about the Jewish roots of Christianity, underlining how the shoot of Jesse flowered in Israel, that the two testaments were indissolubly linked, that the Virgin, Christ and the apostles were all Jews and that Christianity is linked to Judaism like a branch to the trunk that has borne it. Why was so little attention paid to such words?

Certainly, at the doctrinal level, the church was fundamentally opposed to racism for the reasons, both theological and spiritual, which Pius XI expressed so strongly in his encyclical *Mit Brennender Sorge*, which condemned the basic principles of national-socialism and warned Christians against the myth of race and of the all-powerful state. As far back as 1928, the Holy Office had condemned antisemitism. In 1938, Pius XI boldly declared, "Spiritually, we are all Semites." But in the face of the constantly repeated anti-Jewish stereotypes, what weight could such condemnations carry? What weight could the thinking of theologians already referred to carry—thinking which can be found even after 1942 in statements which were not lacking in courage?

In the process which led to the Shoah, we are obliged to admit the role, indirect if not direct, played by commonly held anti-Jewish prejudices, which Christians were guilty of maintaining. In fact, in spite of (and to some extent because of) the Jewish roots of Christianity, and because of the Jewish people's fidelity throughout its history to the one God, the "original separation" dating back to the first-century became a divorce, then an animosity and ultimately a centuries-long hostility between Christians and Jews.

There can be no denying the weight of social, political, cultural and economic factors in the long story of misunderstanding and often antagonism between Jews and Christians. However, one of the essential points in the debate was of a religious nature. This is not to say that a direct cause-and-effect link can be drawn between these commonly held anti-Jewish feelings and the Shoah, because Nazi plans to annihilate the Jewish people has its sources elsewhere.

In the judgment of historians, it is a well-proven fact that for centuries, up until Vatican Council II, an anti-Jewish tradition stamped its mark in differing ways on Christian doctrine and teaching, in theology, apologetics, preaching and in the liturgy. It was on such ground that the venomous plant of hatred for the Jews was able to flourish. Hence, the heavy inheritance we still bear in our century, with all its consequences which are so difficult to wipe out. Hence our still open wounds.

To the extent that the pastors and those in authority in the church let such a teaching of disdain develop for so long, along with an underlying basic religious culture among Christian communities which shaped and deformed people's attitudes, they bear a grave responsibility. Even if they condemned antisemitic theologies as being pagan in origin, they did not enlighten people's minds as they ought because they failed to call into question these centuries-old ideas and attitudes. This had a soporific effect on people's consciences, reducing their capacity to resist when the full violence of national-socialist antisemitism rose up, the diabolical and ultimate expression of hatred of the Jews, based on categories of race and blood, and which was explicitly directed to the physical annihilation of the Jewish people. As Pope John Paul II put it, "an unconditional extermination...undertaken with premeditation."

Subsequently, when the persecution became worse and the genocidal policy of the Third Reich was unleashed within France itself, shared by the Vichy government, which put its own force at the disposition of the occupier, some brave bishops[2] raised their voices in a clarion call, in the name of human rights, against the rounding up of the Jewish population. These public statements, though few in number, were heard by many Christians.

Neither should the many actions undertaken by ecclesiastical authorities to save men, women, and children in danger of death be forgotten; nor the outpouring of Christian charity by the ordinary faithful, shown in generosity of every kind, often at great risk, in saving thousands and thousands of Jews.

Long before this, priests, religious, and lay people—some not hesitating to join underground movements—saved the honor of the church, even if discreetly and anonymously. This was also done, in particular through the publication of *Les Cahiers du Temoignage Chretien* (Notebooks of Christian Witness), by denouncing in no uncertain terms the Nazi poison which threatened Christian souls with all its neopagan, racist, and antisemitic virulence, and by echoing the words of Pius XI: "Spiritually we are all Semites." It is an established historical fact that the survival of a great number of Jews was assured thanks to such gestures of help from among Catholic and Protestant milieux, and by Jewish organizations.

Nevertheless, while may be true that some Christians—priests, religious and lay people—were not lacking in acts of courage in defense of fellow human beings, we must recognize that indifference won the day over indignation in the face of the persecution of the Jews and that, in particular, silence was the rule in the face of the multifarious laws enacted by the Vichy government, whereas speaking out in favor of the victims was the exception.

As François Mauriac wrote, "A crime of such proportions falls for no small part on the shoulders of those witnesses who failed to cry out, and this whatever the reason for their silence."[3]

The end result is that the attempt to exterminate the Jewish people, instead of being perceived as a central question in human and spiritual terms, remained a secondary consideration. In the face of so great and utter a tragedy, too many of the church's pastors committed an offense, by their silence, against the church itself and its mission.

Today we confess that such a silence was a sin. In so doing, we recognize that the church of France failed in her mission as teacher of consciences and that therefore she carries along with the Christian people the responsibility for failing to lend their aid, from the very first moments, when protest and protection were still possible, as well as necessary, even if, subsequently, a great many acts of courage were performed.

This is the fact that we acknowledge today. For, this failing of the church of France and of her responsibility toward the Jewish people are part of our history. We confess this sin. We beg God's pardon, and we call upon the Jewish people to hear our words of repentance.

This act of remembering calls us to an ever keener vigilance on behalf of humankind today and in the future.

Notes

1. John Paul II, *On the Coming of the Third Millennium (Tertio Millennio Adveniente)*, no. 33.

2. In 1942 five archbishops and bishops in the southern (unoccupied) part of France protested against the violation of human rights caused by the rounding up of the Jews. They were Archbishop Saliege of Toulouse; Bishop Theas of Montauban; Cardinal Gerlier of Lyons; Archbishop Moussaron of Albi; and Bishop Daly of Marseilles. Within the occupied zone, Bishop Vansteenberghe of Bayonne published a protest on the front page of his diocesan newsletter September 20, 1942.

3. From the Preface to Leon Poliakov's book, *Bréviaire de la haine* (Breviary of Hate), 1951, p. 3.

PART THREE

Orthodox Christian Statements

61

We Must Be in Unity with the Jews

A Message to the Representatives of the Jewish Community of the United States of America by His Holiness Patriarch of Moscow and All Russia Alexy II, presented to the American Rabbi Arthur Schneier, New York, in November 1991.

Dear brothers, *shalom* to you in the name of the God of love and peace, the God of our fathers, Who revealed Himself to His servant Moses in the burning bush and said: "I am the God of your father, the God of Abraham, the God of Isaac, and the God of Jacob" (Exodus 3:6).

He is the true God, Adonai, God and Father of all, and we are all brothers, for we are all children of His old covenant in the Sinai, which we Christians believe is renewed in the new covenant through Christ; the Sinai covenant (Exodus 24:8) is renewed through the blood of the new covenant. These two covenants are two stages of one and the same "divine-human religion," two moments of one and the same "divine-human process." In this process of formation of God's covenant with humankind, the Israelites became God's chosen people, who were entrusted with the law and the prophets.

This was expressed very well by the distinguished hierarch and theologian of the Russian Orthodox Church, the Archbishop of Kherson and Odessa, Nikanor (Brovkovych), in a sermon given in Odessa in 1884. The main theme of his sermon was the very close relationship between the religions of the Old and the New Testaments. The unity of Judaism with Christianity must be considered not on the basis of indifferentism or some kind of abstract humanistic principles common to all humankind, but on the realistic basis of a spiritual and natural relationship and of affirmative religious interests. We must be in unity with the Jewish people without denying Christianity, and not in defiance of Christianity, but in the name and power of Christianity; and the Jews must be in unity with us not in defiance of Judaism, but in the name and power of true Judaism. We are separated from the Jews because we are not yet "fully Christians," and they, the Jews, are separated from us because they are not yet "fully Jews." For the fullness of Christianity embraces Judaism within itself, and the fullness of Judaism is Christianity (*Pravoslavnoe Obozrenie* [Orthodox Review] 1884, May–June).

The basis for Archbishop Nikanor's comments was the idea of mutual understanding and dialogue between the Orthodox Church and the Jewish people.

These were not the only aspirations for rapprochement and dialogue within our Church.

Already in 1861 the Bishop of Nizhny Novgorod, Chrysanf (Retivzev), called upon the Church to facilitate the cessation of hostility and the implementation of a relationship with the Jewish people based on dialogue and rapprochement (*Trudy Kievskoj Duxovnoj Akademii* [Kiev Seminary Studies] 1861, September, pp. 1–2).

Archbishop Nikolai (Ziorov) also addressed the Jewish people in the spirit of dialogue and rapprochement. "The Jewish people are close to us in faith. Your law is our law; your prophets are our prophets. The Ten Commandments of Moses are obligations of Christians as well as Jews. We wish to live with you in peace and harmony, so that there be no misunderstandings, no enmity, and no hatred between us" (*Varshavskie besedy i rechi* [Warsaw Discussions and Discourses] Vol. 3, St. Petersburg, 1911).

Based upon such religious-pedagogical and theological convictions, the hierarchy, clergy and theologians of our Church have resolutely and openly condemned any and all manifestations of antisemitism, hostility and pogroms in regard to Jews.

During the well-known trial of Beilis [M. M. Beilis, 1873–1934], experts of our Church (Kiev Seminary professor the Rev. Alexander Glagolev and St. Petersburg Seminary professor Ivan Troicky) firmly defended Beilis and resolutely spoke out against the accusations of ritual murders supposedly committed by Jews. The Metropolitan of St. Petersburg, Antony (Vadkovsky), also did much to defend Jews against antisemitic attacks by extreme radical-right organizations.

Separate notice must be taken of the defense of Jews against all kinds of antisemitism by many of our theologians and leading religious thinkers such as, for example, Vladimir Soloviev, Nikolai Aleksandrovich Berdyaev, and Rev. Sergei Bulgakov. Soloviev considered the defense of the Jews one of the most important tasks of his life from a Christian point of view. For him, the issue of the Jews was not a question of good or bad Jews, but rather a question of good or bad Christians.

Much also was contributed to the Christian-Jewish dialogue and rapprochement by our famous orthodox religious thinkers and philosophers who were Jews by birth, S. L. Frank and L. Shestov. Nevertheless, not only our famous hierarchs and theologians participated in this noble cause. Many parish priests actively defended and rescued Jews from pogroms. During World War II and the Nazi occupation, the clergy and faithful of our Church saved and hid Jews, thereby risking their lives. Classic examples are Mother Maria (Skobcova), Rev. Dimitri Klepinin, Rev. Aleksei Glagolev and many others. All of us should know about their heroic deeds and write about their sacrificial service in the rescue of their Jewish brothers and sisters. Unfortunately, the manifestations of antisemitic sentiments and actions have found a place in our lives in the current, difficult time of crisis for our society, a time of disintegration, of the growth of national isolation as well as of ethnic chauvinism; moreover, they have a nurturing socio-political sphere in which they can grow and spread among the worst extremists of radical right-wing chauvinistic groups. Our Church's task is to help our people overcome this problem and to defeat the evil of isolation, of ethnic hostility, and of narrowly egoistic national chauvinism. In this—for us difficult—matter, we hope for understanding and help from our Jewish brothers and sisters, in the establishment through our mutual efforts of a new democratic, free, open and just society for all who live among us. It should be a society which no one would wish to leave and where Jews would live in peace and tranquility, in an atmosphere of friendship, creative cooperation and brotherhood of all the children of Abraham, children of the One God the Father, the God of Abraham, Isaac, and Jacob, the God of your fathers and our fathers.

With joy I must bear witness here to the fact that dialogue and rapprochement with the Russian Orthodox Church always found a positive response and support from the civic and spiritual leaders of Jewish communities in our country, leaders of the Ashkenazi as well as the Sephardi. Among the more famous, one can mention Yitzak Ber Levinson in the first half of the nineteenth century, who was not only the father of the Haskala movement, a movement of high spirituality among the Jews of Russia, but also the initiator on the Jewish side of the dialogue between the Jews and the Russian Church.

With such dialogue in mind, Levinson turned to Archimandrite Christofor, rector of the Kremenec Seminary in Volyn, where they both lived and worked. Levinson's book (1834) about the dialogue with the Orthodox, "Enough Blood," was translated into Russian and became very popular. It was so popular among the Orthodox that our reactionaries condemned it as dangerous for Orthodox clergy (*Perezhytoe* [My Experiences], St. Petersburg, 1911, p. 16).

In connection with the Jewish-Orthodox dialogue one also should mention Rabbi Shmuel Aleksandrov from Bobrujsk, the well-known Jewish cabalist who was influenced by Vladimir Soloviev and killed by the Germans in 1941, as well as Rabbi Lejb Jeguda don Jaxija from Chernigov (Ukraine), who was influenced by Tolstoy, whom he often cited in his sermons. In speaking about the relationship of Jews to our Church, it behooves us also to remember professor Michael Agursky from Jerusalem, who did so much for our rapprochement and was an expert on the history of Jews in Russia. He recently came from Jerusalem to Moscow to attend the Congress of the Russian Diaspora and unexpectedly died. May his memory live forever and his soul rest in the bosom of Abraham, Isaac, and Jacob.

In general, Jews in our country have regarded our Church and its clergy well and with respect. It is not just a coincidence that the defender of Metropolitan Veniamin of St. Petersburg at the 1922 trial concerning so-called "church valuables" was a Jew (Gurovich), who, forgetful of self, defended the Metropolitan, and stated that the Jews thereby were repaying their debt to the Russian Church for its defense of Beilis at the Kiev trial, at which reactionary circles attempted to place blame on all of Jewry.

On the iconostasis of the Russian Church in Jerusalem are inscribed the words of the Psalmist: "Pray for the peace of Jerusalem" (Psalm 122). That is what all of us need today, your people as well as our people, and therefore all other people as well, for as our God is the only Father of all people, so is His peace (*shalom*) one and indivisible for all His children.

62

Address of Ecumenical Patriarch Bartholomew at the United States Holocaust Memorial Museum

Delivered by the Ecumenical Patriarch of Constantinople (Greek Orthodox Church) at the United States Holocaust Memorial Museum, Washington, DC, on October 20, 1997.

To our beloved sisters and brothers in the Lord,
To our friends and all who seek God's love,
May the Lord have mercy on us all.
May the memory of those who died in the Holocaust be eternal.

We are moved to address you today conscious of our tour of this great museum of human suffering and human triumph. Our modesty is touched by the extraordinary achievement that this monument represents to the spirit of truth and the depth of human pain that has plagued this century.

We address you this day with mixed emotions, joyful at being here with you to bask in the fruits of those Jews and Orthodox Christians who have worked so tirelessly for understanding between our houses, that our reasoning together might lead to mutual respect and love for one another. We are also deeply moved, saddened by what we have seen and experienced here today.

We have seen the face of evil, an evil that we note with profound sorrow. However, we have today seen this hideous evil transformed, preserved by the power of love and memory. This place resolves us to assure all humankind that the unfathomable, unspeakable terror of genocide will never again enter into the realm of human action.

The images of this place, the terror which we glimpse but for a moment here, was suffered in the unspeakable depths of living images of God—men, women and children. To even attempt to contemplate this depth of human suffering is almost too much to bear.

Yet we must try.

We must understand that such depravity of human action was caused by a deprivation of human spirit.

We cannot help but see in this place that Jews and Christians bear a special responsibility toward the hope and guarantee that this terrible evil must never again take root within the human psyche.

As Jews and Christians, we have a special responsibility toward preserving a common memory of this Holocaust and of others as well, that they might be avoided.

Our history together is plagued by too many sad instances of fear and loathing and yet it is, here and there, rich with numerous examples of the Almighty's love for us as individuals and as peoples.

Were it not so, the fratricide we know was our inheritance, whose evil fruits we see here, could not now be transformed into an icon of love and fraternal unity.

The story of Yolanda Willis's survival, and the story of our ever-memorable brother in the Lord, Bishop Chrysostomos of Zakynthos, who when forced to list the Jews of the island by the Nazi authorities wrote but one name—his own, and many others in occupied Greece are the true lessons of love. They are icons of Christ's truth, spoken with courage to the dark principalities and powers of this world (cf. Ephesians 6:12).

In this sacred memorial to the Holocaust, the singular icon of our century's evils has been transformed into an instrument of spiritual renewal. In repenting of our species' most terrible crimes, we begin to find the road toward the love for one another that has eluded us for so much of our collective histories. That is the highest achievement of this great museum. In this structure's evocation of the dark nadir of human depravity, this nation has enshrined a memorial to an evil that sadly has echoed in too many times and places of this fading century.

In creating this memorial, and framing this icon of evil as the antithesis of humanity, the United States Holocaust Memorial Museum has simultaneously created an icon of human hope.

The Museum has assured the posterity of human memory that it will never forget its darkest moments so that it might always strive to live out its highest aspirations.

Our humble person is shattered by the experience of this sacred memorial just as we were when we visited Yad Vashem in Israel.

We respect the role of Israel as a guarantor of the Jewish people's existence.

Since every person is created in the image and likeness of God (cf. Genesis 1:27), the evildoers and the good, the perpetrators and the victims, we are left to sort out the difference between obedience to the will of God, and contradicting the commandments of love that are planted by Him in our hearts.

The dreadful indifference of so many peoples as their neighbors were taken away against their will comprises a thorn in the side of the history of the human race. The thorn in humanity's side is its persistent weakness in its relationship with God.

The bitter truth for so many Christians of that terrible time was that they could not connect the message of their faith to their actions in the world. They were unable to manifest their faith from their deeds (James 2:18).

The Ecumenical Patriarchate has sought to remind her spiritual children and all who profess a love for the Divine, that there has never been a greater need for religious people to go out into the world and witness the true fruits of the Spirit, among which are love, joy and peace (cf. Galatians 5:22).

We boldly proclaim to all, to our own spiritual children and to our brothers and sisters in the entire oikoumene, that silence in the face of injustice, silence in the shadows of helpless suffering, silence in the darkness of Auschwitz's bitter night will never again be allowed. True Christian faith ought to be manifest toward every people of faith, any faith. For the Christian's obligation is the preservation of human life with every sacrifice, even with the sacrifice of his own life. Many say that this suggests a level of faith that is impossible to achieve. But we are creatures who are possessed of a self-reflexive understanding of ourselves.

We have the knowledge of the difference between good and evil.

We shall know joy in the Lord in our desire to do His will.

The rescuers of Jews and others from the fires of evil on earth overcame the bitter snare of fear and faithlessness, self-interest and hatred.

They overcame evil with good (Romans 12:21).

All who died in the Holocaust are martyrs, witnesses that point the way for us to God's love.

Aionia ee mnimi afton.

May their memory be eternal.

63

Religion and Peace in Light of Abraham

Address by His All Holiness Ecumenical Patriarch Bartholomew (Greek Orthodox Church) at an interfaith conference held in Mardin, Turkey, in May 2004.

With profound appreciation for this opportunity to share with you a reflection on our father, Abraham, I greet you in peace! For it is indeed peace, with justice and righteousness that is central to the legacy of Abraham we share as his sons and daughters in faith.

As we all know from the ageless story handed down to us, the Lord came to visit Abraham and his wife Sarah in the form of three men. Of course, tradition has identified these men as angels of the Lord, and in Christian theology these angels form the symbol of the Trinity, as artistically represented in the Trinitarian icons so familiar in Orthodox churches worldwide.

During this visit, according to the Hebrew Scriptures, the Lord made an interesting comment as he contemplated telling Abraham of his intentions with regard to the city of Sodom: "Shall I hide from Abraham what I am about to do, seeing that Abraham shall become a great and mighty nation, and all the nations of the earth shall bless themselves by him? No, for I have chosen him, that he may charge his children and his household after him to keep the way of the Lord by doing righteousness and justice; so that the Lord may bring to Abraham what he has promised him" (Gen. 18:18–19).

"…that he may charge his children and his household after him to keep the way of the Lord by doing righteousness and justice." This is a legacy left to us by our father, Abraham. If we are to be recognized as his descendants—either by blood, by promise, or by adoption—we are to be a people who pursue righteousness and justice, and thus pursue peace.

Jews, Christians and Muslims all claim to be descended from Abraham. Our faiths are very clear that we are all somehow his children. But it is interesting to note in this passage that what is characteristic of his children is that they are pursuers of peace. In other words, what should characterize us, his children, is our dedication to the pursuit of peace.

In today's world, it seems that pursuers of peace are few. Terrorists wantonly kill innocent people to make a political statement. Countries go to war against other countries without justification. Ethnic groups commit genocide against other ethnic groups. Racism still causes enmity between people. Children are killed daily, either in war by conventional weapons or in urban street violence by small arms. Even religious rhetoric is often filled with hate speech directed against other religions. And the list of horrors goes on and on.

In the midst of all these troubles, where are those who pursue peace?

Certainly, there must be peacemakers among us. Certainly, there are those who cry out in a seemingly lonely voice to heaven for God to establish peace. Certainly, there are men and women in this world who, in the spirit of the prophets, seek justice in order to lay the foundation for peace. If we are true to our respective faiths, Jews, Christians and Muslims have no option. If we are true to our father Abraham, to seek peace must be our task.

———————

I once heard an interpretation of the Lord's visit to Abraham that might be useful in the context of our reflection. What if, the story goes, the three angels returned to visit Abraham, and one of them was a Jew, one of them was a Christian, and one of them was a Muslim? What would Abraham say to them? The question I would pose to you, my friends, is this: what would Abraham say to the three visitors today? What would he say to us if we were standing in his presence? What would be our answer?

Theologically, our answer would be based on the principles that all of us hold in common. Indeed, we may differ theologically—we each profess ultimate truth claims that cannot be entirely reconciled, either through the covenant with Moses, the revelation in Jesus Christ, or the words of the Prophet Mohammed. But we also share theological principles that must be affirmed, especially in light of our common ancestor Abraham.

We all uphold belief in God as that which leads to the fulfillment of the human person. We all uphold the dignity of the human person as the basis for relationship among all people. We all uphold justice for all people as the goal of our efforts as faithful children of God. Certainly based on at least these three shared principles, we can stand together before our father, Abraham.

These three theological principles lead to the search within our respective traditions for imperatives that motivate us to pursue peace. And these imperatives lead us to concrete action.

Belief in God, and in his sovereignty and love, compels us to love one another, and to desire for the well being of all. This leads us to work on behalf of the others whose fulfillment is thwarted by evils in the world. For example, it leads us to do all we can to minister to those suffering from HIV/AIDS, to teach and preach against the stigmatization that this disease often brings, to care for the families of those affected by the disease, and ultimately to support the scientific research that would eliminate the scourge of this disease from the earth. Some might ask why I include responding to HIV/AIDS as an example of peacemaking. To me, the answer is clear: HIV/AIDS is destroying the infrastructure of countries throughout the African continent, and if we do not find a solution, the hopelessness and violence that result there will affect all people of the world.

Belief in the dignity of the human person demands that we treat all people with respect. This leads us to speak out against those who would humiliate, oppress, and commit violence against others. For example, it leads us to condemn terrorism and war, comfort prisoners, and seek to heal the divisions among people. I am sure that no one in this room, given current events, would question the importance of this example.

Belief in justice requires that we bring an end to injustice. This leads us to seek sustainable development for the economic well being of all. It leads us to address the root causes of terrorism. It leads us to foster reconciliation between enemies. For example, it leads us to try to eliminate the crushing poverty that is the cause of alienation, desperation, and all other manner of hopelessness, and thus of the spontaneous eruptions of violence that result from such hopelessness. It is up to religious communities to call upon societies to solve these problems, so that all people experience the wholeness that is offered by God to his creation. This example, which is often lost in secular circles, is certainly the responsibility of religious voices to raise.

Even as we pursue peace through these types of action, religious communities have other resources that they have traditionally shared, and must continue to share, with those in need. Religious communities offer refuge to those affected by the storms of life. Religious communities offer charity to those who hunger and thirst. Religious communities offer healing to those who are sick, those who mourn and those who are at enmity with one another. Certainly we have done much; certainly there is more we can do.

These resources have over the years demonstrated the faithfulness that is at the heart of every religion. Not surprisingly, they are at the heart of what it means to be the inheritors of Abraham's legacy. For as Jews, Christians and Muslims recall, Abraham offered shelter, a meal, and even a challenge to overlook the sins of others, to his heavenly visitors. If Abraham could be so faithful in the presence of the Lord, it is incumbent upon us to be so faithful in the presence of all people created in the Lord's image.

My friends, this is what it means for religions to seek peace in the light of Abraham. As war rages in the biblical home of our father, Abraham, the importance of this legacy is even more pronounced.

Let us seek peace. Let us work for peace. And let us pray for the peace of God, which is the basis for all peace on earth. In this way, it can thus be as written in the Hebrew Scriptures: "...and by your descendants shall the nations of the earth bless themselves..." (Gen. 22:18a).

64

Communiqué regarding Antisemitic Posters

Issued by the Holy Synod of Bishops of the Serbian Orthodox Church, March 24, 2005.

Upon learning the facts with regard to the antisemitic posters and graffiti that appeared in Belgrade on March 22 of this year, as well as of earlier, similar and in some cases even more blatant, inhumane and malicious demonstrations of prejudice and intolerance toward the Jewish people, the Holy Synod of Bishops of the Serbian Orthodox Church, convened today, March 24, in prayerful memory of the innocent victims of the bombing by the NATO alliance, wishes to communicate the following:

Once again, as we have done in previous years, we most strongly condemn every form and every manifestation of antisemitism. This phenomenon is unacceptable theologically, morally, civilizationally and in every other respect.

At the same time, we decisively and unconditionally reject every attempt, regardless of its origin, to deny, devalue or minimize the Holocaust against the Jews in World War II. Such attempts are especially painful and insulting to us now, upon the commemoration of the sixty-year anniversary of the closing of the death camps in Auschwitz and Jasenovac, where Serbs and Jews together suffered persecution and died solely because of who they were. Empathy and compassion toward the suffering and losses of the Jewish people must be demonstrated exceptionally by us as Serbs, both as Orthodox Christians and as a people that in its distant and not so distant past has itself been subjected to great suffering, and continues to suffer today in Kosovo and Metohija. If our own wounds pain us, and they pain us, then we must also be pained by the wounds of all people and all nations, and especially a nation whose losses to genocide number in the millions.

We also reject and condemn all calumny and false attributions regarding the supposed criminal psychological makeup of the Jewish people. Our people and our faithful are very well aware of what it means to be calumnied, excluded and vilified. The Jewish people knows this through its own painful experience better than any other people. Hence the sin of those individuals and groups that undertake a campaign of calumny against the Jews is all the greater.

We are convinced that the appropriate state authorities will undertake all measures to prevent such unfortunate incidents. Peace, freedom, safety and joint life for all people and all ethnic and religious communities in mutual respect and cooperation for the common good does not merely represent a modern European code for public and private behavior or an international responsibility on the part of all member states of the United Nations; more than that, for centuries it has represented a moral imperative that follows from our faith in the God of love and peace, and from our Christian and Orthodox conscience. This spiritual value is without doubt shared with us by other Christians, as well as by the faithful of other religious communities, first of all the Jews, to whom, according to the words of the Holy Apostle Paul, "belong the sonship, the glory, the covenants, the giving of the law, the worship, and the promises; to them belong the patriarchs, and of their race, according to the flesh, is the Christ. God who is over all be blessed for ever. Amen" (Rom 9:4–5). Elsewhere the same Apostle says in his own name and in ours: "Glory and honor and peace for every one who does good, the Jew first and also the Greek" (Rom 2:10).

65

To Recognize Christ in His People

The final declaration by the "Christian Roundtable" of Eastern Orthodox priests and cultural representatives from Greece, Georgia, Italy, Russia, and Ukraine visiting Jerusalem, April 20–24, 2007.

For centuries Jews and Christians have been both united and separated by the relation to Christ. St. Peter said: "The God of Abraham, and of Isaac, and of Jacob, the God of our fathers, has glorified his Son Jesus; whom you delivered up, and denied him in the presence of Pilate, when he was determined to let him go" (Acts 3:13). Yet if the Apostle's words "you delivered" could refer only to the crowd that screamed "Crucify him!" then the reference of "the God of our fathers [who] has glorified his servant Jesus" is forever pointed at all the Jews and all the Christians. It is as eternal as the Covenant made at Sinai.

The God of Abraham, and of Isaac, and of Jacob, the God of Moses, David, Solomon, the God of Isaiah, Ezekiel, and Daniel, the God of Judas the Maccabean, the God of Anna the Prophetess and Simon the God Bearer, was, is, and will always be the God of Israel and the Father of our Lord Jesus Christ. The idea of succession is conveyed particularly vividly in the anaphora of Vassily the Great's Liturgy. Jesus was, is, and will be the true son of the Jewish people and the true and only and profoundest revelation of the Father that is given us in the Holy Spirit.

For centuries the links of Jesus to His people have been in the shadows. Yet it is the words "you delivered" that came in the foreground and became the basis for an ideology, for contempt, for rejection, for the ghetto, the pale, the hate, the pogroms, and ended in the Holocaust…We propose to reflect why enraged cries of the people who were not aware of what they were doing made an imprint in the

Christians' memory, while the Lord's prayer of forgiveness was lost, or why were not heard the words of St. Peter: "...And now, brethren, I know that through ignorance you did it, as did also your rulers. But those things, which God before had showed by the mouth of all his prophets, that Christ should suffer, he has so fulfilled" (Acts 3:17–18).

Yet even after the death of six million people antisemites feel no guilt. On the contrary, antisemitism is growing in Moslem and former Communist countries. As a totalitarian ideology, antisemitism is in the state of spiritual obsession that continually invents new enemies in old disguise. In any form it is a poison that contaminates a Christian soul. And he who in our day uses the word "Jew" as a curse lies when he calls himself a Christian. As we go over the tragedy of the Holocaust, we are being called on to discover something on a truly evangelic scale: to know Christ who is being crucified with His people. The Holocaust is an obvious sign that points at the anti-Christ nature of the replacement theology. It must lead us to atonement and [to] search for new paths, including theological ones. It is time that we called antisemitism a grave sin against God and man.

What befogs our eyesight?

We worship Christ as True God and True Man. We know that the Divine Word addressed to all people first sounded in the native language of Jesus, who read the Testament that laid down the law of the people to whom He belonged. But so badly did the rejectionist position befog our eyesight that we could neither utter nor even conceive of things so evident. We forgot that Jesus who was originally sent only to the lost sheep of the House of Israel, healed and resurrected the people of this House, that he loved them and bemoaned them as His brothers and sisters. This love permeates the entire Gospel—is it not the expression of his True Humanity that we worship?

And this True Humanity of our Lord cannot be dissolved into abstract universality. Christ the God-man, the New Adam, who sacrificed Himself for the world's sins, was and is also the Son of "Blessed among Women" and the Son of His People in flesh. Whatever brings us the new knowledge of Christ as He was in his earthly sojourn can only enrich our faith.

Gifts without repentance

St. Paul's words, "For the gifts and calling of God are irrevocable" (Romans 11:29), never reached the Christians' hearts in their fullness. They were replaced by the so-called "replacement theology" whose lack of justification was revealed by the Holocaust. The conflict between two Israels does not follow from the Revelation and is not etched forever in the Christian consciousness. The New Israel does not cancel out the Original one. In order to know the mystery of coexistence of two Israels we have to start with a prayer for reconciliation.

We must reflect on the fact that the gifts received by the Jews still remain outside the reality of our experience. Our faith should help us understand Judaism more profoundly. We have to admit that a theological substitute for "replacement theology" has not yet been offered. Yet we place our hopes in the Christian—better yet, joint—prayer of reconciliation. Reconciliation does not signify theological, liturgical, or confessional mixture. Instead, it brings atonement, forgiveness, and love.

Our heritage

In the spirit of this love we must review our own hymnal heritage (in particular, certain hymns of the Passion Week). We should make sure that everything here is in the spirit of the charity that "suffers long, and is kind; charity envies not; charity vaunts not itself, is not puffed up, does not behave itself unseemly, seeks not her own, is not easily provoked, thinks no evil; rejoices not in iniquity, but rejoices in the truth" (1 Corinthians 13:4–6).

Ridding ourselves of poison

Indifference to promulgating antisemitic literature in the church shops of Orthodox communities and cathedrals; ignoring and even encouraging of this regrettable activity—all these contradict Christian ethics. We expect this practice to be eliminated.

Martyr experience

The Christians have undergone an incredible experience of martyrdom. In the course of this experience sometimes it was very hard to distinguish proper martyrdom for faith from passion-suffering, i.e., dying not in the name of Christ, but in the spirit of Christ, in the spirit of a voiceless "lamb to the slaughter" (Isaiah 53:7). Can one not see this Lamb in all the Jewish victims of pogroms and genocides?

Right to land

If we are to realize the Jews' centuries-long suffering, we should actively acknowledge their right to their own land and their own country. Looking back on their own history, the Christian community should not forget that they failed to guarantee the security of the Jews in their midst. Therefore it is the duty of all men of goodwill today to promote peace and security for the State of Israel. The pilgrims to the Holy Land ought to remember that this Land is on the territory of a state with a history that stems from the Bible. Onc cannot fail to see a God's sign in reviving this state nineteen centuries after its destruction. This does not imply supporting any nationalism and indicates respect for rights and dignity of all the people residing in the Holy Land.

Condemnation of terrorism

One of the most important conditions of the necessary dialogue between Christians and Moslems is the demand of unconditional condemnation of terror in all its forms on the part of Moslem religious leaders. We should show zero tolerance to terror, as well as its inspirers and champions.

Dialogue with Judaism

For centuries Jewish theologians ignored the very existence of the Prophet from Galilee. In the second half of the last century the situation finally changed. Besides the turning of Christians to Judaic heritage, the Jews also showed interest in Christian heritage, as shown by the research and publications of Jewish scholars (Flusser, Klausner, Shuraki, etc.). Of course for us Jesus is not merely a historical personality, not merely a teacher, not merely a prophet. For us, there is no Jesus outside the Holy Spirit that gives us faith, outside the Holy Trinity, or outside Resurrection. Yet we are prepared to meet even such interest with understanding and sympathy. Especially notable in this context is the *Dabru Emet* (Jews on Christians and Christianity) declaration adopted by rabbis and Jewish scholars in 2000 [Document 94 below].

Israel and reconciliation among Christians

The connection between reconciliation between Christians and Israel, on the one hand, and among Christians, on the other, becomes more indisputable. This does not mean that we would instantly forsake our traditions and centuries-long discords; rather, it suggests that, while staying faithful to our traditions, we should time and again turn to the mystery of reconciliation in the living and blessed feeling of Christ who carries and saves mankind.

We call on Christians, people of goodwill, to join us in this declaration.

Fr. Vladimir Zelinsky, church writer, ITALY
Fr. Innokenty (Pavlov), PhD, church historian and writer, RUSSIA
Hieromonch Fr. Joseph, Christian writer, GREECE
Valery Kajaya, journalist, RUSSIA
Fr. Kalenike Kapanadze, geographer, GEORGIA
Alexander Nezhny, writer, RUSSIA
Yulia Nezhnaya (Yermolenko), journalist, RUSSIA
Valentin Nikitin, philologist, academician, Raen, RUSSIA
Bishop Ioann Sviridov, editor-in-chief, Christian Church Public
    Radio, RUSSIA
Sergei Serov, art historian, Academy of Graphic Design, RUSSIA
Fr. Shio (Gabrichidze), Father Superior, St. George Monastery in
    Shavnabad, GEORGIA
Vadim Zalevsky, jurist, UKRAINE

66

Address of Ecumenical Patriarch Bartholomew to Members and Leaders of the Jewish Community, New York

Delivered at the Park East Synagogue, New York, October 28, 2009.

Rabbi Arthur Schneier,
Distinguished leaders of the Jewish community,
Beloved friends,

It is indeed a real joy for us to be afforded the opportunity to visit this blessed Park East Synagogue in the heart of this extraordinary city. We are familiar with your spiritual leaders; we are acquainted with your religious and social programs; and we admire your diverse educational initiatives for the formation of your faithful. More particularly, however, we are aware of the extraordinary work for religious freedom by Rabbi Schneier through the Appeal of Conscience Foundation, for which our dear friend has deservedly received the Patriarch Athenagoras Human Rights Award of the Greek Orthodox Archdiocese in America from the hands of our Exarch, Archbishop Demetrios.

Yet, our visit here is more than simply a formality; it transcends a mere courteous visit of a Christian leader to a Jewish leader. Even as the successor of St. Peter, our brother, His Holiness Pope Benedict XVI, visited here last year, we also come, the successor of Peter's earthly brother, the First-Called Apostle Saint Andrew, inspired by our fervent conviction that the most urgent task that lies before all faith communities is our global cooperation for the promotion of greater tolerance and understanding among the peoples, races and religions of our planet. This is why, accompanying us today is His Eminence Metropolitan Emmanuel of France, who facilitates and chairs the international academic consultations between Orthodox Christianity and Judaism, initiated by the Ecumenical Patriarchate since the mid-1970s. There is no doubt in our mind that interfaith dialogue is a responsibility and obligation for all religious leaders of our time. For not only do we have common ground that unites us—such as the sacred Scriptures that we cherish, as well as the Patriarchs and Prophets that we venerate—but we also have common issues that we face in our world.

Foremost among these crucial issues is the preservation of God's creation, the natural environment that we are commanded to "till and keep" (Genesis 2:15) as priestly stewards of the earth. As you are aware, we have just completed our eighth ecological symposium on the Mississippi River in New Orleans, where we raised awareness to the vast ethical and social problems intimately related to the devastation of the world's natural resources as a result of human arrogance and greed.

From the outset of our environmental initiatives, we recognized the importance of working together with [people in] other disciplines (such as scientists and policy makers) as well as other confessions and religions. For the environment surely transcends doctrinal boundaries; it is something for which we are collectively responsible; it is something that we can only address together and not in isolation. And faith communities in the United States have an increased responsibility and obligation to educate their faithful about the grave impact of first-world nations on the planet's capacity for survival.

Other issues of common concern for the world's faith communities include the rising fundamentalism and fanaticism in religious circles, as well as the escalating racism and terrorism in the world. That is why we joined with Rabbi Schneier and we continue to work with the Appeal of Conscience Foundation to encourage greater understanding and tolerance among religions, and when necessary to speak the truth in love and to declare, as was first declared in Bern and reaffirmed in Istanbul: "A crime committed in the name of religion is a crime against religion."

We owe it—as Jews and Christians—to our common heritage, to imitate our forefather Abraham, who received the unexpected visit of the three strangers under the shade of the oak trees in Mamre (described in Genesis 18). Israel's patriarch did not consider these strangers a threat or danger to his ways or possessions. He was not accursed by xenophobia—the fear of the stranger, but rather he was consumed by philoxenia, the love of the stranger. Instead, he sponta-neously shared with them his friendship and his food, extending such generous hospitality that the just treatment and compassionate care of strangers is enshrined in the Torah, and in the Orthodox Christian tra-dition—this scene has been interpreted and identified with the life of God!

Dear friends, we are called to become prophetic communities of transformation in a world of stagnation, prophetic communities of peace in a global society threatened by war, prophetic communities of dialogue in a culture characterized by conflict, and prophetic commu-nities of reconciliation with God's creation at a time when the earth's future is at risk.

We all have great exemplars to follow. For us Christians, we shall never forget the heroes of Bulgaria and Greece who, during the Second World War, risked their own lives to save their Jewish friends and neighbors from the outrageous horror of the Holocaust. And for you, children of Abraham, we have those heroes who, against all odds, established a new nation to safeguard the tradition of the people of Israel. Neither of these efforts was perfect—only a handful were saved, and today we behold how difficult it is to establish security and justice for all in the Middle East. Nevertheless, we are not dismayed. We are emboldened to continue our common struggle.

Let us face these tasks together. Let us hold our hands not only in prayer, but also in solidarity with one another. We owe it to our God, to our common patriarchs Abraham, Isaac and Jacob, to each other, and to the world.

PART FOUR

Ecumenical Christian Statements

(Protestant–Catholic–Orthodox)

67

The Churches and the Jewish People: Toward a New Understanding

Issued by the Consultation on the Church and the Jewish People, a unit of the World Council of Churches, at its meeting in Sigtuna, Sweden, October 31–November 4, 1988.

A. Preamble

We live in an age of worldwide struggle for survival and liberation. The goals of "breaking down of barriers between people and the promotion of one human family in justice and peace," as expressed by the Basis of the World Council of Churches, constitute priorities among all people of living faiths. Through the "Guidelines on Dialogue with People of Living Faiths," adopted by the Central Committee in 1977 and 1979, the World Council of Churches has encouraged the growth of mutual respect and understanding between and among religions as an important basis for human cooperation and harmony. Christians confess that God, whom they have come to know in Jesus Christ, has created all human beings in the divine image and that God desires that all people live in love and righteousness. The search for community in a pluralistic world involves a positive acceptance of the existence and value of distinct historical communities of faith relating to one another on the basis of mutual trust and respect for the integrity of each other's identities. Given the diversity of living faiths, their adherents should be free to "define themselves," as well as to witness to their own gifts, in respectful dialogue with others.

While the promotion of mutual respect and understanding among people of all living faiths is essential, we as Christians recognize a special relationship between Jews and Christians because of our shared roots in biblical revelation. Paradoxically, this special relationship has often been a source of tension and alienation in history with destructive consequences for our Jewish neighbors. We believe that an honest and prayerful consideration of the ties and divergences between Jewish and Christian faiths today, leading to better understanding and mutual respect, is in harmony with the will of one living God to whom both faith communities confess obedience.

B. Historical Note

Since the end of World War II the WCC [World Council of Churches] and its various agencies have shown serious, albeit periodic, concern regarding Jewish-Christian relations. The First Assembly in Amsterdam (1948) acknowledged "the special meaning of the Jewish people for Christian faith" and denounced antisemitism "as absolutely irreconcilable with the profession and practice of the Christian faith" and "a sin against God and man" [*Bridges*, Vol. 1, Document 4]. The Third Assembly in New Delhi (1961) [*Bridges*, Vol. 1, Document 44] reaffirmed the WCC's previous repudiation of antisemitism and, at the same time, rejected the notion that Jews today share in guilt for the death of Christ:

> In Christian teaching the historic events which led to the cru-
> cifixion should not be so presented as to fasten upon the Jewish
> people of today responsibilities which belong to our corporate
> responsibility.

The Commission on Faith and Order at its Bristol meeting (1967) accepted and commended for further theological study a report [*Bridges*, Vol. 1, Document 46] that called for a systematic rethinking of the Church's theological understanding of Judaism. This important proposal was based especially on the following points:
1. Affirmation of the continuity between the Church and the Jewish people, "Christ himself (being) the ground and sub-stance of this continuity";
2. Affirmation of the positive significance of the continuing existence of the Jewish people as "a living and visible sign" of God's faithfulness and love;
3. Rejection of the notion that the sufferings of the Jews are proof of any special guilt before God and recognition of

guilt on the part of Christians who have persecuted Jews or have often stood on the side of the persecutors;

4. Acknowledgment that disobedience before God has in various ways marked not only Jews, as often assumed by Christians, but also Christians themselves, and that therefore both "can live only by the forgiveness of sin, and by God's mercy";

5. Recognition that Christians honestly disagree among themselves regarding "the continued election of the Jewish people alongside the Church" and also regarding the nature of Christian witness to Jews, whereas arrogance, paternalism, and coercive proselytism are rejected by common agreement;

6. Recommendation that misconceptions of Jewish teaching and practices in Christian instruction, preaching, and prayers or anything that may foster prejudice and discrimination against Jews, should be properly corrected.

Although the Bristol report's call for the renewal of Christian thinking on Judaism did not receive wide attention within the WCC, constructive work continued during the 1970s through the Consultation on the Church and the Jewish People (CCJP), resulting in the "Ecumenical Considerations on Jewish Christian Dialogue," a document received and commended for study and action by the Executive Committee of the WCC (1982) [*Bridges*, Vol. 1, Document 51]. These "Ecumenical Considerations" pointed out that the Church, in the process of defining its own theological identity, traditionally assigned to Judaism negative roles and images in the history of salvation by teaching:

1. the abrogation of the Sinai Covenant;
2. the replacement of Israel as God's people by the Church;
3. the destruction of the Temple as proof of divine rejection of the Jewish people;
4. and that ongoing Judaism is a fossilized religion of legalism.

The "Ecumenical Considerations" urged a renewed study of Judaism in historical context and appreciation of the fact that Rabbinic Judaism, the Mishnah, and the Talmud have given the Jewish people spiritual power and structures for creative life through the centuries. While recognizing the diversity and difference between Jews and Christians, as well as among themselves, the "Ecumenical Considerations" also pointed out basic commonalities rooted in biblical revelation and called upon Christians: (1) to see that "for Judaism the survival of the Jewish people is inseparable from its obedience to God and God's covenant" and (2) to learn "so to preach and teach the Gospel as to make sure that it cannot be used toward contempt for Judaism and against the Jewish people."

It is important also to note the position of Vatican II (1963–65) regarding other living faiths, including Hinduism, Buddhism, Islam and Judaism, on the basis of the solidarity of humankind under God for the purpose of fostering unity and love among all people. With respect to the Jewish people, Vatican II stated that "the Jews still remain dear to God because of their fathers, for He does not repent of the gifts He makes nor of the call He issues (cf. Rom 11:28–29)," thus affirming the theological value of the witness of Judaism [cf. *Bridges*, Vol. 1, Document 30]. The *Guidelines and Suggestions for Implementing* Nostra Aetate (1974) [*Bridges*, Vol. 1, Document 38] also point out that the question of Jewish-Christian relations is intrinsic to the Church's own self-definition, since in "pondering its own mystery" the Church encounters the "mystery of Israel." While Vatican II held that "the Church is the new people of God" it also clearly rejected the notion that "the Jews should...be presented as repudiated or cursed by God, as if such views followed from the Holy Scriptures." Vatican II expressed gratitude for the Church's spiritual heritage received from and shared with Jews. Furthermore, Vatican II condemned all "displays of antisemitism" and admonished that:

> all should take pains, lest in catechetical instruction and in the preaching of God's word they teach anything out of harmony with the truth of the gospel and the spirit of Christ.

In recent times, a number of member churches of the WCC and/or church conferences to which they belong, following a similar direction, have issued separate official statements dealing with such topics as (1) antisemitism and the Shoah (Holocaust), (2) covenant and election, (3) the land and State of Israel, (4) the Scripture, (5) Jesus and Torah, (6) mission, and (7) common responsibilities of Jews and Christians. When examined in their totality, these statements significantly advance the Christian understanding of Judaism and Jewish Christian relations on the basis of key points:

1. that the covenant of God with the Jewish people remains valid;
2. that antisemitism and all forms of the teaching of contempt for Judaism are to be repudiated;
3. that the living tradition of Judaism is a gift of God;
4. that coercive proselytism directed toward Jews is incompatible with Christian faith;
5. that Jews and Christians bear a common responsibility as witness to God's righteousness and peace in the world.

The churches still struggle with the issue of the continuing role of Jesus and the mission of the Church in relation to the Jewish people and with the question of the relation between the Covenant and the Land, especially in regard to the State of Israel. We need also to give attention to the self-understanding of those Jews who declare their faith in Jesus as messiah, yet consider themselves as remaining Jewish.

C. Affirmations

In the light of the growth of the Christian understanding of Judaism in the past several decades, we welcome the new appreciation of the faith and life of the Jewish people. We as Christians firmly hold to our confession of faith in Jesus Christ as Lord and God (John 20:28), in the creative, redemptive, and sanctifying work of the triune God, and in the universal proclamation of the gospel. We therefore feel free in Christ to make the following affirmations.

1. We believe that God is the God of all people, yet God called Israel to be a blessing to all the families of the earth (Gen 12:3) and a light to the nations (Isa 42:6). In God's love for the Jewish people, confirmed in Jesus Christ, God's love for all humanity is shown.
2. We give thanks to God for the spiritual treasures we share with the Jewish people: faith in the living God of Abraham, Isaac, and Jacob (Exod 3:16); knowledge of the name of God and of the commandments; the prophetic proclamation of judgment and grace; the Hebrew Scriptures; and the hope of the coming kingdom. In all these we find common roots in biblical revelation and see spiritual ties that bind us to the Jewish people.

3. We recognize that Jesus Christ both binds together and divides us as Christians and Jews. As a Jew, Jesus in his ministry addressed himself primarily to Jews, affirmed the divine authority of the Scriptures and the worship of the Jewish people, and thus showed solidarity with his own people. He came to fulfill, not to abrogate, the Jewish life of faith based on the Torah and the Prophets (Mt 5:17). Yet Jesus, by his proclamation of the dawn of the eschatological kingdom, call of disciples, interpretation of the Law, messianic claims, and above all his death and resurrection, inaugurated a renewal of the covenant resulting in the new movement of the early Church, which in important ways proved also discontinuous with Judaism.

4. We affirm that, in the words of Vatican II, "what happened in his (Jesus's) passion cannot be blamed on all the Jews then living, without distinction, nor upon the Jews of today" (*Nostra Aetate* [*Bridges*, Vol. 1, Document 30] 4). We reject, as contrary to the will of God, the view that the sufferings of Jews in history are due to any corporate complicity in the death of Christ.

5. We acknowledge that the saving work of Christ gave birth to a new community of faith within the Jewish community, a fact that eventually led to tensions and polemics over the issues of the manner of incorporation of gentiles into the elect people of God and the role of the Mosaic Law as a criterion for salvation (Acts 15:1). The majority of Jews, in their understanding of Torah, did not accept the apostolic proclamation of the risen Christ. The early Christians, too, regarded themselves as faithful Jews, but in their understanding of the eschatological events, opened the doors to the gentiles. Thereby two communities of faith gradually emerged, sharing the same spiritual roots, yet making very different claims. Increasingly, their relations were embittered by mutual hostility and polemics.

6. We deeply regret that, contrary to the spirit of Christ, many Christians have used the claims of faith as weapons against the Jewish people, culminating in the Shoah, and we confess sins of word and deed against Jews through the centuries. Although not all Christians in all times and all lands have

been guilty of persecution of Jews, we recognize that in the Christian tradition and its use of Scripture and liturgy there are still ideas and attitudes toward Judaism and Jews that consciously or unconsciously translate into prejudice and discrimination against Jews.

7. We acknowledge with the apostle Paul that the Jewish people have by no means been rejected by God (Rom 11:1, 11). Even after Christ, "They are (present tense) the Israelites, and to them belong (present tense) the sonship, the glory, the covenants, the giving of the law, the worship, and the promises" (Rom 9:4). In God's design, their unbelief in Christ had the positive purpose of the salvation of gentiles until, in God's good time and wisdom, God will have mercy on all (Rom 11:11, 25, 26, 32). Gentile Christians, engrafted as wild olive shoots on the tree of the spiritual heritage of Israel, are therefore admonished not to be boastful or self-righteous toward Jews but rather to stand in awe before the mystery of God (Rom 11:l8, 20, 25, 33).

8. We rejoice in the continuing existence and vocation of the Jewish people, despite attempts to eradicate them, as a sign of God's love and faithfulness towards them. This fact does not call into question the uniqueness of Christ and the truth of the Christian faith. We see not one covenant displacing another, but two communities of faith, each called into existence by God, each holding to its respective gifts from God, and each accountable to God.

9. We affirm that the Jewish people today are in continuation with biblical Israel and are thankful for the vitality of Jewish faith and thought. We see Jews and Christians, together with all people of living faiths, as God's partners, working in mutual respect and cooperation for justice, peace, and reconciliation.

68

Christian-Jewish Dialogue beyond Canberra '91

Adopted by the Central Committee of the World Council of Churches in August 1992 as a basis for the ongoing Christian-Jewish dialogue, and sent to the member churches for study and action.

The relationship between the World Council of Churches and the Jewish community is as old as the Council itself. It has grown and changed over the years. Much progress has been made after many centuries of controversies in the history of Christian-Jewish relations. On several painfully divisive issues we have come closer to reconciliation. New problems and concerns have, however, come up that need to be addressed.

"Come Holy Spirit, Renew the Whole Creation" was the prayer and theme for the World Council of Churches Assembly in Canberra 1991. There the churches renewed their commitment to seek Christian unity. In doing so they saw that this Christian unity cannot be achieved without wrestling with questions of the wider unity of all humankind.

To its member churches the Assembly reported that, "Today in many parts of the world religion is used as a divisive force, with religious language and symbols being used to exacerbate conflicts...We need to build mutual trust and a culture of dialogue. This begins at the local level as we relate to people of other faiths, and take common action especially in promoting peace and justice. The first step is to come to know and to trust each other telling our stories of faith and sharing mutual concerns. Both the telling and the hearing of faith are crucial in discerning God's will."

To peoples of other faiths, among whom were Jews, the Assembly affirmed: "In the presence of the representatives of other faiths who have been our guests during this Assembly, we commit ourselves to refuse to be separated from brothers and sisters of other faiths…and to join them in prayers and common endeavors for peace in anticipation of the day when we all may live together in peace and mutual respect."

More than forty years of hard work by some truly committed people have been summed up in "The Theology of the Churches and the Jewish People" (WCC Publications, Geneva 1988). This publication furthers the reflection on the "Ecumenical Considerations on Jewish-Christian Dialogue" received and commended to the churches for study and action by the Executive Committee of the World Council of Churches, 1982.

A statement "The Churches and the Jewish People: Toward a New Understanding" [Document 67 above] was adopted by the members of the World Council of Churches' Consultation on the Church and the Jewish People (CCJP) in Sigtuna, Sweden, in 1988. The main points of the Sigtuna statement make up a foundation for a continued demanding search for better understanding and for tackling new threats and tensions arising in our time. In summary it says:

    a. That the covenant of God with the Jewish people continues and that Christians are to thank God for the spiritual treasures which we share with the Jewish people.

    b. That antisemitism and all forms of teaching of contempt are to be repudiated.

    c. That the living tradition of Judaism is a gift of God and that we, with St. Paul in his letter to the Romans, recognize the continuing vocation of the Jewish people and the promises given to them as a sign of God's faithfulness.

    d. That proselytism is incompatible with Christian faith and that claims of faith when used as weapons against anyone are against the spirit of Christ.

    e. That Jews and Christians each from their unique perspective have a common responsibility as witnesses in the world to God's righteousness and peace and that they as God's partners have to work in mutual respect and co-operation for justice, reconciliation and the integrity of creation.

The Sigtuna statement reaffirms the unique relationship between Jews and Christians and our shared biblical heritage. We appreciate these important points and trust them to contribute to the strengthening of the foundation of Christian-Jewish dialogue.

Developing Commitments

We are called to attend to a variety of commitments, concerns and challenges, among which are the following:

A. Continuing That Which Is Already in Process

Relationships already established between the WCC and the Jewish community are valued, and will be continued. At the same time new channels and partners for communication and co-operation will be sought. Among suggestions being made as program priorities for the Jewish-Christian dialogue are consultations on spirituality and liberation theology. The role and participation of women in Jewish-Christian dialogue is of pre-eminent importance. There is a call and demand for Orthodox Christian-Jewish dialogues. The WCC will assist the churches to understand the theological significance of living Judaism, to examine contemporary theological affirmations vis-à-vis Judaism and the Jewish people, and to foster implementation of churches' recommendations in Christian teaching, mission and liturgical life.

B. Inviting Diversity in the Christian-Jewish Dialogue

We live in an increasing diversity within our own Christian community. Issues of Christian-Jewish relations, as well as those of other interreligious relationships, can and do divide the churches. This is a challenge both to Christian unity and to the building of human community. We seek a widened spectrum of Christian participation in this dialogue. The presence in the Jewish-Christian dialogue also of Christians from Africa, Asia and Latin America would accentuate the universality and diversity of the church and expand the scope of Christian concerns.

We need to open ourselves to the diversity of subjects and partners appropriate to Christian-Jewish conversation. All issues of substance which arise in any segments of our communities are worthy of exploration, not only those which have been on the agenda for official consultations.

C. *Addressing Christian-Jewish Relationships vis-à-vis Concerns for Religious Liberty*

Christians, like Jews, are committed to preserve and promote religious liberty for all persons. This implies protesting against violations of those liberties. This perspective intensifies our resolve, rooted in our understanding of Christian history and theology, to oppose vigorously antisemitism in all its forms. We have been clear in our stance against antisemitism. The First Assembly gathered in Amsterdam in 1948 stated unequivocally: "We call upon all the churches we represent to denounce antisemitism, no matter what its origin, as absolutely irreconcilable with the profession and practice of Christian faith. Antisemitism is sin against God and man."

In a letter to member churches the General Secretary, Emilio Castro, writes: "There is a special obligation for Christians to make sure that antisemitism is combated wherever it appears...The Christian churches are still committed to look into their own traditions, where teachings of contempt for Jews and Judaism proved a spawning ground for the evil of antisemitism. This is why I appeal to Christians in countries where the specter of antisemitism again haunts the Jewish people, not to fail in their resolve to take action against these acts of racism and to be available in human solidarity." We are now especially aware of the challenge facing many of our communities in Eastern Europe to safeguard religious liberty in their societies, and to address emerging antisemitism. We will strengthen and uphold all such efforts.

D. *Relating Dialogue and Political Advocacy*

The organizations in the Christian and Jewish communities that engage each other in dialogue are also, for the most part, engaged in expressing their commitment to justice and their concern for the life and witness of their respective communities. Such advocacy is an authentic part of the life of both our communities.

We are called to ensure that dialogue will not undermine, or be unrelated to, forthright conversation about divergent political positions. Attempts to influence or change each other's public positions are an intrinsic part of dialogue and should be more frankly acknowledged.

In this regard, we assume that criticism of the policies of the Israeli government is not in itself anti-Jewish. For the pursuit of justice invariably involves criticism of states and political movements, which does not imply denigration of peoples and much less of faith communities. Expressions of concern regarding Israel's actions are not statements regarding the Jewish people or Judaism, but are a legitimate part of the public debate. The same holds true for a critique—from within or from without—of states and political movements that claim a Christian foundation for their basic values.

E. Living in Christian-Jewish Relationship as People Committed to Justice for All

As people of God, we are called to seek justice, peace and truth, to make common cause with those who are suffering injustice, and with others who are also seeking to be peace-makers. We are committed to work with the Jewish community to the fullest extent possible.

Justice, too, must be the guiding commitment for the WCC in regard to its approach to the Middle East, including the Israeli-Palestinian conflict. The WCC has consistently affirmed that there must be justice and security for the Jewish people in Israel. The Seventh Assembly in Canberra reiterated that the WCC repeatedly has advocated "the right of every state in the area, including Israel, to live in peace within secure and recognized boundaries free from threats or acts of force." We have on many occasions stated clearly that "the mutual recognition of the Israeli and Palestinian people on the basis of equality is the only guarantee for peace in the region." The dialogue about justice and peace for all peoples of this region is, and will remain, an essential part of our involvement in Christian-Jewish dialogue.

F. Following the Spirit in Dialogue

The Seventh Assembly of the WCC [Canberra 1991] stated that "The need for reconciliation and building mutual trust leads us to move beyond meetings, exchanges and formal encounters to what we might call a 'culture of dialogue.'" We are convinced that it is the Spirit that leads us into ever deepening relationship with the Jewish people as an integral part of God's economy of salvation for the world.

In this regard, we feel the need to reassess the institutionalized relationships between our communities at all levels. We renew our commitment to promote Christian-Jewish conversation in regions of the world other than the North Atlantic, in order to bring into a productive encounter the theological insights and experience of Christians and Jews from different parts of the world. The emergence of various theologies of inculturation has taken place for the most part in isolation from developments in Christian-Jewish understanding. The Spirit calls us to bring these living streams of insight into both intra-Christian conversations and Christian-Jewish dialogue.

There is a growing quest of spirituality in the world of today. Spiritual values are shared. Spiritual experiences from faith-to-faith meetings abound. We believe that also the Jewish-Christian dialogue can offer spiritual insights. As Christians we can be greatly enriched by the heritage of Jewish spirituality. We affirm the great value of dialogue at the level of spirituality in coming to know and understand Jews as people of prayer and spiritual practice. Such a dimension in the Jewish-Christian dialogue might strengthen a common commitment to justice, peace and truth and to a partaking and creative involvement in the struggles of the world.

69

Statement on the Fiftieth Anniversary of the Deportation of Hungarian Jews

A joint statement of the Roman Catholic Bishops of Hungary and the Ecumenical Council of Hungarian Churches, December 1994.

The Hungarian Roman Catholic bishops and the Hungarian member churches of the Ecumenical Council and leading clergy, in the name of their communities which they represent, remember with reverence that fifty years ago the deportation and cruel killing of Jews in concentration camps took place.

We consider the extinguishing of hundreds of thousands of lives only because of their origin, the twentieth century's disgrace. We respectfully pay tribute to the victims on the anniversary of these painful events. We all consider the Holocaust—on the grounds of the teaching of holy scripture—as a sin crying to heaven and a sin which burdens our history and our communities and, over and above our remembrance of it, urge our expiatory obligation.

On the occasion of this anniversary we have to agree that not only the perpetrators of this senseless wickedness were responsible for this tragedy, but also those who, though professing to be members of our churches, yet out of fear, cowardice and compromise did not raise their voices in protest against the mass humiliation, deportation and murder of their fellow Jewish citizens. Before God we ask pardon for their negligence and omission in the face of this catastrophe fifty years ago. We regard with respect and gratitude those who laid down or risked their lives for their Jewish compatriots in those inhuman, brutal times and protested against the satanic schemes.

It is a duty of conscience for us all to strengthen the service of reconciliation in the life of our communities to ensure that every person is equally esteemed in mutual understanding and affection. In the spirit of the Gospel we must strive for real humane development so that once and for all antisemitism and all forms of discrimination may cease and the sins of the past never again repeated.

70

New Threats of Antisemitism
in the Baltic Area

Report from a World Council of Churches consultation on "New Threats of Antisemitism" held in Warsaw, Poland, October 1999.

A paragraph, and particularly the last sentence of that paragraph, in the "Ecumenical Considerations on Jewish-Christian Dialogue" (World Council of Churches, 1982) [*Bridges*, Vol. 1, Document 51], could be seen as prompting the recently held consultation of church and societies in the Baltic Area on "New Threats of Antisemitism," Warsaw, October 16–19, 1999. It reads: "The World Council of Churches Assembly at its first meeting in Amsterdam, 1948, declared: 'We call upon the churches we represent to denounce antisemitism, no matter what its origin, as absolutely irreconcilable with the profession and practice of the Christian faith. Antisemitism is sin against God and man.' This appeal has been reiterated many times. Those who live where there is a record of acts of hatred against Jews can serve the whole Church by unmasking the ever-present danger they have come to recognize." It is important to underline that a resolute position and stance against antisemitism is not a favor to be done to Jews. Antisemitism is, as someone has said, a Christian problem and not a Jewish problem.

The presence of antisemitism cannot easily be explained. It is linked to political, economic and societal developments in many parts of Europe and has surfaced again within our societies, to some extent related to the upheavals in Europe of the last decade.

Addressing the question of the presence of antisemitism in a particular society is sometimes met with quite a bit of defensiveness. No country likes to admit that antisemitism is alive and well in [its] midst. This is particularly the case in some of the countries of the former Soviet Union. Churches here are not an exception and some prefer to dodge the issue. It was important in the planning of this consultation not to put anyone up against the wall, inviting a defensiveness which is not constructive. It seemed important to find partners in the struggle against antisemitism instead of labeling this or that country as a haven for antisemitism. An intentional search for a partnership as to the context for the consultation was therefore a priority. The Theobalt network proved to be such a partner.

Theobalt, a network of churches in the Baltic region for common reflection and the sharing of experiences regarding their role in society, meets every third or fourth year. In between gatherings of the full participation of the churches in the nine countries around the Baltic Sea, initiatives are taken to call smaller consultations or meetings on specific issues of concern to one or several churches within the region. Theobalt conferences have been arranged in Visby on Gotland from the beginning of the 1980s. The new openness between the nations around the Baltic Sea after 1989 has made it easier and more urgent to meet. The churches in the area are in many ways facing the same challenges on the threshold of the new millennium, requiring renewed reflection on societal values and new possibilities for cooperation and exchange.

In many of the main folk church-traditions around the Baltic Sea there are—as a response to the appearance of antisemitism—documents and statements that deal with the basic theological and moral issues involved. This is the case for the Roman Catholic Church with the Vatican II documents *Nostra Aetate* [*Bridges*, Vol. 1, Document 30] and several subsequent documents and statements. Although there are no documents from Orthodox churches in the Baltic region, there are some statements by the Patriarch of Moscow and other church leaders [cf. Documents 61 and 62 above]. For the member churches of the World Council of Churches there is the statement from the Amsterdam Assembly [*Bridges*, Vol. 1, Document 4] as well as the Ecumenical Considerations on Jewish-Christian Dialogue, a letter by Emilio Castro to the churches in Europe addressing new threats of antisemitism (1990) and the Central Committee document "Christian-Jewish Dialogue beyond Canberra '91" (1992) [Document 68 above].

In a joint effort, the desk on Jewish-Christian relations and the Theobalt network invited church representatives and experts on Jewish-Christian relations from the region to come to Warsaw for a first and tentative discussion on new signs of antisemitism in the societies of which the Theobalt churches are part. The intention was to have a first and tentative deliberation on how to go from official documents and statements to their practical implementation within our churches and within the societies in which the churches live and witness.

Experiences from within the Baltic Context

There was from the beginning a rich contribution. Participants had many insights into the problem that was to be faced through personal experiences or through the experience of their churches. During a first session, such experiences were shared.

The "new threats of antisemitism" have several dimensions where differences are blurred and seldom distinct. The contexts of antisemitism have different facets and are varied.

There is a political context, where the Jewish origin of political opponents is an issue, where there is a supposed Jewish conspiracy against the country or against nationalist leaders or a perceived Jewish implication in ethnic or territorial conflicts.

There is a context related to debates on the catastrophic situation of the economy, on the social and political models to be followed to overcome the crisis and political instability.

There is a context related to ideological debates on national problems: modernity vs. traditionalism, clerical vs. lay leadership, Western-style democracy vs. an ethnocratic state following an autochtonous tradition. There is a context related to interpretations and polemics on the national heritage: the responsibility for the mass crimes of World War II; the causes for the advent of the communist regimes and the disasters provoked by it.

These contexts pertain to confrontations with national identity and myths: the nationalistic tradition, the revaluation of former political leaders and nationalist ideologies.

Finally there is the dimension which is related to theological argumentation: the Christian replacement theology vis-à-vis Judaism, the question of deicide, etc.

The pattern of finding scapegoats to explain societal or personal failures is not a new phenomenon. As there is a long tradition, not least within the Christian societies, to blame the Jews for what is wrong, financially, morally, etc.; this attitude easily comes to the surface, particularly in times when society is in turmoil. Jews, then, are seen as leading within the financial circles. Jews are responsible for moral depravation through films, music, theatre, etc. Jews are looked upon as responsible within society for the introduction of communism, for the collapse of Communism, for the hardships in a market economy, for enriching themselves at the misfortune of other people.

Russian participants reported that Jews are blamed for the iconoclastic movement, for Protestantism, liberalism and ecumenism. Extreme nationalist groups see the murder of the Tsar and his family as an example of ritual murder.

This kind of antisemitism is a poison to society and an evil growth that produces evil fruits: neo-Nazi ideas, xenophobia, violence such as the desecration of Jewish burial yards and threats to and even murder of people who speak publicly or work against the spread of antisemitic propaganda.

The theological anti-Judaism is another kind. It is of a more subtle kind and difficult to come to terms with. Antisemitism has its origin in the anti-Judaism that has its roots in the Christian faith tradition. As the Christian tradition has developed over the centuries, there are expressions and phrases in prayers, hymns and liturgical passages as well as in popular piety that has changed from this in-built tension between Jewish and Christian faith claims into a general anti-Jewishness that then again easily links to antisemitism. When churches are faced with questions regarding their liturgical praxes or theological thought-patterns, there are two ways of reacting. Either there is a defensive attitude, saying that this is part of the revealed truth and therefore not to be given up. Or, there is an awareness of the dangers to the faith and to the sobriety of the society in some of these traditional expressions and consequently a willingness to exchange them for more sound, biblical and healing wordings.

Historical Research and Proven Facts

During a session with a historical perspective on antisemitism in Christian dominated areas in Eastern and Western Europe, it became even clearer that, although they are intertwined, it is necessary to make a distinction between anti-Judaism and antisemitism.

The antagonism between Christian and Jewish truth claims is one thing, which can lead to and regrettably often leads to an anti-Jewish attitude. But it seems that it is when nationalist, ethnic and other societal concerns are mixed with a need for someone to blame, a scapegoat, that things easily develop into antisemitism in the sense that it is the Jew, as a Jew, who is a threat to the society and to societal order.

Also, it is important to realize different manifestations of antisemitism, antisemitism from above and antisemitism from below. Before the disastrous events in Europe in the twentieth century, particularly in its central and eastern parts, during the Nazi reign and the Holocaust, there was an antisemitism from above. Governments, politicians and public persons could use the Jews as scapegoats, blamed responsible for things that had gone wrong in terms of finance, moral or societal orders. After the Holocaust, governments, churches, political parties have made it a point to speak up against antisemitism in all its forms as an evil and a threat to society. Officially there is no defense for antisemitism.

What seems to be a breeding ground for new forms of antisemitic propaganda and actions is an antisemitism from below, from the streets in the form of wall scribbling, various types of popular publications and newspapers. Surveys of the present situation in the countries around the Baltic Sea give the picture of a creeping antisemitism in underground circles, nurturing the idea that there is a "plot" against the old good society. In such a strange plot there are several suspect components: The European Union, NATO, the Western world in general, etc. and among them often "the Jews."

In some of the countries on the eastern side of the Baltic there is a specific problem in that people do not know the Holocaust phenomenon as a historical event and fact. It has not been part of the curricula of the schools, the universities nor even in theological institutions. The truth is not revealed to those who ought to know. Therefore the link between antisemitism and the death camps is not known, nor the link to xenophobia in other directions than the Jews.

A specific problem in societies where there was, or is, a substantial Jewish population, one would easily point out that there were, or are, many Jews in the top Communist leadership, among the top bankers, leading artists, film producers, etc. In such a perspective, antisemitism is often an expression of envy.

Church Documents

A session on church documents on antisemitism showed that many churches had tried to come to terms with their history in this respect and the history of their societies. The first assembly of the World Council of Churches in Amsterdam declared that "antisemitism is sin against God and man." The motives for the statement might have been mixed, but it stands as a starting point for hard work within many member churches on the relations to the Jewish people. The Roman Catholic Church, after having wrestled with its heritage, embarked upon a new relationship to Judaism and the Jewish people during the Second Vatican Council.

The document *Nostra Aetate* has been followed by several official writings explaining church teachings, stressing the particular relationship between Christians and Jews.

Patriarch Alexy II of Moscow in a speech in the United States [Document 61 above] took a clear stand against antisemitism, which gave a signal in the Orthodox context on the importance of the issue. The ecumenical bodies, the World Council of Churches and the Lutheran World Federation, have worked out substantial documents to be studied in the member churches. Thus there are documents and statements in which past mistakes and dangerous interpretations regarding the relationship between Christian and Jewish faith claims are pointed out and the way ahead to avoid stereotypes, general anti-Jewishness and antisemitism in particular is lined out. Several churches have applied such theological and historical insights to their own context in public documents, others are still working on a clarification of their stand, while some churches have not said anything in clear wording. Orthodox participants reminded the meeting that the Orthodox Church does not have a tradition of issuing documents on any subject, let alone the subject of antisemitism.

For the sake of clarifying the Christian position, there was a strong wish among the participants that the churches of the Baltic region—in view of new threats of anti-Semitism—should be of service to their societies by stating publicly their stand in principle on antisemitism and antisemitic propaganda. As long as it seems unclear what the official line of a country is, the reputation of that country is at stake and the country as such and its citizens easily get a bad name. The churches, particularly so if they do it together in a given context, can take a lead and thereby not only reject open antisemitism but also the evils that follow in the wake of antisemitism such as caricatures of disliked neighbors, xenophobia in general, acts of violence toward minorities and an anthropology that sees "the image of God" only in people of one's own ethnic group, race, nation, etc. and not in "others."

Suggestions for the Future

As for concrete suggestions the Warsaw meeting saw the following tasks and possibilities:

To emphasize the area of education, informing a new generation about what is at stake when antisemitism surfaces, providing knowledge about what has happened within the European context in relation to antisemitism, and particularly the Holocaust, which physically took place in the Baltic region.

To link persons and groups within the region who are counteracting such ideologies and thought patterns which lead to and stimulate antisemitic acts and propaganda, and to encourage personal testimonies from inside the region, in order to avoid the impression of an imposition and interference from outside, from abroad.

To search for ways to make books and substantial articles available in local languages and to support historians and theologians who can write on relevant themes from within their contexts.

To encourage an inter-Christian wrestling with the problem of antisemitism, as it is manifested within official or semi-official circles or in the margins of the Christian faith tradition, and to explore certain themes that might provide an opening, for example the theme of suffering in Jewish, Christian and general humanistic thinking.

To support and, whenever possible, participate in the reflection and study process on the issue of Jewish-Christian relations—historical and actual—that has begun in Latvia and to encourage an attempt to gather those who are involved in church education in St. Petersburg for an ecumenical reflection process of the same kind.

To contact those who are responsible for web sites on the Internet for Christian-Jewish relations to ensure that there are references through links from antisemitic entries on the net to sound and scientifically researched material on their own web sites.

To explore the possibility to connect centers, places and key persons within the Baltic area for a joint study, preferably inter-confessional, on old and new forms of antisemitism and their effect on the political and spiritual climate and on the basic value systems of the societies around the Baltic Sea.

71

An Ecumenical Response to *Dabru Emet*

Issued by the Interfaith Relations Commission of the National Council of Churches of Christ in the USA, meeting in Houston, Texas, in February 2001.

The Interfaith Relations Commission of the National Council of Churches of Christ in the USA, meeting in Houston, Texas, expresses its deep gratitude to the scholars and rabbis who wrote and issued the statement *Dabru Emet* ("Speak the Truth") [Document 94 below]. We also call on the leaders of the member communions of the National Council of Churches, and on all Christians, to read and carefully consider the affirmations and the invitation to further dialogue which the statement offers.

Released in Baltimore and New York on the eve of Yom Kippur (the Day of Atonement), September 10, 2000, *Dabru Emet* is addressed to both Jews and Christians. It is a response to the many public statements that Christian churches and councils have made in recent years, making clear the churches' rejection of antisemitism, and asserting their conviction that the Jewish people continue as recipients of God's love and grace.

We welcome this public recognition by Jewish leaders of the changes that have begun and continue within our churches in relation to the Jewish community and in our teaching about Jews and Judaism. It is with thankful and humble hearts that we, as Christians, find ourselves given the grace, after such a history of animosity and violence, to now be in a renewed, renewing and reconciling relationship with Jewish sisters and brothers.

We welcome, also, the "eight brief statements" made in *Dabru Emet*, and commend them to our churches and fellow Christians for study, and as gateways to further dialogue. The document addresses theological issues as well as the meaning and conduct of everyday relations between our two communities. While we may not agree with all that is affirmed in the document, there is much in it that many among us will readily embrace.

The careful wording of these eight points is itself a helpful contribution toward our understanding of each other, and provides a very useful basis for further Jewish-Christian dialogue. Discussion of *Dabru Emet* will certainly figure in the agenda of future theological reflection of our Interfaith Relations Commission. We commend it to Christians in the United States for individual reading and reflection, and for use as a resource in conversations between local churches and synagogues, and in other arenas of inter-religious dialogue.

We thank the drafters of this statement for their work, which is a gift to all those who seek understanding and the life of the kingdom of God. To God be all glory and our humble thanksgiving that, "made in God's image, we are created to live a life of relationship and called to claim the unity in our human diversity" ("Interfaith Relations and the Churches," NCCC Policy Statement, November 1999).

72

Charta Oecumenica: Guidelines for the Growing Cooperation among the Churches in Europe (excerpt)

The Charta Oecumenica was issued jointly by the Conference of European Churches, which includes almost all Orthodox, Protestant, Anglican, Old-Catholic, and independent churches in Europe, and the Council of European Bishops' Conferences, which includes all Roman Catholic Bishops' Conferences in Europe, meeting in Strasbourg, France, in April 2001.

Participating in the Building of Europe

Through the centuries Europe has developed a primarily Christian character in religious and cultural terms. However, Christians have failed to prevent suffering and destruction from being inflicted by Europeans, both within Europe and beyond. We confess our share of responsibility for this guilt and ask God and our fellow human beings for forgiveness.

Our faith helps us to learn from the past, and to make our Christian faith and love for our neighbors a source of hope for morality and ethics, for education and culture, and for political and economic life, in Europe and throughout the world.

The churches support an integration of the European continent. Without common values, unity cannot endure. We are convinced that the spiritual heritage of Christianity constitutes an empowering source of inspiration and enrichment for Europe. On the basis of our Christian faith, we work toward a humane, socially conscious Europe, in which human rights and the basic values of peace, justice, freedom, tolerance, participation and solidarity prevail. We likewise insist on the reverence for life, the value of marriage and the family, the preferential option for the poor, the readiness to forgive, and in all things compassion.

As churches and as international communities we have to counteract the danger of Europe developing into an integrated West and a disintegrated East, and also take account of the North-South divide within Europe. At the same time we must avoid Eurocentricity and heighten Europe's sense of responsibility for the whole of humanity, particularly for the poor all over the world.

We commit ourselves
- to seek agreement with one another on the substance and goals of our social responsibility, and to represent in concert, as far as possible, the concerns and visions of the churches vis-à-vis the secular European institutions;
- to defend basic values against infringements of every kind
- to resist any attempt to misuse religion and the church for ethnic or nationalist purposes.

Reconciling Peoples and Cultures

We consider the diversity of our regional, national, cultural and religious traditions to be enriching for Europe. In view of numerous conflicts, the churches are called upon to serve together the cause of reconciliation among peoples and cultures. We know that peace among the churches is an important prerequisite for this.

Our common endeavors are devoted to evaluating, and helping to resolve, political and social issues in the spirit of the Gospel. Because we value the person and dignity of every individual as made in the image of God, we defend the absolutely equal value of all human beings.

As churches we intend to join forces in promoting the process of democratization in Europe. We commit ourselves to work for structures of peace, based on the non-violent resolution of conflicts. We condemn any form of violence against the human person, particularly against women and children.

Reconciliation involves promoting social justice within and among all peoples; above all, this means closing the gap between rich and poor and overcoming unemployment. Together we will do our part toward giving migrants, refugees and asylum-seekers a humane reception in Europe.

We commit ourselves
  - to counteract any form of nationalism which leads to the oppression of other peoples and national minorities and to engage ourselves for non-violent resolutions;
  - to strengthen the position and equal rights of women in all areas of life, and to foster partnership in church and society between women and men.

Safeguarding the Creation

Believing in the love of the Creator God, we give thanks for the gift of creation and the great value and beauty of nature. However, we are appalled to see natural resources being exploited without regard for their intrinsic value or consideration of their limits, and without regard for the well-being of future generations.

Together we want to help create sustainable living conditions for the whole of creation. It is our responsibility before God to put into effect common criteria for distinguishing between what human beings are scientifically and technologically capable of doing and what, ethically speaking, they should not do.

We recommend the introduction in European churches of an Ecumenical Day of Prayer for the Preservation of Creation.

We commit ourselves
  - to strive to adopt a lifestyle free of economic pressures and consumerism and a quality of life informed by accountability and sustainability;
  - to support church environmental organizations and ecumenical networks in their efforts for the safeguarding of creation.

Strengthening Community with Judaism

We are bound up in a unique community with the people Israel, the people of the Covenant which God has never terminated. Our faith teaches us that our Jewish sisters and brothers "are beloved, for the sake of their ancestors; for the gifts and the calling of God are irrevocable" (Rom 11:28–29). And "to them belong the adoption, the glory, the covenants, the giving of the law, the worship and the promises; to them belong the patriarchs, and from them, according to the flesh, comes the Messiah" (Rom 9:4–5).

We deplore and condemn all manifestations of antisemitism, all outbreaks of hatred and persecutions. We ask God for forgiveness for anti-Jewish attitudes among Christians, and we ask our Jewish sisters and brothers for reconciliation.

It is urgently necessary, in the worship and teaching, doctrine and life of our churches, to raise awareness of the deep bond existing between the Christian faith and Judaism, and to support Christian-Jewish cooperation.

We commit ourselves
- to oppose all forms of antisemitism and anti-Judaism in the church and in society;
- to seek and intensify dialogue with our Jewish sisters and brothers at all levels.

Cultivating Relations with Islam

Muslims have lived in Europe for centuries. In some European countries they constitute strong minorities. While there have been plenty of good contacts and neighborly relations between Muslims and Christians, and this remains the case, there are still strong reservations and prejudices on both sides. These are rooted in painful experiences throughout history and in the recent past.

We would like to intensify encounters between Christians and Muslims and enhance Christian-Islamic dialogue at all levels. We recommend, in particular, speaking with one another about our faith in one God, and clarifying ideas on human rights.

We commit ourselves
- to conduct ourselves towards Muslims with respect;
- To work together with Muslims on matters of common concern.

Encountering Other Religions and World Views

The plurality of religious and non-confessional beliefs and ways of life has become a feature of European culture. Eastern religions and new religious communities are spreading and also attracting the interest of many Christians. In addition, growing numbers of people reject the Christian faith, are indifferent to it or have other philosophies of life.

We want to take seriously the critical questions of others, and try together to conduct fair discussions with them. Yet a distinction must be made between the communities with which dialogues and encounters are to be sought, and those which should be warned against from the Christian standpoint.

We commit ourselves

- to recognize the freedom of religion and conscience of these individuals and communities and to defend their right to practice their faith or convictions, whether singly or in groups, privately or publicly, in the context of rights applicable to all;
- to be open to dialogue with all persons of good will, to pursue with them matters of common concern, and to bring a witness of our Christian faith to them.

73

A Sacred Obligation:
Rethinking Christian Faith in Relation
to Judaism and the Jewish People

Issued by the Christian Scholars Group on Christian-Jewish Relations, an ecumenical association of scholars in this field, in September 2002 as a complement to the Jewish statement Dabru Emet *(Document 94 below).*

Since its inception in 1969, the Christian Scholars Group has been seeking to develop more adequate Christian theologies of the church's relationship to Judaism and the Jewish people. Pursuing this work for over three decades under varied sponsorship, members of our association of Protestant and Roman Catholic biblical scholars, historians, and theologians have published many volumes on Christian-Jewish relations.

Our work has a historical context. For most of the past two thousand years, Christians have erroneously portrayed Jews as unfaithful, holding them collectively responsible for the death of Jesus and therefore accursed by God. In agreement with many official Christian declarations, we reject this accusation as historically false and theologically invalid. It suggests that God can be unfaithful to the eternal covenant with the Jewish people. We acknowledge with shame the suffering this distorted portrayal has brought upon the Jewish people. We repent of this teaching of contempt. Our repentance requires us to build a new teaching of respect. This task is important at any time, but the deadly crisis in the Middle East and the frightening resurgence of anti-semitism worldwide give it particular urgency.

We believe that revising Christian teaching about Judaism and the Jewish people is a central and indispensable obligation of theology in our time. It is essential that Christianity both understand and represent Judaism accurately, not only as a matter of justice for the Jewish people, but also for the integrity of Christian faith, which we cannot proclaim without reference to Judaism. Moreover, since there is a unique bond between Christianity and Judaism, revitalizing our appreciation of Jewish religious life will deepen our Christian faith. We base these convictions on ongoing scholarly research and the official statements of many Christian denominations over the past fifty years.

We are grateful for the willingness of many Jews to engage in dialogue and study with us. We welcomed it when, on September 10, 2000, Jewish scholars sponsored by the Institute of Christian and Jewish Studies in Baltimore issued a historic declaration, *Dabru Emet*: A Jewish Statement on Christians and Christianity [Document 94 below]. This document, affirmed by notable rabbis and Jewish scholars, called on Jews to re-examine their understanding of Christianity.

Encouraged by the work of both Jewish and Christian colleagues, we offer the following ten statements for the consideration of our fellow Christians. We urge all Christians to reflect on their faith in light of these statements. For us, this is a sacred obligation.

1. God's covenant with the Jewish people endures forever.

For centuries Christians claimed that their covenant with God replaced or superseded the Jewish covenant. We renounce this claim. We believe that God does not revoke divine promises. We affirm that God is in covenant with both Jews and Christians. Tragically, the entrenched theology of supersessionism continues to influence Christian faith, worship, and practice, even though it has been repudiated by many Christian denominations and many Christians no longer accept it. Our recognition of the abiding validity of Judaism has implications for all aspects of Christian life.

2. Jesus of Nazareth lived and died as a faithful Jew.

Christians worship the God of Israel in and through Jesus Christ. Supersessionism, however, prompted Christians over the centuries to speak of Jesus as an opponent of Judaism. This is historically incorrect. Jewish worship, ethics, and practice shaped Jesus's life and teachings. The scriptures of his people inspired and nurtured him. Christian preaching and teaching today must describe Jesus's earthly life as engaged in the ongoing Jewish quest to live out God's covenant in everyday life.

3. Ancient rivalries must not define Christian-Jewish relations today.

Although today we know Christianity and Judaism as separate religions, what became the church was a movement within the Jewish community for many decades after the ministry and resurrection of Jesus. The destruction of the Jerusalem Temple by Roman armies in the year 70 of the first century caused a crisis among the Jewish people. Various groups, including Christianity and early rabbinic Judaism, competed for leadership in the Jewish community by claiming that they were the true heirs of biblical Israel. The gospels reflect this rivalry in which the disputants exchanged various accusations. Christian charges of hypocrisy and legalism misrepresent Judaism and constitute an unworthy foundation for Christian self-understanding.

4. Judaism is a living faith, enriched by many centuries of development.

Many Christians mistakenly equate Judaism with biblical Israel. However, Judaism, like Christianity, developed new modes of belief and practice in the centuries after the destruction of the Temple. The rabbinic tradition gave new emphasis and understanding to existing practices, such as communal prayer, study of Torah, and deeds of loving-kindness. Thus Jews could live out the covenant in a world without the Temple. Over time they developed an extensive body of interpretive literature that continues to enrich Jewish life, faith, and self-understanding. Christians cannot fully understand Judaism apart from its post-biblical development, which can also enrich and enhance Christian faith.

5. The Bible both connects and separates Jews and Christians.

Some Jews and Christians today, in the process of studying the Bible together, are discovering new ways of reading that provide a deeper appreciation of both traditions. While the two communities draw from the same biblical texts of ancient Israel, they have developed different traditions of interpretation. Christians view these texts through the lens of the New Testament, while Jews understand these scriptures through the traditions of rabbinic commentary.

Referring to the first part of the Christian Bible as the "Old Testament" can wrongly suggest that these texts are obsolete. Alternative expressions—"Hebrew Bible," "First Testament," or "Shared Testament"—although also problematic, may better express the church's renewed appreciation of the ongoing power of these scriptures for both Jews and Christians.

6. Affirming God's enduring covenant with the Jewish people has consequences for Christian understandings of salvation.

Christians meet God's saving power in the person of Jesus Christ and believe that this power is available to all people in him. Christians have therefore taught for centuries that salvation is available only through Jesus Christ. With their recent realization that God's covenant with the Jewish people is eternal, Christians can now recognize in the Jewish tradition the redemptive power of God at work. If Jews, who do not share our faith in Christ, are in a saving covenant with God, then Christians need new ways of understanding the universal significance of Christ.

7. Christians should not target Jews for conversion.

In view of our conviction that Jews are in an eternal covenant with God, we renounce missionary efforts directed at converting Jews. At the same time, we welcome opportunities for Jews and Christians to bear witness to their respective experiences of God's saving ways. Neither can properly claim to possess knowledge of God entirely or exclusively.

8. Christian worship that teaches contempt for Judaism dishonors God.

The New Testament contains passages that have frequently generated negative attitudes toward Jews and Judaism. The use of these texts in the context of worship increases the likelihood of hostility toward Jews. Christian anti-Jewish theology has also shaped worship in ways that denigrate Judaism and foster contempt for Jews. We urge church leaders to examine scripture readings, prayers, the structure of the lectionaries, preaching and hymns to remove distorted images of Judaism. A reformed Christian liturgical life would express a new relationship with Jews and thus honor God.

9. *We affirm the importance of the land of Israel for the life of the Jewish people.*

The land of Israel has always been of central significance to the Jewish people. However, Christian theology charged that the Jews had condemned themselves to homelessness by rejecting God's Messiah. Such supersessionism precluded any possibility for Christian understanding of Jewish attachment to the land of Israel. Christian theologians can no longer avoid this crucial issue, especially in light of the complex and persistent conflict over the land. Recognizing that both Israelis and Palestinians have the right to live in peace and security in a homeland of their own, we call for efforts that contribute to a just peace among all the peoples in the region.

10. *Christians should work with Jews for the healing of the world.*

For almost a century, Jews and Christians in the United States have worked together on important social issues, such as the rights of workers and civil rights. As violence and terrorism intensify in our time, we must strengthen our common efforts in the work of justice and peace to which both the prophets of Israel and Jesus summon us. These common efforts by Jews and Christians offer a vision of human solidarity and provide models of collaboration with people of other faith traditions.

Signed by members of the Christian Scholars Group on Christian-Jewish Relations, September 1, 2002.

Institutions listed only for identification purposes.
Dr. Norman Beck, Poehlmann Professor of Biblical Theology and Classical Languages, Texas Lutheran University, Seguin, Texas
Dr. Mary C. Boys, SNJM, Skinner & McAlpin Professor of Practical Theology, Union Theological Seminary, New York City, New York

Dr. Rosann Catalano, Roman Catholic Staff Scholar, Institute for Christian & Jewish Studies, Baltimore, Maryland

Dr. Philip A. Cunningham, Executive Director, Center for Christian-Jewish Learning, Boston College, Chestnut Hill, Massachusetts

Dr. Celia Deutsch, NDS, Adj. Assoc. Prof. of Religion, Barnard College/Columbia University, New York City, New York

Dr. Alice L. Eckardt, Professor emerita of Religion Studies, Lehigh University, Bethlehem, Pennsylvania

Dr. Eugene J. Fisher, U.S. Conference of Catholic Bishops, Bishops' Committee for Ecumenical and Interreligious Affairs, Washington, DC

Dr. Eva Fleischner, Montclair [NJ] State University (emerita), Claremont, California

Dr. Deirdre Good, General Theological Seminary of the Episcopal Church, New York City, New York

Dr. Walter Harrelson, Distinguished Professor emeritus of Hebrew Bible, Vanderbilt University, Nashville, Tennessee

Rev. Michael McGarry, CSP, Tantur Ecumenical Institute, Jerusalem

Dr. John C. Merkle, Professor of Theology, College of St. Benedict, St. Joseph, Minnesota

Dr. John T. Pawlikowski, OSM, Professor of Social Ethics, Director, Catholic-Jewish Studies Program, Union, Chicago

Dr. Peter A. Pettit, Director, Institute for Christian-Jewish Understanding, Muhlenberg College, Allentown, Pennsylvania

Dr. Peter C. Phan, Warren-Blanding Professor of Religion and Culture, The Catholic University of America, Washington, DC

Dr. Jean-Pierre Ruiz, Associate Professor and Chair, Dept. of Theology and Religious Studies, St. John's University, New York

Dr. Franklin Sherman, Associate for Interfaith Relations, Evangelical Lutheran Church in America, Allentown, Pennsylvania

Dr. Joann Spillman, Professor and Chair, Dept. of Theology and Religious Studies, Rockhurst University, Kansas City, Missouri

Dr. John T. Townsend, Visiting Lecturer on Jewish Studies, Harvard Divinity School, Cambridge, Massachusetts

Dr. Joseph Tyson, Professor emeritus of Religious Studies, Southern Methodist University, Dallas, Texas

Dr. Clark M. Williamson, Indiana Professor of Christian Thought emeritus, Christian Theological Seminary, Indianapolis, Indiana

74

Canadian Church Leaders' Letter against Antisemitism

The following letter was addressed by the undersigned church leaders "to the churches of Canada, the Jewish community in Canada, and to all people of good will," December 8, 2003.

We, the leaders of nine Christian churches in Canada, speak to you together through the facilitation of the Canadian Council of Churches, of which we all are members. In this letter, we are addressing one situation only, which is a Canadian one. While we recognize that there are other serious situations here in Canada and throughout the world, which demand the faithful attention of all people of good will, we have become profoundly concerned and deeply dismayed by the alarming increase of antisemitism in Canada. This antisemitism has taken many forms, including violence against Jewish persons—simply because of their ethnic or religious background, and the desecration of holy places and cemeteries. We have become alerted to this resurgent evil through our own witness, through the media, and through the concern of others, including members of the Court of Appeal for Ontario and the Ontario Superior Court of Justice.

We, the undersigned, representing many of the Christian churches in Canada, are fully aware of and deeply grateful for the Jewish roots of our faith traditions. In the Epistle to the Romans, chapter 11, verses 17 and 18, St. Paul wrote,

> *You Gentiles are like a branches of a wild olive tree that*
> *were made to be a part of a cultivated olive tree...*
> *you enjoy the blessings that come from being part*
> *of that cultivated tree... Just remember that you*

are not supporting the roots of that tree.
Its roots are supporting you.
   (Contemporary English Version)

Therefore we would declare our unqualified gratitude for the gifts of the Jewish people to world civilization in general and Canadian society in particular.

We acknowledge with sadness and regret, and with no little shame, the historic burden of persecution, which Jews have borne throughout Western history; a burden all too often inflicted by Christians, who have maligned Jesus' own people in Jesus' name.

We challenge all churches, parishes, congregations and people of good will to find ways and means to expose and eradicate antisemitism within and from Canadian society.

We must not be silent.

We urge all within our church communities and indeed, all Canadians, to exercise the greatest diligence on behalf of our Jewish friends and neighbors, that when they come under attack, and their sacred places desecrated, that they find true solidarity in establishing security and in redressing wrong.

We invite all our people, where the opportunity exists, to become acquainted with our Jewish brothers and sisters and with their places of worship in communities from coast to coast, celebrating all that we share with our Jewish friends and neighbors, and respecting our differences.

We commit ourselves to demonstrating not only through words but through united action, our determination to confront antisemitism on every front.

This we pledge in the unwavering conviction of the eternal love of Almighty God for all peoples and nations, in the unwavering conviction that we are, Jews and Christians alike, brothers and sisters, children of one God, heirs in faith of Abraham and Sarah.

Signed by:
The Most Rev. Michael G. Peers, Primate, Anglican Church of
   Canada
The Rev. Dr. Kenneth Bellous, Executive Minister, Baptist
   Convention of Ontario and Quebec

The Rev. F. Thomas Rutherford, Regional Minister, Christian
  Church (Disciples of Christ) in Canada

The Most Rev. Brendan M. O'Brien, Archbishop of St. John's,
  President, Canadian Conference of Catholic Bishops

The Rev. Raymond Schultz, National Bishop, Evangelical Lutheran
  Church in Canada

The Rev. P. A. (Sandy) McDonald, Moderator, The Presbyterian
  Church in Canada

The Rev. Siebrand Wilts, Stated Clerk, Regional Synod of Canada,
  Reformed Church in America

M. Christine MacMillan, Territorial Commander, The Salvation
  Army, Canada & Bermuda Territory

The Right Rev. Peter Short, Moderator, The United Church of
  Canada

75

The Holocaust/Shoah: Its Effects on Christian Theology and Life in Argentina and Latin America

Final Declaration of the First International Symposium of Christian Theology, held in Buenos Aires, Argentina, in May 2006.

To the Christian Communities of Latin America and the Caribbean

To All Those Who Search for Justice, Peace, and the Integrity of Creation

1. We are Christians, women and men, convoked by the Judeo-Christian Confraternity of Argentina, the Faculty of Theology of the Universidad Católica de Argentina (UCA) and the Instituto Universitario ISEDET (Protestant) of Buenos Aires. We have gathered in Argentina, in the presence of brothers and sisters from different Jewish communities, in order to hold the First International Symposium of Christian Theology in the San Martín Palacio of the Argentinean Chancellery, offered by the Secretaría de Culto (secretariat for religious affairs) of the Republic, co-organizer of the meeting. Over the course of three days we have reflected upon the relationship between Christians and Jews, beginning with the theme, Holocaust/Shoah: Its Effects on Christian Theology and Life in Argentina and Latin America. As we end our meeting, we want to bring together and share the meditations that have blossomed from our interchanges.

2. We have been recalling the Shoah within its meanings of razing, destruction and annihilation. We have focused our attention on that vast collection of horrors suffered by the Jewish people within the context of the Second World War, fruit of a long period of preparation and incubation, when perverted Nazi ideology moved depraved intentions

to eliminate an entire people. We have taken note of the extent to which this unique and monstrous act shook the very foundations of the social contract, with the ethical and religious proposals in effect up to that moment. Christianity in particular, owing to its being in the majority in the countries where the massacre was perpetrated, was obliged to consider its own responsibilities and to rethink its own principles, above all when many Christians either participated in such atrocities or failed to protest enough against them.

3. We believe that when attempting to explain why the Shoah was possible, we must examine the religious causes. A long history of Christian anti-Judaism and of Christian violence against the Jews prepared the road for Nazi ideology. The fundamental weakness, and even the failure, of the Christian vision before the Shoah resided basically in a declaration of the uselessness or irrelevancy of the Jewish people. This is the key to understanding the theological roots that lie behind the events.

4. As then, so also in our own day, certain ways of understanding and preaching Christian doctrine end up offering a framework of containment, approval and reaffirmation of anti-Jewish convictions. Today, some still think that the Jews have nothing in particular to offer, because the religious faith that identifies them is considered to have already fulfilled its historic function. This mentality feeds into the idea, more or less conscious, that their eventual disappearance would not affect humanity. Anti-Zionism, inasmuch as it denies the right of Israel to exist as a state, and even regarding it as a danger to humanity, is a manifestation of this deplorable anti-Judaism yet present and active among us.

5. In Argentina, and in Latin America in general, even after the Shoah, reactionary conservative Christian sectors survived believing that their faith offered bases for their anti-Judaism. Argentina is one of the nations with a major Jewish population, and the Jews have enriched the life of the country with numerous and extremely valuable contributions. However, Argentina has been and still is the stage for persecutions or insults directed at Jewish persons and institutions, even on the part of convinced Christians.

6. Therefore, we are persuaded that theologians must critically reexamine the whole of their own traditions in light of the Shoah. Theology has to ask itself in what way do the theological roots of this event still continue to be present, and put all its efforts into extirpating

them, so that no one can in any manner base his or her anti-Jewish statements on any supposed Christian doctrine, and so that any Christian [who] listens to anti-Jewish statements can energetically respond. Otherwise, theologians become accomplices of those who tolerate Nazism, or of those who continue to believe that Christian faith and anti-Judaism are compatible.

7. It becomes necessary to affirm that, after Jesus, the Jewish people in their concrete historic and religious reality, in our present day and at all times, has an irreplaceable mission, and that Christians are in permanent need of Judaism's contribution.

8. Although we recognize important advances in reflection and dialogue among religious authorities and within specialized circles, the formation that students of theology, preachers and catechists receive must be revised, in order to achieve the definitive removal of statements that express anti-Jewish convictions, or that devalue the Jewish contribution, from both popular and academic language.

9. Dialogue between Christians and Jews permits us to recognize better that the Creator offers us grace, and requires us to cooperate in a communitarian manner, in order to confront the forces of evil that assault human dignity. We Christians, more than ever, are trying to recognize the presence of Jesus in the poor and suffering, and we understand that, on the Cross, he identified himself with all of them. But we believe that the Old Testament, the living and present Word of our God, contributes more than enough foundations for the social efforts of Jews and Christians. The Jews of Argentina are noted for a preaching style that beautifully brings out the social and civic consequences of faith, which coincide with the new accents in Christian theology. Taking into account the frequent violations of human rights in our country and in Latin America, we believe that the same God— Blessed be he—calls us to an ongoing reflection and cooperation ordered to the birth of a new world of fraternity, justice and peace, which will bring the Messiah whose coming, or return, we await.

PART FIVE

Joint Christian-Jewish Statements

76

A Common Declaration on the Family

Issued by the International Catholic-Jewish Liaison Committee, a joint instrumentality of the Holy See's Commission for Religious Relations with the Jews and the International Jewish Committee for Interreligious Consultations, at its meeting in Jerusalem in May 1994.

Jewish and Christian understandings of the family are based upon the biblical description of the dual creation of the human being—man and woman—in God's image, and on the dual nature of God's covenant with the Patriarchs and Matriarchs—as with Abraham and Sarah together. We affirm the sacred value of stable marriage and the family as intrinsically good. We also stress its value in transmitting the religious and moral values from the past to the present and to the future.

The Jewish People and the Catholic Church represent two ancient traditions that have supported and been supported by the family through the centuries. We can, today, make together a solid contribution to the overall discussion of these themes in this International Year of the Family.

The family is humanity's most precious resource. Today it is faced with multiple crises throughout the world. So that families can meet the obligations placed on them and respond to the challenges facing them, they should have the support of society.

The family is far more than a legal, social or economic unit. For both Jews and Christians, it is a stable community of love and solidarity based on God's covenant. It is uniquely suited to teaching and handing on the cultural, ethical, social and spiritual values that are essential for the development and well-being of its members and of society. The rights and obligations of the family in these areas do not come from the State but exist prior to the State and ultimately have their source in God, the Creator. Family and society have living, organic links. Ideally, they will function to complement each other in furthering the good of humanity and of each person.

Parents, who gave life or have adopted their children, have the primary obligation of bringing them up. They must be the principal educators of their children. Families have an essential right to exercise their responsibilities regarding the transmission of life and the formation of their children, including the right to raise children in accordance with the traditions and values of the family's own religious community, with the necessary instruments and institutions.

Appropriate marriage preparation and parent formation programs can and should be developed by each of our religious communities on the national and local levels. These can assist parents to meet their responsibilities to each other and to their children, and guide the children to meet their obligations to their parents. Religious communities need to create a variety of support systems for families, just as many of our respective religious rituals have done so effectively over the centuries.

The family should provide a place in which different generations meet to help each other to grow in human wisdom. It should enable family members to learn to accommodate individual rights to other requirements of social life within the larger society. Society, for its part, and in particular the State and international organizations, have an obligation to protect the family by political, social, economic, and legal measures that reinforce family unity and stability, so that the family can carry out its specific functions.

Society is called upon to support the rights of the family and of family members, especially women and children, the poor and the sick, the very young and the elderly, to physical, social, political and economic security. The rights, duties and opportunities of women both in the home and in the larger society are to be respected and fostered. In affirming the family, we reach out at the same time to other persons such as unmarried persons, single parents, the widowed and the childless, in our societies and in our Churches and Synagogues.

In view of the worldwide dimension of social questions today, the role of the family has been extended to involve cooperation for a new sense of international solidarity.

While Jews and Catholics have significant differences in perspective, we also have a solid ground of shared values upon which to build our common affirmation of the essential role of the family within society. In turn, these values will only be fully realized through concrete applications in differing cultures and societies. We offer this declaration to our own communities and to other religious communities in the hope that it may be of service to them in their efforts to respond to the challenges which the family is facing today.

77

A Common Declaration on the Environment

Issued by the International Catholic-Jewish Liaison Committee, a joint instrumentality of the Vatican's Commission for Religious Relations with the Jews and the International Jewish Committee for Interreligious Consultations, at its meeting in Vatican City in March 1998.

Across the world people are becoming increasingly aware that certain forms of human activity are leading to environmental damage and seriously limiting the possibility of a sustainable development for all. Climate change, air and water pollution, desertification, resource depletion, and loss of biodiversity are among the consequences. While many have contributed to this damage, all must learn to live in a way which respects the integrity of the delicate balance that exists among the earth's ecosystems. Nor can we ignore the relation between the effect on the environment of population increase in certain areas and of heightened economic expectation among peoples.

Governments, commerce, industry, and agriculture must also collaborate if individuals and communities are to be able to exercise their right to live in a sound and healthy environment.

Concern for the environment has led both Catholics and Jews to reflect on the concrete implications of their belief in God, Creator of all things. In turning to their sacred scriptures, both have found the religious and moral foundations for their obligation to care for the environment. While they may differ in interpretations of some texts or in their methodological approaches, Jews and Catholics have found such broad agreement on certain fundamental values that they are able to affirm them together.

1. All of creation is good and forms a harmonious whole, rich in diversity (Genesis 1–2).

God created everything that exists, each according to its kind. "And God saw that it was good." Nothing, therefore, is insignificant; nothing should be recklessly destroyed as if devoid of purpose. Modification of species by genetic engineering must be approached with great caution. Everything is to be treated with reverence, as part of a whole willed by God to be in harmony. It was a willful act of disobedience that first broke this harmony (Genesis 3:14–19).

2. The human person—male and female—is part of creation and yet distinguished from it, being made in the image and likeness of God (Genesis 1:26).

The respect due to each person, endowed with a God-given dignity, allows for no exception and excludes no one. Life is precious. We are to affirm it, to promote it, to care for and cherish it. When harm is done to the environment, the lives of both individuals and communities are profoundly affected. Any social, economic, or political activity that directly or indirectly destroys life or diminishes the possibility for people to live in dignity is counter to God's will.

3. The human person, alone of all creation, has been entrusted with the care of creation (Genesis 1:26–30; 2:15–20).

The human person has an immense responsibility, that of caring for all of creation. No person or group can use the resources of this earth as proprietor, but only as God's steward who destined these goods for all. Assuring that individuals and communities have access to what is necessary to sustain life in dignity is an expression of this stewardship, as is a reverent and moderate use of created goods.

4. Land and the people depend on each other (Leviticus 25; Exodus 23; Deuteronomy 15).

We all depend on the land, source of our sustenance. While human activity renders the land productive, it can also exhaust it, leaving only desolation. In the Jubilee Year, a time for God, liberty is to be proclaimed throughout the land, debts forgiven, and slaves freed. Also the land is to lie fallow so that it, too, can be restored.

A recognition of the mutual dependence between the land and the human person calls us today to have a caring, even loving, attitude toward the land and to regulate its use with justice, the root of peace.

5. Both Jews and Catholics look to the future, a time of fulfillment.

Our responsibility for all that dwells in the earth and for the earth itself extends into the future. The earth is not ours to destroy (cf. Deuteronomy 20:19), but to hand on in trust to future generations. We cannot, therefore, recklessly consume its resources to satisfy needs that are artificially created and sustained by a society that tends to live only for the present. We also need to act, together whenever feasible, to assure that sound practices, guaranteed by law, are established in our countries and local communities for the future preservation of the environment.

Care for creation is also a religious act. Both Catholics and Jews use water, fire, oil, and salt as signs of God's presence among us. As part of God's creation, we offer its fruits in prayer and worship, and the Psalmist does not hesitate to summon all of creation to join in praising God (Psalms 96, 98, 148).

Respect for God's creation, of which we are a part, must become a way of life. We therefore call upon our respective religious communities and families to educate children, both by teaching and example, to fulfill the trust that God has confided to us.

The earth is the Lord's and the fullness thereof; the world and those who dwell therein (Ps 24:1).

78

The Spirituality of the Psalms and the Social Morals of the Prophets

A statement issued by the International Jewish-Christian Symposium held in July 1998 at the Durau Monastery in Neamt County, Romania, and hosted by the Orthodox Metropolitanate of Moldavia and Bucovina.

This meeting between representatives of the Jewish religion and Orthodox Christian theologians gathered major personalities of the Jewish spirituality in different countries, representatives of the Romanian Government and of the Israeli Embassy, representatives of the Catholic Church in Romania, and professors of Biblical Theology from the Orthodox Faculties in Bucharest, Sibiu, and Iasi. From the lectures that were given and from the ensuing dialogues emerged the common wish to further deepen the relations that exist between the two great spiritual traditions (Jewish and Christian) and to search for solutions by developing inter-human and interreligious relations.

The following aspects were emphasized in particular:

1. The international Jewish-Christian meeting at Durau of 20–22 July 1998 was a blessed and meaningful event, being the first meeting of this kind in Romania.

2. The theme of this meeting, "The Spirituality of the Psalms and the Social Morals of the Prophets," was approached in an atmosphere of prayer, of theological thought, of dialogue and friendship.

3. The Jewish-Christian meeting in Romania emphasized the common belief that the spirituality of the Psalms and the morals of the Prophets contain the life-giving Word of God and constitute a permanent value for the religious, moral, and social life.

4. The representatives of the two religions (Jewish and Christian) participating in this meeting expressed their common belief that the Psalms and the Prophets call us to always praise the Eternally Living

God, the Maker of heaven and earth, the Lord of History, to love God and to reject all idols brought by sin and egotism, by the desire toward domination and materialism. The closer we get to God, the closer we get to one another.

5. The Psalms and the Prophets call us to defend and promote the dignity of every human being created in the image and likeness of God, to reject extremism, xenophobia, fanatical fundamentalism, and violence, to search for peace, to promote tolerance, to help the poor and the widow, to search for justice, and to show love in all circumstances, to search for God and for the life blessed by Him.

6. The Psalms and the Prophets call all humans and all peoples to repentance for sins, to good deeds, to salvation and eternal life. The Psalms and the Prophets show us the holiness and the merciful love of God for the whole of humanity and urge people to search for holiness, justice and peace.

7. The Jewish-Christian meeting in Romania constituted an important moment of affirming the common Biblical traditions, of mutual understanding and dialogue between the representatives of the Jewish religion and of the Christian religion, and of cooperation between Romania and Israel. This meeting increased the wish of many Christians in Romania to better know the Jewish tradition and the Holy Land.

79

Protecting Religious Freedom and Holy Sites

Issued by the International Catholic-Jewish Liaison Committee, a joint instrumentality of the Vatican's Commission for Religious Relations with the Jews and the International Jewish Committee for Interreligious Consultations, at its meeting in New York in May 2001.

Religious Freedom under Attack

In recent years, inter-religious and anti-religious violence has been on the rise. In some places thousands of people have been killed and thousands more left homeless, even made refugees. Assassination of religious leaders and lay workers has become a frequent occurrence. Shrines, monuments and houses of worship have come under attack, been damaged or destroyed. The rights of many hundreds of thousands of believers have been violated. The offenders are occasionally individuals. More often they have been groups, whether mobs, terrorist organizations, or people with authority: police, military personnel or even governments.

We are troubled by assaults on religious freedom wherever they occur. We are all the more disturbed when members of our own religious communities have been the offenders. Assembled for this International Catholic-Jewish Liaison Committee meeting, we affirm once again before God and the world community our common commitment to the protection of religious freedom and to the security of holy places.

Respect for Holy Places

From the dawn of human consciousness, men and women have experienced the holy in locations that they have designated as sacred.

Throughout recorded history, various groups have felt special attachment to places that they considered holy. The sacred texts of the great historical religions include accounts of specific places where individuals or groups experienced significant encounters with God.

Holy places set aside in memory of these encounters with the divine are a part of the character of every religious tradition. The faithful are drawn to them out of reverence for the great events or personalities they commemorate, and as loci for especially fervent prayer. Each of the great religious traditions of humanity has places that it holds to possess special sanctity. Holy places are as much a common feature of the religious traditions of humanity as are sacred time or prayer.

Paradoxically, one of the results of the identification of locations as sacred is that these places can become the focus for the tensions between the members of different religious communities. A place that is considered holy by one group can come to be claimed by adherents of another tradition. As a result, holy places can become the source of conflict as much as of spiritual expression.

Tragically, as religious communities fall into estrangement or antagonism, the holy places of each community often become the target of violence or vengeance instead of veneration and reverence. People act out their contempt and anger through various forms of violation: occupation, desecration, even destruction. So too, when holy sites are used for military purposes, their sacred character is defiled. One group can take physical possession of the holy place of another and eradicate traces of its earlier identity. Objects of veneration can be defaced. Holy places have been reduced to rubble.

As people of faith, we know how important our own holy places are in our religious and communal lives. Each of our communities of faith has also experienced the desecration of spaces sacred to us. We know the intense pain that arises from that experience. It is out of this history that we condemn all violence directed against holy places even by members of our own communities.

Protecting Religious Freedom

Freedom of religion and of conscience, including the rights of religious communities within society, derive from and are rooted in the liberty of persons before God. As Christians and Jews, we find the religious roots of such respect in the dignity of all persons created "in the image and likeness of God" (Gen 1:26). Religious freedom is realized through the exercise of specific rights. Among these are: freedom of worship, liberty in public manifestation of one's belief and the practice of one's religion, the freedom of religious communities to organize themselves and conduct their own affairs without interference, the right to show the implications of one's beliefs for society, the right to hold meetings, and the right to establish educational, charitable, cultural and social organizations in keeping with the religious orientation of one's own religious tradition.

Protecting religious liberty requires the efforts of many parties. Looking at our own task, we must do more as religious leaders to teach our fellow believers respect for people who belong to other religious traditions. Religious leaders should also take initiatives to foster a climate of respect. They must be ready to speak out against violations of religious liberty committed against people of other religions.

We encourage religious bodies to institute regular programs of interreligious education, dialogue and exchange. When members of other faiths, particularly minority religions, come under attack, we urge people of good will to speak out in defense of the religious liberty and the human rights of the minority, to offer them support and to share with them public signs of solidarity. Religious leaders should never use their declarations for incitement or make shrines and houses of worship havens for hostile political action.

We ask all believers to work amicably across religious lines to resolve religious disputes and to follow the ways of peace together. Complaints about violations of religious liberty, freedom of conscience or the sanctity of holy places should be subject to careful examination and must never be an occasion for recrimination or defamation. Rather we must always strive to establish an atmosphere of openness and fairness in which disputes may be resolved.

Governments and political authorities bear special responsibility for protecting human religious rights. Those responsible for law, order and public security should feel themselves obligated to defend religious minorities and to use available legal remedies against those who commit crimes against religious liberty and the sanctity of holy places. Just as they are prohibited from engaging in anti-religious acts, governments must also be vigilant lest by inaction they effectively tolerate religious hatred or provide impunity for the perpetrators of anti-religious actions.

Armed forces ought to be vigilant in avoiding violent action against religious minorities and attacks against places of worship and holy sites. In the interest of securing religious liberty in times of conflict, armed personnel should be trained to respect the rights of religious minorities and holy sites and held accountable for their actions. When conflicts arise between legitimate defense needs and religious immunity, ways must be found to avoid, or at least minimize the infringement of religious rights.

Conclusion

We stand together as representatives of the Catholic and Jewish communities of faith in calling on men and women of all faiths to honor religious liberty and to treat the holy places of others with respect. We call on all people to reject attacks on religious liberty and violence against holy places as legitimate forms of political expression.

We look forward, prayerfully, to the time when all people shall enjoy the right to lead their religious lives unmolested and in peace. We long for the time when the holy places of all religious traditions will be secure and when all people treat one another's holy places with respect.

80

Message of the Christian-Jewish Consultation in Yaoundé, Cameroon

Issued by the International Jewish Committee for Interreligious Comsultations and World Council of Churches, November 2001.

I.

The first Christian-Jewish consultation to be held in French-speaking Africa took place in Yaoundé, Cameroon, from 8 to 13 November 2001 under the auspices of the International Jewish Committee for Interreligious Consultations (IJCIC) and the World Council of Churches (WCC), with participants from Benin, Burundi, Congo/Brazzaville and Democratic Republic of the Congo, France, Israel, Ivory Coast, Kenya, Rwanda, South Africa, Switzerland, Togo, the United States, and Cameroon.

The meeting took place in the facilities of the Protestant Theological Faculty of Yaoundé in a warm and fraternal atmosphere, and dealt with the following topics:

Shalom and Ubuntu [Humaneness, or Humanity]
Memory and the Experience of Violence
The Challenge of Peace-Building

The consultation was distinguished by a combination of deep scholarly research and experiential participation in our respective faiths, including the celebration of the Sabbath and of Christian Sunday worship. Residing together has been a catalyst for authentic and joyful exchanges that have enabled us to appreciate the richness of our differences rather than looking at them with fear and hesitation.

There was evident during the sessions an intense listening and attention, which bore witness to the reciprocal curiosity and mutual respect among the participants.

II.

We have particularly noticed convergences between certain concepts found in our lived traditions and our respective histories:
- Shalom and Ubuntu;
- the role of the word in Judaism and of palaver [discussion, consensus-formation] in African cultures;
- the idea of tikkun [repair] and the theology of reconstruction.

Unhindered by the bilateral disputes underlying the Jewish-Christian dialogue in Europe, our encounter here has been able to establish itself on a positive basis, free from suspicion and resentment, and emphasizing:
- the centrality of the biblical text in the Jewish and Christian traditions of all the participants;
- the convergence of Jewish and African memories.

III. Recommendations:

- Each participant will endeavor to give a media echo to this consultation.
- The participants pledge to transmit the message in their respective religious communities.
- We would like to see the minutes of this consultation published in order to bring it to the attention of a wider audience.
- We envision a study of biblical sources, particularly in Hebrew, that make reference to the African people.
- We propose creating a Jewish-African anthology.
- We would like to meet in the near future in Jerusalem.
- We encourage the idea of itinerant lecturers.
- We will undertake a study of biblical texts that can be used to support concrete struggles such as various social injustices, the condition of women, AIDS, conflicts, etc.
- We propose to set up an Internet forum for the sharing of knowledge, reflections, and information.

Condemning racist and antisemitic prejudices, we pledge to stay together, in our communities and wherever we find ourselves, as artisans of peace.

"Depart from evil and do good; seek peace and pursue it." (Psalm 34:14)

81

Joint Statement on Antisemitism

Issued by the Presidents of the Council of Christians and Jews (U.K.) on January 27, 2004.

Since its inception sixty years ago during the darkest days of World War Two, the Council of Christians and Jews [CCJ] has continued to confront the evil of antisemitism with a message of healing and mutual respect between our communities.

We believe the warm friendship between Britain's Christian and Jewish leaders—nourished by the work of CCJ at local level—has had an influence that extends beyond our two faiths. It has helped to set a tone for tolerance and respectful diversity across religious and ethnic boundaries in Britain.

Today, however, antisemitism is resurfacing as a phenomenon in many parts of the world. There have been fatal attacks on Jewish people, destruction and desecration of synagogues and cemeteries and the fire-bombing of Jewish schools. Incitement to hatred and violence against Jewish people has increased.

Britain has been less affected than many other countries but has certainly not been immune. We recognize that many in the Jewish community feel vulnerable and afraid. They seek and deserve the support that we as religious leaders can offer.

It is against this background that, as the Presidents of CCJ, we agree on the following:

- Antisemitism is abhorrent. It is an attempt to dehumanize a part of humanity by making it a scapegoat for shared ills. We reject utterly the politics of hate and we pledge ourselves once more to combat antisemitism and all forms of racism, prejudice and xenophobia.
- We celebrate the fact that Jewish people have made a vast contribution to humanity; that Judaism is a valued voice in the conversation of mankind; and that, along with people of other

445

faiths, Jews and Christians are called by God to work for peace, human dignity and respect for all people.

- We recognize that the suffering of the Jewish people is a stain on the history of Europe. Today, our total rejection of anti-semitism, amid evidence of its resurgence, is a signal that we will not permit it to stain our continent's future as it has its past. This is our common pledge and one we call on others to join.
- We acknowledge that criticism of government policy in Israel, as elsewhere, is a legitimate part of democratic debate. However such criticism should never be inspired by antisemitic attitudes, extend to a denial of Israel's right to exist, or serve as justification for attacks against Jewish people around the world.
- We share with so many others a deep longing for peace, justice and reconciliation in the Holy Land and we believe that achieving this would help to make it harder for antisemitism to flourish.

As religious leaders we reject the misuse of religion and religious language in seeking to address political challenges. We seek instead to speak and be heard together in our shared confidence that, in the mercy of God, the wounds of the world can be healed.

Signed by the Joint Presidents of the Council of Christians and Jews:
    The Archbishop of Canterbury
    The Cardinal Archbishop of Westminster
    The Chief Rabbi
    The Archbishop of Thyateira and Great Britain
    The Moderator of the Free Churches' Council
    The Moderator of the Church of Scotland
    Rabbi Dr. Albert Friedlander

82

Joint Declaration of the Archbishop of Canterbury and the Chief Rabbis of Israel

Issued in London on September 5, 2006, by the Archbishop of Canterbury, Dr. Rowan Williams, together with Chief Rabbi Shlomo Amar and Chief Rabbi Yonah Metzger.

1. [Introduction]

2. We meet today as religious leaders, Anglican Christians and Israeli Jews, each part of the wider world community of Christianity and Judaism. We seek a dialogue which draws both on our particularity and also on the universal nature of our respective communities and which makes its contribution to the wider dialogue of the religions of the world in which we share.

3. Our meeting forms a further and hopeful chapter in the long story of the relationship between Christianity and Judaism. It is a story in which Christianity emerges from within Judaism, but includes down the centuries all too many times of violence and persecution by Christians of Jews. It also includes significant signs of redemption and hope for a fruitful future together, not least in the United Kingdom where the resettlement of the Jewish communities after three and a half centuries of exile is being celebrated this year. The United Kingdom, encouraged by its Christian community, was involved in the origins of the State of Israel and the Church of England was instrumental in initiating the first Council of Christians and Jews in the dark days of 1942. Since those terrible times of the Holocaust a relationship between our communities, nationally and internationally, has grown from the steady work of encounter, discussion, reflection and reconciliation.

4. This relationship has not been without setbacks and difficulties, but for the Church of England and the Anglican Communion this is a commitment that reflects a continued determination to honor the

covenant made by God with Abraham. The outworking of this deter-mination is found in many places: in our welcome for the foundational document *Nostra Aetate*[1] of our sister Roman Catholic Church in 1965 which has happily led to her present relationship of dialogue with rep-resentatives of the Chief Rabbinate of Israel; in the recommendations of the Lambeth Conferences of 1988 and 1998 and the document "Sharing One Hope";[2,3] in the joint declaration by the Presidents of the Council of Christians and Jews on antisemitism in 2001;[4] in the work of the office of the Archbishop of Canterbury toward the Alexandria Declaration in 2002;[5] in our strong support for the inauguration of a national Holocaust Memorial Day in the United Kingdom; and in the statements made by the Archbishop on those occasions.[6] Our prayer is that the Almighty will redeem our past and direct our future.

5. The dialogue between religions is an essential need of our time and requires that all people of faith bend their best efforts to this com-mon task. In this connection we are sensitive in particular to the importance of continuing to develop our relationships of trust with Islam, nationally in our two countries and internationally. For Christians and Jews, however, the task of building mutual relationship has a different and prior basis than our dialogue with any other reli-gion. Our relationship is unique, not only historically and culturally, but also scripturally, and for both religions, is rooted in the one over-arching covenant of God with Abraham to which God remains faithful through all time. It is unique historically through the interaction of the Christian and Jewish communities, especially in Europe down to the Holocaust; and it is unique in the contributions made through the arts, science and humanities to a common culture.

6. Our meeting today builds also on the personal relationships which have grown between us from our previous occasions of personal meeting in Europe and in Israel and from our correspondence. We expect and intend that the friendship and respect that we hold for each other will continue to grow and provide an example to our communities.

7. We consider that the purpose of this and future meetings is to provide new opportunities for dialogue between us. Dialogue has pro-found value in its own right and its purposes are mutual understand-ing and respect of each others' traditions and beliefs; the sharing of common concerns; the development of personal human relationships, and in all these things an openness to God's initiative. Neither evan-gelism nor conversion has a place amongst the purposes of the dia-logue and we emphasize the importance of respect for each other's

faith and of rejecting actions intended to undermine the integrity of the other.

8. We recognize that we meet in the context of troubled times in many parts of a world where religious faith has an increasingly significant place in shaping the thoughts and actions of people and communities. We note both signs of hope and of concern and we seek to play our part in enabling mutual understanding between religions for the good of the world.

9. Amongst our profound concerns is the rise of antisemitism in Britain and the rest of Europe, in the Middle East and across the world at the present time. This is a scourge that we are committed to struggle against. Where it is fostered within communities of faith we have particular responsibilities which we will not shirk; where it is fostered by governments or political parties we will openly oppose it; at all times we will seek to educate the coming generations in the history of antisemitism, recognizing that there have been times when the Church has been complicit in it.

10. The Holy Land has a very special place in our heritage, as it also has for Muslims. We long for the time of peace and justice spoken of by Isaiah: "I will make a new heavens and a new earth. They will neither harm nor destroy on all my holy mountain," but we are also conscious that we are far from such a time. The Holy Land and its people, Jewish, Christian and Muslim, continue to suffer all forms of violence and its consequences. Terrorism remains rife. Governments and political and religious movements deny the very right to existence of the State of Israel. There is no agreement on the rights of the Palestinian people and the means to mutual well-being and flourishing.

11. In these circumstances we commit ourselves afresh to the task of peace making in the Holy Land and we believe that our meeting today is both a sign and a potentially fruitful action to that end.

12. We reaffirm for ourselves today the condemnations of violence made by our colleagues and predecessors such as in the 2002 Alexandria Declaration. We reaffirm our belief in the rights of the state of Israel to live within recognized and secure borders and to defend itself by all legal means against those who threaten its peace and security. We condemn without reserve those who deny a place for Israel and especially those who engage in the evil work of seeking to bring about its destruction. We warmly encourage all forms of constructive engagement, whether religious, humanitarian or economic, which seek to enable closer bonds between individuals and communities.

13. In our meeting today, we have listened carefully to each other and have taken note of those aspects of our common experience and current situations which can form the basis for further discussion and reflection. In this connection we note in particular our respective relationships with national governance and the potential for good and for ill that this offers; our common hopes for the good of our societies; our concern to find ways in which our younger generations will understand and appreciate their faith; and in these times when worldwide the bonds of family and community are weakened, we hope to share the possibilities open to us to seek together ways to their strengthening.

14. In all these matters we have at heart the imperative to seek ways to show the love of God to our fellow human beings and our communities with whom we share our times and places. Our hope is that by this dialogue we may allay some of the misunderstandings and anxieties in our countries by showing a mutual concern for peace, security and mutual respect.

15. Conscious of the above, we express our mutual desire to begin a time of dialogue and conversation in the coming years. We affirm that this will be a dialogue of mutual respect in which we seek only to understand each other better and to strengthen our own communities and their affection and respect for each other. To this end we commit ourselves to further meetings in Jerusalem and at Lambeth and to invite others in our wider communities to join with us. We charge our colleagues together to put in hand the necessary arrangements which will make for further fruitful meetings.

[Signed]
Chief Rabbi Shlomo Amar of Israel
Chief Rabbi Yonah Metzger of Israel
The Most Reverend Dr. Rowan Williams, Archbishop of Canterbury

September 5th, 2006 / 12th of Elul, 5766

Notes

1. 1965 "Declaration on the Relation of the Church to Non-Christian Religions" [*Bridges*, Vol. 1, Document 30].

2. 1988 and 1998 Lambeth Conferences. "Jews, Christians and Muslims: The Way of Dialogue" [Document 25 above].

3. 2001 *Sharing One Hope? The Church of England and Christian-Jewish Relations.* Church House Publishing.

4. Joint declaration by the Presidents of the Council of Christians and Jews on Antisemitism in 2004 [Document 81 above].

5. Alexandria Declaration in 2002.

6. 2006 Holocaust Memorial Day statement by the Archbishop of Canterbury. Available at http://www.archbishopofcanterbury.org/

83

Religious Liberty and the Relationship between Freedom and Religion

Communiqué of the Sixth Academic Meeting between Judaism and Orthodox Christianity, Jerusalem, March 1–15, 2007.

The Sixth Academic Meeting between Judaism and Orthodox Christianity on "Religious Liberty and the Relationship between Freedom and Religion" took place from March 14–15, 2007, in the Jurisdiction of the Greek Orthodox Patriarchate of Jerusalem and held at the Van Leer Institute. The meeting was also made possible with the generous support of the Sapir Center for Jewish Education and Culture and of the Archons of the Order of St. Andrew, Ecumenical Patriarchate. The meeting was co-chaired by Chief Rabbi David Rosen, President of the International Jewish Committee on Interreligious Consultations and His Eminence Metropolitan Emmanuel of France, who heads the office of Interreligious and Intercultural Affairs in the Liaison Office of the Ecumenical Patriarchate to the European Union, Brussels.

The opening of the meeting began with the reading of a message from His All Holiness the Ecumenical Patriarch Bartholomew I, and the meeting was honored by the presence of His Beatitude Patriarch Theophilos III of Jerusalem and [the] Chief Rabbi of the State of Israel, Rabbi Yonah Metzger. Patriarch Theophilos III also presented his message at the opening session and hosted a reception at the Patriarchate.

Greek government officials who sent their greetings to the participants included Her Excellency Mrs. Dora Bakogiannis, Minister of Foreign Affairs and His Excellency Mr. Thodoris Roussopoulos, Minister of State and Government Spokesman. Greetings were also delivered by Mr. Andrew Athens, Honorary President of the World

Council of Hellenes and Archon of the Ecumenical Patriarchate. Chief
Rabbi Rosen opened with welcoming remarks followed by the introductory address of Metropolitan Emmanuel of France.

Forty delegates were present at the meeting representing Judaism
and Orthodoxy. Among the observers were representatives from the
Vatican as well as the Ecumenical Theological Research Fraternity in
Israel.

The subject of the first session was "Religious Freedom and Law
in our Sources." Presentations were made by Chief Rabbi Mordechai
Piron, Chairman of the Sapir Center for Jewish Education and Culture
in Jerusalem and Professor Vlassios Phidas of the University of Athens,
representing the Ecumenical Patriarchate. The presentations of the
second session, on "Faithfulness to a Religious Identity in the Modern
World," were delivered by Rabbi Dr. Richard Hirsch, President of the
World Union of Progressive Judaism in Jerusalem and Reverend
Professor Thomas Fitzgerald, Dean of the Holy Cross Greek
Orthodox School of Theology in Brookline, MA, representing the
Ecumenical Patriarchate. Papers for the third session on "Addressing
the Challenges from Concrete Contexts," were presented by Rabbi Dr.
Richard Marker of New York and Reverend Dr. Sergey Hovorun of
the Department for External Church Relations of the Patriarchate of
Moscow.

The following principles were affirmed by the consultation:

a. The principle of religious freedom is a fundamental right
   that flows from our mutual biblical affirmation that all
   human beings are created in the image of God (Gen.
   1:26–27). Freedom is a divine gift and religious value and as
   such must be respected and protected.

b. Because freedom enables us to choose between good and
   evil, the gift of freedom requires the exercise of responsibility. The manner in which we express our responsibility profoundly affects human dignity and wider contexts in which
   the person lives: family, community, nation and humanity.
   We are, therefore, endowed with an ethical responsibility to
   pursue righteousness, and to confront evil wherever we find
   it. Personal freedom, morality and responsibility are all
   interconnected.

c. Freedom of religion, freedom of conscience for all individuals and freedom to exercise one's worship and practices at

the national, regional and international levels must be guaranteed. Otherwise, societies fail to respect the inviolable rights of persons of diverse religions as well as of those of no religion at all.

d. Religious communities are entitled to defend their own authentic religious identities against attempts to undermine them.

e. The preeminent value of the human person obliges us to respect all forms of religious and secular expression, as long as they do not infringe upon or threaten the security and religious freedom of individuals, communities and societies. Conversely, where militant secularism and religious extremism pose such a threat, they must be repudiated and combated.

Following on from the above principles, we call upon governments to recognize the important role of religion within their states and broader society, and to implement the above-listed principles in all state legislation impacting religious practice and expression.

84

A Time for Recommitment: Building the New Relationship between Jews and Christians ("The Twelve Points of Berlin")

Issued by the International Council of Christians and Jews at its meeting in Berlin, Germany, in July 2009.[1]

In the summer of 1947, sixty-five Jews and Christians from nineteen countries gathered in Seelisberg, Switzerland. They came together to express their profound grief over the Holocaust, their determination to combat antisemitism, and their desire to foster stronger relationships between Jews and Christians. They denounced antisemitism both as a sin against God and humanity and as a danger to modern civilization. And to address these vital concerns, they issued a call in the form of ten points to Christian churches to reform and renew their understandings of Judaism and the relationships between Judaism and Christianity.

Now, more than sixty years later, the International Council of Christians and Jews issues a new call—this one to both Christian and Jewish communities around the world. It commemorates the anniversary of the Seelisberg gathering, which was also the genesis of the International Council of Christians and Jews. Today's call reflects the need to refine the Ten Points of Seelisberg, consistent with the advances in interreligious dialogue since that groundbreaking document of 1947.

This new call contains twelve points—presented as goals, and addressed to Christians and Jews, and to Christian and Jewish communities together. After listing the twelve points and several specific tasks for each one, the document reviews the history of the relationship between Christians and Jews, which has provided the contextual framework and impetus for our initiative.

We members of the International Council of Christians and Jews speak together in this new call as active members of our traditions with a centuries-long history of alienation, hostility and conflict, punctuated by instances of persecution and violence against Jews in Christian-dominated Europe, as well by as moments of graciousness and mutual recognition from which we can take inspiration

Spurred by the Seelisberg initiative, we have worked to overcome the legacy of prejudice, hatred and mutual distrust. Through a serious commitment to dialogue, self-critical examination of our texts and traditions, and joint study and action for justice, we better understand each other, accept each other in the fullness of our differences, and affirm our common humanity. We understand that Jewish-Christian relations are not a "problem" that is going to be "solved," but rather a continuing process of learning and refinement. Perhaps most important, we have found friendship and trust. We have sought and found light together.

The journey has been neither simple nor easy. We have encountered many obstacles and setbacks, including conflicts—some quite serious—over theological or historical developments. But our determination to pursue the dialogue in spite of difficulties, to communicate honestly, and to assume our partners' good will has helped us stay the course. For these reasons, we believe that the history, the challenges, and the accomplishments of our dialogue are relevant for all those who are dealing with intergroup and interreligious conflicts.

In that spirit, we issue this call to Christian and Jewish communities around the world.

A TIME FOR RECOMMITMENT: THE TWELVE POINTS OF BERLIN

A Call to Christian and Jewish Communities Worldwide

We, the International Council of Christians and Jews and our member organizations, resolve to renew our engagement with the Ten Points of Seelisberg that inspired our beginnings. Therefore, we issue these calls to Christians, Jews, and all people of good will:

A CALL TO CHRISTIANS AND CHRISTIAN COMMUNITIES

We commit ourselves to the following goals and invite all Christians and Christian communities to join us in the continuing effort to remove all vestiges of contempt toward Jews and enhance bonds with the Jewish communities worldwide.

1. To combat religious, racial and all other forms of antisemitism

Biblically
- By recognizing Jesus' profound identity as a Jew of his day, and interpreting his teachings within the contextual framework of first-century Judaism.
- By recognizing Paul's profound identity as a Jew of his day, and interpreting his writings within the contextual framework of first-century Judaism.
- By emphasizing that recent scholarship on both the commonality and gradual separation of Christianity and Judaism is critical for our basic understanding of the Jewish-Christian relationship.
- By presenting the two Testaments in the Christian Bible as complementary and mutually affirming rather than antagonistic or inferior/superior. Denominations that use lectionaries are encouraged to choose and link biblical texts that offer such an affirming theology.
- By speaking out against Christian misreadings of biblical texts regarding Jews and Judaism that can provoke caricatures or animosity.

Liturgically
- By highlighting the connection between Jewish and Christian liturgy.
- By drawing upon the spiritual richness of Jewish interpretations of the scriptures.
- By cleansing Christian liturgies of anti-Jewish perspectives, particularly in preaching, prayers and hymns.

Catechetically
- By presenting the Christian-Jewish relationship in positive tones in the education of Christians of all ages, underlining the Jewish foundations of Christian belief and accurately describing

the ways Jews themselves understand their own traditions and practices. This includes the curricula of Christian schools, seminaries and adult education programs.

- By promoting awareness of the long-lived traditions of Christian anti-Judaism and providing models for renewing the unique Jewish-Christian relationship.
- By underscoring the immense religious wealth found in the Jewish tradition, especially by studying its authoritative texts.

2. To promote interreligious dialogue with Jews

- By understanding dialogue as requiring trust and equality among all participants and rejecting any notion of convincing others to accept one's own beliefs.
- By appreciating that dialogue encourages participants to examine critically their own perceptions of both their own tradition and that of their dialogue partners in the light of a genuine engagement with the other.

3. To develop theological understandings of Judaism that affirm its distinctive integrity

- By eliminating any teachings that Christians have replaced Jews as a people in covenant with God.
- By emphasizing the common mission of Jews and Christians in preparing the world for the kingdom of God or the Age to Come.
- By establishing equal, reciprocal working relationships with Jewish religious and civic organizations.
- By ensuring that emerging theological movements from Asia, Africa and Latin America, and feminist, liberationist or other approaches integrate an accurate understanding of Judaism and Christian-Jewish relations into their theological formulations.
- By opposing organized efforts at the conversion of Jews.

4. To pray for the peace of Jerusalem

- By promoting the belief in an inherent connectedness between Christians and Jews.

- By understanding more fully Judaism's deep attachment to the Land of Israel as a fundamental religious perspective and many Jewish people's connection with the State of Israel as a matter of physical and cultural survival.
- By reflecting on ways that the Bible's spiritual understanding of the land can be better incorporated into Christian faith perspectives.
- By critiquing the policies of Israeli and Palestinian governmental and social institutions when such criticism is morally warranted, at the same time acknowledging both communities' deep attachment to the land.
- By critiquing attacks on Zionism when they become expressions of antisemitism.
- By joining with Jewish, Christian and Muslim peace workers, with Israelis and Palestinians, to build trust and peace in a Middle East where all can live secure in independent, viable states rooted in international law and guaranteed human rights.
- By enhancing the security and prosperity of Christian communities both in Israel and Palestine.
- By working for improved relations among Jews, Christians and Muslims in the Middle East and the rest of the world.

A CALL TO JEWS AND JEWISH COMMUNITIES

We commit ourselves to the following goals and invite all Jews and Jewish communities to join us in the continuing effort to remove all vestiges of animosity and caricature toward Christians and to enhance bonds with Christian churches of the world.

5. To acknowledge the efforts of many Christian communities in the late twentieth century to reform their attitudes toward Jews

- By learning about these reforms through more intensive dialogue with Christians.
- By discussing the implications of changes in Christian churches regarding Jews and their understandings of Judaism.
- By teaching Jews of all ages about these changes, both in the context of the history of Jewish-Christian relations and according to the appropriate stage of education for each group.

- By including basic and accurate background information about Christianity in the curricula of Jewish schools, rabbinic seminaries and adult education programs.
- By studying the New Testament both as Christianity's sacred text and as literature written to a large degree by Jews in a historical-cultural context similar to [that in which] early Rabbinic literature [was produced], thereby offering insight into the development of Judaism in the early centuries of the Common Era.

6. To re-examine Jewish texts and liturgy in the light of these Christian reforms

- By grappling with Jewish texts that appear xenophobic or racist, realizing that many religious traditions have uplifting, inspirational texts as well as problematic ones. The emphasis for all religious traditions should be on texts that promote tolerance and openness.
- By placing problematic texts within their historical context, in particular writings from the times when Jews were a powerless, persecuted and humiliated minority.
- By addressing the possible re-interpretation, change or omission of parts of Jewish liturgy that treat others in problematic ways.

7. To differentiate between fair-minded criticism of Israel and antisemitism

- By understanding and promoting biblical examples of just criticism as expressions of loyalty and love.
- By helping Christians appreciate that communal identity and interconnectedness are intrinsic to Jewish self-understanding, in addition to religious faith and practice, therefore making the commitment to the survival and security of the State of Israel of great importance to most Jews.

8. To offer encouragement to the State of Israel as it works to fulfill the ideals stated in its founding documents, a task Israel shares with many nations of the world.

- By ensuring equal rights for religious and ethnic minorities, including Christians, living within the Jewish state.
- By achieving a just and peaceful resolution of the Israeli-Palestinian conflict.

A CALL TO BOTH CHRISTIAN AND JEWISH COMMUNITIES AND OTHERS

We commit ourselves to the following goals and invite Jews, Christians and Muslims, together with all people of faith and goodwill, always to respect the other and to accept each other's differences and dignity.

9. To enhance interreligious and intercultural education

- By combating negative images of others, teaching the foundational truth that each human being is created in the image of God.
- By making the removal of prejudices against the other a high priority in the educational process.
- By encouraging mutual study of religious texts, so that Jews, Christians, Muslims and members of other religious groups can learn both from and with each other.
- By supporting common social action in the pursuit of common values.

10. To promote interreligious friendship and cooperation as well as social justice in the global society

- By rejoicing in the uniqueness of each person, and promoting everyone's political, economic and social well-being.
- By recognizing as equal citizens members of faith traditions who have migrated to new homelands where they may have become part of a religious minority.
- By striving for equal rights for all people, regardless of their religion, gender or sexual orientation.
- By recognizing and grappling with the fact that feelings of religious superiority—and an accompanying sense that other religions are inferior—are present in each tradition, including one's own.

11. To enhance dialogue with political and economic bodies

- By collaborating with political and economic bodies whenever possible to promote interreligious understanding.
- By benefiting from political and economic groups' growing interest in interreligious relations.
- By initiating discussion with political and economic bodies around the urgent need for justice in the global community.

12. To network with all those whose work responds to the demands of environmental stewardship

- By fostering commitment to the belief that every human being is entrusted with the care of the Earth.
- By recognizing the shared Jewish and Christian biblical duty toward creation, and the responsibility to bring it to bear in public discourse and action.

To all these challenges and responsibilities, we—the International Council of Christians and Jews and its member organizations—commit ourselves.

Note

1. The full document "A Time for Recommitment" also includes, following the material given here, an essay on the history of Christian-Jewish relations and of the International Council of Christians and Jews, entitled "The Story of a Transformed Relationship." See http://www.ccjr.us/images/stories/ICCJ_Time-for-Recommitment.pdf.

85

Journeying Together in Mutual Respect

A joint statement on the dialogue between Jews and Protestants in Switzerland, issued by the Protestant-Jewish Dialogue Commission of the Federation of Swiss Protestant Churches and the Swiss Federation of Jewish Communities in October 2010.

A. PROLOGUE

This statement by the Protestant-Jewish Dialogue Commission established by the Swiss Federation of Jewish Communities and the Federation of Swiss Protestant Churches is the first official joint statement of Jews and Christians on a dialogue that began more than sixty years ago. The fact that it is a joint declaration marks a milestone in the history of Christian-Jewish relations in this country. It reflects the development of a dialogue process that began after the Shoah and that has taken place, and continues today, in the framework of personal encounters, Jewish-Christian working groups, and contacts between the two communities at the national level. Out of this dialogue process grew many efforts by Protestant churches, in the second half of the twentieth century, to express a respectful relationship with Jewish people. This has borne fruit in areas such as Christian education and adult education.

In the course of this dialogue process, mutual understanding and mutual trust have been growing steadily. Given this experience, the present Joint Statement does not seek to set forth a common theological definition of the relationship between the church and Judaism. Rather, the focus is on the nature and significance of the dialogue itself, for genuine dialogue presupposes that no group exercises pressure on the other or casts doubt on the other's right to religious self-determination.

It is for this reason that this statement begins with the concept of freedom, which plays a central role both in the modern perspective and in the Bible, even if this is understood differently by Jews and Christians. Also constitutive of both traditions is the belief that freedom includes responsibility. Further, the orientation to Scripture is foundational for both traditions. Hence the theses below, after introductory comments about the dialogue, have three sections: Freedom—Scripture—Responsiblity. This statement will serve as a basis for the further development, broadening, and deepening of a culture of respect and dialogue. It is directed to the members of the Jewish and Protestant communities, especially those who are involved in preaching, teaching, and education.

B. INTRODUCTION

1. Identity and Dialogue

Human beings are shaped by their origins, their lives, and their encounters with others. Their identity derives from their inheritance from family, community, and society as well as their membership in particular local, linguistic, cultural and religious groups, as well as ever-new encounters. The human being lives in these multiple dimensions. A person's identity is never simple, but always complex. We enter the dialogue with the awareness that our identity is shaped by our respective heritages and is formed in relationships with others.

In dialogue we meet one another with the acknowledgment of the diverse and multiple dimensions of our identity and in respect for the beliefs of others. Dialogue presupposes that the other person is fully respected in his or her otherness. The unconditional integrity of the other permits neither assimilation nor appropriation. But if the other is recognized precisely as the other, this can also enrich oneself.

2. The dialogical encounter of Jews and Christians

The dialogical encounter that has developed in recent decades between Jews and Christians signifies a fundamental redefinition of Jewish-Christian relations.

Along with increased knowledge of the other comes the elimination of stereotypes. On the Christian side, in the face of centuries of hostility toward and persecution of Jews, the key task is to overcome anti-Jewish stereotypes and caricatures. This is documented in various church pronouncements. A culture of respect is increasingly taking hold, one that aims to overcome the "teaching of contempt" and make possible a real dialogue.

The prerequisite for constructive dialogue is listening to the other without prejudice. In recent years, this dialogue has helped develop trust by the two parties in one another. Trust creates mutual commitment and responsibility toward the other.

On the basis of this increasing trust, the Protestant-Jewish Dialogue Commission, established by the Swiss Federation of Jewish Communities and the Federation of Swiss Protestant Churches, has formulated the following theses. [Note: capitalized and asterisked terms in the section immediately following (C. Theses) refer to the corresponding terms in the subsequent section (D. Comments).]

C. THESES

FREEDOM – SCRIPTURE – RESPONSIBILITY

1. Freedom

Presupposition: We who engage in Religious/Jewish-Christian dialogue assume that God has destined human beings for FREEDOM.*

a. The gift of freedom
God gives humans freedom as liberation from BONDAGE* and from foreign domination, but also from any behavior that is not worthy of our humanity. This freedom includes life in a community. It is freedom for serving—freedom, therefore, means to be in an ongoing dynamic process.

b. Living in freedom in a dialogue of communities
As humans, trusting in God, decide for freedom, they are part of a community of the free. In encounter, the free person/the free community owes it to the other to follow its own path, true to its own heritage. God helps us to preserve this freedom. Jews find this help in the Torah (INSTRUCTION).* Christians experience it in Jesus Christ.

c. Freedom to live in responsibility
To live in freedom means to take responsibility. The mutual dependence of individuals on one another as well as the mutual dependence of
the individual and the community implies mutual responsibility for one
another: the individual for other individuals, the individual for the
community, and the community for its members.

2. The Scriptures

Presupposition: We who engage in religious/Jewish-Christian dialogue
find in the Scriptures the basic orientation for our faith and our
actions.

a. Revelation
REVELATION* begins for Jews with the giving of the Torah on
Mount Sinai and continues in the constant encounter and debate with
it, aimed at keeping the COMMANDMENTS.* For Christians, God's
revelation centers in Jesus Christ.

b. The idea of a Holy Scripture
Common to both Jews and Christians is the idea of a HOLY SCRIP-
TURE.* For Jews, this is the Hebrew Bible (Tanach). According to the
traditional enumeration it includes twenty-four books, in three sec-
tions: Torah (Pentateuch), Neviim (Prophets) and Ketuvim (Writings).
For Christians, Holy Scripture includes both the books of the OLD
TESTAMENT* (the twenty-four books just mentioned) and of the
NEW TESTAMENT.*

c. Interpretation of Scripture
Every generation has the task of interpreting the Scriptures for its own
time. The Bible itself already exhibits various interpretation processes.
Among both Jews and Christians, Scripture is interpreted differently
depending on various theological traditions or worldviews. This diversity of interpretations of Scripture testifies to its richness and its vitality. What all these efforts have in common is the goal that what is
"holy" in Holy Scripture might ever and again become evident and
effective for the contemporary situation.

d. Dialogical interpretation

Dialogical interpretation of Scripture means seeking a dialogue not only with the text, but also with the conversation partner. Even with a common reading of Scripture, there are different interpretations. The freedom of interpretation resulting from the dialogue with the text is also granted to the dialogue partner. This opens into the recognition of the other as an equal counterpart whose opinion is respected and understood, without having to be adopted.

3. Joint Responsibility

Presupposition: We who engage in religious/Jewish-Christian dialogue assume that according to the Scriptures freedom obligates us not only to responsibility for one another, but also to a shared responsibility for the world.

a. Responsibility as response to God's call

The believing community's response to the call of God heard in Scripture inescapably includes responsibility toward one's fellow humans and toward the environment.

b. Responsibility for others as God's creatures

In freedom for serving justice, we take responsibility for others as GOD'S CREATURES.* This common responsibility is grounded in the call of God the Creator to help to shape the creation.

c. Responsibity before God for peace and justice

Supported by God's promise of a NEW WORLD,* we are obliged, in responsibility before God and to the GLORY OF GOD,* to work for PEACE* and to contribute to building a just world.

D. COMMENTS

FREEDOM: Human beings always live in relationships that are determined by domination and power relations. But since humans were created in God's image, thus as free creative beings, the state of the subjugation of one person to another is contrary to that person's dignity. The project of the Torah is to realize human dignity by freeing people to serve God. Therefore, in the Bible, the history of Israel begins with its enslavement by the Egyptians and its liberation by God. This freedom is fundamentally at risk if it becomes an end in itself, and hence must always be protected. This happens only through humans being placed in the service of God.

BONDAGE: The story of the beginnings of the Jewish people in Egyptian bondage not only presents the story of a dramatic rescue; it also became a model for the Jewish conception of time (from creation to redemption) and space (from the desert to the Promised Land) and for the struggle against political injustice (Exodus 22:20: "You shall not wrong or oppress a resident alien, for you were aliens in the land of Egypt") and against religious discrimination.

In connection with God, the term bondage is a symbol for liberation: according to rabbinic opinion, the one who serves God is free from all the determinisms and conditionalities of human existence. It is in this sense that the Jewish people understands itself as God's servant.

Like any culture of that time, also ancient Judaism knew slavery. Special laws of the Torah served to counteract the oppression this involved. The New Testament contains no initiative to abolish slavery in principle. What does appear, however, within the early Christian communities, which from the beginning included slaves, is the astonishing tendency that life together in the community is not oriented to the different social status of slave and free. Paul states this programmatically: "There is no longer slave or free...for all of you are one in Christ Jesus" (Galatians 3:28).

Further, the New Testament speaks figuratively of humans as "slaves of sin" (John 8:34, Romans 6:17, 20). Those who let themselves be dominated by selfish and inordinate desires and instincts fail [not] only in their duty to their neighbor, but also to themselves. The freedom given by God means freedom from such a self-centered existence to a freedom that manifests itself in love (Galatians 5:13).

JUSTICE: "Justice, and only justice shall you pursue, so that you may live and occupy the land that the Lord your God is giving you" (Deuteronomy 16:20). This verse epitomizes the centrality of justice in the Jewish tradition: according to the Torah, the Jewish people can secure its existence in the land promised by God only through justice.

Justice, *tzedek* in Hebrew, is the seminal principle not only for relations among humans, but also for relations between humans and God. God binds humans to the practice of justice; it is part of election (Genesis 18:19). The fundamental importance of justice also to God is cited: "Shall not the Judge of all the earth do what is just?" (Genesis 18:25).

Tzedakah means the loving righteousness of God that Israel is obliged to imitate. Thus it signifies in Judaism also an act of charity and love (*hesed*, Proverbs 21:21).

In the New Testament justice or righteousness is a central, and at the same time an ambiguous term, connected to both ethics and the doctrine of salvation. Thus in Paul, "righteousness of God" is a key term denoting God's saving act in Jesus Christ. According to Romans 1:17, God's righteousness is revealed in the gospel (of Jesus' death and resurrection, 1 Corinthians 15:15). This means that God has shown his justice or righteousness in offering believers salvation solely out of grace, through his act in Christ.

At the same time justice is required of humans in the sense of acting justly. Thus the followers of Jesus are enjoined, according to Matthew 6:33, to strive first for the kingdom of God and his righteousness. Justice or righteousness is essentially a relational term. It refers to the behavior appropriate to one's relationship with God as well as to how God by his saving turn toward us in Christ fulfills his promises and thereby proves his own justice toward humanity.

INSTRUCTION is the literal translation of Torah. The word Torah is derived from the root *y-r-h* ("instruct" or "teach"). Torah can be rendered "teaching" or "instruction" as well as "law."

The giving of the Torah to Israel is the expression of God's love for his people. From a Jewish perspective, the Torah is the basic and permanently binding "pointing of the way" for life. It is understood as created by God and as an ordering principle that undergirds all of life.

With the rendering of Torah as *nomos* in the Greek translation of the Hebrew Bible (the Septuagint) and in the New Testament, the range of meanings of Torah now was narrowed to "law."

In early Christianity, different positions developed vis-à-vis the Torah. According to Matthew, Jesus did not "come to abolish the law or the prophets," but to fulfill the law (Matthew 5:17). In the Christian reception of the Torah, the Decalogue and love of neighbor are central.

REVELATION: The Jewish tradition understands revelation as the act of handing over the Torah by God to the people of Israel at Mount Sinai. The Torah includes a written part (*Torah shebichtav*)—the five books of Moses—and an oral part (*Torah shebe'al-peh*), handed down since the Sinaitic revelation and committed to writing between the second and sixth centuries of the Common Era in the Mishnah and Talmud.

According to rabbinic opinion the divine character of the Torah, its eternal nature, is expressed in its written form only in an abbreviated and implicit way, so that the Torah is not immediately understandable. The Torah requires interpretation. The keys to interpretation are an inherent part of the Sinaitic revelation. Only in studying the Torah is it received. In grappling with the text of the Torah, scholars participate in the revelatory event; they themselves stand on Mount Sinai, as it were.

The purpose of interpretation is the translation of the Word of God into ever-changing human reality. Both this work of translation work as well as its results, namely, concrete religious instructions, are oral Torah.

According to the Christian understanding, God has revealed himself in Jesus Christ, and that in two ways. First, Jesus himself—to whom Christian faith ascribes, in his status as Son of God, a unique knowledge of God (Matthew 11:27; John 1:18; 1 John 5:20)—in his preaching and his dealings with people reveals God as the loving Father, who accepts sinners (e.g., Luke 15:11–32). Secondly, God is revealed in what Christ underwent—in Jesus' death and resurrection—as the life-creating God who justifies and saves. If God reveals himself in Christ first and foremost as a gracious God, it is incontestable, in the New Testament, that communion with God also involves a turning, a reorientation toward God's will.

The biblical writings are not in themselves the Word of God or the revelation of God; rather, they are the authoritative, proclaimed witness to God's revelatory actions.

COMMANDMENTS: *Mitzvah*, the Hebrew word for commandment, is the heart of Jewish religious culture. Judaism knows 613 *mitzvahs* (*mitzvot*). The word mitzvah derives from the Hebrew root z-w-h ("order" or "command"). A *mitzvah* is a duty or an obligation, one that God expects humans to obey. It is not simply a good deed; it is not voluntary. To grasp the meaning of *mitzvah* it is essential to recognize that the good in people only comes to expression in practical deeds. From the Jewish perspective, the fulfilling of the commandments is a source of joy.

HOLY SCRIPTURE: The holiness of Scripture consists in its being understood as the Word of God. Critical to the classical Jewish understanding is the idea that Moses wrote the Torah at the behest of God. As a consequence, every single letter of Scripture is sacred. None may be altered or erased. Only in grappling with Scripture do humans have access to an ever-new understanding of God's Word.

For Christians, the holiness of Scripture consists in God's speaking through it God's liberating and guiding word.

OLD AND NEW TESTAMENT: Speaking of "old" and "new" in this connection refers to Jeremiah 31:31–34, where God announces a new covenant with the house of Israel. In the Jewish tradition, this new covenant has a messianic quality: it is understood as God's creating in the heart of the people of Israel an inner readiness to obey the commandments of the Torah.

The terms "Old Testament" and "New Testament" correspond to the way in which, from the beginning, the Christian tradition has received the Bible and has articulated salvation history: the Old Testament requires a new reading in the sense of a dynamic reappropriation. The fact that the term "Old Testament" was often used pejoratively and polemically emphasizes the ambiguous and easily misunderstood nature of this term, including the possibility of slipping into a theology of substitution. In the final analysis, to speak of "Old" and "New" Testaments means for Christians to take full responsibility for their history. In these phrases is crystallized both the continuity of Christianity with its Jewish heritage and its break with that heritage.

CREATURE OF GOD: According to Genesis 1:26, the human being is created in God's image. This verse is interpreted differently by and in the two traditions. When the Bible says that God made the human being "a little lower" than himself (Psalm 8:6), it emphasizes that there is an insurmountable distance between the creature and the Creator.

All persons have an inherent dignity because they were created in the image of God. That makes them worthy in the eyes of God and of humanity. And because they thereby participate in the creative act of God, human beings are empowered and obliged to continue this act of creation (Genesis 1:28, 2:15). This is the human being's responsibility. It is this for which humanity is called to answer. This is the essence of being human, and is what sets humans apart from other creatures. One is worthy as a human being before oneself and before God when one protects in every living being that being's gift of God-given life; when, before God, one honors the humanity of every person and discharges one's responsibility for the creation.

NEW WORLD: The promise of the creation of a new earth and a new heaven appears in the Bible in Isaiah 65:17: "For I am about to create new heavens and a new earth; the former things shall not be remembered or come to mind."

The earth and the heavens, taken together, constitute for the ancient Near Eastern mind the whole of reality, the cosmos. God will renew the heavens and the earth. This verse is one of the roots of the Jewish messianic hope, looking toward an end time of a just and peaceful world (cf. Isaiah 11:5–9).

In the New Testament, the promise of Isaiah 65:17 appears, among other places, in 2 Peter 3:13: "But, in accordance with his promise, we wait for new heavens and a new earth, where righteousness is at home." According to Christian hope, the recreation of the cosmos is the goal (*telos*, in Greek) of the history of salvation. With Christ, this has already begun, bringing with it the creation of a new humanity (1 Corinthians 5:17). One who is justified by faith acts in accordance with God's will.

GLORY OF GOD: This phrase translates the Hebrew word *kabod*. In the biblical context and in the broader Jewish tradition, the term "glory of God" refers, on the one hand, to the many manifestations of God (compassion, grace, patience, kindness—cf. Exodus 34:6) that constitute his majesty. On the other hand, it signifies the reverence and praise that humans owe to God. From the Jewish perspective, it is linked to the fulfillment of the Torah. Inherent in it is respect for the dignity of the human being, who is created in the image of God (Genesis 1:27). In the Greek version of the Hebrew Bible, *kavod* is rendered with *doxa* ("glory," "honor," "fame," etc.); this determines, to no small extent, the Christian understanding of God's glory. It refers to the divinity of God that God reveals in the creation and in Christ. The appropriate behavior of humans in the face of this is praise of God and love of neighbor (cf. Proverbs 14:31).

PEACE: *Shalom*, the Hebrew word for peace, is derived from the root *sh-l-m* ("perfect," "complete"). In the Hebrew Bible, the word *shalom*, on the one hand, refers to the level of the individual. It means that one is inwardly at peace with oneself (Genesis 28:21). On the other hand, it means the absence of war (Leviticus 26:6) and the comprehensive material and spiritual well-being of society (Ezekiel 37:26).

Peace is not a state that humans discover; on the contrary, they must seek it diligently and pursue it (Psalm 34:14) The same goes for the righteousness that is closely linked to peace (Deuteronomy 16:20; Isaiah 11:1–9).

The Torah was given for the purpose of peacemaking (Babylonian Talmud, *Gittin* 59b) and can be read as a guide to compassion (Psalm 145:9) and peacefulness (Proverbs 3:17).

For the Christian tradition, "peace" can signify the contents of the Gospel (Ephesians 2:7). Inasmuch as we are declared righteous by faith, we have peace with God through Jesus Christ (Romans 5:1). The reconciliation of people with God enables them to live in peace with one another.

In the Messianic age, a world-embracing, final peace will prevail (Isaiah 11:5–10).

PART SIX

Jewish Statements

86

Address by Rabbi Mordecai Waxman on the Twentieth Anniversary of *Nostra Aetate*

Delivered by the Chairman of the International Jewish Committee on Interreligious Dialogue during an audience of the International Catholic-Jewish Liaison Committee with Pope John Paul II in the Vatican, October 28, 1985.

Your Holiness:

October 28, 1965, was both a historic and revolutionary date. It marked a turning away from eighteen centuries often characterized by both misunderstanding and persecution, toward a dialogue in which we explored our common spiritual roots and confronted our disagreements frankly but in a spirit of mutual understanding and respect.

In the ensuing years, the Episcopates in the United States, Latin America, and Europe have made the spirit of *Nostra Aetate* [*Bridges*, Vol. 1, Document 30] their own, carried its doctrines even further, and sought to translate them into modes of action and behavior.

Your Holiness personally has given great depth to the dialogue and evoked a warm response from Jews and, indeed, from many Catholics throughout the world through your own statements. These included your declaration in Mainz in 1980 [*Bridges*, Vol. 1, Document 34] in which you affirmed, "The people of God of the Old Covenant [which] was never repudiated by God..." That was supplemented by your statement in Rome in 1982 that we pursue "diverse but, in the end, convergent paths with the help of the Lord."

There is a Hebrew proverb that says, *D'vorim hayotzim me'im ha-lev, nichnasim al ha-lev* ("Words which come from the heart, speak to the heart"). The warmth with which you have spoken today of our common spiritual heritage, our common concerns, and our common goals enables us, in turn, to speak from the heart.

We appreciated, in *Nostra Aetate* and in the declarations which have flowed from it, the ability of a great faith to examine itself and to chart new directions.

The repudiation of the false teachings—responsible for so much hatred and persecution—that all Jews, then and now, were responsible for the death of Jesus, encouraged Jews everywhere to feel that there was a new spirit in the Christian world. We have noted with distress lapses from time to time into the old and repudiated language by some Catholic authorities. Nonetheless, the wide acceptance of the new approach in the Catholic world has been for us a source of hope.

The further recognition in *Nostra Aetate* and in the *Guidelines* that the Jewish religious tradition has continued to evolve and grow through the centuries to the present day and has much to contribute to our world, and the assertion that every effort must be made to understand Judaism "in its own terms," as it sees itself, made dialogue possible.

But, in these same years, the Jewish people have been undergoing a profound transformation of our own. The Nazi Holocaust shook us to the core of our being. The creation of the State of Israel restored us as a factor in history but, even more, restored us religiously and spiritually. For the third time in Jewish history, the pattern of exile and redemption was reenacted. The implications are incalculable, but we are confirmed in biblical belief that the Covenant with the land established by the God of Abraham and his descendants endures, even as the Covenant of the Torah abides. It said to us in the words of the Torah portion read this week throughout the Jewish world that "Abraham still stands before the Lord."

We are deeply moved by the knowledge that Your Holiness has testified to this truth through your apostolic letter in April 1984:

> For the Jewish people who live in the State of Israel and who preserve in that land such precious testimonies to their history and their faith, we must ask for the desired security and the due tranquility that is the prerogative of every nation and condition of life and of progress for every society.

Thus, a renewed Jewish people, restored to Jerusalem and to human dignity, can engage in dialogue with the Catholic Church, confident that we have spiritual riches to cherish and to share, aware that we both have a common obligation to engage in *Tikkun Olam*—the improvement and perfecting of our world. On this anniversary of *Nostra Aetate*, we are conscious that much of its vision has yet to be translated into reality and universal acceptance. But we look forward to the creation of structures and programs which will translate our dialogue into actions which will move the hearts of the members of our respective faiths in the joint quest for universal peace, for social justice and human rights, and for upholding the dignity of every human being created in the Divine image.

Your Holiness, in recognition of the common spiritual heritage we share and in consideration of the fact that the Catholic and Jewish world are commemorating the 850th anniversary of the birth of one of our greatest figures, we wish to present you with a copy of the beautiful Kaufman manuscript of the *Code of Maimonides*. With it, we offer the hope that the final line of the *Code* will be fulfilled through our continuing dialogue which shall, with God's will, grow in depth and understanding so that "the earth may be filled with the knowledge of the Lord as the waters cover the sea."

87

Address by Prof. Giacomo Saban on the Occasion of the Visit of Pope John Paul II to the Great Synagogue of Rome

Delivered by the President of the Jewish Community of Rome on April 13, 1986.

Your Holiness:

I have the honor of being the first to welcome you to this major temple on the banks of the Tiber. I greet you on behalf of the most ancient Jewish community of the Diaspora, a community that I have been given the privilege of serving. In expressing our satisfaction at seeing a Roman pontiff for the first time cross the threshold of a synagogue, I feel it my duty to recount briefly the history of the Jewish community of this city, a history which goes back several thousand years.

Having settled on the banks of the Tiber almost two centuries prior to the destruction of the Second Temple, the fathers of the Jews who lived in Rome for centuries lived here as free Roman citizens. They wept, together with the multitude, over the mortal remains of Caesar; they applauded, together with the delirious populace, the triumph of Augustus. They were not spared, however, during the reigns of less glorious emperors, suffering, together with the rest of the inhabitants of Rome, from their wickedness and tyranny.

Their number grew with the arrival of the prisoners of the Jewish wars, and—at first slaves, but then quickly freed—they enjoyed a relatively tranquil life. Witness to this fact is a stone tablet between the fourth and the fifth mile of the ancient Appian Way...But I am here speaking of the majority, because there were also those who came to Rome to ascend the glorious stairway of martyrdom, and the names of some of these are inscribed in the lists of the Mamertine Prison, from

Aristobulus, son of Herod the Great, the victim of dark political designs, to Simon bar Ghiora, who fought relentlessly for our people's freedom.

Contrary to the legislation of Augustus Caesar, which, inscribed in bronze tablets and hung in the forums of the principal cities of the Empire, safeguarded the rights of our ancestors, the Theodosian Code limited their freedom, activity, and development. Nonetheless, they remained—faithful to the city—perhaps the only constant component in the mosaic of populations that converged on Rome from throughout the Empire. Nor did their life consist only of trade and commerce; our commentators speak of flourishing rabbinical academies, and many inscriptions in the catacombs witness to the fact that they constituted an inviting center of spirituality and a source of pure monotheistic faith in the midst of a world in which paganism was moving toward its extinction.

The dark centuries which followed and which saw, together with the end of the Western Empire, the decline of the city, were borne by this community with serene courage. Shortly after the end of the first millennium, when the temporal power of the popes was being consolidated, a son of this community, Nathan hen Jechiel Anav, whose house is found in Travestevere, not far from here, wrote in Rome the *Arukh*, the first normative compendium of the Judaism of the Diaspora.

This community escaped the massacres that were inflicted upon Judaism on the other side of the Alps by croziers and crusades; it did not, however, remain indifferent to the lot of those brothers in the faith, as is documented by the ancient funerary liturgy still in use among the Jews of Rome.

The first centuries after the year 1000 were difficult and painful for both the Jews and the rest of the population of Rome. Relations with the ruling power went through alternating phases, and violent acts were inflicted upon this community in the persons of its teachers. But those were the years in which Dante showed his appreciation of Immanuel Romano, who entered the world of Italian literature, bringing his meter, style, and same poetic structures into Jewish literature.

The year 1492 saw the community grow with the arrival of refugees from Spain, and the liberal attitude of the pope assured them a haven in this city.

In the following half century, the situation was to change radically. In September of 1553, hundreds of copies of the Talmud were burned not far from here, in Campo di Fiori, and this blaze, which was not the first, would be reignited more than once in subsequent centuries. After the accession of Paul IV, with the bull *Cum nimis absurdum* of July 14,1555, the ghetto of Rome was established precisely where we find ourselves today. The measures introduced, harshly restrictive with regard to study and worship, as well as normal everyday activities, reduced the inhabitants of the ghetto to economic and cultural misery, depriving them of some of their most fundamental rights.

Limitations of every sort and lack of freedom were thus the lot reserved to Roman Jews for a period of more than three centuries. It was only 115 years ago that this complex of restrictions, enslavement, and humiliations came to cease, and not without some very sad last eruptions, such as the Caso Mortara…

It took more than sixty years for the community of Rome to begin to refashion a normal existence worthy of the position that it occupies in the framework of Italian Judaism, both in terms of numbers and historical tradition. This process was cruelly cut short by the events immediately preceding the Second World War, with persecutions which were much more horrible in that they aimed at the complete annihilation of Judaism worldwide.

It does not fall to us to judge what took place in Rome during those years, as we are too near in time to those days. What was taking place on one of the banks of the Tiber could not have been unknown on the other side of the river, nor could what was happening elsewhere on the European continent. Nonetheless, many of our brethren found help and refuge through courageous initiatives precisely within those convents and monasteries that they had learned to fear for so many centuries.

An apostolic nuncio who would be called to the papacy fifteen years later was not ignorant of the misdeeds that were being carried out in those days in the heart of our continent.

That pope, John XXIII, wished to see the development of a spirituality suited to the tormented world that was finally experiencing the healing of the atrocious wounds of the war. With the Second Vatican Council he wished to give the Church an opportunity to begin anew to meditate upon fundamental values. *Nostra Aetate*, that Council document which most relates to us [*Bridges*, Vol. 1, Document 30], introduces a different relationship between the faith of Israel and that of the surrounding world, restoring to us not only what for centuries we had been denied, but also the dignity that it had always been our right to see recognized.

The work of that "just man" has always had our praise and total appreciation; that work has been eminently carried on by his successors. That work must continue. The efforts of men of goodwill must in fact tend toward greater understanding of peoples, fully respecting their diversity. It is in this context that I feel I must manifest the aspiration to see abandoned certain reticence regarding the State of Israel. The land of Israel has a role that is central, emotionally and spiritually, in the heart of every Jew, and a change of attitude in its regard would gratify not only those present here, but Judaism worldwide. It would also, in my opinion, make a real contribution to the pacification of a region of the world that today presents threats and perils to the entire Western world.

This would be a further step, then, in the "fraternal dialogue" of which *Nostra Aetate* speaks. I do not hesitate to believe that this step will be taken. Today's visit, Your Holiness, that you have held to be opportune—I would even say necessary—is a lively testimony to the spirit of the Council. It fills us all with joy, inasmuch as it is a sign which foreshadows better days, days in which all those who believe in the One God—may His Holy Name be blessed—will be able, united, to contribute to the creation of a better world.

88

Address by Chief Rabbi Elio Toaff on the Occasion of the Visit of Pope John Paul II to the Great Synagogue of Rome

Delivered on April 13, 1986.

Your Holiness:

As the chief rabbi of this community, whose history goes back thousands of years, I wish to express to you my intense satisfaction at the gesture you have wished to carry out today, visiting a synagogue for the first time in the history of the Church. This gesture is destined to be remembered throughout history. It shows itself linked with the enlightened teaching of your illustrious predecessor, John XXIII, who, one Sabbath morning, became the first pope to stop and bless the Jews of Rome who were leaving this temple after prayer, and it follows the path marked out by the Second Vatican Council, which, with the declaration *Nostra Aetate* [*Bridges*, Vol. 1, Document 30], produced that revolution in relations between the Church and Judaism that has made today's visit possible.

We thus find ourselves before a true turning point in Church policy. The Church now looks upon the Jews with sentiments of esteem and appreciation, abandoning that teaching of disdain whose inadmissibility Jules Isaac—may he be remembered here in blessing—brought to the attention of Pope John.

At this historic moment, my thoughts turn with admiration, gratitude, and mourning to the infinite number of Jewish martyrs who serenely faced death for the sanctification of God's name. Theirs is the merit if our faith has never wavered and if fidelity to the Lord and his Law has not failed in the long course of the centuries. Thanks to them, the Jewish people lives still, the only surviving people from antiquity.

Thus, we cannot forget the past, but today we wish to begin, with faith and hope, this new historical phase, which fruitfully points the way to common undertakings finally carried out on a plane of equality and mutual esteem in the interest of all humanity.

We propose to spread the idea of the spiritual and moral monotheism of Israel in order to bring together mankind and the universe in the love, the power and the justice of God, who is the God of all, and to bring light to the minds and hearts of all men, so as to cause order, morality, goodness, harmony, and peace to flourish in the world.

At the same time, we reaffirm God's universal fatherhood over all men, taking our inspiration from the Prophets, who taught it as that filial love which joins all living beings to the maternal womb of the infinite as to their natural matrix. It is therefore man who must be taken into consideration; man, who was created by God in his image and likeness, with the aim of conferring upon him a dignity and nobility that he can maintain only if he wills to follow the Father's teaching. It is written in Deuteronomy, "You are children of the Lord your God," in order to indicate the relationship that must join men to their Creator, a relationship of Father and child, of love and benevolent indulgence, but also a relationship of brotherhood which must reign among all human beings. If this truly existed, we would not today have to struggle against the terrorism and twisted acts of violence that reap so many innocent victims—men, women, the elderly, and children—as happened not long ago even at the threshold of this temple.

Our common task in society should therefore be that of teaching our fellow man the duty of mutual respect, showing the iniquity of the evils afflicting the world; such as terrorism, which is the exaltation of blind and inhuman violence, and which strikes out against defenseless people, including Jews in every country, simply because they are Jews; likewise, antisemitism and racism, which we vainly felt to be forever vanquished after the last world war.

The condemnation that the Council pronounced against every form of antisemitism should be rigorously applied, as well as the condemnation of all violence, in order to keep all mankind from drowning in corruption, immorality, and injustice.

The invitation that we read in the book of Leviticus—"I am the Lord your God; sanctify yourselves, be holy, because I am Holy"—is meant to be an exhortation to imitate the holiness of the Lord in our lives.

In this way, the image of God in potency in man from the first moment of his creation becomes the image of God in act. The *Kedoshim Tih'yu* is the imitation on the part of man of what are called the "ways of the Lord."

In this way, by seeking to subject all their actions to the spirit, man gives the spirit dominion over material reality.

The reward for this kind of conduct is great, and God already revealed this to Abraham when he brought him out to gaze at the sky on a starry night: "I am the Lord who brought you out of Ur Casdim in order to give you possession of this land." The possession of the promised land is obtained as a reward for having followed the ways of the Lord, and the end of days will come when the people have returned there.

This return is being realized: Those who escaped from the Nazi death camps have found in the land of Israel a refuge and a new life in regained liberty and dignity. It is for this reason that their return has been called by our teachers "the beginning of the coming of final redemption—*Reshit tzemihat ge'ulatenu*."

The return of the Jewish people to its land must be recognized as a good and an inalienable gain for the world, because it constitutes the prelude—according to the teachings of the Prophets—to that epoch of universal brotherhood to which we all aspire, and to that redemptive peace that finds its sure promise in the Bible. The recognition of Israel's irreplaceable role in the final plan of redemption that God has promised us cannot be denied.

We will thus be able to strive together to affirm man's right to freedom, a complete freedom that encounters an inviolable boundary only when it infringes upon or limits the freedom of others. Man is born free, is free by nature; thus all men, no matter to what people they belong, must be equally free, because all have the same dignity and participate in the same rights. There are no men who can consider themselves superior and others inferior, because there is in everyone that divine spark that makes them equal.

Yet even in our own day, there are still countries in the world where freedom is limited and discrimination and alienation are practiced without any hesitation. I am referring in particular to blacks in South Africa, and, as far as freedom of religion is concerned, to Jews and Catholics in the Soviet Union. Our common task ought to be that of proclaiming the fact that from man's fundamental freedom there arise inalienable human rights: like the right to life, to freedom of thought, conscience, and religion.

The right to life must be understood not only as the right to exist, but to see one's life guaranteed, from its birth, to see one's existence assured against every threat, every violence; it means a guarantee of the means of subsistence through a more equitable distribution of wealth, so that there are no longer people dying of hunger in the world. It means the right of each person to see his honor, his good name, safeguarded against calumny and prejudice, including that of a religious nature. It means the condemnation of every attack on a person's self-respect, considered by Judaism to be equivalent to bloodshed. It means to fight against falsehood because of the disastrous consequences it can have on society, and against hate, which provokes violence and is considered by Judaism the same as hate of the Lord, of whom man is the image.

Freedom of thought also includes freedom of conscience and religious freedom. We have to strive with all our power in order to prevent man even today from being persecuted or condemned for the ideas he professes or for his religious convictions.

The concept of freedom—as we see—is a composite one, and if one of its components is suppressed, it is inevitable that sooner or later the whole complex reality of freedom will be lost because it is a unity that has an absolute and indivisible value. It is an ideal in and of itself, one of the objects of that reign of universal justice preached in the Bible, by virtue of which men and peoples have the inalienable right to be their own masters.

Your Holiness, at this very important moment in the history of relations between our two religions, as our hearts open to the hope that the misfortunes of the past might be replaced by a fruitful dialogue that—even while respecting our existing differences—might give us the possibility of a concordant activity, of sincere and honest cooperation toward the realization of those universal ends that are found in our common roots, allow me to conclude my reflections with the words of the Prophet Isaiah: "I will greatly rejoice in the Lord, my soul shall exult in my God; for he has clothed me with the garments of salvation, he has covered me with the robe of righteousness, as a bridegroom decks himself with a garland, and as a bride adorns herself with her jewels. For as the earth brings forth its shoots, and as a garden causes what is sown in it to spring up, so the Lord God will cause righteousness and praise to spring forth before all the nations" [Isa 61:10–11].

89

Address by Rabbi Mordecai Waxman on the Occasion of the Visit of Pope John Paul II to the United States

Delivered in Miami, Florida, September 11, 1987.

It is our honor and pleasure to welcome you to the United States. We do so in behalf of the Jewish organizations who are represented here today; organizations that have been in fruitful conversations with the Roman Catholic Church through the years.

They include representatives of the American Jewish Committee, the American Jewish Congress, the Anti-Defamation League of B'nai B'rith, and the Synagogue Council of America, which is here representing the Union of American Hebrew Congregations, United Synagogue of America, Central Conference of American Rabbis and Rabbinical Assembly. Also present with us this morning are the leaders of other major organizations in American Jewish life, as well as members of the Greater Miami Jewish community.

The men and women assembled here reflect the rich diversity of American Jewish life; we constitute a variety of religious and communal affiliations; American-born and immigrant; some are survivors of the Shoah, the Nazi Holocaust, while others have never experienced the dark shadow of antisemitism in their own lives. We come from all sections of the United States, and we come as full participants in the pluralistic and democratic society that has encouraged us to be proudly American and fully Jewish at the same time.

Your visit to this country happily coincides with the 200th anniversary of the U.S. Constitution, a document that guarantees religious liberty for all American citizens and which has enabled all faith communities to flourish in an atmosphere of religious pluralism. This has made possible a free and flourishing religious life for all.

Second Vatican Council

It has been twenty-two years since the conclusion of the Second Vatican Council and the promulgation of *Nostra Aetate* [*Bridges*, Vol. 1, Document 30]. The broad teachings that emerged in 1965 have been further enriched and strengthened by a series of formal Catholic documents and pronouncements, some of them your own. These statements have transformed Catholic-Jewish relationships throughout the world, and this positive change is especially evident here in the United States.

As the largest Jewish community in the world, we have developed close and respectful ties with many Roman Catholics, both lay and clergy, and we value these warm relationships and treasure these friendships. We particularly cherish our relationship with the National Conference of Catholic Bishops and its Secretariat for Catholic-Jewish Relations. In almost every place where Catholics and Jews live in the United States, we relate to each other in some organized fashion. We constantly exchange views and opinions, and as Jews and Catholics we often share our positions, sometimes agreeing, sometimes disagreeing, but always striving for a spirit of mutual respect and understanding.

Throughout the United States, American Jews and Catholics work in concert with one another on a wide range of social justice issues and fight for global human rights and against all forms of racism and bigotry. Our common agenda has always embraced, and our future agenda will continue to embrace, the many crucial problems of the human family as a whole.

One of the major achievements of our joint encounters is the shared recognition that each community must be understood in its own terms, as it understands itself. It is particularly gratifying that our Catholic-Jewish meetings are conducted in a spirit of candor and mutual respect.

Issue of Waldheim Visit

Such meetings took place last week at the Vatican and at Castel Gandolfo. These conversations, although quickly arranged, were highly significant. You and high church leaders listened to the deeply felt concerns of the Jewish community that were raised following last

June's state visit to the Vatican by Austrian President Kurt Waldheim, who has never expressed regrets for his Nazi past.

Obviously, the differences expressed at last week's meeting have not been resolved. However, this opportunity for us to express the pain and anger of the Jewish community in face-to-face meetings and for you and leaders of your church to listen with respect and openness represents an important confirmation of the progress our communities have made in recent decades. One of the results of those meetings will be an instrumentality to develop closer communication and contact between our communities.

A basic belief of our Jewish faith is the need "to mend the world under the sovereignty of God...*L'takken olam b'malkhut Shaddai.*" To mend the world means to do God's work in the world. It is in this spirit that Catholics and Jews should continue to address the social, moral, economic and political problems of the world. Your presence here in the United States affords us the opportunity to reaffirm our commitment to the sacred imperative of "*tikkun olam*," "the mending of the world."

But before we can mend the world, we must first mend ourselves. A meeting such as this is part of the healing process that is now visibly under way between our two communities. It is clear that the teachings proclaimed in *Nostra Aetate* are becoming major concerns of the Catholic Church and under your leadership are being implemented in the teachings of the church and in the life of Catholics everywhere.

Reconciliation Process

Catholics and Jews have begun the long overdue process of reconciliation. We still have some way to go because Catholic-Jewish relations [are] one of this century's most positive developments.

We remain concerned with the persistence of antisemitism—the hatred of Jews and Judaism, which is on the rise in some parts of the world. We are encouraged by your vigorous leadership in denouncing all forms of antisemitism, and by the church's recent teachings. The church's repudiation of antisemitism is of critical importance in the struggle to eradicate this virulent plague from the entire human family.

Antisemitism may affect the body of the Jew, but history has trag-ically shown that it assaults the soul of the Christian world and all oth-ers who succumb to this ancient, but persistent pathology.

We hope that your strong condemnations of antisemitism will con-tinue to be implemented in the schools, the parishes, teaching materi-als and the liturgy, and reflected in the attitudes and behavior of Catholics throughout the world. Greater attention needs to be paid to the Christian roots of antisemitism. The "teaching of contempt" reaped a demonic harvest during the Shoah in which one-third of the Jewish people were murdered as a central component of a nation's pol-icy. The Nazi Holocaust-Shoah brought together two very different forms of evil: On the one hand it represented the triumph of an ideol-ogy of nationalism and racism, the suppression of human conscience and the deification of the state—concepts that are profoundly anti-Christian as well as anti-Jewish. On the other hand the Shoah was the culmination of centuries of antisemitism in European culture for which Christian teachings bear a heavy responsibility.

Shoah Pronouncements

While your sensitive concerns and your noteworthy pronounce-ments about the Shoah have been heartening, we have observed recent tendencies to obscure the fact that Jews were the major target of Nazi genocidal policies. It is possible to visit Nazi death camps today and not be informed that the majority of its victims were Jews. Your letter about Shoah, sent last month to Archbishop John May, the president of the National Conference of Catholic Bishops, represented a deep level of understanding of that terrible period.

We look forward to the forthcoming Vatican document on the Shoah, the historical background of antisemitism.

Many Catholic schools in the U.S. are already teaching about the Holocaust and efforts are under way to develop a specific curriculum about the Shoah for Catholic students. This material is being jointly developed by Catholic and Jewish educators.

Even though many of the great centers of Jewish learning were destroyed during the Shoah, there has been a remarkable renewal of Jewish religious life throughout the world.

This renaissance of the spirit is taking place not only in the United States, in the State of Israel, and in other lands of freedom, but in the Soviet Union as well. Many Soviet Jews are discovering that the covenant between God and the people of Israel is indeed "irrevocable" as you declared last year at the Grand Synagogue in Rome. The struggle of Soviet Jews to achieve freedom is a major concern of the Jewish community, and we appreciate the support American Catholics have given to this cause.

The return to Zion and the re-establishment of Jewish sovereignty in the land of Israel play a paramount role in Jewish self-understanding today. Because of the importance that the State of Israel occupies in the mind, spirit, and heart of Jews, whenever Christians and Jews meet in a serious conversation, Israel is at the center of that encounter. The re-emergence of an independent Jewish state onto the world stage in 1948 has compelled Christians and Jews to examine themselves and each other in a new light.

Holy See and Israel

We must express our concern at the absence of full diplomatic relations between the Holy See and the State of Israel. We welcome the recent statements from Vatican leaders declaring that no theological reasons exist in Catholic doctrine to inhibit such relations. We strongly urge once again that full and formal diplomatic relations be established soon between the Vatican and the State of Israel. Such a step would be a positive and constructive contribution by the Vatican to the peace process, and it would send a strong signal to the international community that the Holy See recognizes Israel as a permanent and legitimate member of the family of nations.

One of the most welcome results of the recent Catholic-Jewish encounter has been the recognition by Catholics that Judaism has continued and deepened its unique spiritual development after the separation of the Christian church from the Jewish people some 1,900 years ago.

A meeting such as today's is a vivid reminder that we live in a historic moment. Clearly, as two great communities of faith, repositories of moral and spiritual values, Catholics and Jews need to move together in this new moment. The last quarter century has irreversibly changed the way we perceive and act toward each other.

In an age of great challenges and great possibilities there is a compelling need for a "vision for the times," *"Chazon L'moed"* (Habakkuk, 2:3). Our vision for Catholics and Jews is a prayer of the synagogue.

At the end of the Torah reading, the scroll is held high so the entire congregation may see the words of God, and together the congregation prays, *"Hazak, Hazak, v'nithazek,"* "Be strong, be very strong, and let us strengthen one another."

90

Emet ve'Emunah ["Truth and Faithfulness"]: Statement of Principles of Conservative Judaism (excerpt)

The following is the section on "Relations with Other Faiths" of the Statement of Principles, issued jointly in January 1988 by the Jewish Theological Seminary of America, the Rabbinical Assembly, the United Synagogue of America, the Women's League for Conservative Judaism, and the Federation of Jewish Men's Clubs.

From the time of the earliest settlement of Israelite tribes in the land of Canaan, Jews have always lived in close proximity to and in contact with people of other faiths and nationalities. This has been equally true in the Land of Israel and in the Diaspora. Historically, the attitude which a Jewish community has taken toward gentiles has generally depended on the nature of the relations which that community had with its immediate neighbors. The Iberian Jews, during their "Golden Age," had a fairly positive attitude toward the Muslims among whom they lived, while the Jews of the Rhineland, martyred during the Crusades, produced some bitter anti-gentile rhetoric. Yet throughout Jewish history, in all eras and in all lands, there has been a prodigious amount of cultural influence and borrowing, an exchange which has gone in both directions and has benefited both Jews and gentiles.

Jewish culture has been able to grow and develop—and this has been the greatest positive feature of the Diaspora—because of the recognition that our rejection of another people's faith does not entail a rejection of its entire civilization. Although we often have lived in tension with the nations of the world, our Bible developed and adapted some of their myths, our Talmud drew upon their vocabulary and institutions, our poetry used their meters, and the State of Israel has benefited from many aspects of world culture. Conversely, what we have created, in the realms of religion, philosophy, law, social institutions, the arts, and science, has been freely appropriated by the rest of the world.

The contemporary age has not departed from this historical trend. North American Jews enjoy the unprecedented blessing of full partic- ipation in the political life of free nations, and consequently their opportunities for fruitful exchange with other faiths and cultures are manifold. In the United States, Jews have a good deal in common with other religious groups, since we share a fairly recent immigrant history with many of them, and since we are all, as religious groups, set at arm's distance from the official organs of political power in this constitution- ally secular nation. Common agendas have been fairly easy to formu- late in such a setting, and thus North America has seen a very healthy proliferation of programs for interfaith dialogue and cooperation. In the Land of Israel, despite the obvious tensions between Jews and Arabs, there have been mutual influences between Jewish and non- Jewish cultures in the Middle East. Its expansion into the realm of Islamic-Jewish dialogue is devoutly to be wished.

As Conservative Jews, we acknowledge without apology the many debts which Jewish religion and civilization owe to the nations of the world. We eschew triumphalism with respect to other ways of serving God. Maimonides believed that other monotheistic faiths— Christianity and Islam—serve to spread knowledge of, and devotion to, the God and the Torah of Israel throughout the world. Many modern thinkers, both Jewish and gentile, have noted that God may well have seen fit to enter covenants with many nations. Either outlook, when relating to others, is perfectly compatible with a commitment to one's own faith and pattern of religious life.

If we criticize triumphalism in our own community, then real dia- logue with other faith groups requires that we criticize triumphalism and other failings in those quarters as well. In the second half of the twentieth century, no relationship between Jews and Christians can be dignified or honest without facing up frankly to the centuries of preju- dice, theological anathema, and persecution that have been thrust upon Jewish communities, culminating in the horrors of the Shoah (Holocaust). No relationship can be nurtured between Jews and Muslims unless it acknowledges explicitly and seeks to combat the ter- rible social and political effects of Muslim hostility, as well as the dis- turbing but growing reaction of Jewish anti-Arabism in the Land of Israel. But all of these relationships, properly pursued, can bring great blessing to the Jewish community and to the world. As the late Professor Abraham Joshua Heschel put it, "no religion is an island."

Theological humility requires us to recognize that although we have but one God, God has more than one nation. Our tradition explicitly recognizes that God entered into a covenant with Adam and Eve, and later with Noah and his family as well as His special covenant with Abraham and the great revelation to Israel at Sinai. It is part of our mission to understand, respect, and live with the other nations of the world, to discern those truths in their cultures from which we can learn, and to share with them the truths that we have come to know.

91

Response to the Vatican Document "We Remember: A Reflection on the Shoah"

Issued in April 1998 by the International Jewish Committee on Interreligious Consultations.

The document "We Remember: A Reflection on the Shoah" [Document 49 above] was issued in March 1998 and discussed at a meeting of the International Liaison Committee later that month. It has evoked reactions among our member organizations and we wish to summarize these and bring them to your attention.

We would like first to express our appreciation of Pope John Paul II's letter to Cardinal Cassidy expressing the hope for all men of good will to work together, in which we sincerely join. We are keenly aware of the many initiatives of the Pope to improve Catholic-Jewish relations during the twenty years of his papacy and of his personal sensitivity to the horrors of the Shoah.

The Document and Antisemitism

The subject of the document as conceived in 1987 was The Shoah and Antisemitism and we have found those sections warning against the dangers of antisemitism a moving testimony to your determination to fight this evil in any form and in any place. They are pointed and phrased strongly and can leave believers in no doubt, in the oft-repeated words of Pope John Paul II, that antisemitism is a sin. The clear affirmation goes far beyond previous Vatican documents on the subject and we welcome its unequivocal challenge. We are also well aware that this document will reach millions in parts of the world who have never had firsthand contact with a Jew and could help to counteract the traditional prejudices which exist there. We hope that everything will be done to ensure that the message will quickly reach grass roots level.

The Historical Record

Our problems with the document relate to historical presentation and interpretation. However let us first say that the summary of the course of the Shoah, called "a major fact of the history of the century," should render impossible the obscenity of Shoah Denial among Catholics and we see in this one of the major positive aspects of the document.

Our disappointments in the historical treatment were accentuated by the great impression made upon us by the series of statements on the subject published in recent years by National Episcopal Conferences, especially in those countries which were the focus of the Shoah—many on the fiftieth anniversary of the liberation of the camps or the end of the European War. These documents were characterized by clarity, sensitivity and courage and we had hoped that the Vatican document would be written with the same categorical approach. In relating to aspects of the historical record, we will quote from these documents as examples of conclusions we had hoped would be similarly expressed in the Vatican document.

Christianity and Historical Antisemitism

Initial Jewish reactions on the publication of the document were deeply concerned by the incorporation of the quotation from the Pope's speech of 31 October 1997 [Document 33 above] in which he said "In the Christian world—I do not say on the part of the Church as such—erroneous and unjust interpretations of the New Testament regarding the Jewish people and their alleged culpability have circulated for too long." Nobody can doubt the Pope's sincere abhorrence of antisemitism but his apparent absolution of the Church from historical responsibility was, at least, puzzling. Jewish reactions went into great detail concerning the misdeeds of the historical Church. At the meeting of the International Liaison Committee, Cardinal Cassidy explained the perspective of the writers of the document. As summarized in the subsequent communiqué, he said that "the term 'the Church' refers for Catholics to the inerrant mystical bride of Jesus Christ, whereas the term 'sons and daughters of the Church' does not exclude members of the Church at any level." We feel it unfortunate that the distinction was not spelled out in the document as we doubt whether even all believers are aware of this distinction and the statement as it stands could (and did) lead to conclusions different from those intended. Even after the explanation, we find many Church statements confusing—including those of the Bishops' Conferences with their frequent references to failings of "the Church." What are we to make of the statement of the German and Austrian bishops from 1988 which says "The Church, which we proclaim holy and which we honor as a mystery, is also a sinful Church and in need of conversion," which would seem to conflict with the concept of the inerrancy of the mystical Church. We were glad to note that Father Raniero Cantalamessa in his Good Friday sermon delivered in the name of the Pontifical Household quoted the Pope's statement of October 31 but omitted the phrase which we found problematic.

The document does indeed ask some of the pertinent questions that needed to be asked: "Whether the Nazi persecution of the Jews was not made easier by the anti-Jewish prejudices imbedded in some Christian minds and hearts?" "Did anti-Jewish sentiment among Christians make them less sensitive, or even indifferent, to the persecutions launched against the Jews by National Socialism when it reached power?" To these questions a clear answer was expected which would have showed how the teaching of contempt has influenced Christianity throughout the centuries and how it deeply affected the Christian responses to Nazi persecution. This was to be found clearly stated in the documents of the Bishops. For example in the 1995 Statement of the Dutch Bishops: "A tradition of theological and ecclesiastical anti-Judaism contributed to the climate in which the Shoah could take place. A so-called 'Teaching of Contempt' taught that the Jews were a people rejected after Christ's death. These kinds of traditions meant that Catholics kept aloof from Jews and in some cases were indifferent or hostile. We reject this tradition of ecclesiastical anti-Judaism and regret its terrible outcome."

The 1997 Statement of the French Bishops [Document 60 above] expressed the historical aspect with especial clarity: "A tradition of anti-Judaism affected Christian doctrines and teachings, theology and apologetics, preaching and liturgy in various degrees and prevailed among Christians throughout the centuries until Vatican II...To the extent that the priests and leaders of the Church for so long allowed the teaching of contempt to develop and fostered in Christian communities a collective religious culture which permanently affected and deformed mentalities, they bear a serious responsibility."

The relevant paragraph in the Vatican document (page 8 paragraph 1) does indeed refer to the historical record but avoids taking a clear position on the relationship between the teaching of contempt and the political and cultural climate that made the Shoah possible. Sentences such as "Sentiments of anti-Judaism in some Christian quarters and the gap which existed between the Church and the Jewish people led to a generalized discrimination..." or "[Jews] were looked upon with a certain suspicion and mistrust. In times of crisis such as famine, war, pestilence or social tensions, the Jewish minority was sometimes taken as a scapegoat and became the victim of violence, looting, even massacres" overlook the systematic unceasing persecution over sixteen centuries by the Church, its leaders and theologians, priests and laymen. It was not merely "a certain suspicion and mistrust" but an institutionalized policy of humiliation, discrimination and hatred—disseminated in canon law, in the liturgy, the catechism, from pulpits and schools directed to reducing the Jew to a position of total inferiority in every aspect of thought and endeavor. The document only hints at the reality which is succinctly presented in some of the Bishops' statements.

(We welcome the clarification issued by Cardinal Cassidy at the ILC and reiterated in an interview with Reuters on April 2 in which he noted that there was no intention to exclude popes, bishops or any official people from any guilt and agreed that the document could have been clearer on this point.)

The Church and the Shoah

This brings us to the consideration of the role of historical Church antisemitism in the lead-up to the Shoah and the actual behavior of Catholics during those terrible times. First of all a distinction is drawn in the document between antisemitism, based on theories contrary to the constant teaching of the Church on human equality, and anti-Judaism. The National Socialist Regime, it is said, was a thoroughly modern neo-pagan regime whose antisemitism had its roots outside Christianity. Then the right question is asked "Whether the Nazi persecution of the Jews was not made easier by the anti-Jewish prejudices imbedded in some Christian minds and hearts?"

The implication that while Christians have been guilty of anti-Judaism but antisemitism is a contradiction of the teaching of the Church is dubious and it is unfortunate that it is put forward in generalities that could well mislead many for whom this document is intended. There was indeed a change in the main emphases of antisemitism in the late nineteenth century from a religious basis to a more secular prejudice with a pseudo-racialist base. However can it be said that the latter was not influenced by the long centuries of Church conditioning? The antisemitic parties preaching the new ideology from the late nineteenth century often stressed their Christian affiliations. For example, the party of one of the formulators of modern antisemitism in Germany, Adolf Stoecker, was the Christian Social Workers' Party; the party of the antisemitic mayor of Vienna, Karl Lueger (a major influence on Hitler), was the United Christians; while Austria had the Christian Social Club and the Catholic People's Party, France had its Catholic Workers' Club and the Christian Democratic Movement, and the significant role played by the Church in the Dreyfus Affair will be recalled. Thus the statement that this was "an anti-Judaism that was essentially more sociological and political than religious" plays down the fact of the unbroken line of Christian anti-Judaism/antisemitism and its impact throughout Europe. After all the Jew was still the deicide and the traditional anti-Jewish stereotypes were not changed or renounced and were absorbed into the new antisemitism. The Catholic attitude toward the Jews was unchanged and its influence cannot be excluded. This is why the suggestion of a complete dichotomy between "anti-Judaism" and "antisemitism" is misleading. One shades into the other. It was Christian anti-Judaism that created the possibility of modern pagan antisemitism by delegitimizing the Jews and Judaism. (Incidentally ancient paganism was far more tolerant of Jews and Judaism than was the Christian Church).

It is true that the National Socialist regime adopted a pagan ideology which rejected the Church—although this did not mean that all churchmen and believers rejected National Socialism. It may be noted that Hitler, Himmler and the other Nazi leaders were all baptized Christians who were never excommunicated. The same is true of the vast apparatus of killers, the product of Christian Europe. The Church is not accused of direct responsibility for the Shoah but of its legacy of sixteen centuries of conditioning which had created an environment in which a Shoah became possible and many Christians would feel no compunction in collaborating. Pope John Paul II in his speech of October 31 stated, "Erroneous and unjust interpretations of the New Testament regarding the Jewish people and their presumed guilt circulated for too long and contributed to a lulling of many consciences." Here was a clear answer to the question posed in the document "Did anti-Jewish sentiment among Christians make them less sensitive or even indifferent to the persecutions launched against the Jews by National Socialism when it reached power?" We regret that it was not included. Another clear statement was that of the French bishops [Document 60 above]: "It is important to admit the primary role played by the consistently repeated anti-Jewish stereotypes wrongly perpetuated among Christians in the historical process that led to the Shoah." Such simple statements were what had been hoped for in the document rather than the convoluted approach that was taken.

Behavior during the Shoah

"Did Christians give every possible assistance to those being persecuted and in particular to the persecuted Jews" asks the document and replies "Many did but others did not." Jews will ever be grateful for those courageous Christians who saved and helped Jews and in other ways opposed the persecutions and in so doing risked their lives. But these heroes cannot be called the "many." Indeed the statement that "many did" does not do justice to the supreme self-sacrifice of the few (who acted as individuals and seldom received any support from the Church). Their numbers were small compared not only with those who were cowed into inactivity but with those who took an active role in the persecution and extermination (a major group not mentioned in the document). Unlike the German and French documents, where those who stood up and rescued Jews were seen as exceptions, the Vatican document gives the impression that those who were evil, insensitive and acquiesced to the Final Solution were the exception to the overall Christian approach. However, while we feel the document could have been more explicit, we recognize the significance of its statements: "For Christians, this heavy burden of conscience of their brothers and sisters during the Second World War must be a call to penitence. We deeply regret the errors and failures of those sons and daughters of the Church." At the same time, we feel that some of the examples of churchmen standing up to Hitler were unfortunate. Cardinal Bertram may have condemned National Socialism in 1931 but his subsequent record was very different. He opposed all public protest against the deportations and the massacres of the Jews as had been suggested by some of his colleagues and after Hitler's suicide he addressed a circular letter to the priests in his diocese inviting them to celebrate a solemn requiem service in memory of the Fuehrer. In the words of the German Bishops' statement of 1995 [Document 58 above]: "Even the pogroms of November 1938 were not followed by public and expressed protests." This comes precisely into the category of response that we feel is slurred over in the text.

The question of the role of Pope Pius XII is obviously a contentious issue with differing views not only between Jews and Catholics but among Catholic scholars themselves. It would have been preferable to have left this subject to future historians. But once opened, it is a Pandora's box. The statement that the Pope was responsible for saving hundreds of thousands of Jewish lives has not been substantiated by the published documents. A final judgment on this can only be made after the Archives are opened. We are given one generalizing quotation made by Pius XII but no reference to the charge of "silence"—he never once explicitly mentioned the Jews in his public pronouncements during World War II. The issue of silence, not confronted in the document, is faced—at least with relation to the French hierarchy—in the French Bishops' document [*Bridges*, Vol. 1, Document 42] which states frankly: "The vast majority of church officials did not realize their considerable power and influence and that, given the silence of other institutions, the impact of a public statement might have forestalled an irreparable catastrophe. The bishops of France did not speak out, acquiescing through their silence in these flagrant violations of the rights of man and leaving an open field for the spiral of death. Today we confess that silence was a mistake." The document could well have spoken out against the silence of the hierarchies. It is not the place where the dispute on Pope Pius XII's role can be solved. But we do miss the simple statement that the earthly Church as a whole erred during this period and we see the refusal to assign any blame to it as an institution a step backward from the position of the German and French bishops.

We were disappointed by the introduction (at the bottom of page 12 of the document) of a list of calamities experienced by other nations—and in particular "the drama of the Middle East." We with our long record of suffering can profoundly empathize with the tragedies of other peoples. But we can never forget the uniqueness of the Shoah which is the point we would have expected the document to bring out. In no other case, was an entire people doomed to the utmost humiliation and then extermination off the face of the earth—even to the extent of going back generations to identify their "blood." Moreover as Catholic belief as expressed in recent documents clearly links the salvation of Christians with God's redemption of the Jewish people whose covenant with him is irrevocable, Christians cannot view the Shoah as they do other genocides.

We welcome Cardinal Cassidy's suggestion, recorded in the communiqué at the end of the ILC meeting, that a joint team of Jewish and Christian scholars review the relevant material relating to the Catholic Church and the Shoah in the volumes produced by Catholic scholars and if questions still remain, further clarification will be sought. The Vatican archives are the only great archive which remain closed for the World War II period. When they are opened, there will doubtless be both positive and negative disclosures. But only in this way will the historical record be authoritatively established.

We would like to conclude, as we began, on a positive note. We appreciate Cardinal Cassidy's statement that Catholics have much to learn and that the Jewish community needs to understand better how the Catholic Church views itself. Our critique of the document is not meant with any negative intent but as a pointer to the guidelines which we think should be adopted in Catholic teaching of the Shoah. It is in the spirit of Cardinal Cassidy's comment that the document is not a conclusion but rather a step for further development, and that in the words of Pope John Paul II's covering letter, we will "work together for a world of true respect for the life and dignity of every human being." Indeed "We Remember" is not only an indictment of the past but, in its condemnation of antisemitism, a milestone-guideline for the future.

92

Recognizing Bonds between the Jewish and Catholic Communities

Issued jointly in March 2000 by the Central Conference of American Rabbis (Reform) and the Rabbinical Assembly (Conservative).

The Central Conference of American Rabbis (Reform) and The Rabbinical Assembly (Conservative), representing 3,000 rabbis, wish to recognize and acknowledge the growing bonds between the Jewish and Catholic communities. We praise Pope John Paul II's courageous strides in working to heal the historic breach that has separated our communities. The Pope has affirmed the irrevocable nature of God's covenant with the Jewish people. He has condemned antisemitism as a "sin against God." He has forged diplomatic relations with Israel, recognizing the Jewish State's right to exist within secure borders. He has called upon Christendom to engage in *teshuva* for the atrocities of the Holocaust. He has apologized for the excesses of the Crusades and the Inquisition. He has opposed Christian missionizing toward the Jews, instead urging the intensification of Jewish piety. In this context, we welcome and applaud Pope John Paul II's historic liturgy of forgiveness, presented to the global community of Catholics this past Sunday.

Borrowing from the Pope's terminology, we call upon our rabbinic constituents to engage in intensified dialogue and fellowship with our Roman Catholic neighbors. At this historic moment of the first papal pilgrimage to the sovereign Jewish State, may the inspiring leadership of Pope John Paul II lead us toward greater reconciliation, friendship and partnership in effecting *tikkun olam*.

Rabbi Charles Kroloff
President
Central Conference of American Rabbis

Rabbi Seymour Essrog
President
The Rabbinical Assembly

Rabbi Paul Menitoff
Executive Vice President
Central Conference of American Rabbis

Rabbi Joel Meyers
Executive Vice President
The Rabbinical Assembly

93

Address by Prime Minister Ehud Barak of the State of Israel on the Occasion of the Visit of Pope John Paul II

Delivered at Yad Vashem, the Holocaust Martyrs' and Heroes' Remembrance Authority, Jerusalem, March 23, 2000.

Your Holiness, Pope John Paul II,

Allow me to open with a few words in our language, the language of Abraham, Moses and the Covenant, which has once again become the native language of the land of Israel.

> [*In Hebrew:* A 2,000-year-old historical cycle is returning here to its beginning, bearing the weight of remembrance—its richness and pain, its light and shadows, its song and laments. The wounds of time will not be healed in a day, but the path which brought you here leads to a new horizon. This hour will go down in history as a propitious hour, a moment of truth, the victory of justice and hope.]

Your Holiness,

In the name of the Jewish people, in the name of the State of Israel and all of its citizens—Christians, Muslims, Druze and Jews—I welcome you, in friendship, in brotherhood, and in peace, here in Jerusalem, the capital of Israel, the eternal city of faith.

Your Holiness,

We meet today in this sanctuary of memory, for the Jewish people and for all humanity. "Yad Vashem"—literally "a place and a name"—

for the six million of our brothers and sisters, for one and a half million children, victims of the barbarian evil of Nazism.

When the darkness of Nazism descended, and my people were led from all over Christian Europe to the crematoria and the gas chambers, it seemed that no longer could one place any hope in God or man. That in the words of the prophet Joel, "The sun and the moon darkened and the stars withdrew their luster." And the silence was not only from the heavens. During that time, here in the land of Israel, the poet Natan Alterman wrote these searing, tormented verses:

As our children cried underneath the gallows,
the wrath of the world we did not hear...

Your Holiness,

From the depths of that "long night of the Shoah," as you have called it, we saw flickers of light, shining like beacons against the utter darkness around them. These were the righteous gentiles, mostly children of your faith, who secretly risked their lives to save the lives of others. Their names are inscribed on the walls around us here at Yad Vashem; they are forever inscribed on the tablets of our hearts.

You, Your Holiness, were a young witness to the tragedy. And as you wrote to your Jewish childhood friend, you felt, in some sense, as if you yourself experienced the fate of Polish Jewry. When my grandparents, Elka and Shmuel Godin, mounted the death trains at Umschlagplatz near their home in Warsaw, headed toward their fate at Treblinka—the fate of three million Jews from your homeland—you were there, and you remembered.

You have done more than anyone else to bring about the historic change in the attitude of the Church toward the Jewish people, initiated by the good Pope John XXIII, and to dress the gaping wounds that festered over many bitter centuries.

And I think I can say, Your Holiness, that your coming here today, to the Tent of Remembrance at Yad Vashem, is a climax of this historic journey of healing. Here, right now, time itself has come to a standstill—this very moment holds within it two thousand years of history. And their weight is almost too much to bear.

Shortly before setting out on your pilgrimage here, you raised the flag of fraternity to full mast, setting into Church liturgy a request for forgiveness, for wrongs committed by members of your faith against others, especially against the Jewish people.

We appreciate this noble act most profoundly.

Naturally, it is impossible to overcome all the pains of the past overnight. Your Holiness has frequently commented on problems regarding past relations between Christianity and the Jews. It is our wish to continue productive dialogue on this issue, to work together to eliminate the scourge of racism and antisemitism.

Your Holiness,

Mine is a nation that remembers. However onerous the burden of memory, we may not avoid it, because without memory there can be neither culture nor conscience.

The establishment of the State of Israel against all odds, and the ingathering of the exiles not only has restored to the Jewish people its honor and mastery over its fate; it is the definitive, permanent answer to Auschwitz. We have returned home, and since then no Jew will ever remain helpless or be stripped of the last shred of human dignity. Here, at the cradle of our civilization, we have rebuilt our home, so that it may thrive in peace and security. Defending our state has claimed a heavy toll.

We are now resolved to find paths to historical reconciliation. We are in the midst of an enormous effort to secure comprehensive peace with our Palestinian neighbors, with Syria and Lebanon, and with the entire Arab world.

Your Holiness,

We have noted with appreciation your words about the unique bond of the Jewish people to Jerusalem, that, and I quote you, "Jews love Jerusalem with a passion...from the days of David who chose it as a capital, and from the days of Solomon who built the temple there; therefore they turn to it in their prayers every day, and point to it as a symbol of their nation."

I would like to reiterate our absolute commitment to protect all rights and properties of the Catholic Church, as well as those of the other Christian and Muslim institutions; to continue to ensure full freedom of worship to members of all faiths equally; and to keep united Jerusalem open and free, as never before, to all who love her. I know that you pray, as we do, for the unity and peace of Jerusalem:

Pray for the peace of Jerusalem...Peace be within thy walls and prosperity within thy palaces. For my brethren and companions' sake I will now say, peace be within thee.

Your Holiness,

You have come on a mission of brotherhood, of remembrance and of peace.

And we say to you:

Blessed are you in Israel.

94

Dabru Emet ["Speak the Truth"]: A Jewish Statement on Christians and Christianity

Issued in September 2000 by the National Jewish Scholars Project, a group convened by the Institute for Christian & Jewish Studies, Baltimore, Maryland. Authored by the four scholars named at the end, the statement was accompanied by a lengthy list of other Jewish signatories.

In recent years, there has been a dramatic and unprecedented shift in Jewish and Christian relations. Throughout the nearly two millennia of Jewish exile, Christians have tended to characterize Judaism as a failed religion or, at best, a religion that prepared the way for, and is completed in, Christianity. In the decades since the Holocaust, however, Christianity has changed dramatically. An increasing number of official Church bodies, both Roman Catholic and Protestant, have made public statements of their remorse about Christian mistreatment of Jews and Judaism. These statements have declared, furthermore, that Christian teaching and preaching can and must be reformed so that they acknowledge God's enduring covenant with the Jewish people and celebrate the contribution of Judaism to world civilization and to Christian faith itself.

We believe these changes merit a thoughtful Jewish response. Speaking only for ourselves—an interdenominational group of Jewish scholars—we believe it is time for Jews to learn about the efforts of Christians to honor Judaism. We believe it is time for Jews to reflect on what Judaism may now say about Christianity. As a first step, we offer eight brief statements about how Jews and Christians may relate to one another.

Jews and Christians worship the same God. Before the rise of Christianity, Jews were the only worshipers of the God of Israel. But Christians also worship the God of Abraham, Isaac, and Jacob; creator of heaven and earth. While Christian worship is not a viable religious choice for Jews, as Jewish theologians we rejoice that, through Christianity, hundreds of millions of people have entered into relationship with the God of Israel.

Jews and Christians seek authority from the same book—the Bible (what Jews call "Tanakh" and Christians call the "Old Testament"). Turning to it for religious orientation, spiritual enrichment, and communal education, we each take away similar lessons: God created and sustains the universe; God established a covenant with the people Israel, God's revealed word guides Israel to a life of righteousness; and God will ultimately redeem Israel and the whole world. Yet, Jews and Christians interpret the Bible differently on many points. Such differences must always be respected.

Christians can respect the claim of the Jewish people upon the land of Israel. The most important event for Jews since the Holocaust has been the re-establishment of a Jewish state in the Promised Land. As members of a biblically based religion, Christians appreciate that Israel was promised—and given—to Jews as the physical center of the covenant between them and God. Many Christians support the State of Israel for reasons far more profound than mere politics. As Jews, we applaud this support. We also recognize that Jewish tradition mandates justice for all non-Jews who reside in a Jewish state.

Jews and Christians accept the moral principles of Torah. Central to the moral principles of Torah is the inalienable sanctity and dignity of every human being. All of us were created in the image of God. This shared moral emphasis can be the basis of an improved relationship between our two communities. It can also be the basis of a powerful witness to all humanity for improving the lives of our fellow human beings and for standing against the immoralities and idolatries that harm and degrade us. Such witness is especially needed after the unprecedented horrors of the past century.

Nazism was not a Christian phenomenon. Without the long history of Christian anti-Judaism and Christian violence against Jews, Nazi ideology could not have taken hold nor could it have been carried out. Too many Christians participated in, or were sympathetic to, Nazi atrocities against Jews. Other Christians did not protest sufficiently against these atrocities. But Nazism itself was not an inevitable outcome of Christianity. If the Nazi extermination of the Jews had been fully successful, it would have turned its murderous rage more directly to Christians. We recognize with gratitude those Christians who risked or sacrificed their lives to save Jews during the Nazi regime. With that in mind, we encourage the continuation of recent efforts in Christian theology to repudiate unequivocally contempt of Judaism and the Jewish people. We applaud those Christians who reject this teaching of contempt, and we do not blame them for the sins committed by their ancestors.

The humanly irreconcilable difference between Jews and Christians will not be settled until God redeems the entire world as promised in Scripture. Christians know and serve God through Jesus Christ and the Christian tradition. Jews know and serve God through Torah and the Jewish tradition. That difference will not be settled by one community insisting that it has interpreted Scripture more accurately than the other; nor by exercising political power over the other. Jews can respect Christians' faithfulness to their revelation just as we expect Christians to respect our faithfulness to our revelation. Neither Jew nor Christian should be pressed into affirming the teaching of the other community.

A new relationship between Jews and Christians will not weaken Jewish practice. An improved relationship will not accelerate the cultural and religious assimilation that Jews rightly fear. It will not change traditional Jewish forms of worship, nor increase intermarriage between Jews and non-Jews, nor persuade more Jews to convert to Christianity, nor create a false blending of Judaism and Christianity. We respect Christianity as a faith that originated within Judaism and that still has significant contacts with it. We do not see it as an extension of Judaism. Only if we cherish our own traditions can we pursue this relationship with integrity.

Jews and Christians must work together for justice and peace.
Jews and Christians, each in their own way, recognize the unredeemed state of the world as reflected in the persistence of persecution, poverty, and human degradation and misery. Although justice and peace are finally God's, our joint efforts, together with those of other faith communities, will help bring the kingdom of God for which we hope and long. Separately and together, we must work to bring justice and peace to our world. In this enterprise, we are guided by the vision of the prophets of Israel:

> It shall come to pass in the end of days that the mountain of the Lord's house shall be established at the top of the mountains and be exalted above the hills, and the nations shall flow unto it...and many peoples shall go and say, "Come ye and let us go up to the mountain of the Lord to the house of the God of Jacob and He will teach us of His ways and we will walk in his paths." (Isa 2:2–3)

Tikva Frymer-Kensky, University of Chicago
David Novak, University of Toronto
Peter Ochs, University of Virginia
Michael Signer, University of Notre Dame

95

Address by Rabbi David Rosen at the Audience of the International Jewish Committee on Interreligious Consultations with Pope Benedict XVI

Delivered at the Vatican by the Chair of the International Jewish Committee on Interreligious Consultations on October 30, 2008.

Your Holiness,

It was the privilege of the International Jewish Committee for Interreligious Consultations, as the official Jewish partner of the Holy See's Commission for Religious Relations with the Jews, to be received by you here very shortly after the commencement of your Pontificate. This second occasion comes on the eve of the twentieth meeting of our joint International Jewish-Catholic Liaison Committee (ILC)—itself the fruit of *Nostra Aetate*—due to be held in Budapest in ten days time.

The two central themes of the forthcoming twentieth ILC may be viewed as reflecting the key character and purpose of our relationship.

The first is that of the Role of Religion in Secular Society. This reflects our continuous desire as Jews and Catholics to confront the challenges of our time and to draw on our respective traditions—above all upon the values within them that we share, to provide guidance and benefit for society at large.

The second theme of our twentieth ILC meeting is the state of Catholic-Jewish relations in Eastern Europe in particular; and reflects our commitment to combating the tragic blights of the past that have afflicted our relationship—specifically antisemitism, which the late Pope John Paul II described as "a sin against God and man." Renascent nationalism is all too often associated with xenophobia and anti-semitism which regrettably has demonstrated itself to be a powerfully

resistant evil virus, not least of all in those societies where this prejudice has been rife for millennia.

We are profoundly grateful for all that the Holy See has said and
done in recent times to help combat this sin and all forms of bigotry
and prejudice.

Our Budapest meeting will open with a commemoration of
Kristallnacht, the event which, as it were, heralded the darkest period in
Jewish history and which in its own way reflected the tragedy of our past
relationship. For even if, as Your Holiness most importantly declared in
Birkenau, and recently reiterated in Paris, Nazism was in fact an assault
on the roots of the Church itself, nevertheless the fact that the tragedy
could take place with the ease that it did, perpetrated by so many who
were baptized Christians, was a reflection of the degree to which antisemitism had insinuated itself into these societies.

However we give thanks for those Christians who were true to the
most sublime of the teachings of their faith and saved many Jews during that terrible time. In this regard we reiterate our respectful call for
full and transparent access of scholars to all archival material from that
period, so that assessments regarding actions and policies during this
tragic period may have the credibility they deserve both within our
respective communities and beyond.

The fact that in Hungary where half of the Jewish community was
exterminated, Kristallnacht will be commemorated by us together with
the Catholic Church led by His Eminence Cardinal Erdo who has
been publicly recognized by the Jewish community for his work "to
preserve the memory of the Jews killed during the Holocaust and those
who saved Jews," is itself a reflection of how far we have come in trans-
forming the tragedy of the past into a memorial for the future to
advance our friendship and cooperation.

For this we give thanks for Your Holiness' own contribution following in the footsteps of the historic actions and declarations made by
the late Pope John Paul II.

At a Papal audience for the ILC in 1990 celebrating the twenty-
fifth anniversary of *Nostra Aetate* [*Bridges*, Vol. 1, Document 30], Pope
John Paul II emphasized in accordance with that historic document,
that "the Church's very nature is intrinsically linked with her reflection
on the nature of the Jewish People." He then mentioned the challenge
for the Church to further "reflect upon and express more thoroughly
her thinking on the "mystery which is the Jewish people" as "an intimate part of the 'mystery' of revelation and salvation."

During the last year and a half there has been some concern within the Jewish community that the commitment to this charge might be weakening and there were interpretations in the wake of Your Holiness' *Motu Proprio* and reformulation of the Latin rite prayer in the Easter liturgy for the Conversion of the Jews, that portrayed these as a regression in terms of our relationship of mutual respect.

We were accordingly most grateful for the clarifications we received from His Eminence Cardinal Kasper—reiterated by His Eminence Cardinal Bertone in his letter to the Chief Rabbis of Israel—affirming that this prayer is eschatological in nature and in no way reflects any endorsement of proselytization of Jews on the part of the Church.

We are furthermore greatly heartened by the fact that the Synod of Bishops meeting just concluded here in Rome made a point of emphasizing the importance not only of the Hebrew Scriptures themselves for the Church, but also of the place of the people of these Scriptures, the people of Israel, in this regard. Moreover the fact that the Synod was addressed for the first time ever by a rabbi—one of the leading rabbis of Israel—is itself surely a remarkable testimony.

Above all we profoundly appreciate the words of your Holiness at your meeting last month with our co-religionists in France—a meeting which like those held by your Holiness on your visit to the USA, reflected the special regard of the Holy See for the Jewish community. In Paris you emphasized "the eternal Covenant of the Almighty" with the Jewish People, whom the Church sees "as her beloved brothers in Faith." We pray that your emphasis on the eternal validity of the Sinai Covenant will stimulate the charge of your blessed predecessor, to "further reflect upon and express more thoroughly" the meaning of the Church's relationship with the Jewish People; thereby enabling us to continue to grow in mutual respect for one another's integrity.

Before concluding my words, Your Holiness, I wish to express the solidarity of the Jewish community represented by IJCIC, with our Christian brothers and sisters who have been and are suffering from violence and persecution in different parts of the world—especially in Iraq, in India, and in Southeast Asia. We pray for their well being and that the achievements of our own relationship will inspire others to overcome the wounds of the past and live together in the spirit of mutual respect and cooperation.

96

Greetings by Chief Rabbi Riccardo di Segni on the Occasion of the Visit of Pope Benedict XVI to the Great Synagogue of Rome

January 17, 2010

1. First, my greetings and thanks to Pope Benedict XVI, Bishop of Rome, for his act of visiting our Community's most important place of worship.

2. When a new Pope was elected, his pontificate began with a solemn procession through the streets of Rome. The Jews of the city were also required to take part in this procession, decorating part of the route. The decorations included large laudatory panels. Their contents were known but no one in recent times had seen them until not long ago, when a casual discovery in the archives of our Community brought to light a collection of fourteen of these cardboard placards, dating back to the eighteenth century. We have had them restored and organized a special exhibition in our museum. During his visit today, the Pope will be the first person to view these panels. They are a piece of our history as Roman Jews in our two thousand year old relations with the church, just like the historic event taking place today. However, the difference in meaning is great. The panels were the tribute due as barely tolerated subjects, living walled in and limited in their freedom. There were worse ceremonies before the eighteenth century panels: the display of the Torah to the Pope, who reserved the right to deride it. Times have obviously changed and we thank the Lord, Blessed is He, who has brought us an era of freedom. After the liberty conquered in 1870, ever since the time of Vatican II, our relations with the Catholic Church and its Pope are based on terms of equal dignity

and mutual respect. It was the advances of the Council that made this relationship possible. Should they be called into question the possibility of dialogue would no longer exist.

3. The area of Rome that the Jews had to decorate was near the Arch of Titus. This was no accidental choice; it was meant to remind the Jews of their humiliation in the loss of their political independence. However, for us that symbol was never only negative: the Jews were humiliated and without independence, but they continued to live, while the empires that had subjected and defeated them no longer existed.

4. To this miracle of survival, the miracle of the regained independence of the State of Israel was added. Twenty-four years have passed since the historic, unforgettable visit of Pope John Paul II to this Synagogue. At the time, our community leaders made a strong request to the Pope to recognize the State of Israel, and diplomatic relations were established not long afterwards. It was a further sign of changing, more mature times. The State of Israel is a political entity, guaranteed by the right of nations. But in our religious vision, we cannot avoid seeing a design of Providence. The terms "holy land" or "promised land" are commonly used, but with this language, there is a risk of forgetting the original meaning. The land is the land of Israel, and in Hebrew it is literally not the land which is holy. Instead, it is *eretz haQodesh*, the land of He who is Holy. And the promise is the one that G-d made repeatedly to our patriarchs, Abraham, Isaac and Jacob, to give it to their descendants, the children of Jacob-Israel, who actually held it for long periods of time. This is a basic, unassailable fact in the Jewish consciousness and it is important to remember that it is based on the Bible to which, despite the different interpretations, is given a holy meaning by you and by us.

5. There is an ample, significant representation of our Community, together with representatives of external institutions here to welcome Pope Benedict XVI. But perhaps the memories and biographies of each person are more important than the institutions. They are a living, impressive document of Jewish history of the last century. I would like to mention a few names, and hope the others will forgive me. Referring only to the rabbis present, we have Rabbi Brudman, Chief Rabbi of Savion in Israel, who spent three years of his childhood being moved from one concentration camp to another; Rabbi Schneier of New York who was a child in the horrors of Budapest in 1944; Rabbi Shearyashuv

haKohen, Chief Rabbi of Haifa who fought in the Israeli War of Independence in 1948 and was a prisoner of the Jordanians; and Rabbi Arussi, Chief Rabbi of Kiryat Ono, descendant of a family that emigrated from Yemen to Israel. And thinking of our own community, we have a diminishing group of survivors of the death camps of Nazi Germany. I would like to emphasize that their story is not only one of suffering but also one of resistance and loyalty. Some of them might have been saved if they had renounced their faith. But they did not. I would like to quote the simple, touching testimony of Leone Sabatello, who recently passed away.

"At the Military College, where they held us after the round-up of October 16, they asked us if anyone was Catholic, or was willing to become Catholic. Some said yes, but in our family we gathered together and remained what we always are."

6. "We remained what we always are." It is this force, this tenacity, this bond that has made our Community great and makes it grow. We are living in a season of rediscovery of our tradition, of study and observance of the Torah. Our schools are growing, as are our religious services, and the number of synagogues that multiply throughout the city. And all this takes place amidst our full integration in the city, in a spirit of friendship, of welcome, solidarity and open-mindedness.

7. In his visit to this Synagogue, Pope John Paul II described the relationship between Jews and Christians as that between brothers. The narrative of *Sefer Bereshit*, Genesis, gives us some precious suggestions for understanding. As Rabbi Sachs explains, from the beginning to the end of the book, there is a leitmotif tying together the different stories. The relationship between brothers starts out badly, with Cain killing Abel. Another pair of brothers, Isaac and Ishmael, live separated, the victims of an inherited rivalry, but are united in their gesture of compassion when they bury their father Abraham. A third pair of brothers, Esau and Jacob, have an equally conflicting relationship, they meet for a brief reconciliation and an embrace and then their roads separate. Finally, there is the story of Joseph and his brothers, which begins dramatically with an attempted murder and sale into slavery but is resolved with a final reconciliation when Joseph's brothers admit their error and give proof of their willingness to sacrifice themselves one for the other. If ours is a relationship of brothers, we should ask ourselves quite sincerely what point of this journey we have reached, and how far we still have to travel before we recover an authentic rela-

tionship of brotherhood and understanding, and what we have to do to achieve this.

8. What we should and can do together. Here is an example. There is a great deal of talk today about the need to protect the environment. On this point, we have a very special, common vision to transmit. The obligation to protect the environment was born with the first man. Adam was placed in the Garden of Eden with the duty "to work it and to guard it" (Gen 2:15). We must remember that the word nature never appears in the Jewish Bible as an independent entity, but only the concept of the created and creatures. We are all creatures, from rocks to human beings. Francis of Assisi's Canticle of the Creatures is rooted in Biblical spirituality, particularly the Psalms. For that reason, we can all agree on a non-idolatrous project of ecology, without forgetting that summit [the] of the creatures is man, made in the Divine image. Our responsibility is to protect all of creation, but the sanctity of life, the dignity of man, his freedom, his need for justice and ethics are crucial commodities to be safeguarded. These are the Biblical imperatives that we share, together with that of mercy: living one's religion with honesty and humility, as a powerful instrument of growth and human support, without aggressiveness, without political exploitation, without turning it into an instrument of hate, exclusion or death.

9. The terrible responsibility of man. Our Sages often used powerful images to express their thought, seeking allusions in the language of the Holy Scriptures. There is a phrase from Exodus (15:11) that says "Who is like you among the powers, *baelim*, O Lord." Rabbi Ishmael, a witness of historic atrocities, and himself a martyr of the repression of Hadrian, read this phrase with a small variation: *bailemim*, "who is like you, O Lord, among the mute," who witnesses the disasters of the world and does not speak. The silence of G-d, or our own incapacity to hear His voice in the face of the world's evils are an inscrutable mystery. But the silence of man is on a different level; it makes us wonder, it challenges us, and neither does it escape justice.

Jews, Christians and those of other faiths have been and still are persecuted around the world for their beliefs. Only He who is the Lord of forgiveness can forgive all those who persecute us.

9. Despite a dramatic history, the unresolved problems, and the misunderstandings, it is our shared visions and common goals that should be given pride of place.

The image of respect and friendship that emanates from this encounter must be an example for all those who are watching. But friendship and brotherhood must not be exclusive or opposed to others. This is particularly true for all those who acknowledge the spiritual legacy of Abraham. Without exclusion, Jews, Christians, and Moslems are called to this responsibility of peace. The prayer that is raised in this Synagogue is the one for universal peace announced by Isaiah (66:12) for Jerusalem, *kenahar shalom ukh'nachal shotef kevod goi.* "Peace to her like a river and the glory of the nations like a flowing stream."

Thank you. Shalom.

97

Affirming the Image of God: Statement of Jewish Scholars of the Jewish Theology Project

Issued by the Elijah Interfaith Institute, Jerusalem, in May 2010. Signed by twenty-five members of the Jewish Theology Project and Jewish religious leaders from Israel, the United States, the United Kingdom, the Netherlands, France, Poland, and Australia.

Recent weeks and months have brought to public attention the issue of Jewish attitudes to non-Jews, as these are found in some traditional sources and halakhah (Jewish religious law), particularly with reference to Rabbi Yitzchak Shapira's book *Torat Hamelekh* ["The King's Torah," Jerusalem, 2009]. The great liberty with which the author dispenses with the life of non-Jews under various circumstances has become a scandal in the media, a subject for police investigation for incitement, a discussion item on antisemitic websites, and the subject of an appeal to the Supreme Court of Israel. It has engendered heated discussion, most of which has focused on the right to teach Torah and to engage in discussion of halakhah, especially of a theoretical nature, unencumbered by external considerations and factors, such as police and state control. While these issues may be legitimate subjects for discussion, they conceal the main concerns raised by these teachings and their public reception. Many Rabbinical authorities have subsequently failed to condemn these teachings in theoretical and practical terms, leaving the impression that these are indeed appropriate contemporary Jewish attitudes to non-Jews. For this reason, we, rabbis, teachers and scholars of Jewish studies of various disciplines, religious denominations and political perspectives, from different countries worldwide, have come together to express with a united voice our deep disdain for these extremist teachings, which are opposed to fundamental Jewish conceptions of the unity of humanity which all Jews affirm at this time of year on the High Holidays. We assert that the core issue they raise must be given priority in Jewish education and thought. Our view is that Jewish teaching involves more than merely citing texts, whether in or out of context. Teaching and the art of halakhic ruling always reflect a broader religious worldview, guided by core values. In our understanding, the creation of humanity in God's image is the great principle, as our sages recognized.[1] We believe this mandates full respect for the infinite value, equality and uniqueness of every human life, for it is created in the image of God. Our Torah's ways are ways of pleasantness and all her paths are peace.[2] These and other great principles are the guidelines through which we interpret and teach our tradition.[3]

We are working together under the aegis of the Elijah Interfaith Institute, to bring to light teachings of Judaism that cohere to this worldview. Love of one's own group should not be equated with the hatred of others. Israel's calling is harmonious with the well-being of all humanity. We recognize that there are voices in our tradition that have lost sight of these great principles, because of the unspeakable suffering that our people have undergone throughout history. It is, therefore, a contemporary educational and halakhic challenge to confront these extremist teachings, to contain them, and to dissent from them publicly, applying the methods of halakhah, classical interpretation and historical study.

We have been collaborating on a project of developing a contemporary Jewish approach to other religions that would make our students and communities aware of the dangers inherent in such extremist views in our tradition, and that would inspire a broader view of Judaism, its ethical task and its vision for humanity.

Accordingly, we call upon rabbis and educators to take a clear stand against narrow views of Jewish particularity, in favor of a broader vision of Judaism's relations to the other. Our scholars stand ready to debate the views under discussion. Our own critique of *Torat Hamelekh* will shortly be published on this website [www.jewishtheology-elijah.org]. We will also be publishing educational resources that provide an alternative view of the non-Jew in Judaism, that remind us that "The Lord is good to all, and His compassion extends to all His creatures."[4]

Notes

1. See *Sifra Qedoshim* 4; Mishnah *Avot* 3:14.
2. Prov 3:17.

3. We are painfully aware that such problematic theoretical teachings can easily become transformed into practical guidelines for action, as witnessed by horrifying acts such as the Hebron massacre by [Baruch] Goldstein in 1994. We also recall some tragic lessons of our history, and the actions of Israel's enemies in the past century, applying a perverted logic that we should not replicate within Jewish teaching. For example, the right to kill children lest they grow up to threaten us was cited by Otto Ohlendorf of the German Army Einsatzgruppe C at his trial, to justify his unit's shooting of tens or hundreds of thousands of Jewish children among the more than million Jews murdered by the shooting squads in Eastern Europe in 1941–1942.

4. Ps 145:9.

98

Greetings of Chief Rabbi Jonathan Sacks to Pope Benedict XVI at an Interfaith Meeting in London

Address by Rabbi Jonathan Sacks, Chief Rabbi of the United Hebrew Congregations of the Commonwealth, at a meeting of British religious leaders with Pope Benedict XVI at St. Mary's University College, London, on September 17, 2010.

We welcome you, leader of a great faith, to this gathering of many faiths, in a land where once battles were fought in the name of faith, and where now we share friendship across faiths.

That is a climate change worth celebrating. And we recognize the immense role the Vatican played and continues to play in bringing it about. It was *Nostra Aetate* [*Bridges*, Vol. 1, Document 30], forty-five years ago, that brought about the single greatest transformation in interfaith relations in recent history, and we recognize your visit here today as a new chapter in that story, and a vital one.

The secularization of Europe that began in the seventeenth century did not happen because people lost faith in God. Newton and Descartes, heroes of the Enlightenment, believed in God very much indeed. What led to secularization was that people lost faith in the ability of people of faith to live peaceably together. And we must never go down that road again.

We remember the fine words of John Henry Cardinal Newman, "We should ever conduct ourselves towards our enemy as if he were one day to be our friend," as well as your own words, in *Caritas in Veritate*, that "the development of peoples depends...on a recognition that the human race is a single family, working together in true communion, not simply a group of subjects who happen to live side by side."

We celebrate both our commonalities and differences, because if we had nothing in common we could not communicate, and if we had everything in common, we would have nothing to say. You have spoken of the Catholic Church as a creative minority. And perhaps that is what we should all aspire to be, creative minorities, inspiring one another, and bringing our different gifts to the common good.

Britain has been so enriched by its minorities, by every group represented here today and the intricate harmonies of our several voices. And one of our commonalities is that we surely all believe that faith has a major role in strengthening civil society.

In the face of a deeply individualistic culture, we offer community. Against consumerism, we talk about the things that have value but not a price. Against cynicism we dare to admire and respect. In the face of fragmenting families, we believe in consecrating relationships. We believe in marriage as a commitment, parenthood as a responsibility, and the poetry of everyday life when it is etched, in homes and schools, with the charisma of holiness and grace.

In our communities we value people not for what they earn or what they buy or how they vote but for what they are, every one of them a fragment of the Divine presence. We hold life holy. And each of us is lifted by the knowledge that we are part of something greater than all of us, that created us in forgiveness and love, and asks us to create in forgiveness and love.

Each of us in our own way is a guardian of values that are in danger of being lost, in our short-attention-span, hyperactive, information-saturated, wisdom-starved age. And though our faiths are profoundly different, yet we recognize in one another the presence of faith itself, that habit of the heart that listens to the music beneath the noise, and knows that God is the point at which soul touches soul and is enlarged by the presence of otherness. You have honored us with your presence, and we honor you. May you continue to lead with wisdom and generosity of spirit, and may all our efforts combine to become a blessing to humanity and to God.

99

A Jewish Understanding of Christians and Christianity

A statement issued in May 2011 by the Center for Jewish-Christian Understanding and Cooperation (CJCUC), an Israeli Orthodox Jewish study and dialogue center in Efrat.

Many leaders of Christianity today no longer seek to displace Judaism. They recognize the Jewish people's continuing role in God's plan for history, and through their own understanding of the Christian Testament, they understand themselves as grafted into the living Abrahamic covenant.

Christians see themselves not merely as members of the Noahide covenant, but as spiritual partners within the Jewish covenant. At the same time, they believe that God does not repent of his covenantal gifts and that the Jewish people continues to enjoy a unique covenantal relationship with God in accordance with its historical two-thousand-year traditions.

Jewish and Christian theologies are no longer engaged in a theological duel to the death and therefore Jews should not fear a sympathetic understanding of Christianity that is true to the Torah, Jewish thought and values. In today's unprecedented reality of Christian support for the Jewish people, Jews should strive to work together with Christians toward the same spiritual goals of sacred history—universal morality, peace, and redemption under God—but under different and separate systems of commandments for each faith community and distinct theological beliefs.

Nearly all medieval and modern Jewish biblical commentators understood Abraham's primary mission as teaching the world about God and bearing witness to His moral law. Maimonides insisted in his halakhic and philosophical writings that spreading the knowledge of the One God of Heaven and Earth throughout the world was the main

528

vocation of Abraham. Significantly, this understanding of Abraham's religious mission is exactly the role and historical impact of Christianity as understood by great rabbis such as Rabbis Moses Rivkis, Yaakov Emden and Samson Raphael Hirsch.

R. Moses Rivkis (17th century Lithuania):

The gentiles in whose shadow Jews live and among whom Jews are disbursed are not idolators. Rather they believe in *creatio ex nihilo* and the Exodus from Egypt and the main principles of faith. Their intention is to the Creator of Heaven and Earth and we are obligated to pray for their welfare (Gloss on *Shulhan Arukh, Hoshen Mishpat,* Section 425:5).

And Rabbi Jacob Emden (18th century Germany):

The Nazarene brought a double goodness to the world…The Christian eradicated *avodah zarah,* removed idols (from the nations) and obligated them in the seven mitsvot of Noah, a congregation that works for the sake of heaven—people who are destined to endure, whose intent is for the sake of heaven and whose reward will not denied (Seder Olam Rabbah 35–37; Sefer ha-Shimush 15–17).

And Rabbi Samson Raphael Hirsch (19th century Germany):

Although disparaged because of its alleged particularism, the Jewish religion actually teaches that the upright of all peoples are headed toward the highest goal. In particular, rabbis have been at pains to stress that, while in other respects Christian views and ways of life may differ from those of Judaism, the peoples in whose midst the Jews are now living [i.e., Christians] have accepted the Jewish Bible of the Old Testament as a book of Divine revelation. They profess their belief in the God of heaven and earth as proclaimed in the Bible and they acknowledge the sovereignty of Divine Providence in both this life and the next. Their acceptance of the practical duties incumbent upon all men by the will of God distinguishes these nations from the heathen and idolatrous nations of the talmudic era (*Principles of Education,* "Talmudic Judaism and Society," 225–227).

[Further from Rabbi Hirsch]:

Israel produced an offshoot [Christianity] that had to become estranged from it in great measure, in order to bring to the world—sunk in idol worship, violence, immorality and the degradation of man—at least the tidings of the One Alone, of the brotherhood of all men, and of man's superiority over the beast (*Nineteen Letters on Judaism*, Jerusalem, 1995).

When we combine this rabbinic appreciation of Christianity with today's non-replacement Christian theologies toward Judaism, we find fresh possibilities for rethinking a Jewish relationship with Christianity and for fashioning new Jewish-Christian cooperation in pursuit of common values. If so, Jews can view Christians as partners in spreading monotheism, peace, and morality throughout the world.

This new understanding must encompass a mutual respect of each other's theological beliefs and eschatological convictions. Some Christians maintain that Christianity is the most perfect revelation of God and that all will join the church when truth is revealed at the end of time. Jews, too, are free to continue to believe, as Maimonides believed, that "all will return to the true religion" (Mishneh Torah, Laws of Kings, 12:1) and, as Rabbi Joseph B. Soloveitchik declared, "In the ultimate truthfulness of our views, [we] pray fervently for and expect confidently the fulfillment of our eschatological vision when our faith will rise from particularity to universality and will convince our peers of the other faith community" ("Confrontation," from *Tradition: A Journal of Orthodox Thought*, 1964, 6:2 [*Bridges*, Vol. 1, Document 67]).

The new relationship requires that Christians respect the right of all Jewish persons to live as Jews with complete self-determination—free from any attempts of conversion to Christianity. At the same time, Judaism must respect Christian faithfulness to their revelation, value their role in divine history, and acknowledge that Christians have entered a relationship with the God of Israel. In our pre-eschaton days, God has more than enough blessings to bestow upon all of His children.

The prophet Micah offers a stunning description of the messianic culmination of human history:

Come, let us go up to the mountain of the Lord and the God of Jacob, that He teach us His ways, and we will walk in His paths. Let the peoples beat their swords into plowshares and their spears into pruning hooks. Nations shall not lift up sword against nation, nor shall they learn war anymore. Let every man sit under his vine and under his fig tree; and no one shall make him afraid...Let all the people walk, each in the name of his God; and we shall walk in the name of our Lord our God forever and ever. (4:2–5)

Jews and Christians must bear witness together to the presence of God and to His moral laws. If Jews and Christians can become partners after nearly two thousand years of theological delegitimization and physical conflict, then peace is possible between any two peoples anywhere. That peace would be our most powerful witness to God's presence in human history and to our covenantal responsibility to carry God's blessing to the world. It is the very essence of which the messianic dream is made.

Translators of Documents Originally Issued in Languages Other than English

#11. "Statement on the Fiftieth Anniversary of the Pogrom in November 1938" (1988)—translated by Franklin Sherman with Fritz Voll.

#12. "The Church and the Jewish People" (1990)—translated by Franklin Sherman with Fritz Voll.

#15. "Message on the Fiftieth Anniversary of the End of the Second World War and the Fiftieth Anniversary of the Liberation of the Concentration Camp at Auschwitz" (1995)—translated by Franklin Sherman from the German version in Hans Hermann Henrix and Wolfgang Kraus, eds., *Die Kirchen und das Judentum, Bd. II: Dokumente von 1986 bis 2000* (Paderborn: Bonifatius Druck and Gütersloh: Gütersloher Verlagshaus/Chr. Kaiser, 2001), pp. 504–5.

#16. "Origin and Goal of the Christian Journey with Judaism" (1997)—translated by Franklin Sherman with Fritz Voll.

#18. "Time to Turn: The Protestant Churches in Austria and the Jews" (1998)—translated by Franklin H. Littell.

#19. "Christians and Jews: A Manifesto Fifty Years after the Weissensee Declaration" (2000)—translated by Franklin Sherman with Fritz Voll.

#21. "Statement on the Sixtieth Anniversary of the End of the Second World War" (2005)—translated by Franklin Sherman with Fritz Voll.

#61. "We Must Be in Unity with the Jews" (1991)—translated by Albert A. Kipa.

#75. "The Holocaust/Shoah: Its Effects on Christian Theology and Life in Argentina and Latin America" (2006)—translated by Robert Mosher.

#85. "Journeying Together in Mutual Respect"—translated by Franklin Sherman with Fritz Voll.

Note: Organizations that function in several languages often issue English versions of their documents without any identification of their drafters or translators. The above are the items in the present volume for which specific translators could be ascertained.

Index

Titles of Documents

Sources of Documents